A Student's A–Z of Psychology

A Student's **A–Z** of **Psychology**

>> V van Deventer
>> M Mojapelo-Batka

A Student's A-Z of Psychology

First published 2005
Revised reprint 2006
Second edition 2013

Juta and Company Ltd
First Floor
Sunclare Building
21 Dreyer Street
Claremont
7708

PO Box 14373, Lansdowne, Cape Town, South Africa, 7779

ISBN 978-0-70218-905-0

Project Manager: Willemien Jansen
Editor: Wendy Priilaid
Proofreader: Lauri de Jager
Typesetter: ANdtp Services, Cape Town
Cover designer: MR Design

Typeset in Frutiger LT Std 10/14 point

Contents

Preface

A Student's A-Z of Psychology is a response to the requirements of the modern learning environment, namely the need for core, focused texts that provide underpinning knowledge for competency based tasks. This book is suited to an introductory level course in psychology. In addition to the psychological knowledge traditionally required for a first course in psychology, it also contains information on skills based topics, such as presentations, research essays, information modelling and information analysis.

Vasi van Deventer and Mapula Mojapelo-Batka has more than 30 years' experience in teaching introductory psychology. They share a keen interest in new developments in the learning environment. During the last 10 years, they have gained extensive experience in designing competency based courses that do not rely on traditional 'wrapped around a textbook' methodology. Both authors are clinical psychologists by profession. Vasi holds a PhD from the University of South Africa and Mapula a PhD from the University of Pretoria.

They would like to acknowledge the contribution made by Angelo Fynn, Christine Laidlaw, Lebo Makobe and Khuze Skosana to the preparation of this manuscript.

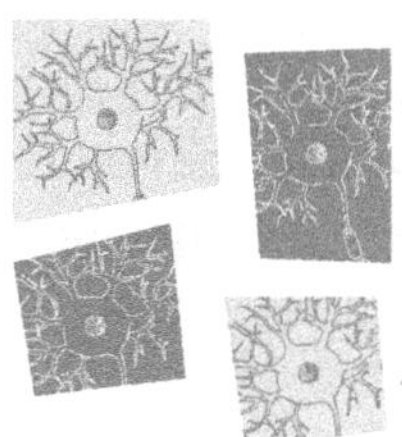

Cognition: Problem solving

Problem solving is often regarded as one of the highest forms of thinking. There are two phases to successful problem solving. First, we need to discover the general properties of a correct solution. This general solution is an overall idea of what is required to solve the problem but without specific detail. Once we have a general solution, we can work on a functional solution with sufficient detail to guide further action to solve the problem.

1 Steps in the process of problem solving

In the process of problem solving, we need to start by knowing just what the problem is. We then think of suitable ways of solving it, which we call strategies. Next we decide on the best solution and finally we evaluate or assess this solution to see whether it has been effective.

1.1 Identify the problem and define it clearly

Problem solving starts with the recognition that there is a problem and this is followed by a definition of the problem. The way we recognise and define a problem influences the way we go about solving it. For example, you may think that you would like to have a big family, perhaps six children, but then you realise that you do not earn enough money to provide properly for them. This realisation means that you recognise the problem. If you define the problem as not having enough money, then the solution to your problem would be to find ways of supplementing your income. However, if you define the problem as placing too many demands on your resources (that is, your income), then your solution would be to have fewer children so that you can provide for them properly with your available resources.

1.2 Explore various strategies

Problems can be solved in various ways, one of which may be to apply a set of rules. For example, you see a man standing next to the freeway looking for a lift. You are not sure whether you should stop or not. The rules of the road say that hitchhiking is not allowed on freeways and therefore you do not stop. Another way of problem solving may mean looking at a task or problem situation in different ways in order to find a solution. For example, your daughter is unemployed and wants you to buy a television because she is bored at home. You cannot afford one so you look at other ways of solving the problem (of boredom), like encouraging her to join a volunteer programme or to participate in sport. Here are some strategies for problem solving:

1.2.1 Trial and error approach

A trial and error approach to solving a problem is called a mechanical approach, because it involves applying a set of rules or discovery by rote. Trial and error thinking involves trying all possibilities more or less randomly. For example, you know that one of the keys in a bunch fits a particular lock, but you do not know which is the right one. The trial and error approach would be to try each key one by one, in any order, until you find it.

1.2.2 Heuristic strategies

If you cannot solve the problem mechanically or by habitual ways of thought; however, you may need to adopt an approach based on understanding. An understanding approach to the lock and key problem may involve an examination of the type of lock and trying only those keys that are likely to fit it. This is an example of a heuristic strategy, which means that you try the likeliest solution first and reduce the alternatives that have to be considered. In everyday life, we often use heuristic strategies to reduce the number of alternative options in solving problems. The heuristic approach increases the odds of success, but does not guarantee a solution.

Here are some examples of heuristic strategies that can help us to solve problems:

- Try working backwards from the desired goal to the current situation. For example, you want to buy a pair of shoes that costs R450, but the problem is that you do not have enough money. You decide that you can save R100 each month by cutting back on other expenditures.
- Identify the way that the current situation differs from your desired goal and identify the steps you need to take to reduce the difference. This may mean that you have to break up your desired goal into several smaller goals (or sub-goals), so that you can identify the means to achieve the end goal or aim. For example, in order to save the money for the shoes, you have to decide what you can do without. Each month, you may have to cut back on something and this constitutes a step or sub-goal towards achieving your main goal of buying the shoes.

- Adopt an analogical approach by thinking of a similar problem and considering whether the solution to the similar problem will work for your present problem. For example, you may remember that in the past you saved money to help out a family member. Think of what you did then to save money and see if you can apply the same strategy now.
- Make a list of your assumptions or questions and systematically challenge or test each one, which may suggest ideas for solving the problem. In the problem situation described here, your questions may be, for example, 'Are the shoes worth R450?'; 'Can I find similar shoes at a better price?'; 'Should I look for other shoes?'; 'Why do I want these particular shoes?'; and so on.

1.3 Explore possible solutions

Several possible solutions may have emerged from the previous phase of problem solving and each one needs to be considered. You may need to ask what the particular solution would bring about or how it would change the problem situation, what the advantages and disadvantages would be and what the cost of implementing the solution may be. There may not be definite answers to these questions, but they should help you consider different ideas and possible solutions. The only way you can test the effectiveness of a possible solution is by taking some action to try it out.

1.4 Evaluate and learn from the solution

It may happen that each potential solution you try gives rise to other problems, but again you can deal with each one until you find a satisfactory solution. You have to assess each solution to find out whether it has solved the problem effectively.

2 Insight

Sometimes an answer to a problem appears suddenly and we wonder why we did not see it before. This is called gaining insight into a problem. It often happens when we re-organise the elements of a problem, selecting those that are relevant and ignoring those that are not, or selectively combining bits of useful information that may not seem related at first. Insight also involves the comparison of new problems with old information, or information about problems that have already been solved (Coon, 2004).

3 Restricted thinking

Sometimes we seem to get stuck in our thinking. We cannot find a solution to a problem or we may be unable to see alternatives. One of the explanations of why we get stuck is that of mental set or fixation. Fixation is an example of restricted thinking. Another way of describing it is the tendency to evaluate a problem situation in a particular way and to stick to that evaluation.

Here is an example of restricted thinking: Anna has been told from when she was little that it is cruel to keep birds in a cage, so she gets upset whenever she sees a bird in a cage. Getting upset is the result of a mental set. Sometimes it is cruel to keep birds in cages, but there are other ways of looking at this situation. Maybe the bird was injured and by keeping it in a cage, the owner is saving its life because it would never be able to fend for itself in the wild. And maybe the owner uses the example of the injured bird to raise awareness of caring for the environment and to improve the lives of other birds.

The following are four other common barriers to problem solving (Coon, 2004):

1. *Emotional barriers.* Sometimes we are unable to solve problems because our emotions get in the way of thinking clearly. For example, the fear of being embarrassed or of making a mistake may prevent us from trying to solve problems.
2. *Learned barriers.* We may think that something can only be done in one way because that is the way we have learned to do it, but there are other ways of problem solving in addition to the old ways.
3. *Perceptual barriers.* Sometimes we tend to see only one aspect of a problem and ignore others. This can get in the way of solving problems.
4. *Cultural barriers.* Our cultural values may lead us to believe that reason and logic are the best means of solving problems and that fantasy and play are a waste of time. In this way we do not explore the various ways of solving problems.

Bibliography

Coon, D. 2004. *Introduction to psychology.* 10th edition. Belmont, CA: Wadsworth.

Jordaan, W. and Jordaan, J. 1998. *People in context.* 3rd edition. Johannesburg: Heinemann.

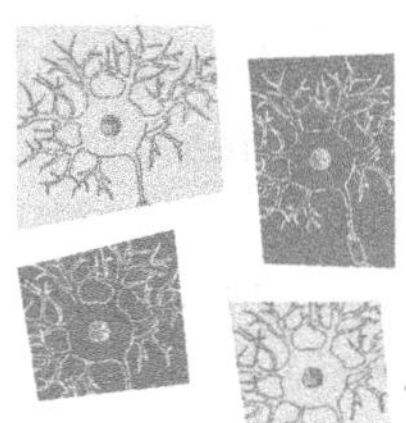

Cognition: Reasoning

Reasoning is one form of thought. Reasoning can be defined as a process of goal-directed thinking that draws conclusions from a set of facts. When we reason, we compare different bits of information. Some of the information may provide evidence to support our ideas and other information may not. On the basis of reasoning about the information, we can come to some conclusion. Look at the following example of reasoning. 'I would like to make my grandmother happy. I know my grandmother likes chocolate cake. I think I will make a cake for her.' In this example you are reasoning that, since your grandmother likes chocolate cake, you will make her happy by baking a cake for her.

1 The structure of reasoning

We all use reasoning for various needs and purposes, but we do not necessarily all use reasoning well. The quality of reasoning depends very much on the suitability or relevance of the reasons we present to support our point of view. This implies that reasoning has a certain structure. There are two main structures inherent in reasoning – a premise and a conclusion.

A premise is the statement from which the conclusion is inferred. When you reason, the viewpoint you adopt or the claim you make is the conclusion. The premise provides the evidence that supports your conclusion. For example, someone may say: 'I think that the South African team will beat the Zimbabwean team because the South Africans have won the last two matches against Zimbabwe'. In this example, the view that 'the South African team will beat the Zimbabwean team' is the conclusion. The premise or evidence from which the conclusion is inferred is the fact that the South Africans have a stronger team because they have won the previous two matches against Zimbabwe. If the person just says: 'I think that the South African team will beat the Zimbabwean team', the person is merely expressing an opinion. It is not an example of reasoning because the statement does not contain the structure of reasoning – that is, a premise and a conclusion.

The relevance of the premise to the conclusion determines how well the person is reasoning. If, for example, the person had said the South Africans would beat the Zimbabweans because he does not like the look of the Zimbabweans, the premise is not relevant to the conclusion. In everyday life, the relevance of the premise you use to support your point of view is crucial if you want to avoid faulty reasoning. Unfortunately, there are often subjective reasons (such as social and emotional needs) why irrelevant reasons or faulty premises are used to support a conclusion or point of view. For example, if you say: 'Jane should win the award for singing because she is my cousin', you are using faulty reasoning because the conclusion is not based on a relevant premise. It may be true that Jane is your cousin, but an award for singing should be based on singing ability and not on relationships.

If you have difficulty identifying premises and conclusions, here are two general guidelines: In order to identify a conclusion, you can ask yourself what the speaker (or writer) is trying to indicate or impress on you. The premises can be identified by asking what evidence or information the speaker presents to support the conclusion.

2 Reasoning based on formal rules of logic

When we reason, information from the environment and information stored in memory are used according to a set of rules for transforming that information. There are two main types of reasoning: deductive and inductive (Coon, 2004; Jordaan and Jordaan, 1998).

2.1 Deductive reasoning

Deductive reasoning refers to the process of drawing a conclusion that follows logically from two or more statements or premises. Deductive reasoning is based on the logical rule that, if the premise(s) is (are) true, then the conclusion is true (and cannot possibly be false). Here is an example of deductive reasoning: A student, Sofia, arranges with a friend, Noleen, to meet in the library. Sofia tells Noleen that if she is not at her desk in the study area on the seventh floor, she will be in the photocopying section. Noleen does not find Sofia in the study area but finds her in the photocopying section. This is deductive reasoning because the premise was true (Sofia was either in the study area or the photocopying section) and therefore the conclusion is guaranteed (Noleen did not find Sofia in the study area and therefore knew that she would be in the photocopying section).

2.2 Inductive reasoning

Inductive reasoning uses available evidence to generate a conclusion about the likelihood of something. In inductive reasoning, conclusions are based on premises, but premises do not guarantee conclusions. They only provide some support for the likelihood or probability of conclusions. Look at the following example: 'There are clouds in the sky [premise]. I think it is going to rain.' This is an example of inductive reasoning because the presence of clouds in the sky increases the likelihood of rain but does not guarantee it. The clouds may not build up to rain clouds, or the sun may come out or the wind may blow the clouds away and therefore it may not rain. If you had said: 'I see raindrops falling on my hand. It is raining', this would be an example of deductive reasoning because seeing drops of rain necessarily means that it is raining. Through inductive reasoning we can make conclusions on the basis of limited information. However, it must be remembered that these conclusions are only assumptions; they are not certainties and therefore they are not facts. When people use these assumptions as facts, errors of reasoning occur.

Inductive reasoning is used when we form analogies or comparisons. Analogical reasoning means that you infer patterns of relations between things. For example, let us find the missing word in the following analogy: 'Left is to right as up is to ...'. Left and right are concepts that are linked through the relation of direction. Left and right are opposite directions. The analogy suggests that the second clause should match the first and so the missing word should be something that is related to the word 'up' by opposite directionality. It therefore makes sense that the missing word is 'down'. We use analogical reasoning to find patterns in events. For example, when you describe the similarities and differences between two things or events, you are using analogical reasoning.

3 Differences between formal and informal reasoning

So far in this section, we have looked at reasoning based on formal rules of logic. Although we do not stop and think about premises and conclusions when we are discussing things with our friends, knowledge of rules of formal reasoning helps us to decide on the quality or relevance of people's reasoning. Descriptions of formal reasoning merely spell out the basis of everyday reasoning. According to Jordaan and Jordaan (1998), the main differences between formal and everyday or informal reasoning are as follows:

- In formal reasoning the premises are stated explicitly and in informal everyday reasoning they are more implied than explicit.
- In formal reasoning the problem that is being reasoned about (or argued) is generally not personally relevant; informal reasoning usually has personal consequences for everyday life.
- The personal relevance of informal reasoning can lead to weaknesses in reasoning. Reasons for this may be that: (1) we may accept a premise as true without thinking carefully about its accuracy; or (2) we may accept a conclusion because it agrees with our own personal viewpoint without thinking carefully about the evidence on which it is based.

- The structures and rules of formal reasoning are more obvious than in informal everyday reasoning.
- In formal reasoning there is usually only one correct solution; in informal everyday reasoning there are generally several possible solutions because of the practicalities of everyday life.

4 Fallacies

Conclusions are sometimes based on fallacies or misleading arguments. People may use fallacies when they want us to change the way we believe. Fallacies use irrelevant premises to support a conclusion, as if those premises are relevant. Here are some different types of fallacy:

- Playing on someone's sympathies to get something done – for example, a student who fails an exam asks the lecturer to give him a pass mark because he has difficult personal circumstances. This is poor reasoning, because the student's personal circumstances are not relevant criteria for passing the exam from an academic point of view. Many students who have difficult personal circumstances pass exams by mastering the necessary course work.
- Trying to discredit an issue by discrediting the person who supports the issue – for example, you may say you do not believe what a person says because you do not like the appearance of that person. Again, the premise (appearance) is irrelevant to the conclusion (that the person's views are worthless).
- Relying on the characteristics of a certain group in order to gain support for a particular conclusion – for example, an advertisement which states that 'real men drink beer' is playing on the sentiments of men who want to be seen as manly. The premise is irrelevant to the conclusion (that is, if you drink beer you will be manly).
- Using a false analogy – this means implying that things that are similar are actually identical. Look at the following example: 'Nomsa loves her husband and is happy to be a housewife. If you would rather work than be a housewife, then you do not love your husband'. In this example, the analogy is based on the comparison of Nomsa and you as wives, implying that you are identical. This analogy is false because there may be lots of reasons why Nomsa is happy to be a housewife and Nomsa's situation may be quite different from yours. You can still work and love your husband.
- Using a slightly changed version of someone else's point of view as a basis for your reasoning – for example, Mary says she can understand that some people have reasons for agreeing with abortion. Sam then claims that Mary is in favour of abortion. The error in reasoning here is that Mary was expressing her understanding of some others who support abortion and is not necessarily in favour of abortion herself.

5 Critical reasoning

In order to prevent misunderstandings, it is important that we should be able to evaluate the information we receive, that we should reason correctly and that we should make good judgements. This is what is meant by the term 'critical reasoning'. You are not necessarily criticising someone if you use critical reasoning. The term implies that you are thinking critically about the information you have. Critical reasoning means that you look at all the options and various explanations for something and do not merely accept one point of view or the explanation that suits you. Critical reasoning helps you to cope better with situations in daily life. Using critical reasoning helps you to gain greater insight into things, to be better informed, to be open-minded and to make good decisions.

The following are steps you can take to improve your critical reasoning ability (Jordaan and Jordaan, 1998):

5.1 Identify the problem

Before you can deal with a problem, you have to acknowledge that there is a problem and define what it is.

5.2 Keep an open mind

Being open-minded means that you do not just accept an opinion or view (even your own) as being true or relevant. There are ways in which you can facilitate open-mindedness:

- Avoid either/or categorisation. This means that you should avoid seeing things as extremes, such as either right or wrong, good or bad, or true or false. Such extremes are seldom applicable.
- Believing that you are totally right and another is totally wrong may cause you to overlook other factors that could play a role in explaining why you are having difficulties. Try to look for other possibilities or positions in the middle (called the 'middle ground').

5.3 Remember the difference between language and reality

Language is a system of symbols and is therefore not the same as reality. We use language to describe our reality, but they are not the same thing. We can compare this to the relation between a painting of a bunch of flowers and the actual bunch of flowers. The artist selects certain detail and colours to create an attractive painting, but it is not necessarily exactly the same as the real bunch of flowers. In fact, it is not a bunch of flowers at all, but a *representation* of a bunch of flowers. In the same way, language is not reality but a means of representing it. People who are critical thinkers can identify the aspects of a situation that others may not have described or included, or help to adopt a new perspective. This can make people annoyed, but it helps to clarify the situation. In other words, we should try to see beyond the painting or beyond the words; we should try to see the reality of things as clearly as possible and understand that language represents it in many different ways.

5.4 Use open-ended questions

If you ask questions in a certain way, you may get only 'yes' or 'no' answers. If you phrase the questions differently, you can get a great deal more information and you are more likely to find solutions for problems. For example, you are concerned that your teenage son is not paying enough attention to studying because he enjoys socialising and when he indicates that he is going out, you ask: 'Should you be going out tonight?' This implies that you think he should not be going out and this may lead to resentment and a breakdown in communication. However, if you ask your son what plans he has made to manage his studies while still being able to enjoy his social life, the matter is open to discussion of various options that are acceptable to both of you.

5.5 Avoid over-generalisations

An over-generalisation means using a conclusion that is based on very little evidence or that is based on one instance of an event and making this conclusion a rule. For example, you see a young man driving recklessly and you generalise your observation to reach the conclusion that he is a bad person or that all young men drive recklessly. This is clearly not the case.

5.6 Be empathetic

Empathy means understanding fully. Empathy can generally be attained by putting yourself in the other person's position and trying to think what it must be like or what he or she is feeling. Empathy is different from sympathy, which means feeling sorry for someone. Empathetic openness allows you to be aware of various people's positions, or to listen to all sides of the story. Empathetic openness not only helps you to understand others but makes you more sensitive to what they are experiencing. This encourages people to say what they need to say and facilitates communication.

5.7 Obtain relevant information

In order to make the right decisions, you need to have as much information as possible about the relevant issue. Because all the necessary information is not always readily available, you need to know where to find information (what the right sources are).

5.8 Use informal knowledge

Although we gain a great deal of information from formal sources, such as studying, there is also a great deal to be obtained from informal sources. Informal knowledge refers to the information and experience that people obtain from practical experience in everyday life, which is not necessarily written down in books.

5.9 Develop collective thinking

We live in an information society and it is seldom possible for one person to have all the information needed to deal with a particular problem or situation. Collective thinking means thinking in a group, where information is combined from various sources. Collective thinking is successful when certain rules are followed. For example, a strict task orientation should be maintained; discussion should be summarised and clarified on an ongoing basis; all contributions from group members should be acknowledged; conflict and disagreement should be recognised without choosing sides; and people should aim for compromises to ensure everyone's co-operation.

Bibliography

Coon, D. 2004. *Introduction to psychology.* 10th edition. Belmont, CA: Wadsworth.

Jordaan, W. and Jordaan, J. 1998. *People in context.* 3rd edition. Johannesburg: Heinemann.

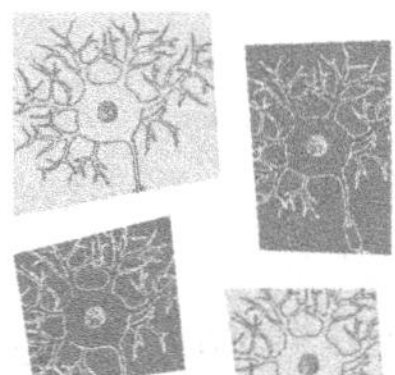

Cognition: Thinking

1 The nature of thought

Thinking has many forms, like day dreaming, or reasoning and problem solving, but whatever the form, thinking refers to mentally processing information. Perception is the first step in processing information. Perception is a form of knowing about the world, based on information obtained from our sensory systems. Sensory information is then compared with mental structures or internal representations so that the input is identified and can further guide our actions. Thought processes comprise another step in the sequence of processing information.

Thinking is a complex process of transforming available information to form new representations. In other words, through thinking we process symbolic representations of things. It is another form of knowing. When we think about something, we do not need to have that thing in front of us. We can represent things (for example objects, situations or people) in our minds and even combine thoughts to make new representations. For example, when you lie in bed at night and think about what you are going to say at a student meeting the next day, you are using a mental language to represent the events that may occur and to plan how to respond. You may also think about a car or a jacket you would like to buy and even see it in your mind's eye – that is, a visual representation. These things (thoughts about the meeting, a car or a jacket) are regarded as symbols. The thoughts are symbols or representations of the actual objects or events because they exist inside our heads. As you can see from these examples, symbolic representations are based not only on concrete objects (like a car) but can also be based on abstract ideas (like democracy or feelings).

On the most basic level, thinking is the internal representation of a problem or situation. When we are thinking, we make use of certain mental structures or systems of symbols. The three main symbol systems that are covered here are images, concepts and language.

1.1 Images

Images are the symbolic representations of objects and their characteristics. In other words, an image is a mental representation that has picture-like qualities. We can form an image of something in our thoughts even if that thing is not present. For example, when you are far away from someone you love, you can form a mental image of that person in your mind. Your image is based on what the person looks like and perhaps the way the person smiles or moves. We can also form auditory images, based on a person's voice for example. You can form an image of a place based on the sounds you associate with it; for example, an image of the sea could be based on the sound of waves breaking on the rocks. An image is therefore more than just a picture. For example, your image of a holiday at the sea may relate to a visual image, as well as the sound of the waves and the smell of the salty sea air.

Images play an important role in our thoughts and can even help us think more effectively. Forming an image of something can help us to remember information about it. For example, if we try to remember someone's name, it helps to have an image of what that person looks like. Forming images can also help us to remember unrelated things. For example, you may find it difficult to remember a list of unrelated words like 'window', 'spoon', 'dress', 'stove', 'hand', 'sun' and 'shoes'. You would probably remember the words better if you formed a mental image of a woman in a dress and shoes standing at a stove preparing food with a spoon in her hand and looking at the sun shining through the window.

People also use images to help them solve problems by retrieving images stored in memory to apply to a current problem. For example, by manipulating mental images, a scientist can think about different ways to solve a particular physics or chemistry problem without actually doing the experiment several times over. In this way, the scientist uses stored images (from memory) to apply past experience or knowledge in order to solve a current problem. Images are not only retrieved from memory but can be created or invented. For example, an artist may have an image of a picture before it is actually painted. When we speak of visual images, we must remember that they are seldom complete detailed pictures, but are more like broad outlines of something. For example, if you try to think of the face of someone you know well, you will probably be unable to visualise detail but you get an overall picture instead.

1.2 Concepts

A basic process in thinking is to categorise experiences. The categories we form as mental representations of groups of related items are called concepts. These are the building blocks of thinking and they help us to organise knowledge in systematic ways

(Morris and Maisto, 2003). A concept may be related to physical objects; for example, 'food' is a concept that refers to various things we can eat. 'Meat' is an example of the concept of 'food', but 'meat' is also a concept in itself because it refers to many kinds of meat. A concept may also be something abstract; for example, 'democracy' is a concept referring to the characteristics that define democracy. Concepts may represent the properties of objects, such as colour or size and therefore 'red' and 'large' are also concepts. Concepts may also refer to relations between objects, such as the concepts of 'bigger' or 'heavier' when comparing things.

1.2.1 Hierarchical organisation of concepts

Using concepts is a form of thinking that classifies things in our world and makes sense of it. Concept formation is based on experience. Through our interaction with the world, we learn about the characteristics of things and place them in categories or groups. Concepts can also form networks – that is, they may be interrelated – and one concept can be part of others. For example, the concept of 'fruit' is part of the concept of 'food', but 'fruit' also includes concepts such as 'apples'. To make sense of the world, people tend to organise related concepts in a hierarchy, which means in an organised way. A hierarchy organises things from the general to the specific. For example, the broad category of food has several sub-categories, such as fruit and meat, which are also divided into types such as apples and steak. A conceptual hierarchy is made up of at least three levels: a superordinate (or top) level, an intermediate (or middle) level and a subordinate (or bottom) level (Jordaan and Jordaan, 1998). Things that have common attributes fall on the same level.

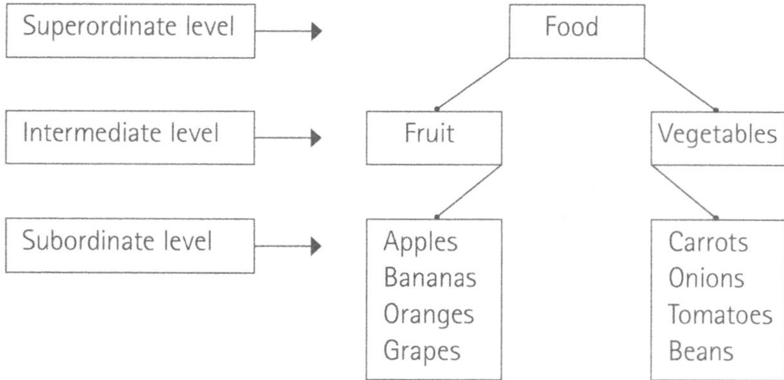

Figure 1 An illustration of a conceptual hierarchy

The concept on each level includes all the concepts on lower levels. Let us look at the conceptual hierarchy of food as an example. We can say that the concept of 'food' is on the superordinate level because it is based on the unique characteristic of things that can be eaten and that provide nutrition. The concept of 'food' includes the concepts of 'fruit' and 'apples'. The concept of 'fruit' falls on the intermediate level because it is one form of the concept of 'food', but there are other types of food that do not share the same characteristics as fruit, such as the concepts of 'meat' or 'vegetables' (see Figure 1). 'Apples' are on the subordinate level because they are one specific type of the concept of 'fruit' and there are other different types of fruit. Both apples and fruit are members of the general concept of 'food' (Coon, 2004).

1.2.2 *Conceptual rules*

We rely on conceptual rules to decide whether or not something belongs to a certain concept. For example, the conceptual rule for deciding whether something belongs to the concept of 'food' may be that it is an edible substance that is taken into the body to maintain life and growth. Using this conceptual rule, we can conclude that chewing gum is not food because it does not maintain life and growth, even if it can be eaten. We do not often use this kind of formal conceptual hierarchy in everyday life. Formal conceptual hierarchies are based on exact definitions or agreements about attributes in an objective sense. This type of definition is called the *denotative meaning* of a concept. Informal conceptual hierarchies are based on subjective or personal experience and emotions. For example, if you asked several people to compile a hierarchy of their goals in life, you would get very different answers. Personal meanings of concepts are called the *connotative meanings* of concepts.

1.2.3 *Conceptual errors*

The inaccurate use of concepts can lead to errors of thinking. If we oversimplify a complex category, this can result in the formation of stereotypes or rigid ways of thinking. For example, the view of a woman as someone who runs a household and raises children is a *stereotype* that gets in the way of seeing a woman as an individual who may have other abilities, roles and preferences.

Problems are also created by all-or-nothing or one-dimensional thought. This kind of thought leads to the classification of things at extremes and not seeing the differences in between. All-or-nothing thought may lead to the classification of something as absolutely right or wrong, whereas we know that there can be states in between when something can be partly right or partly wrong. Consider, for example, the statement that it is wrong to speak your mind. Believing totally in the statement is an example of all-or-nothing thought. While it is generally a good thing to be controlled and sensitive to the needs of others, there may be situations where you have to speak your mind to clarify a situation to the benefit of everyone.

1.2.4 Prototypes

The process of concept formation is part of the mind's attempt to function economically; that is, to minimise processing time and effort wherever possible. We respond most effectively to concepts on the most basic level. For example, if you look at an apple, the first thing that comes to mind is that it is an apple rather than a piece of fruit. Thinking of it as a piece of fruit rather than an apple is higher up the conceptual hierarchy and requires greater abstraction and effort. If you were shown a picture of an apple, your reaction time in identifying it as an apple would be quicker than the time taken to identify it as a piece of fruit.

Another way of thinking efficiently is by forming *prototypes,* or ideal models of concepts. A prototype helps us to identify things efficiently. For example, when you think of fruit, you do not make a mental list of the features of fruit. We mentally compare the things we see to prototypes and this helps us to identify them efficiently. An example of a prototype is the following: the prototype of a table is a flat surface with four legs attached at right angles to it. Tables may differ in height, shape or type of material, but they are all based on the same design principle.

1.3 Language

Most thinking relies a great deal on language. The relationship between language and thought is a complex one. Language can be defined as a system of symbols to represent thoughts. Language is used as a way of making sense of things and a means of communicating with others, based on a shared system of meaning. For example, the word 'happy' refers to an emotional state and a word of the same meaning is used in many different languages to refer to the same state.

1.3.1 Inner speech

One way in which language influences thought is seen in our use of *inner speech.* Language is not only used to communicate with others, but can also be used to direct our own thoughts and actions. For example, you may find that when you have to carry out a complex task for the first time, you say things out loud to yourself as you go along in order to make the task clearer or simpler. This is called inner speech or implicit speech. Inner speech consists of key words and phrases, not complete and grammatically correct sentences. For example, if you are driving in an unfamiliar city, you may repeat phrases relating to the directions you have been given in order to locate landmarks, such as 'public telephone on corner ... turn right'. Inner speech is an example of the way in which language plays a role in thought.

1.3.2 Language and thought

Although there is a relationship between language and thought, we must remember that they are not identical. There is evidence that thinking can take place without language. For example, studies on the early cognitive development of deaf children have shown that they are able to think before they acquire a language (Braden, 1984). Another example is seen in people with damage to the language area of the brain who are still capable of thinking and problem solving, even though their language usage is impaired (Banich, 2001). Experiments have shown that chess players rely on thinking about the spatial organisation of the pieces on the board and not on inner speech to plan their moves. Too much inner speech can in fact slow down the process of visual problem solving.

Language does help us to form concepts through naming and classifying perceptions, but we must remember that words and concepts are not one and the same. An illustration of the idea that words and concepts are not identical can be found in children's behaviour, which demonstrates that they know a concept even before they have a word for it. For example, very young children can group blocks of the same colour before they can actually name the colour. This demonstrates that they understand the concept of colour before they have words for colours.

Bibliography

Banich, M. 2001. *Cognitive neuroscience and neuropsychology.* 2nd edition. Boston, MA: Houghton Mifflin.

Braden, J.P. 1984. The structure of non-verbal intelligence in deaf and hearing subjects. *American Annals of the Deaf,* 130, 496–501.

Coon, D. 2004. *Introduction to psychology.* 10th edition. Belmont, California: Wadsworth.

Fine, R. 1965. The psychology of blindfold chess: An introspective account. *Acta Psychologica,* 24, 352–370.

Jordaan, W. and Jordaan, J. 1998. *People in context.* 3rd edition. Johannesburg: Heinemann.

Morris, C.G. and Maisto, A.A. 2003. *Understanding psychology.* Englewood Cliffs, NJ: Prentice Hall.

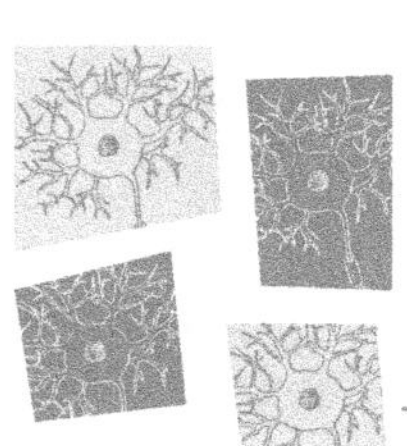

Consultation scenario for a psychological research project

1 The scenario

Dr Matoane is a consulting psychologist. A non-profit governmental organisation (NGO) for community development approaches him to do research on a national project, called the People for Community Project (PfCP). He sets up a consultation meeting with the project co-ordinator to discuss the matter.

During the meeting, Dr Matoane learned that the PfCP is a project that aims at getting people involved in the development and improvement of their own communities. According to the project co-ordinator, the PfCP wants to make an impact not only in impoverished communities but also in socio-economically well-developed ones. In this respect, the PfCP differs significantly from community development projects that the NGO for community development had introduced before. Previous projects focused on underdeveloped and disadvantaged communities. Some of these projects were successful, but a large number of them failed. The NGO now believes that the high failure rate was due to the underlying assumptions about community. These programmes were all based on the CNP development premise, in which C stands for community (define the community), N for needs (identify the community needs) and P for programme (develop a programme to address the needs).

The problem was that the nature of the community was defined in advance. After the community was defined, the needs of the people who were perceived to be members of the community were identified and these needs were interpreted in terms of the definition of the community. This meant that programmes were developed for predefined communities. The people were never consulted about the nature of their community and although they were consulted about their needs, these were then interpreted in terms of a predefined nature of the community. It is possible that the interpretations of these needs distorted the needs to such an extent that they could no longer be seen as the needs of the people involved. Moreover, the people involved were perceived to be members of the defined community, but they were never consulted on the degree to which they associated themselves with the community as it was defined.

In the PfCP, the NGO is now opting for a different approach to creating community development programmes. It thinks the nature of communities should not be predefined but should be defined by the people themselves. This approach causes some difficulties. For example, people certainly differ with regard to what they perceive to be the nature of the community they belong to. In addition, an individual may perceive him- or herself to be a member of more than one community, therefore it becomes more difficult to define the target community for a development programme (the target community is the community that the programme aims to develop).

This is where the NGO needs the consultant's assistance. They want Dr Matoane to help them find a method for defining target communities in such a way that it incorporates the complexities of people's perceptions of their community.

Dr Matoane listens carefully to the project manager because he wants to understand exactly what the problem is and he wants to manage their expectations within the scope of his limitations so that a workable plan of action can be agreed upon.

He tells the project manager that he needs time to explore the matter further in order to be able to define the problem more clearly, to consider the problem within a field of existing knowledge and to design the study that would be required to investigate methods that could be used to define target communities.

2 The interpretation of the scenario

In this scenario, the consultant's client is the NGO for community development. The project co-ordinator is not the client. He is the consultant's contact person at the NGO. The contact person represents the client. The interview between the consultant and the client's contact person contains the following elements:

- The *concern* raised by the client. The NGO is concerned about the large number of community projects that fail.
- The *need* indicated by the client. The NGO wants to change the premise on which it bases its community programmes. Previously it worked with predefined communities. It wants to change this approach and work with communities that are defined by themselves.
- *Contextual* information that helps the consultant form a better understanding of the client's needs. The project co-ordinator provides contextual information about the project (PfCP) and also about the theoretical approach on which it is based. The PfCP aims to get people involved in the development and improvement of their own communities. It is a national project and it is

implemented not only in impoverished communities but also in socio-economically well-developed communities. The theoretical basis of the project is the CNP development premise.

- The *request* made by the client. The NGO wants the consultant to help find a method for defining target communities in such a way that it incorporates the complexities of people's perceptions of their community.
- Managed *expectations*. The client's request is quite complex, which means the client has high expectations. Dr Matoane manages these expectations by indicating that further exploration is required to clarify the problem and to consider it in terms of existing knowledge in the field and to design a suitable research study.
- A provisional *plan of action*. The provisional plan of action is that Dr Matoane undertakes to explore the matter further and to return with a clear definition of the problem and an understanding of how it could be seen in terms of existing knowledge in the field and with a proposal for a study that could be undertaken to investigate methods that can be used to define target communities.

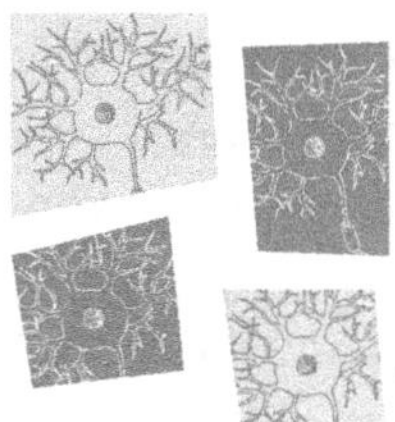

Consultation scenario for a stress management programme

1 The scenario

Dr Lydia de Bruyn is a consulting psychologist. She is in her office when the telephone rings. The person who telephones her introduces himself as the personnel manager of a company called InfoTech SA. He explains that they obtained Lydia's name from another company she did consultation work for some time ago. He tells her that the other company was very impressed with her professional and ethical approach and because the work she did for them was based on sound psychological theory. He explains that his company is experiencing personnel problems and that they are hoping to consult with Lydia on how to solve them. Lydia agrees on a date and time to meet with the personnel manager. She prefers to meet at the personnel manager's office because it provides an opportunity to see the environment in which the company's personnel work.

Lydia's first priority is to clarify her task. She has to listen very carefully to her clients to get an idea of their problems and their expectations. She has to find out what their problems are and what they expect her to do about it.

During the interview, she learns that the company is an information technology company doing business on a global scale. The company operates in a stressful environment. Because they do business all over the world, they have to work a 24-hour day. In other words, they can expect queries from their clients at any time during the day or night. The environment in which they function is highly competitive. There is constant pressure to respond to their clients as quickly as possible. There is also constant pressure to update products and to develop new products to stay ahead of the competition.

It is very difficult for individuals to maintain the high levels of performance required by their work circumstances. The company's sick-leave records show higher than normal levels of absenteeism. More individuals are becoming sick and are staying sick for longer periods of time. People at all levels in the company are complaining about the stress they feel and the frustrations they experience. Some individuals are becoming apathetic and despondent about their work. The company sees these phenomena in a serious light because production goes down and production standards are compromised.

The company wants Lydia to advise them on intervention strategies that would enable people to function better. The company cannot change the global environment in which it operates, but it can try to create an internal work environment in which people can cope with stressful demands. The personnel manager explains that they need the help of a psychologist to design and implement intervention strategies that would help individuals to cope better in a high-stress environment.

After listening very carefully to the personnel manager, Lydia indicates that she could help the company define the problem in terms of psychological theory and that she will be able to design an appropriate intervention strategy and help the company implement it. She explains that there are psychological issues that have to be considered in order to understand the current situation in the company and that her focus will be on the psychology of the individual. She does not plan to consider the psychology of the organisation.

She explains that she has to consider psychological issues to form a *psychological* understanding. In other words, she wants to look at the ways in which employees behave in the company and then try to look beyond their behaviour patterns to try to see the psychology that explains the behaviour. She has to understand the psychology behind the behaviour if she wishes to design an intervention strategy because this is designed in terms of the psychology behind the behaviour and not in terms of the behaviour itself. A psychological intervention strategy aims to change people at a psychological level. If a person's psychology changes, then his or her behaviour pattern changes.

The situation described by the personnel manager indicates to Lydia that she has to consider the concept of stress to understand what happens to people when they find themselves in stressful situations. She realises she has to look at the psychology of work to understand the context in which stress occurs. She also has to explore human motivation to understand what motivates people to act in particular ways. And finally, she has to consider the idea of self-concept to understand how people see and appreciate themselves in the contexts in which they find themselves.

Towards the end of the interview, Lydia summarises the main points discussed during the interview to make sure she understands the situation correctly. The personnel manager clarifies a couple of minor points and the two of them agree that they have similar perspectives. Lydia's next step is to work out a realistic schedule for the execution and completion of the task. She asks the personnel manager when the company wants to start implementing the intervention strategy. She explains to him that she needs time to design it and that the design and implementation process have to be discussed with him before the strategy can be implemented. She explains the steps required to design and implement an intervention programme. They discuss the programme outcomes and the dates by which these have to be achieved and they decide on a project implementation plan that will enable them to achieve the outcomes on time. Then Lydia says goodbye, gets into her car and drives back to her office where the hard work is to begin.

2 The interpretation of the scenario

In this scenario Dr Lydia de Bruyn is the consultant and her client is a company called InfoTech SA. The personnel manager is not the client. He is the consultant's contact person at InfoTech SA. The contact person represents the client. The interview between Lydia and the personnel manager contains the following elements:

- The *concern* raised by the client. The company is concerned about the higher than normal levels of employee absenteeism, the complaints about personal stress and frustrations, the fact that people are becoming apathetic and despondent towards their work and the effect this has on production levels and standards.
- The *need* indicated by the client. The company wants to improve the level of functioning of its employees, in particular to cope better with stressful demands. It envisages doing this by implementing intervention strategies.
- *Contextual information* that helps the consultant form a better understanding of the client's needs. The personnel manager provides contextual information about the environment in which the company operates and also about the environment in which employees operate within the company. The company operates in a 24-hour global business context, which is very competitive. This means quick response times and constant innovation, which creates a stressful environment for individuals.
- The *request* made by the client. The company wants the consultant to design and implement intervention strategies that would help individuals cope better in the high-stress environment.
- Managed *expectations*. To avoid any misunderstandings, the consultant makes sure that there is agreement on all points between her and the personnel manager. She indicates that she will be able to meet the client's expectations to design and implement an intervention strategy. However, she limits her intervention to the individual and states that it does not include intervening at an organisational level. She also explains that the intervention is based on psychology and also that she needs time to design and implement intervention.

- A provisional *plan of action.* The consultant explains the steps required to design and implement an intervention programme. The consultant and the client agree on a project implementation plan that will allow them to achieve the required outcomes. The first step is for the consultant to design an intervention programme based on appropriate psychological theory and to discuss this and its implementation with the personnel manager.

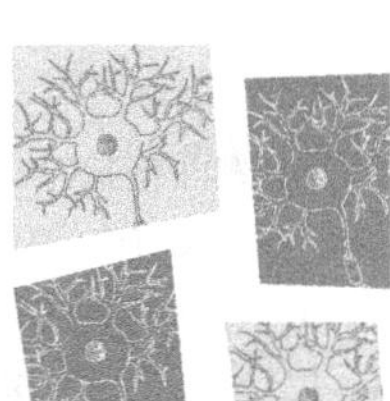

Consultation scenario for a study management programme

1 The scenario

Lesiba is a psychological counsellor at a university and Brian telephones him to ask for assistance because he has failed his exams. Lesiba agrees on a date and time for Brian to come and see him in his office.

Lesiba's first priority is to clarify his task. He has to listen carefully to Brian to get an idea of his problems and his expectations.

During the interview, Lesiba learns that Brian is employed full time as an administrative clerk at a big company. He waited a year before he found the job, so he is very pleased to be working there. Brian would very much like to work in the human resources department of the company, but he does not have the necessary qualifications. However, he has been told that if he studies part time he will be given credit and when he has the necessary credits he will be considered for a position in the human resources department. Brian is very keen to get on with his studies. Although he has not studied at university level before, he decides to register for six modules for the first semester in the hope that he will finish his studies more quickly.

Brian's parents live in a rural area, so he is staying with his uncle. The house is quite near to Brian's place of work; however, his uncle has a large family and the house is full. Brian receives his study package, but because he doesn't have a desk to put it on, he stores it under his bed. Brian enjoys his life. He likes to play soccer in his free time and to socialise with his friends. Before he realises it, a month has passed and he has not started his studies. He is happy to see that assignments are not compulsory and he thinks he will catch up with the work in time for the exams. Brian takes two weeks' leave to prepare for the exams. He is very disappointed when he gets his results and sees that he has failed four of the six modules.

Lesiba decides to ask Brian what he thinks the problem is. Brian says it is not his fault that he failed, but that the exam papers were too difficult. He thinks that he should have passed the four that he failed because he managed to pass two others. When Lesiba asks him for other possible reasons, he says he would pass if he had a place of his own. He also wonders if the lecturers do not want him to pass because he is from a disadvantaged background. Lesiba then asks Brian about his study habits at present. He describes a rather haphazard pattern of studying irregularly for brief times without any systematic approach to his studies. He tends to give up easily.

Brian would like Lesiba to advise him on an intervention strategy that will enable him to pass his exams. He cannot change his environment, but he can try to find a solution that will help him to cope better with the demands of his chosen objectives (that is, to succeed with his studies). Lesiba agrees to help Brian to develop a problem-solving strategy and then to draw up a psychological programme to assist him to deal with the management of his studies through behaviour modification. He explains to Brian that he (Lesiba) needs to draw on psychological knowledge to develop an intervention strategy that will work best for Brian. Lesiba knows that one needs to consider psychological theory relating to thinking, reasoning and problem solving in order to help Brian to get a clear picture of his problem. One also needs to consider psychological theory relating to learning and memory in order to identify the factors that will help Brian study more effectively and keep to his programme.

Towards the end of the interview, Lesiba summarises the main points discussed during the interview to make sure that both of them understand the situation correctly. The next step is to work out a realistic schedule for the execution and completion of the programme. Lesiba warns Brian that the intervention programme will mean hard work and dedication on Brian's part. He asks Brian when he will be ready to start implementing it. They establish the time required to achieve the desired outcome and also discuss the number of meetings that may be required. Lesiba has to find appropriate times for meeting with Brian in between other appointments. They consult their diaries and agree on a date for the next appointment, which will also be when they start implementing the programme.

2 The interpretation of the scenario

In this scenario, Lesiba is the consultant and the student, Brian, is his client. The consultation interview between Lesiba and Brian contains the following elements:

- The *concern* raised by the client. The client's concern is that he failed his examinations. This concern is explicit, but there is also an implicit concern, namely that Brian will not be considered for a position in human resources if he does not progress in his studies. The concern is implicit because it is not explicitly stated by Brian, but implicated in the contextual information he provides.
- The *need* indicated by the client. Brian wants to become a successful student – that is, one who passes his exams. He needs to learn how to cope better

with the demands posed by his objectives (to pass his exams and to work in human resources). He needs somebody to help him achieve this.

- *Contextual information* that helps the consultant form a better understanding of the client's needs. Brian provides contextual information about his personal circumstances, the reasons for his studies and his understanding of what it means to study. Brian comes from a rural, disadvantaged background. He stays with his uncle near his place of work, but in overcrowded circumstances. He embarked on his studies to obtain credits that would allow him to be considered for a better job; however, Brian does not really understand what it means to study. He does not take personal responsibility but blames his failure on other factors (difficult exam papers, not having a place of his own and lecturers being biased against him). He is not disciplined, socialises too much, puts off his studies and tries to make up for lost time by cramming for exams.
- The *request* made by the client. Brian wants Lesiba to advise him on an intervention strategy that will enable him to pass his exams.
- Managed *expectations*. Lesiba agrees to help Brian develop problem-solving and study management strategies. To avoid any misunderstanding, he makes sure that there is agreement on all points. He also warns Brian that the intervention programme will mean hard work and dedication on Brian's part.
- A provisional *plan of action*. Lesiba and Brian discuss the time required for the programme and decide on a realistic schedule for the execution and completion of the programme as well as the number of meetings that will be required. They fix a date for the next appointment. Before their next meeting, Lesiba has to compile an intervention programme based on psychological theory relating to thinking, reasoning, problem solving, learning and memory.

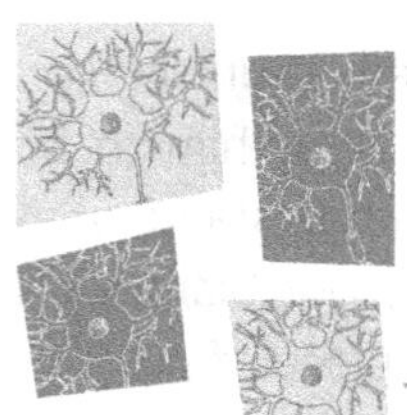

Consultation interview

Consultation services became popular during the latter half of the 20th century, as the world moved into the information age. The information age caused major changes in the structure of organisations, which had to become more focused and efficient in a world that required specialised services and faster reaction times. Many of the services that were previously part of an organisation but that were not directly concerned with its core business were sourced out to be provided by external, specialised service providers. For example, in many of the smaller companies, personnel departments were closed down and sourced out to external service providers who specialised in personnel matters. Many governments followed suit and today it is not unusual to see public sector functions delivered by private companies. Sourcing out non-core business services makes for smaller, leaner and more efficient organisations. External service providers are focused on what they do and are able to provide the required services more efficiently and effectively.

1 What does it mean to consult?

When an organisation requires a service that it does not provide itself, it consults with an external service provider to provide the required service. Consultants are specialists. They are knowledgeable and skilful in their domains of operation; however, the work of a consultant is not easy. Consultants have to move into an organisation that they do not know. They have to form relationships with individuals they have never met before. They have to orientate themselves quickly and they have to learn fast. One of the most fundamental skills any consultant has to master is how to be effective in a consultation interview.

2 The consultation interview

There are many different kinds of consultation interview. When you walk into the hardware store and ask the assistant's advice on which kind of paint to buy, you are in fact consulting the assistant. Going to a doctor's rooms with a health complaint is another example of consulting. When somebody considers taking a psychology course that you have just finished and asks for your opinion, he or she is in fact consulting you about the course.

Although consultation interviews may differ for different kinds of consultation, all consultation interviews have some basic elements in common. If you are a consultant, you have to listen carefully to what your client says. At some stage during the interview the client will raise a *concern*. If you listen carefully, you will learn what the client wants. In other words, you will learn what the client's *needs* are. You will hear that the client wants you to do something. In other words, the client will raise a *request*. Sometimes you will have to ask questions to clarify the client's needs and to understand what exactly it is the client expects of you.

In addition, you have to focus on the context in which the problem occurs to gain a better understanding of the client's needs with regard to the situation in question. In other words, you have to *contextualise* the problem presented by the client. Once you are certain you understand the client's needs and his or her request, you will have to manage the client's *expectations*. The problem is that clients may have expectations that you may not be able to fulfil, thus you have to guide them to be more realistic. You have to explain to them what your strengths and weaknesses are. You have to indicate your limitations and manage their expectations. Only after you and your client seem to understand each other are you in a position to suggest a *plan of action*. A plan of action is often referred to as a project plan. Once you decide on a plan of action, it is up to you, the consultant, to deliver on that plan and to do so on time.

3 Summary

All consultation interviews contain the following elements:

- A *concern* raised by the client. The concern is what the client finds wrong or problematic. It is the problem that spurs the client into action.
- *Needs* indicated by the client. The client's needs follow from the concern. These are embedded in the differences between the client's current situation and the future situation desired by the client. The question is: What does the client want to do about the concern?
- *Contextual information* that helps the consultant form a better understanding of the client's needs. The client's problem is embedded in a particular context and is better understood if the problem is contextualised – that is, if the problem is understood in terms of the relevant issues that surround the problem.

- A particular *request* made by the client. At some stage during the interview, the client will raise a particular request, asking the consultant to provide advice, to offer a service or to conduct an intervention.
- Managed *expectations.* The consultant has to make sure the client understands what can and cannot be offered by the consultant. The client may be unrealistic in his or her expectations of the consultant. The consultant has to manage the client's expectations to make them more realistic.
- A provisional *plan of action.* Once the consultant and his or her client have agreed upon the request made by the client and the consultant's ability to deliver on the request, the consultant provides a provisional plan of action. At the very least, the consultant and the client decide on the next step to be taken.

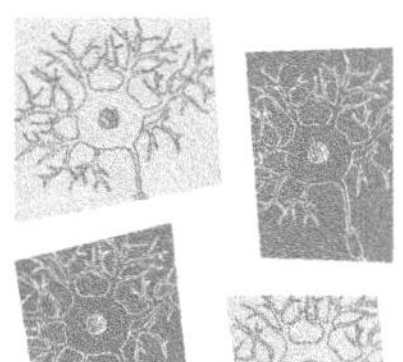

Emotion and motivation

The term *motivation* refers to an internal state that activates and gives direction to our thoughts, feelings and actions. Morris and Maisto (2003) define a motive as a specific need or desire that arouses the organism and directs its behaviour towards a goal. All motives are triggered by some kind of stimulus. For example, a motive for hunger can be triggered by a bodily condition, such as a low blood sugar level, or a cue in the environment, such as an advertisement on TV for a juicy steak, or a feeling such as boredom and loneliness.

Emotion refers to the experience of feelings of such as fear, joy, anger, etc. Like motives, emotions also activate and affect behaviour, but it is difficult to predict the kind of behaviour that a particular emotion will prompt. For example, if a man is hungry, we can be reasonably sure that he will seek food. If the same man experiences the feeling of anger, he may react in a variety of ways and we cannot know with certainty what he will do.

Motivation and emotions are closely linked concepts for three reasons:

- Both motives and the arousal of emotions activate behaviour (for example, you may study hard because you are motivated by your friend or because you fear failure).
- Motives are often accompanied by emotions (for example, the motive to succeed or perform well in the exam is often accompanied by feelings of anxiety).
- Emotions typically have motivational properties of their own (for example, because you are in love, you are motivated to be with the one you love) (Lahey, 2002).

Bibliography

Lahey, B. 2002. *Essentials of psychology.* Boston, MA: McGraw-Hill.

Morris, C.G. and Maisto, A.A. 2003. *Understanding psychology.* Englewood Cliffs, NJ: Prentice Hall.

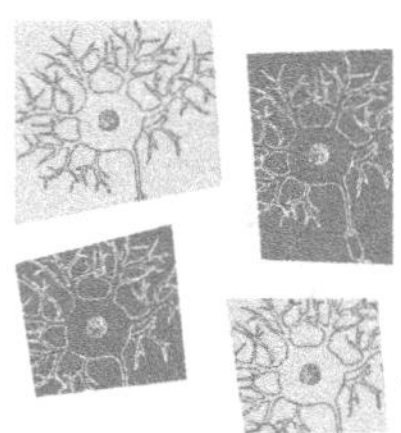

Emotion: Classification of

Many researchers have tried to classify emotions experienced by humans. The following criteria will be used to identify and describe the various emotions.

1 Primary and secondary emotions

Some years ago, Robert Plutchik (1994) proposed that there are eight primary or basic emotions: fear, surprise, sadness, disgust, anger, anticipation, joy and acceptance. Combinations of these primary emotions lead to the generation of other emotions. For example, the combination of joy and acceptance may give rise to the emotion of love; anticipation and joy may lead to optimism; and surprise and sadness may lead to disappointment. In addition, according to Plutchik's model, different emotions may combine to produce an even wider and richer spectrum of experience. For example, love can be accompanied by sadness or by joy.

It is important to remember that there are enormous differences in the ways that different cultures view and categorise emotions. Some do not have words for anxiety or depression or guilt. Some have one word encompassing love, sympathy, pity and liking, which are all distinct emotions in other cultures. Because of cultural differences in the experience of emotions, the tendency now is to distinguish between primary and secondary emotions. Primary emotions are those emotions shared by people throughout the world, regardless of the culture. Most researchers use four criteria to identify primary emotions: (1) they must be evident in all cultures; (2) they must contribute to survival; (3) they must be associated with a distinct facial expression; and (4) they must be evident in non-human species (for example, anger is expressed by revealing the teeth in humans and animals, such as dogs or baboons). There is still no conclusive agreement on which emotions qualify as primary emotions. Secondary emotions are those that are found in some cultures but not in all of them.

Secondary emotions may be considered as the various combinations of primary emotions as influenced by the cultural background (Morris and Maisto, 2003).

Not all psychologists agree on Plutchik's eight basic emotions. Most people agree that there are about six basic emotions and are easily able to recognise facial expressions of happiness, surprise, fear, sadness, anger and disgust. Some psychologists suggest that it is not possible to explain human emotional experience by combining a set of basic emotions. They suggest that we should think of these as basic response components that are shared by a wide variety of emotional experiences. For example, a frown (or furrowed forehead) is often part of the expression of anger, but when someone frowns it does not necessarily mean that the person is angry. A frown may indicate that the person is somehow blocked from reaching a goal and may indicate frustration, concentration or confusion.

2 Positive and negative emotions

Emotions may be experienced as positive or negative. Positive emotions like joy, love and acceptance are usually experienced as pleasurable and rewarding. Positive emotions may create an urge to be creative, to explore, to seek new experiences and to grow. In short, positive emotions encourage personal growth and social connection. A capacity for having positive emotions is a basic human strength and may lead to the development of emotional intelligence (see 'Emotional intelligence' on pages 42–44).

Negative emotions, on the other hand, are usually experienced as unpleasant. Intense negative emotions involve arousal of the sympathetic nervous system, which prepares the individual to either run away in fear or to fight in anger. When physiological arousal is prolonged or unresolved, negative emotions may contribute to the development of physical illnesses, such as headaches, stomach ache or ulcers and psychological problems such as depression or anxiety.

3 Emotions of various intensity

The intensity of emotions varies on a continuum, ranging from extremely low to extremely high intensity. For example, if you are angry you may feel annoyance or rage. Annoyance is a less intense emotion, while rage may be classified as a more intense one. The intensity of feelings interacts with your level of physiological arousal and the quality of the emotion you are experiencing. At the low level of psycho-physiological arousal, the emotions experienced are of low intensity. In this case, the quality of the experience is neutral in the sense that it is neither clearly pleasant nor clearly unpleasant. Emotions like acceptance, boredom and annoyance belong to this group. At a high level of psycho-physiological arousal, emotions experienced are usually of high intensity and the quality of the emotion can in most instances be clearly defined as either pleasant or unpleasant. These imply that there can be major differences in the intensity of primary emotions like joy, anger or fear.

4 Internally and externally expressed emotions

Emotions are expressed and recognised in different ways. For example, we can distinguish between internal and external expressions of emotions. Physiological changes are internal expressions of emotions. Research has shown that there are subtle but distinct physiological changes associated with specific emotions (Levinson, Ekman and Friesen, 1990).

Emotions can also be externally expressed through words (for example, anger or frustration can be verbally expressed by swearing or shouting at someone) and through non-verbal communication such as facial expressions, gestures and body movement, or tone of voice. If these external expressions are viewed in relation to the context in which they are expressed, they are useful tools in identifying and recognising the nature and the intensity of the expressed emotion.

Bibliography

Levinson, R., Ekman, P. and Friesen W. 1990. Voluntary facial action generates emotion-specific autonomic nervous system activity. *Psychophysiology,* 27, 263–283.

Morris, C.G. and Maisto, A.A. 2003. *Understanding psychology.* Englewood Cliffs, NJ: Prentice Hall.

Plutchik, R. 1994. *The psychology and biology of emotion.* New York: Harper Collins.

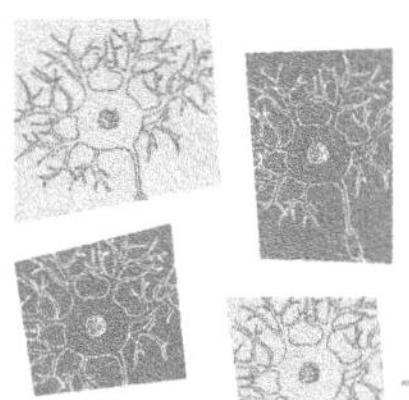

Emotion: Concept of

1 Definition of the concept of emotion

Every day of our lives we experience a variety of feelings. Emotions are one type of feeling. Emotions are feelings that are clearly linked to the meaning of a particular situation. The way in which people express, describe, define or recognise their emotions is related to several factors, such as the situation they are in, age, gender and cultural factors.

According to Coon (2004), the word *emotion* means 'to move'. For example, an emotion may move us to do something, like fear may move us to run away from danger. In explaining what takes place during the experience of an emotion, we need to understand how bodily arousal, behaviour, cognitions and expressions are interrelated. The concept of emotion, therefore, can be defined as a combination of physiological arousal (for example alteration in heart rate, blood pressure and other involuntary movements) combined with perceptual-cognitive processes (for example thinking and subjective experience) and observable behavioural expressions (such as crying or laughing).

2 Components of emotion

We are now going to look at the important components of emotion: physiological arousal, cognitive processes and behavioural expression.

2.1 Physiological component

Emotions are closely tied to physiological processes, but the interconnections are very complex. Physiological arousal associated with emotions occurs through the actions of the autonomic nervous system, which regulates the activity of glands, smooth muscles and blood vessels. There are two divisions of the autonomic nervous system, called the sympathetic nervous system and the parasympathetic nervous system. These two systems are active at all times and work together to bring about balance in the person's functioning.

When an emotion is experienced, arousal increases and the sympathetic system activates the body for emergency action (for example for 'fighting' to protect the person, or 'fleeing' from danger). The arousal leads to purposeful bodily changes that improve the chances of surviving an emergency. If there is sudden intense emotion, the sympathetic effects may be strong enough to bring about a heart attack or sudden death in older persons or those with heart problems. Continued high levels of arousal resulting from the action of the sympathetic nervous system can be damaging, therefore the body has a counterbalancing mechanism – the parasympathetic nervous system – which can reverse the effects of emotional arousal. After a period of intense emotion, activation of the parasympathetic nervous system has the following effects: heart rate slows, the pupil size returns to normal and blood pressure drops. In this way, the parasympathetic system restores the balance and helps build up and conserve body energy.

The parasympathetic system responds much more slowly than the sympathetic system. After a strong emotional shock or intense emotion and increased physiological arousal, the parasympathetic system may overreact, causing a response called parasympathetic rebound. This means that the parasympathetic system continues to act even though balance has been restored. Depending on how severe the parasympathetic rebound is, it may lead to a lower blood pressure, dizziness, fainting and even sudden death.

The connection between emotion and autonomic arousal provides the basis for the use of devices like a lie detector, more accurately called a polygraph. A lie detector is a device that is usually used by the police to record physiological changes in the body (such as a change in the heart rate, breathing rate and blood pressure) as they question a person. The lie detector does not in actual fact detect lies but rather measures emotional arousal by monitoring heart rate, blood pressure, breathing rate and the amount of sweat on the hands while the person responds to questions. The idea is that lying causes an increase in physiological arousal, which is picked up by the lie detector and this can indicate whether the person's response to a question is a lie or not.

2.2 Cognitive-perceptual component

Emotions are highly personal and relate to subjective experience (this means that an emotional experience depends on the way you as an individual interpret a situation). In understanding emotions, we usually rely on individual or subjective verbal reports of what it is people are experiencing. People's cognitive processes about events in their lives are therefore the key determinants of the emotions they experience.

A specific event, such as driving a car for example, may be very pleasurable for some people but highly threatening and thus anxiety-provoking for another. The emotions relating to driving depend on what a person thinks about driving, the context of driving, past experiences regarding driving and present needs. For example, a young person who gets freedom and independence by driving is likely to see driving as an enjoyable experience, whereas a person who has recently been involved in a motor vehicle accident may view it as scary and unpleasant. Some theorists believe that the cognitive process about an event (or the interpretation of the event) is as important as the event itself.

2.3 Behavioural component

Although we can talk about our emotions, they are usually expressed in body language or non-verbal behaviour. Bodily gestures and facial expressions are used to show a variety of basic emotions. For example, imagine that you see a girl who has tears in her eyes, with the corners of her mouth turned down and perhaps trembling lips, who says little and sits slumped over. On the basis of her facial expression and body language, it is likely that you will conclude that this girl is sad and despondent, even though you have not spoken to her.

Basic facial expressions like anger, fear, disgust, sadness and happiness appear to be fairly universal. This means that these facial expressions are interpreted in the same way by all cultures; however, the interpretation of many facial expressions can be shaped by learning. As a result, some facial expressions are found only in specific cultures. For example, among many African cultures, sticking out the tongue is a gesture of disrespect or teasing. For a person from a Chinese culture, sticking out the tongue is a gesture of surprise. If a person comes from another culture, it is important to know the social context in which a facial expression developed in order to make sure that the expressed emotion is not misunderstood.

Bibliography

Coon, D. 2004. *Introduction to psychology.* 10th edition. Belmont, CA: Wadsworth.

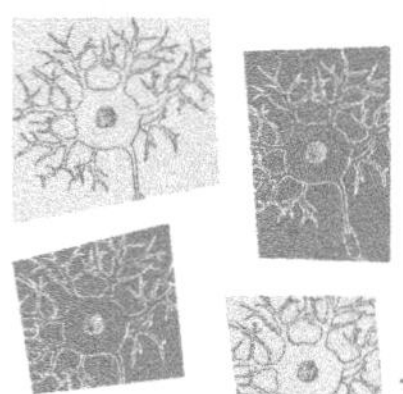

Emotion: Theories of

The experience of emotions is the result of the interaction between physiological and psychological arousal. Psychological arousal is the process whereby people become aware of situations and feelings through conscious thinking. Arousal that involves both physiological and psychological arousal is called psycho-physiological arousal. There is a continuum of physiological arousal, which means that one's emotions and behaviour become more intense and change qualitatively as the level of physiological arousal rises. However, feelings are not determined by physiological arousal in itself. The meaning that one ascribes to a situation (that is, the cognitive content), in conjunction with physiological arousal, determines the nature and intensity of one's feelings. The exact nature of the interaction between arousal, behaviour, cognitions, expressions and feelings remains a subject of speculation. Several theories have been developed to explain the role of these factors in emotion. Some of the important theories will be discussed here.

1 Schachter's two-factor theory of emotion

According to Schachter (1964), emotions occur when we apply a particular label to general physical arousal. The experience of emotion therefore depends on two factors: (1) autonomic arousal; and (2) cognitive interpretation of that arousal. Schachter's theory was based on the following study: People were given an injection of a hormone that caused physiological arousal such as increased heart rate and blood pressure. However, they were told that the injections were vitamins and were not told that they would experience physiological arousal. The people who received the injections were then placed in different situations – a happy one where people laughed and played with paper aeroplanes and an unhappy one where an angry atmosphere was created by complaints about filling in a long questionnaire.

When asked afterwards, the people in the happy situation reported feeling happy and they smiled. The people in the unhappy situation reported feeling angry and their facial expressions showed anger. Schachter concluded that because the people did not know what caused their physiological arousal, they looked for other causes in the environment. They used environmental cues (from the happy and unhappy situations) as the cause of their arousal and then reported being happy or angry accordingly.

Below is a schematic representation of Schachter's two-factor theory:

Stimulation → Arousal + Label/Appraisal → Emotion + Behaviour

The following is an example of an application of the two-factor theory. The theory would predict that if you met a lion while walking in the bush, you would be aroused. If the lion seemed aggressive, you would interpret your arousal as fear. However, if the lion offered a paw to shake your hand, you would be happy, amazed and relieved. This example makes it clear that emotion is much more than just an agitated body. Schachter believed that when we are aroused, we have a need to interpret our feelings, therefore the type of emotion we experience depends on our interpretation (cognition) of the arousal, according to the context. Schachter concluded that the conscious experience of the physiological arousal (for example increased heart or respiration rate and sweating) and the conscious experience of the meaning of the stimulus situation (cognitive content) are equally important and integrated components of emotions.

This theory has been criticised by people who say that emotions may occur without first experiencing physiological arousal.

2 Cognitive appraisal theory

Unlike Schachter's two-factor theory, the cognitive theory of emotion claims that the components of physiological arousal and cognitive processes are not equally important in the interpretation of emotion (Sdorow and Rickabaugh, 2002). It is suggested that the way we think about (or make cognitive appraisal of) a situation results in emotions (Lazarus, 1991). According to the cognitive appraisal theory, the important requirement for the interpretation of emotion is the cognitive content of the stimulus situation – that is, the meaning attached to the stimulus situation at that moment is more important than the physiological arousal. In other words, our interpretation (or appraisal) of the situation or event is the primary cause of emotions and can result in our experiencing different emotions.

Using the example of the lion again, the sequence of events in the interpretation of the emotion, according to the cognitive appraisal theory, may be as follows:

1. You perceive the stimulus situation and categorise it according to the concepts that you are familiar with: you see and know that it is a lion.
2. Primary appraisal occurs: on the basis of past experience or knowledge, you

appraise or weigh up the situation as either threatening or non-threatening. In this case, your past knowledge of lions tells you that they are dangerous.

3. The emotion is differentiated: depending on the nature of the primary appraisal, an appropriate emotion differentiates. This means that the type of emotion you experience depends on your interpretation of the situation. For example, if your appraisal leads to the interpretation that the situation is threatening or dangerous, you will experience fear and if you interpret it as non-threatening, you will not experience fear.
4. Physiological arousal or body changes (e.g. shaking knees) accompany or follow the event. For example, body changes such as shaking knees or a loud heart beat may increase your feeling of fear and encourage the desire or impulse to run away.

Below is a schematic representation of cognitive appraisal theory:

Stimulation → Primary appraisal → Differentiation of emotion → Physiological arousal

The cognitive theory adds two further steps in the differentiation of emotion. This involves secondary appraisal and coping strategies in reaction to a situation (Jordaan and Jordaan, 1998). Secondary appraisal refers to the consideration of how to act and the consequences of the various courses of action. For example, your primary appraisal may lead to the interpretation that the situation is dangerous and result in the experience of fear. When you think about the situation again (secondary appraisal), you think about how to act and what the consequences of your actions may be.

Secondary appraisal of the situation can lead to the two possible coping strategies. The first is direct action, where you face the threatening situation by fighting or fleeing. For example, you may consider running away from the lion, but then you think that you will never run faster than a lion and decide to take other action, such as making a noise to chase the lion away. The second option is reappraisal, which means the reconsideration of the situation, especially in the light of new or additional information that was not available when the emotion was initially experienced. For example, if the lion had offered his paw as a handshake, the secondary appraisal may be benign in that you may think that perhaps the lion is not hungry and may not eat you, in which case you are in no danger. The effect of benign reappraisal in view of the additional information may give rise to a totally different cognitive appraisal, emotion and direct action. By reappraising situations and considering different coping strategies, it may be possible to gain cognitive control over the quality and intensity of emotions that result from primary appraisal.

The cognitive appraisal theory suggests that thinking occurs before feeling.

Sometimes emotions occur very quickly and it is not clear that thinking occurs before feeling. For example, when you hear that you have won the lotto, you react with joy before really thinking about it. Researchers suggest that we do actually think first in these situations, but that the thinking occurs at an unconscious level without us really being aware of it (Plotnik, 2002).

Bibliography

Jordaan, W. and Jordaan, J. 1998. *People in context.* 3rd edition. Johannesburg: Heinemann.

Lazarus, R. 1991. Cognition and motivation in emotion. *American Psychologist,* 46(4), 352–367.

Plotnik, R. 2002. *Introduction to psychology.* 6th edition. Pacific Grove, CA: Wadsworth.

Schachter, S. 1964. The interaction of cognitive and physiological determinants of emotional state. In L. Berkowitz (Ed), *Advances in social psychology, volume 1.* New York: Academic Press.

Sdorow, L. and Rickabaugh, C. 2002. *Psychology.* 5th edition. New York: McGraw-Hill.

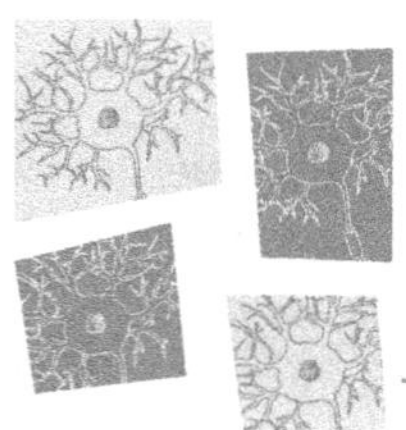

Emotional intelligence: Concept of

Many years ago the philosopher Aristotle wrote that it is easy for anyone to become angry, but that it is not easy to become angry at the right person, in the right way, at the right time, or for the right reason. Today we call this ability to know and manage our own emotions: *emotional intelligence.*

Emotional intelligence refers to a combination of skills, including empathy (understanding what others are experiencing), self-control, self-awareness, sensitivity to the feelings of others, persistence (keeping on going even when the situation is difficult) and self-motivation (doing things for yourself and not relying on other people or things to motivate you). Emotional intelligence provides the link between feelings, character and moral values. The way we approach life (and our ethical standards) depends on our emotional capacities. For example, we need the skills of empathy and sensitivity in order to read emotions in others before we can care about others and their well-being. We cannot care about others if we do not sense their needs or distress. We cannot have a strong will and good character if we cannot control our own impulses.

You may have wondered why people with roughly the same opportunities, schooling and intellectual ability differ in the success they attain in life. Emotional intelligence, not IQ, may be the answer. This expands our ideas of what it means to be intelligent and puts emotions at the centre of aptitudes for living. Being emotionally intelligent means using and expressing our emotions wisely and appropriately. The psychologist and writer, Daniel Goleman (1997), believes that people who do well in life tend to be emotionally intelligent. Good self-control, sensitivity to others and the appropriate expression of emotion help us have good relationships, be successful at work and protect our health and well-being. Emotional intelligence (sometimes referred to as EQ) can be as powerful as, or even more powerful than, intellectual ability (IQ). Emotion is necessary for effective thought, but bad emotions can interfere with effective thinking. For example, you have probably heard people who are worried or upset say they cannot think straight. This is an example of how emotion can disrupt thinking.

We have already mentioned that genetic heritage determines our temperament, but we must remember that temperament is not destiny. This means that we may have a certain temperament but it is not the only factor determining the way we behave. We can modify temperament with emotions. The emotional lessons that children learn at home and at school make an important contribution to the development of the essential emotional habits that can govern our lives. While emotional balance can help protect our health and well-being, bad emotions can put our physical health at risk. Goleman suggests that deficiencies in emotional intelligence increase the risk for problems such as depression, aggression and violence, anxiety, eating disorders and drug abuse. He believes that the solution is to teach young people self-awareness, self-control and empathy and the abilities of listening, resolving conflicts and co-operation. We cannot do without emotions, but we need to control and express them appropriately.

The following are examples of the abilities of people with high emotional intelligence:

- They motivate themselves and keep on trying in the face of frustrations.
- They control impulses and delay gratification.
- They regulate moods and do not allow emotions to interfere with their ability to think.
- They recognise emotions in others.
- They have hope.

The first step in gaining emotional intelligence is to know one's own emotions through self-awareness and recognising a feeling as it happens. If you can manage your emotions, you will probably handle relationships well and be socially more competent. If you manage your relationships well, you will probably be more popular, have better leadership ability and be more effective in your interactions with others.

The absence of emotional intelligence can have high costs. The result may be withdrawal from others (for example preferring to be alone and feeling unhappy); feeling anxious or depressed (for example feeling nervous or unloved, needing to be perfect); or having attention or thinking problems (for example being too nervous to concentrate and doing badly at school or work). In severe cases, the result may be socially unacceptable behaviour such as telling lies and cheating, arguing a lot, being mean, demanding attention, being destructive, being stubborn and moody, or being quick-tempered. As a result of knowledge about emotional intelligence, many psychologists believe that schools should promote emotional competence as well as intellectual skills. The result they hope for would be greater self-control and compassion, which are the basic capacities needed for people to thrive.

Bibliography

Goleman, D. 1997. *Emotional intelligence.* New York: Bantam Books.

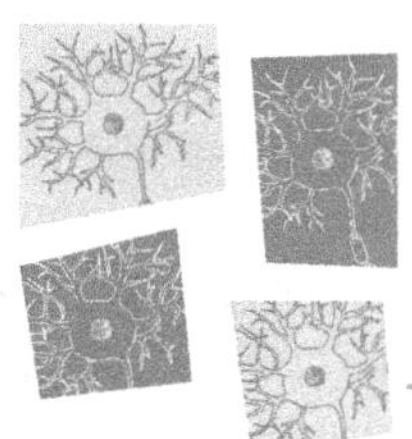

Emotions: Interpretation of

1 Gender and emotions

Women have a reputation of being more emotional than men. In one study, when men and women saw movies of people in distress, the men showed little emotion, but the women expressed feelings of concern for those in distress. However, physiological measures of their emotional arousal (such as heart rate and blood pressure) showed that the men in the study were actually just as affected as the women were. The men simply inhibited the expression of their emotions, whereas the women were more open about their feelings (Morris and Maisto, 2003).

Certain emotional expressions are expected from women, whereas they are not expected of men. As a result, men learn to suppress their emotional expression from a very early age. Emotions such as sympathy, sadness and distress and expressions of these emotions, such as crying, are often considered unmanly in many cultures. Boys are trained from an early age to suppress these emotions in public. This may explain why men are less likely than women to seek help in dealing with emotional issues. For many men, an inability to express feelings is a major barrier to having close, satisfying relationships with others.

Men and women are also likely to react with very different emotions to the same situation. For example, a man may react to betrayal by feeling angry, whereas a woman may react by feeling sad, hurt or disappointed. And when men get angry, they generally turn their anger outward against other people or the situation in which they find themselves. And women generally turn their anger inward. These gender-specific reactions are consistent with the fact that men are four times more likely than women to become violent in the face of life crises. Women are more likely than men to become depressed because they direct their emotions inwards.

Men and women also differ in their ability to interpret non-verbal cues of emotions (for example a sad face, an angry face or a happy face). Hall (1984) found that women were more skilled than men in noticing and interpreting the facial expressions, body cues and tone of voice of others. An explanation for this difference may be that women tend to be the primary caregivers for very young infants and therefore they need to become more attuned to the subtleties of emotional expressions than men need to be (Morris and Maisto, 2003). Another explanation of gender differences in emotional sensitivity is based on the relative power of women and men. There is evidence that, regardless of gender, followers are more sensitive to the emotions of leaders than vice versa. Women generally occupy less-powerful positions than men and this reinforces the tendency that women are more sensitive to the emotional displays of others, particularly those in powerful positions (who are usually men). In South Africa, many women are occupying positions of power that were previously held by men. Women who occupy the types of job traditionally held by men (for example train drivers or mining engineers) are often called on to regulate, manage or otherwise alter their emotional expression. This may change the traditional relation between emotion and gender in future.

2 Cultural differences in emotional experiences

There are also cultural differences in the way people think about or interpret and express their emotions, as well as the way that different cultures group emotions (Plotnik, 2002). For example, people from different cultural backgrounds are usually able to interpret, identify or express a happy or an angry face. However, the fact that certain facial expressions, gestures and postures occur in all cultures does not mean that the interpretations of these expressions are the same for all cultures. For example, in Western cultures it is acceptable for a man to greet another man with a smile, but in some African cultures it is not acceptable for a man to greet another man with a smile as this may imply a sexual connotation.

There are also many cultural differences in the way people think about or interpret and express their emotions as well as in the way that different cultures group emotions. Some categories or groups of emotions that are universally understood in Western cultures seem to be unknown, unrecognised or unnamed in many non-Western cultures. For example, the concept of depression seems to be more recognised in many Western cultures than in non-Western cultures, including the Sotho-speaking people of South Africa.

A similar conclusion can be drawn about non-verbal expression of emotions. Although many natural expressions associated with basic emotions (for example fear, joy, anger, etc) appear to be similar in many cultures, culture influences the ways people learn to control and modify these expressions. The principle called display rules (Ekman, 1994) refers to culture-specific rules that govern how, when and why expressions of emotions are appropriate. These rules concern the circumstances under which it is culturally acceptable for people to show emotions. For example, research has shown that groups of people from different cultural backgrounds expressed different emotions at different times and places when shown a video that provoked anger (Ekman, Friesen and Ellsworth, 1972). We can see this in everyday life too. For example, traditional African cultures encourage and indeed expect crying and outward expressions of grief at funerals, while Western cultures are more restrained and tend to disapprove of uninhibited expressions of grief. Display rules differ greatly from culture to culture and therefore non-verbal expressions of emotions vary across cultures because of culture-specific attitudes and display rules (Morris and Maisto, 2003).

From the above discussion, it is clear that our culture helps shape the interpretation and expression of our emotions. The main differentiating factor appears to be whether the worldview of the culture is predominantly individualist (that is, the focus is mainly on the interests of the individual, as in many Western cultures) or is predominantly collectivist (that is, the focus is on the group, as in many non-Western and African cultures). These differences in the interpretation and expression of emotions suggest that learning plays an important role in emotions. For example, some cultures encourage free emotional expression, whereas others teach people through modelling (that is, observing others) and reinforcement (that is, through punishment and/or reward for appropriate behaviour) to reveal little emotion in public. It therefore makes sense that people raised in different cultures may learn to interpret emotional stimuli differently.

3 The context of emotion

Knowledge of the context (or circumstances) in which an emotion is expressed is important in accurately understanding and interpreting the expressed emotion. People usually use facial expressions, body gestures, tone of voice and language to interpret the nature and intensity of emotions. These cues, if used in isolation, may lead to an incorrect and/or inadequate interpretation of somebody's emotion. For example, a woman crying on her wedding day may be interpreted by many as a sign of joy. After getting the fuller context of the woman's situation or the circumstance around the marriage, this interpretation may be different. For example, the woman may actually be sad and the tears may be a sign of frustration because of an abusive relationship or forced marriage. Without the knowledge of the context in which the emotion is expressed, therefore, the correct interpretation or understanding of the nature and intensity of emotions may be very difficult.

Bibliography

Ekman, P. 1994. Strong evidence for universals in facial expression. *Psychological Bulletin,* 115(2), 268–367.

Ekman, P., Friesen, W. and Ellsworth, P. 1972. *Emotion in the human face.* Elmsford, New York: Pergamon.

Hall, J. 1984. *Nonverbal sex difference: Communication accuracy and expressive style.* Baltimore: Johns Hopkins University Press.

Morris, C.G. and Maisto, A.A. 2003. *Understanding psychology.* Englewood Cliffs, NJ: Prentice Hall.

Plotnik, R. 2002. *Introduction to psychology.* 6th edition. Pacific Grove, CA: Wadsworth.

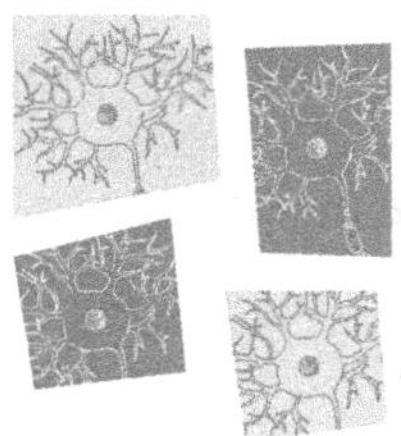

Groups: Attributes of human groups

Group is a term we use loosely to refer to a collection of things, yet there is also something special about a group. Somehow, a group is more than the things that constitute it. We think of these things as the members of the group, who belong because they have something in common, which is what makes us think of them as belonging together. So, in the abstract technical sense, we can consider a group to be a collection of elements that share a particular attribute. However, a collection of things can also form a group because they relate to one another in a specific manner. A more inclusive definition of a group would therefore be a collection of elements that share attributes and/or relate to one another in specific ways.

A collection of balls may be grouped on the basis of their colour (that is, all red balls in one basket and all yellow balls in a different one). However, the balls may also be grouped because they relate to one another in a certain way. For example, a board game may require a set of balls of different colours – such as a set consisting of a red ball, a white ball and a blue ball. These balls are grouped on the basis of their belonging to the same game. The relationship among the three balls reflects a sharing that is more abstract and not directly visible in the balls themselves.

Not all groups are the same. Because they differ from one another, groups themselves have specific characteristics. A group normally gets its characteristics from those of its elements. For example, the group consisting of red balls could be called the red group. This is the wonderfully logical thing about groups: they can be grouped. A group can be an element of a larger group. In other words, one can have a group that consists of other groups as its elements.

The notion that groups can be the elements of other groups is a powerful idea because it allows us to use the concept of a group to model complex structures and phenomena. The method is simple. It does not matter how much the degree of complexity increases at each level because we merely have to consider what the group looks like at that level and what its subgroups (elements) are. An example may help to explain the idea. We can consider a community in terms of the number of groups in it and then consider society in terms of the communities that constitute it. At each level of study, we have elements that constitute a group. At the first level we have groups of people that constitute a community and at the second level we have communities that constitute society. If we know the theory of groups in general, we can apply it at different levels of complexity and use the same theory to describe more and more complex structures.

So what are the general characteristics of groups? What makes a group a group?

1 The general characteristics of groups

A group has structure and process. The structure of a group refers to its elements and the way in which these are organised. The process of a group refers to the way in which the elements of the group interact and how these interactions evolve over time.

1.1 Group structure

A group is structured in a circular way. On the one hand, the group is made up of certain elements. In a sense, the group's characteristics come from those of its elements. On the other hand; however, membership of a group is determined by the characteristics of the group. There is a group norm that determines whether or not an element can be considered a member of the group.

The circular relationship between a group and its elements is also evident in the relationship among the elements. Elements that form part of a group share particular characteristics and are therefore related to one another. The strengths of these relationships are an indication of the cohesion of the group, but a group need not be uniformly cohesive. In other words, not all elements relate to each other to the same degree. Some elements may be strongly related, while others may have much weaker relationships. However, the fact that these elements belong to a group already presupposes a certain level of cohesion among them. In other words, the group imposes a certain level of cohesion.

1.2 Group process

Apart from structure, groups also have process. Process indicates change over time, thus the group does not remain static, neither does it fluctuate randomly. Process means the group evolves in a certain direction and this may not happen smoothly. The group may move in various (even opposing) directions, because process involves interactions among the elements of the group. These interactions may not 'pull' in the same direction, but may oppose one another, leading to unexpected movements of the group as a whole. Some elements may interact more strongly than others, which may exert a dominant influence on the direction in which the group progresses.

2 Attributes of human groups

So far we have considered the nature of groups in abstract terms, but how do the abstract characteristics of groups square up with groups of human beings? We should realise that, as a member of a group, a human being is a special kind of element. This is because, although human beings can be grouped using characteristics such as race and gender, they can also think for themselves, thus they are elements that can (at least to some extent) decide for themselves whether or not they belong to particular groups. We should therefore distinguish between objective and subjective factors of group membership (Moghadham, 1998). This leads to a slightly more complex definition of a human group, namely that it exists when people define themselves as members of a group and when the existence of this group is recognised by others who do not consider themselves to be members of the group (Brown, 1988).

Jordaan (1998) and Swart (2004) identify the following 10 attributes of groups that seem to be common in the work of group theorists:

- Awareness of group membership
- Interaction among members
- Common goals
- Cohesiveness
- Socio-metric structure
- Group norms
- Group polarisation
- Group think
- Group conflict
- Patterns of leadership and followership

In the following sections, we consider these attributes in terms of group structure and group process.

2.1 The structure of human groups

2.1.1 Human membership

For human groups, it is not sufficient simply to assign a person to a group. The members need to be aware that they are members of the group and this means they have to have the experience of belonging to it. To experience group membership, the members have to have at least one thing in common. They have to believe that the benefits of membership outweigh the disadvantages and gradually become more committed to the group and socially more integrated into it.

2.1.2 Group norms

Group norms are shared expectations about the kinds of behaviours that are required by all group members (Swart, 2004). These norms are rules that prescribe and forbid certain behaviours and to be a group member, one has to submit to them. Group norms thus put pressure on members to conform and in this sense, they determine group membership. Group norms originate in three ways. They are: (1) formulated by group leaders; (2) the product of group experience; and (3) transferred from other groups.

2.1.3 Group cohesion

Group cohesion refers to the strength of the relationships among group members. We can recognise highly cohesive groups by the behaviour of their members. Members of a highly cohesive group identify strongly with the group and they defend it against outside criticism. The cohesion of a group is forced from the inside as well as from the outside. Group members may form a tight group because they have a strong sense of joint destiny (inside force), or they may stand together because their group is threatened by other individuals (outside force).

2.1.4 Socio-metric structure

Group members are not equally attracted to each other. In general, some members are better liked than others and particular group members have particular preferences as to whom they like and dislike. These patterns of liking and disliking form a group's socio-metric structure, which is influenced by the group's degree of task orientation. If a group is strongly task oriented, there is less opportunity for it to concentrate on interpersonal relationships.

The socio-metric structure and the nature of the tasks performed by the group lead to identifiable communication patterns. Groups often develop particular patterns of communication, which structure the way information flows within them. A group's pattern of communication is known as its communication network. The network determines the hierarchy of communication (who speaks to whom), its frequency and the number of people involved in it (the bandwidth of the communication).

2.2 The process of human groups

All group processes start with interaction among group members. In fact, group membership itself depends on interaction. If there is not sufficient interaction among group members, there is no reason for the individuals to be members of the group. As groups develop, there are significant changes in the patterns and frequency of interaction among group members. One can see interaction patterns in the way in which group members communicate as well as in the way in which they exert effort in their actions. The communication patterns have a significant impact on the interactions in a group. They determine which members interact directly and which interact indirectly with one another. Interaction patterns also show up in how much effort group members put into the actions that are required of them.

There is a phenomenon called the Ringelmann effect (Sdorow and Rickabaugh, 2002:494). An agricultural engineer called Max Ringelmann found that when people work in groups they exert less effort than when working alone. Today, this effect is called *social loafing.* Social loafing occurs when group members feel that their individual performance is not evaluated and acknowledged, thus they are less motivated to exert the required effort. Social loafing can be reduced by convincing group members that they are held accountable. This means that their individual efforts are evaluated, or that these contribute significantly to the group's overall performance.

Groups normally have specific purposes, which can be implicit (that is, not clearly formulated) or explicit (that is, clearly formulated). A group's purpose defines its goals and its development and functioning are determined by them. To achieve the group's goals, members have to perform specific roles. There are two types of role, namely instrumental and affiliative. Instrumental roles are aimed at executing tasks and affiliative roles are aimed at support and interpersonal contact. Both role types are required for groups to develop and function properly, but the purpose of a group determines the emphasis it places on its role types.

If the purpose of a group is to produce a particular product, its members are required to be task oriented. In other words, the instrumental role type is emphasised in this group. Of course, group members still have to work together and therefore still have to fulfil an affiliative role, but in this group affiliation (the relationships among group members) is less important than the tasks the members have to complete. On the other hand, if the purpose of the group is to support its members, affiliation is more important than instrumental roles.

As groups develop, they may change the way in which they emphasise the different role types. Typically, when a group starts up, it has to put some emphasis on the affiliative role because people have to learn to work together even if the purpose of the group is to produce a particular product. They have to learn how to relate to one another.

2.2.1 Group polarisation

The interactions among group members and the fact that they share common goals have a moderating effect on the personal views that individual group members have. Therefore, groups serve to temper extreme views and group norms tend to move towards moderate positions. However, this may not necessarily be the case. Sometimes, group views swing towards extreme positions. This is known as group polarisation. Group polarisation occurs when existing individual opinions, views, ideas and positions become more extreme during group discussions. This may happen when group members get information from one another that supports and augments their initial individual positions and the group norm may then shift from a moderate to a more radical position.

2.2.2 Group conflict

The interaction among group members may not always go smoothly. In fact, group conflict between members is inevitable in the life of any group. Jordaan (1998) indicates a number of possible sources of conflict. Members may have different expectations of the group they belong to. These may be about what the group means for them, or what they can get out of it. They may not agree about the group's goals or the methods of achieving them. They may differ about the way in which resources are distributed in the group and they may experience threats to self-esteem, identity and security. This may lead to negative feelings about one another and to attempts to push some members out of the group. Whether or not conflict spirals out of control depends on the strength of the purpose of the group and the degree to which the members share the group's goals. Groups with strong purpose and clearly shared goals usually withstand the turbulence of group conflict.

2.2.3 Group think

If conflict can threaten a group's existence, the other side of the coin is equally dangerous. In groups that are highly cohesive, group members may become overly aligned with the group's goals. This can lead to a phenomenon known as *group think*. This occurs in cohesive groups when the group places unanimity ahead of critical thinking (Sdorow and Rickabaugh, 2002:493), thus decisions are taken in an unconsidered and uncritical way. This can happen when the group has a directive leader who limits the alternatives for group members and who makes them feel that they have to toe the line. It can also happen when the group is under pressure to take a consensual decision. When these factors are present in highly cohesive groups, the chance of group think increases. However, in the absence of these factors, cohesive groups do not necessarily resort to group think. One should also keep in mind that group think is not necessarily a bad thing, because it does not always lead to bad decision making. According to Jordaan (1998), catastrophic decisions occur when the following happen:

- When group cohesion creates an illusion of invulnerability and limitless power
- When the group relies on the stereotyping of people and situations rather than actual observations and tested facts
- When the group believes strongly in the inherent morality of its own right of existence, methods and decisions
- When the illusion of unanimity in the group puts pressure on members to keep quiet about their misgivings

Jordaan (1998) suggests that groups can counter the tendency to group think by taking the following measures:

- Having strong leaders withdraw from decision-making processes

- Instructing particular group members to play the role of devil's advocate
- Bringing in outside observers to monitor the group's decision-making process

2.2.4 Patterns of leadership and followership

Although some groups may be uniform, affording equal status to every member in the group, this is the exception rather than the rule. In most groups, members have particular tasks. The status of members varies depending on the nature of their tasks and the level of responsibility they have to carry in the group. These differences are reflected in the interaction patterns in groups. The question is: How do leaders and followers merge in groups? According to Jordaan (1998), this is a question of leadership. Certain individuals emerge as leaders in their groups. How do they guide and direct the behaviour of group members? There is a vast literature of research into leadership qualities and processes, but most theories belong to one or more of the following categories (Abrahams and Ruiters, 2003):

- Leading through personal traits
- Charismatic leadership
- Transformational leadership
- Super leadership

The *personal-trait* approach to leadership postulates that leaders have special characteristics such as drive and energy, honesty and integrity, self-confidence, intelligence and expertise. Such leaders are driven by their ambition and need for power, but group members feel safe with them and are willing to subject themselves to their control. However, the traits associated with leaders do not seem to be the required characteristics for good leadership. In other words, there are leaders who do not display these traits. Furthermore, trait theories do not explain how leaders lead group members through the changes that occur as groups develop. Leaders need to be charismatic to effect changes.

Charismatic leaders demonstrate the important leadership traits, but they also have self-confidence and a sense of purpose and are able to articulate their visions clearly. They motivate group members and guide them with clear purpose.

Transformational leaders understand the circumstances and the needs of group members. These leaders are flexible and they adapt their style of leadership to the specific demands of the situation and to group members' needs. Depending on the situation, these leaders may choose to do one of the following:

- Delegate (achieve the group goal by assigning separate tasks to specific team members)
- Follow a participatory style (achieve the group goal by assigning certain aspects of tasks – instead of whole tasks – to group members so that everybody works together towards completing the task)

- Follow a selling style (achieving the group goal by getting people enthusiastic about what they do)
- Follow a telling style (achieving the group goal by giving clear instructions to be followed by everybody)

In addition, transformational leaders help group members buy into group goals and purpose. Group members feel supported. They pledge their loyalty to and put their trust in their leader. Super leaders lead others to lead themselves. These leaders are transformational leaders, but they act as teachers and coaches and they empower group members to manage themselves. This approach increases members' feelings of personal control and encourages them to become intrinsically motivated.

Bibliography

Abrahams, F. and Ruiters, R.R. 2003. Industrial psychology: Selected topics. In L. Nicholas, *Introduction to psychology.* Cape Town: UCT Press.

Brown. R. 1988. *Group processes: Dynamics within and between groups.* Oxford: Blackwell.

Jordaan, W. 1998. Group functioning. In W. Jordaan and J. Jordaan, *People in context.* 3rd edition. Johannesburg: Heinemann.

Moghadham, F.M. 1998. *Social psychology: Exploring universals across cultures.* New York: Freeman.

Sdorow, L. and Rickabaugh, C. 2002. *Psychology.* 5th edition. New York: McGraw-Hill.

Swart, T. 2004. Group concepts, processes and dynamics. In L. Swartz, C. de la Rey and N. Duncan (Eds), *Psychology: An introduction.* Cape Town: Oxford University Press.

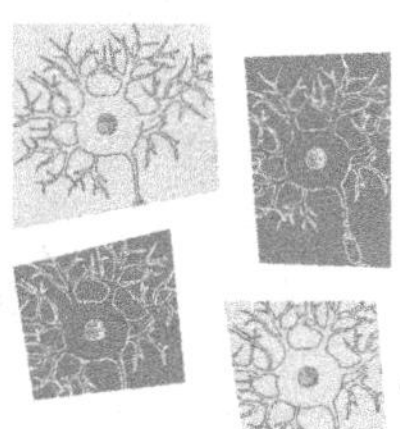

Groups: Differentiation of groups

How do human groups form? How do they come into existence? In some instances, for example in the work situation, groups are constituted to perform specific tasks. These groups are known as task teams. However, there are various other kinds of groups that are not as actively and as purposefully constituted as is the case with task teams. What processes are at work when these groups form?

Jordaan (1998) identifies three main processes at work in group formation. These are social categorisation, stereotyping and identification.

1 Social categorisation

There are many variables in terms of which people differ from each other. However, these variables do not only serve to differentiate people, but also to group those who are similar with regard to the variable in question. Gender, eye colour and mother tongue are examples of such variables. Gender does not only distinguish males from females, but also serves to divide males and females into two separate groups. A group is formed when a number of individuals are seen to be similar in some respect, but also to differ from others with regard to the matter in question. For example, students in a psychology class belong together because they share the fact that they study psychology and in this respect they differ from those who do not. This kind of distinction leads to a distinction between the *in-group* and the *out-group*. Members of the in-group refer to themselves as 'us' and they indicate members of the out-group as 'them'. Jordaan (1998) refers to this process of differentiation as *social categorisation*. In other words, the process of social categorisation is at work when in-groups and out-groups are differentiated.

The dynamics of social categorisation are complex because they involve two opposing terms – *similarity* and *difference* – at the same time. Social categorisation is an interplay between similarity and difference. In technical terms, we would indicate this interplay as a double logic. There is the logic (a way of thinking) that brings about similarity, but simultaneously there is a logic (a way of thinking) that brings about difference and these two play on each other. The complexity that is associated with a double logic is the reason why groups form in dynamic and unpredictable ways. We cannot indicate group formation on a single scale that combines similarity and difference – a scale that measures from different to similar. We need two scales: one to indicate the degree of similarity and another to indicate the degree of difference (see Figure 1).

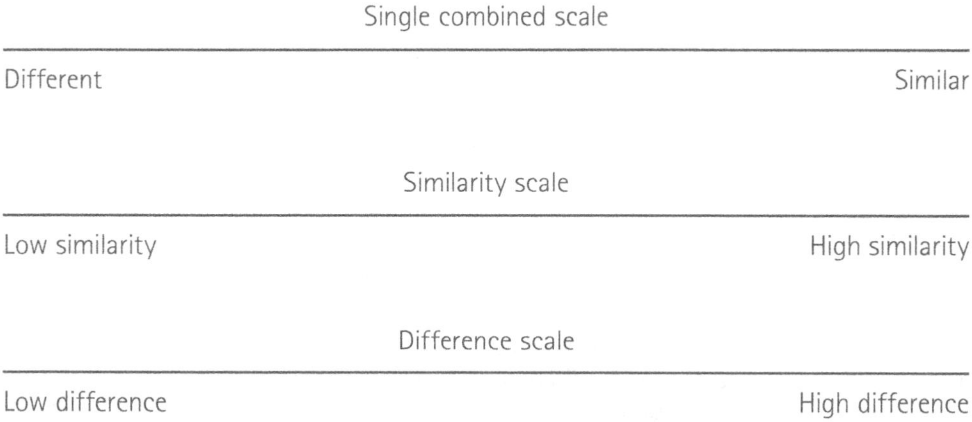

Single combined scale

Different — Similar

Similarity scale

Low similarity — High similarity

Difference scale

Low difference — High difference

Figure 1 The double logic of group formation requires a double scale – one for similarity and one for difference

If we measure group formation on a single combined scale, less difference means more similarity and less similarity means more difference. This would mean that the more similar in-group members are to each other, the more they differ from the out-group members, or that greater difference from the out-group indicates a higher degree of similarity among in-group members. This is not the case. When we separate the scale into a similarity scale and a difference scale, it is clear that in-group members can have a low degree of similarity amongst themselves but still be very different from the out-group and vice versa. However, in group formation, the logic of similarity and the logic of difference play upon each other. In other words, the two scales are not independent of each other. This is the reason why groups form in dynamic and unpredictable ways.

2 Social stereotyping

We all have a tendency to jump to impressions of what other people are like. These stereotypes, which are general beliefs and expectations about people.

These expectations can be negative or positive. Stereotypical thinking reflects our tendency to simplify large amounts of information. We simplify complexity by systematising and ordering information into categories and we then think in terms of these categories instead of detailed facts. When stereotypical thinking is applied to groups of people, we refer to this as social stereotyping, which is a process of simplifying information about groups. The danger of this process is that it easily leads to oversimplified ideas about the stereotyped group. According to Jordaan (1998), stereotyping involves unqualified generalisations of some aspect of the group. Information that affirms the stereotype is recognised, while information that questions or refutes it is ignored. This kind of selective perception leads to self-fulfilling prophecies. Stereotypes create expectancies that allow us to perceive selectively, recognising information that confirms our expectations and overlooking that which refutes them, thus perpetuating the stereotypes we have. The real danger is that stereotypes may create prejudice and social distance. When this happens, groups may begin to develop ideologies based on stereotypes of groups (Foster, 2003).

It is not difficult to see that stereotypical thinking can easily creep in when groups differentiate into in-groups and out-groups. In-group members base their image of the out-group on oversimplified ideas of how the out-group differs from them. This view of the out-group is oversimplified and impoverished because the in-group views the out-group in terms of its own (in-group) ideas. The in-group members enforce their own ideologies on the out-group. They define the out-group in terms of how it differs from the in-group. In this process, the in-group ignores the essential nature of the out-group. They do not look at the out-group and see its members for what they are, thus stereotypical thinking often plays a significant role in group formation.

3 Social identity

According to social identity theory, an individual's self-concept has two components, namely personal identity and social identity (Foster, 2003). Most individuals have more than one social identity because most of us belong to more than one of the following groups: ethnic, religious, political and vocational and most of us play more than one role in the interpersonal domain (for example being a mother, a lover or a teenager). When individuals belong to a group, they automatically think of it as their group (the in-group). This happens because everybody needs a positive self-image (Santrock, 2003:668). People have a natural feeling of belonging to particular groups because their membership enables them to compare their groups with less-favourable stereotypical images of other groups, making them feel good about themselves. Groups are formed because people want to belong to one or more groups that have desirable attributes. If they are a member, they can claim the group attributes as their own and create a positive image of themselves.

Bibliography

Foster, D. 2003. Social psychology. In L. Nicholas (Ed), *Introduction to psychology.* Cape Town: UCT Press.

Jordaan, W. 1998. Group functioning. In W. Jordaan and J. Jordaan, *People in context.* 3rd edition. Johannesburg: Heinemann.

Santrock, J.W. 2003. *Psychology.* 7th edition. New York: McGraw-Hill.

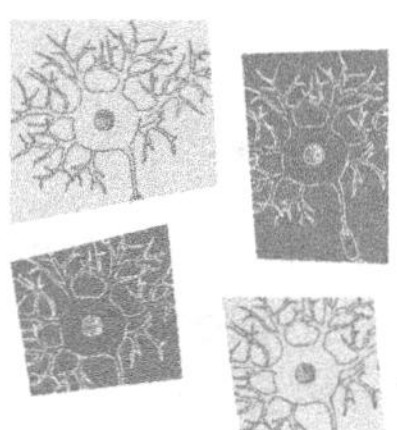

Groups: Interaction of groups

Group formation is a complex process of social categorisation that leads to in-groups and out-groups. This raises the question of intergroup relationships. Intergroup behaviour occurs when members of one group act toward members of another and when these actions happen in terms of group membership rather than in terms of the members' individual capacities (Swart, 2004). How can the rivalry that is inherent in the differentiation between us-groups and them-groups be overcome to ensure good intergroup co-operation?

1 Levels of explanation of intergroup relations

There is no shortage of explanations of intergroup relations. Swart (2004) distinguishes four levels at which explanations of intergroup relations are offered.

These are as follows:

- *Individual-level explanations.* These are explanations that try to explain the nature of intergroup relations in terms of individual dynamics and personality factors.
- *Interpersonal-level explanations.* The explanations that fall in this category deal with theory that explains interpersonal interactions, for example the theory that interpersonal interactions are based on economic principles. In terms of the economic model, people interact with others on a reward versus costs basis. In other words, people are only inclined to interact if the interaction offers a psychological reward that is greater than the psychological costs involved.
- *Positional-level explanations.* The theories in this category deal with group-type interactions. An example is the realistic conflict theory proposed by Sherif (in Swart, 2004). According to this theory, group conflict results

from incompatible group goals, or from competition between groups over scarce resources.

- *Ideological-level explanations.* Explanations in this category refer to general belief systems in society, which determine the way groups behave in society. Groups may experience conflict when they adhere to belief systems that are incompatible.

2 A practical framework for intergroup co-operation

Although there is no shortage of explanations of intergroup behaviour (whether harmonious or conflicting types of behaviour), the theories seldom proceed to practical solutions. In this sense, Jordaan (1998) makes a worthwhile contribution with his practical framework for intergroup co-operation. Jordaan suggests the following:

2.1 Create a social norm

Creating a social norm affirms and legitimises the commonality of the various groups.

Groups exist within wider contexts. Various groups may share a particular context. However, the contexts of groups are not always visible to the individual group members. This is so because the groups that members belong to constitute the contexts for them. The broader context within which the groups exist contains a number of attributes that are common to the groups. For example, groups that exist within the context of human society share the attribute of being human groups. They share the fact that they consist of human beings. Groups that exist within a particular organisation share the fact of their organisational membership. The groups may have different functions and may differ in a number of respects, but they exist because the organisation exists and they share the goals and purposes of the organisation. Group members need to be made aware of the wider context shared by the various groups. Group leaders can play an important role in this regard. They entice group members to look beyond the limits of their respective groups and to share in the common goals that may exist in the context the group shares with other groups.

2.2 Maintain equality of status

The equal status of members of different groups should be maintained in intergroup contact situations.

Groups are not similar. Group differences are a major reason for group differentiation. Groups may differ in a number of respects and may be organised hierarchically in terms of particular attributes. However, no single group is superior in all respects regarding the way it differs from other groups and likewise, no single group can be low on all counts of difference. Groups normally average out on their highs and lows. In other words, groups can be organised hierarchically with regard to a particular aspect of difference, but are pretty much on a par when all possible aspects of difference are taken into account. In intergroup contact situations, there is therefore no reason to assign a lower status to representatives of one group relative to those of another. Even if the groups are organised hierarchically with regard to a particular concern, the representatives of the less important group should still have equal status with those of the more important one and the status of equality should be taken seriously.

2.3 Maintain interpersonal contact

Maintaining interpersonal contact between groups reduces perceptions of in-group heterogeneity and demolishes perceptions of out-group homogeneity.

Group members are aware of the differences among themselves. However, they are not aware of those inside the groups of which they are not members. Out-group members are thus perceived as 'all alike' – as being homogeneous – whereas in-group members are perceived as a heterogeneous group. The understanding that out-group members are not all the same comes about through interpersonal contact with members of the out-group. Once we begin to see the heterogeneity of the out-group, it becomes more difficult to stereotype the group members. It is also more difficult to maintain strict borders between groups if we cannot frame people according to their stereotypes. The variation (heterogeneity) among the group members of the various groups makes it clear that group members cannot be restricted to one particular group. It becomes clear that their group membership is one which is based on a particular aspect of their lives and not on their entire lives (their stereotyped lives).

2.4 Maintain co-operative activities

Co-operative activities may be maintained by setting common goals and allowing the groups to develop common interests and values and to look for solutions to problems together.

When groups work together to realise common goals, they become aware of the broader context in which they exist. Group members work together to realise group goals. If they are not aware of the way in which group goals come together to realise the goals shared by the groups that exist in the broader context, they cannot see how the groups function in harmony for a greater good.

2.5 Develop a multicultural ethos

The term *multicultural* is used mostly in the context of society, referring to the fact that modern societies consist of various cultural groups. However, any context in which we find more than one group can be termed 'multicultural' in the sense that the groups differ from one another. A multicultural ethos refers to the fact that group members should become aware that, apart from being members of a particular group, they also have membership of the broader context in which their group exists. This dual membership is a basic factor in forming a multicultural identity. Membership of the broader context means our identity includes the cultural diversity of the various groups, but also that we still have an identity attached to our primary group.

2.6 Develop a critical consciousness of oppressive patterns

Replacing an oppressive system with another one, or simply switching the roles of the oppressed and the oppressor within a particular system are not cures for oppression. When the oppressed becomes the oppressor, the process of oppression is simply repeated and the oppressive pattern is perpetuated. We need a critical consciousness of these patterns to cure oppression. It is important to remember that oppression starts the very moment that we do not treat and respect another human being as a human being in his or her own right – that is, the moment we do not allow others to develop their self-esteem and to realise themselves as human beings.

Human beings have a natural tendency to want to belong to groups. This is because groups are stronger and richer than their individual elements. In the same way, groups that work together are both stronger and richer than individual ones. Jordaan's suggestions for group co-operation provide a useful framework within which groups can learn to work together. The double logic of difference and similarity that plays itself out when a group is formed should also be applied at the level of intergroup co-operation. Even when groups compete for scarce resources, the interplay of difference and similarity should be maintained as a primary mechanism. Groups can only survive if they acknowledge that they are simultaneously similar and different.

Bibliography

Jordaan, W. 1998. Group functioning. In W. Jordaan and J Jordaan, *People in context.* 3rd edition. Johannesburg: Heinemann.

Swart, T. 2004. Group concepts, processes and dynamics. In L. Swartz, C. de la Rey and N. Duncan (Eds), *Psychology: An introduction.* Cape Town: Oxford University Press.

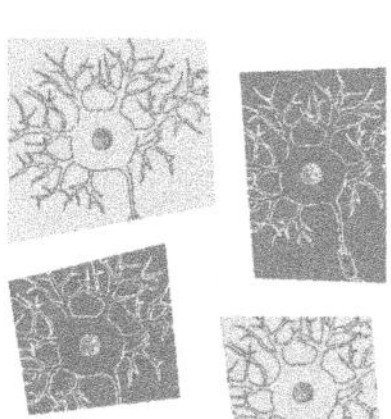

Human nervous system: Impulse conduction in the neuron

Neurons are the building blocks of the human nervous system. A neuron on its own cannot do much, but when neurons work together and form large networks, they produce complex behaviours. These networks are really large and consist of millions of neurons. The human body contains such a network. In the human body, millions of neurons are constantly relaying messages to produce ordinary human behaviour. Even a brief thought needs a large number of neurons. All human behaviour, such as thinking, learning, watching, feeling, planning or taking action, is based on the complicated interactions among neurons in the nervous system.

Messages are relayed from the sensory organs (such as the eye and the ear) to the brain. These organs are stimulated by information from the environment. In the sensory organs, this information (called stimuli) is translated into energy that can be relayed by the neurons. For example, when a sound reaches the ear, the energy of the sound (the auditory stimulus) stimulates the ear, which translates it into electrochemical energy that stimulates the neuron. When the neuron is stimulated, it generates a nerve impulse. In other words, the sensory organs translate external stimuli into internal stimuli which are conducted to the brain and also inside the brain, in the form of nerve impulses. The process by which messages are relayed in neurons and from one neuron to the next is called impulse conduction.

Impulse conduction in the nervous system is made up of two main processes:

- *Electrical.* The nerve impulse begins in the first segment of the axon and travels down the axon to the terminals because of electrical events at the cell membrane.
- *Chemical.* The passage of the nerve impulse from one neuron to another is a chemical process. There is a small gap (called a synapse) between the structures of one neuron and another (for example between the dendrites of one neuron and the axon terminals of another) and chemical processes

determine whether or not the impulse will be conducted across the gap to the next neuron.

In this section we consider the electrical process of impulse conduction. The chemical process is considered in the next section (*Human nervous system: Impulse conduction in the synapse*).

1 The neuron is electrically charged

Each neuron is like a small electric battery. A battery has two poles, one positive and the other negative. The difference between the positive and negative poles is called a potential difference. When a battery is charged, there is a large potential difference between the two poles, but as the battery runs down the difference between the poles decreases. The battery is flat when there is no potential difference left between the two poles. When the battery is recharged, the potential difference between the positive and negative poles is increased again.

The potential difference between the poles of a battery (that is, the electrical charge of the battery) is brought about by splitting chemical particles into positive and negative parts, which are called ions. When a battery is being charged, the positive ions are pushed to one side of a barrier and the negative ones to the other side. A charged battery has a large number of positive ions on one side of a barrier and a large number of negative ions on the other. The battery's positive pole is positive because it is on the side of the barrier where all the positive ions are assembled. The negative pole is negative because it is on the side where all the negative ions are gathered. When the two poles are connected (which is what happens when we use a battery) the connection forms a bridge across the barrier and the positive and negative ions can join up again to form neutral particles. Once all the positive and negative ions have joined up again, the battery is flat with no difference in potential between the positive and negative poles. The battery has to be recharged, which means the neutral chemical particles have to be split into positive and negative ions again.

To see why a neuron is like a battery one has to keep in mind that there is fluid inside the neuron and that the neuron itself lies in fluid. In other words, there is fluid inside and outside the neuron. The membrane of the neuron forms a barrier between the inside and the outside fluids. The fluid contains various kinds of chemical particles, some of which are ions because they are electrically charged. There are positive and negative ions. Because these ions are unevenly distributed on either side of the cell membrane, there is a potential difference between the inside and the outside of the neuron, therefore the neuron is electrically charged.

2 The resting membrane potential

An impulse is conducted when the electrical charge across the cell membrane of the neuron changes, but before an impulse can fire (or be conducted), there must be a condition of readiness in the neuron. This is called the *resting membrane potential*, which is an electrical charge brought about by the difference between the positive and negative ions inside and outside the neuron. If the ions were distributed equally inside and outside the cell membrane, there would be no electrical charge and no potential. When the neuron is in a condition of readiness, the fluid inside the neuron is negative relative to the fluid outside, therefore the resting membrane potential means negative inside and positive outside the neuron.

There are different mechanisms that create the resting membrane potential. Ions move about constantly in the fluid inside and outside the cell. One of the reasons for this is because ions naturally move from areas where there is a high concentration of ions to areas where this is low. Another reason for their movement is that ions with opposite charges attract each other while those with similar charges move away from each other. If left to their own devices the ions would eventually even out on either side of the cell membrane and there would be no charge, but to move about, they have to pass through the membrane. The membrane contains mechanisms that allow some ions through and prohibits others. Sometimes the membrane plays an active role in separating ions. For example, sodium and potassium ions move back and forth across the membrane, but the membrane contains sodium and potassium pumps that push the sodium back outside and the potassium back inside. The cell membrane thus plays an important role in creating and maintaining potential differences between the inside and the outside of the neuron.

Sodium ions are positively charged, therefore the high concentration of sodium ions on the outside of the membrane creates a positive electrical charge. The potassium ions inside the neuron are also positively charged, but the total electrical charge on the inside of the membrane is not positive. It is negative because the fluid on the inside of the membrane also contains proteins and nucleic acid molecules that are negatively charged. The proteins are too big to pass through the membrane. The negative charge of the proteins and nucleic acid molecules outweighs the positively charged potassium ions and therefore the total charge on the inside of the neuron is negative relative to the positive outside.

The resting membrane potential occurs when the neuron is in an inactive (resting) but polarised state. The neuron is polarised (that is, it has a negative and a positive pole) because a potential difference exists across its membrane, with the inside being negative relative to a positive outside. When there is a resting membrane potential, the neuron is ready to receive information (messages) in the form of electrical impulses and to conduct these impulses along its axon to the next neuron.

3 The action potential

The soma receives information from the synaptic connections between itself and other neurons. This information comes in the form of changing potentials across the soma's membrane. The membrane potentials propagate towards the axon hillock (a specialised part of the soma that connects to the axon) where they are summed. When the total potential reaches a particular level in the axon hillock, an action potential is triggered in the axon. The axon must have a resting membrane potential for an action potential to be triggered and the summed potential in the axon hillock must exceed the resting potential by a particular amount, called the threshold. An axon potential is therefore triggered only when the summed potential in the axon hillock reaches the threshold potential. The threshold potential is more than the axon's resting membrane potential.

As indicated earlier, the resting membrane potential means the axon is negatively charged on its inside and positively on its outside. The axon's membrane is polarised because there is a difference in potential across the membrane. This occurs when there is a high concentration of positively charged sodium ions on the outside of the axon's membrane and a high concentration of positively charged potassium ions on the inside of the membrane, together with negatively charged proteins and nucleic acids. Because the negative charge obtained from the proteins and nucleic acids is more than the positive charge of the potassium, the total charge on the inside is negative relative to the outside.

When an action potential is triggered, the membrane becomes permeable to sodium ions, which rush into the axon, moving from the high sodium concentration on the outside of the neuron to the low sodium concentration on the inside. The influx of positively charged sodium ions means the neuron becomes less negative on the inside. When the charges on outside and on the inside of the neuron even out, the membrane is depolarised, which happens when there is no potential difference between the inside and the outside of the axon. The influx of sodium ions stops when the inside becomes slightly more positive than the outside. At this stage the membrane ceases to be permeable to sodium ions but now becomes permeable to potassium. The positively charged potassium ions move from the high concentration on the inside of the axon to the low concentration on the outside. The outside becomes positive again because it gains positively charged ions and the inside becomes negative because it loses them. The membrane repolarises, once again, gaining a potential difference between the inside and the outside. The process continues until there are more potassium ions on the outside than there are sodium ions on the inside. At this stage the axon membrane is hyperpolarised (that is, more polarised than in its resting phase). This phase does not last long before the axon starts to return to its resting membrane potential.

The axon is now in a refractory period. During this period the membrane returns the sodium and potassium ions to their original states. It pumps the sodium to the outside of the neuron and the potassium back to the inside. At the beginning of the refractory period, the neuron does not respond to any stimulus. This is called an absolute refractory period. At this stage the axon cannot conduct an impulse. Towards the end of the refractory period when most of the sodium and the potassium have been returned to the outside and the inside respectively, a very intense stimulus can trigger an impulse. This is a relative refractory period. Once the initial balance of sodium (outside) and potassium (inside) has been regained, the neuron enters a polarised resting phase with the normal resting membrane potential fully restored. The neuron stays in the resting phase until another action potential is triggered at the axon hillock.

4 Characteristics of impulse conduction

Once the impulse is initiated at the axon hillock, it is rapidly conducted along the axon. The impulse does not happen simultaneously everywhere along the axon. It propagates down the axon from the axon hillock to the axon terminals, thus the changes in the axon's membrane (that occur during impulse conduction) spread from one segment of the axon to the next. Once a segment of the membrane changes (for example becomes more permeable to sodium ions), the adjacent section also starts to change. In this way changes spread down the axon from one neighbouring segment to the next.

When a segment finishes conducting the impulse, it enters a refractory period, thus the refractory period follows the impulse down the axon. This means the impulse can be conducted in one direction only. It cannot start moving back up the neuron in the direction of the axon hillock because the segments where the impulse has passed are in various stages of a refractory phase and therefore they cannot conduct the impulse, which can only move forward towards the telondendria.

The refractory period also prevents the nervous system from overstimulation. To understand why, one has to be familiar with the relationship between stimulus intensity and impulse conduction. When a stimulus becomes more intense (for example when a louder sound is heard, or when a brighter light is seen) the impulse does not become more intense. In other words, more intense stimuli do not cause bigger changes in membrane potentials and therefore bigger impulses or faster impulses. They cause more frequent impulses. Thus as the intensity of a stimulus increases the frequency of impulses increases. A loader sound means more impulses are propagated down the axon while a softer sound means fewer impulses are conducted, but the impulses that are conducted are always of the same magnitude.

Impulse conduction is an all-or-nothing affair. An impulse is either fired or not fired – there is no in-between. Once the potential difference at the axon hillock reaches a certain level (the threshold), the impulse is triggered and once an impulse has been triggered it is conducted with the same strength and the same speed along the entire axon. It does not slow down or wither away halfway down the axon.

This is true for the axon, but not for the soma. In the soma, a more intense stimulus causes more intense potential differences across the membrane and the threshold at the axon hillock is reached more quickly. In the case of very intense stimuli, the threshold is constantly exceeded and the axon would have had to conduct impulses in very quick succession. If this were to happen, the axon would totally deplete the sodium and potassium balance in the nervous system. Fortunately, due to the refractory period, the rate at which a neuron can conduct impulses is limited. A neuron does not conduct an impulse before its sodium and potassium balance has been restored or has come very close to being so.

There are two more aspects of impulse conduction that are important to note, both of which concern the speed of the impulse. Although the strength and speed of an impulse is constant in a particular neuron, it can vary with nerve fibres of different thickness. The larger the nerve fibre (the greater the diameter or width), the stronger the impulse and the faster it is conducted. For example, thick fibres can conduct impulses at a speed of about 100 metres per second, but fibres with a smaller diameter conduct them more slowly – at speeds as comparatively low as 100 centimetres per second.

The second factor that has an impact on the speed of an impulse is whether or not the axon is myelinated. An axon is myelinated if it is enclosed in a white fatty sheath called myelin. These sheets insulate the neuron except at small gaps, called the nodes of Ranvier. These gaps separate the sheaths and contain the sodium and potassium ion channels required for impulse conduction. Impulses travel faster along axons that are myelinated because the impulse jumps from node to node instead of moving smoothly along the axon as in the case of un-myelinated axons. This also means there are two kinds of impulse conduction – the one in myelinated axons where the impulse jumps from node to node and the other in un-myelinated axons where the impulse propagates smoothly. In myelinated axons, impulse conduction is known as salutatory conduction and in un-myelinated axons it is called action potential conduction.

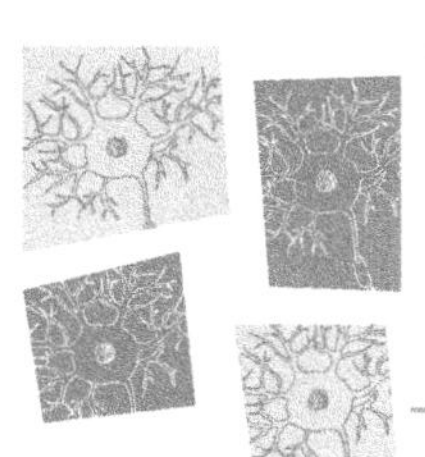

Human nervous system: Impulse conduction in the synapse

Neurons relay information by conducting electrical impulses. They form large networks to produce complex behaviour. Although a huge amount of information is processed in the way impulses are conducted within neurons, the connections between neurons are equally important. The conduction of a nerve impulse in a neuron is primarily electrical, but the communication between different neurons is primarily chemical.

1 The synapse

There is a microscopically small gap between the axon terminal of one neuron and the dendrite or soma of another. The membrane of the axon terminal is the presynaptic membrane and the membrane of the dendrite or soma is the postsynaptic membrane. The gap is known as the synaptic cleft. The presynaptic and postsynaptic membranes together with the synaptic cleft is the synapse.

When an action potential reaches the tips of the axon terminals, it causes chemicals to be released into the synaptic cleft which allow contact to take place across it. These chemicals are called neurotransmitters and they can alter activity in neurons.

Figure 1 shows the connections between two neurons. A close-up of one of these connections (the one indicated in the circle) is shown in the diagram on the right. The diagram depicts the synaptic cleft between a terminal button of a presynaptic neuron and a dendrite membrane of a receiving (postsynaptic) neuron.

Communication between neurons occurs because of the movement of chemicals across the synaptic cleft. When a neuron fires, the action potential is conducted toward the axon terminals, which causes the vesicles (with their neurotransmitters) to move closer and attach themselves to the presynaptic membrane. At the point where they attach, the membrane opens and the neurotransmitters pass into the synaptic cleft. The neurotransmitters mix with the fluid outside the cells and combine with the receptors in the postsynaptic membrane.

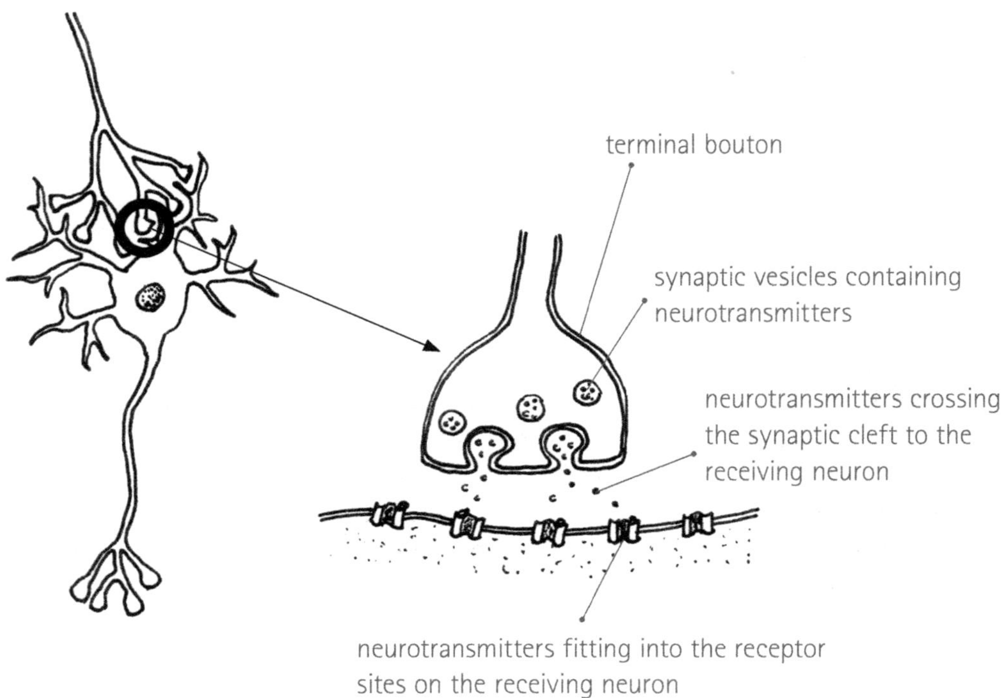

Figure 1 Synaptic transmission

Different neurons use different chemicals as their neurotransmitters but each neuron releases the same chemical from all branches of its axon. The neurotransmitter molecules diffuse across the synapse to the postsynaptic neuron (the neuron on the receiving end of the synapse). There the neurotransmitter molecules attach to receptors on the other neuron's dendrites or cell bodies causing channels in the postsynaptic membrane to open or close.

2 Postsynaptic potentials

Some neurons release neurotransmitters that excite the next neuron (that is, stimulate it to fire an impulse). This means the neurotransmitter can make the next neuron more likely to produce an action potential, which is called a postsynaptic potential. Other neurons release neurotransmitters that *inhibit* the production of an action potential in the next neuron (that is, try to stop the impulse firing). After a neurotransmitter excites or inhibits a receptor in the next neuron, several things can happen to the neurotransmitter. It could become reabsorbed by the axon that released it (through a process called re-uptake), it could diffuse away or become broken up by enzymes, or it could bounce around for a while and then return to the postsynaptic receptor again. The longer the neurotransmitter stays in the synaptic cleft, the more likely it is to affect the other neuron.

At any one time, a neuron may receive hundreds or thousands of inputs from other neurons because it has many dendrites connecting to many axon terminals. Each one of these connections form a synapse and each of these synapses produces an excitatory or inhibitory potential. These potentials spread along the neuron's dendrites and across its soma towards the axon hillock. The sum total of the excitatory and inhibitory potentials has to exceed the neuron's threshold for it to generate an impulse. For example, if several axon terminals discharge a neurotransmitter with an excitatory function at the same time, the postsynaptic potentials may exceed the neuron's threshold and generate an impulse. However, the opposite may happen if a significant number of axon terminals discharge a neurotransmitter with an inhibitory function. In this case the inhibitory potentials may keep the excitatory potentials below the threshold, preventing an impulse in the postsynaptic neuron.

It is important to remember that a postsynaptic potential is not an all-or-nothing event. It is a graded potential. The potentials generated in the postsynaptic membranes become weaker as they travel along the dendrites and across the soma. These potentials also impact on each other. Excitatory potentials add towards greater excitation, inhibitory potentials add towards greater inhibition and excitatory and inhibitory potentials tend to cancel each other out.

These processes involve temporary and spatial summation. Spatial summation occurs when a postsynaptic potential is reinforced by action potentials from the terminals of several axons reaching the same synapse at more or less the same time. The action potential is reinforced because more of the neurotransmitter is released and accumulates in the synaptic cleft, strengthening the postsynaptic potential. Temporal summation occurs when the same axon discharges repeatedly, also causing the release and accumulation of more of the neurotransmitter in the synaptic cleft. Spatial and temporal summation increase the chance of a neuron firing in the case of excitatory postsynaptic potentials and reduce the chances of neurons firing in the case of inhibitory postsynaptic potentials.

3 The nature of neurotransmitters

Neurotransmitters can be excitatory or inhibitory, but may also have both inhibitory as well as excitatory effects at times. Whether the neurotransmitter has an excitatory or inhibitory effect depends on the following:

- The nature of the neurotransmitter
- The place where it acts

- The quantity of neurotransmitter in relation to the enzyme that destroys it
- The amount of inhibitory neurotransmitters in relation to the amount of excitatory neurotransmitters at a particular synapse

What are neurotransmitters? They have certain identifying characteristics:

- They are chemicals that are present in or synthesised (made) by neurons.
- When the neuron is active, a chemical is released and produces a response in a target cell.
- There is a mechanism for removing the neurotransmitter from the synaptic cleft once its work is done.

There are many neurotransmitters and more are likely to be discovered, but the following are regarded as the 'classic' neurotransmitters, mainly because we know more about them than others (Morris and Maisto, 2003).

Acetylcholine (ACh)

ACh is released by cells in the brain and spinal cord, as well as by the parasympathetic nerves and its effects vary. For example, it causes skeletal muscles to contract. The effect can be seen in a poison (called curare) used on arrowheads by traditional hunters, which prevents acetylcholine from reaching the receptors. This causes paralysis of the muscles so that the animal is unable to breathe and therefore suffocates. Acetylcholine is also believed to be related to memory, probably because it supports normal wakeful behaviour and mental alertness. An insufficiency of acetylcholine in some brain areas of patients with Alzheimer's disease may explain the progressive decline in their cognitive functioning.

Adrenalin (epinephrine)

Adrenalin is released by the sympathetic nerves and the adrenal glands. It increases the heart rate and the contraction of blood vessels, skeletal muscles and heart muscle. It also speeds up metabolism and the release of glucose into the blood.

Noradrenalin (NA)

NA is also called norepinephrine (NE). It is released by brain cells and sympathetic nerves as well as the adrenal glands and has an excitatory effect. A lack of NA is associated with depression and an excess with mania.

Dopamine (DA)

DA is associated with good mental health; however, an excess of dopamine is believed to be associated with schizophrenia, a mental disorder characterised by loss of contact with reality. DA is also involved in the control of motor behaviour. Too little can result in muscle rigidity and tremor. For example, an insufficiency of DA in the brain contributes to Parkinson's disease, a form of mental disorder characterised by disturbances of movement and dementia.

Serotonin

Serotonin is found in the brain, digestive tract and blood. Serotonin helps to regulate the sleep–wake cycle and temperature. It is also associated with seasonal depression, a mood disorder that occurs in autumn and winter. Several types of antidepressants obtain their effect through modulation of serotonin at synapses.

Gamma-aminobutyric acid (GABA)

Although GABA is excitatory in the developing brain, it is the main inhibitory neurotransmitter in the adult brain. It regulates excitability throughout the human nervous system, controls muscle tone and helps to manage aggression and appetite.

Endorphin

Endorphin is a neurotransmitter involved in the experience of pleasure and the suppression of pain. It is produced during 'feel-good' activities, such as laughter, love and especially exercise, where it is associated with a phenomenon known as 'runner's high'. During strenuous exercise people may exceed what they would normally call their physical limit and afterwards experience euphoria and feelings of well-being.

4 The effect of drugs on synaptic processes

Some knowledge of neurotransmitters helps us to understand the effect of drugs on behaviour because the drugs work by affecting synaptic processes. There are two main classes of drug: agonists are those that have a similar effect to some neurotransmitters and antagonists are those that block the action of some neurotransmitters. For example, the opiate-sensitive receptors in postsynaptic neurons are highly receptive to narcotics like morphine and codeine (pain killers). Morphine and codeine are therefore agonists. Anaesthetic drugs and barbiturates (which are sedatives) are antagonists because they increase the sensitivity of postsynaptic receptors to inhibitors, which prevents excitation of the neurons. Drugs are generally classified on the basis of their effects on behaviour.

Bibliography

Morris, C.G. and Maisto, A.A. 2003. *Understanding psychology.* New Jersey: Prentice Hall.

Weiten, W. 2001. *Psychology: Themes and variations.* 5th edition. California: Wadsworth.

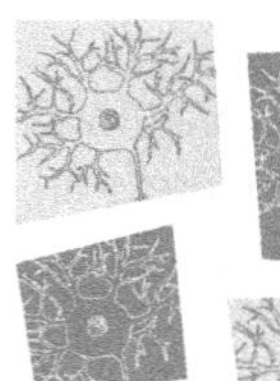
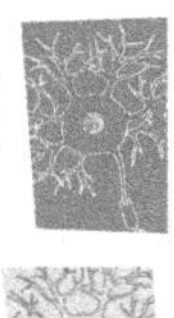

Human nervous system: Structure and function

The parts of the nervous system, individually and working together, are responsible for various aspects of behaviour. However, it is important to keep in mind that this is only one way of describing behaviour and there are other viewpoints, such as looking at the contribution of thoughts or social experiences in shaping our behaviour.

The human nervous system is a very complex communication system that functions in a highly organised and integrated way. In order to get an overview of this system, it is necessary to classify its component parts.

The nervous system comprises two main parts – the central nervous system and the peripheral nervous system. The *central nervous system* is made up of the brain and spinal cord. It can be compared to a central control room that sends and receives information to and from the body and the outside world. The *peripheral nervous system* is made up of the neurons and organs that lie outside or beyond the brain and spinal cord. It has two main parts – the somatic nervous system and the autonomic nervous system.

1 The central nervous system

The brain and spinal cord are protected by bones (the brain is protected by the skull and the spinal cord by the bones of the spinal column, called vertebrae) as well as three strong membranes. The outer membrane is called the dura mater, which is very strong and thick. The middle membrane, called the arachnoid, is also thick but more flexible. The inner membrane, called the pia mater, is soft and flexible. The brain and spinal cord each are made up of two almost identical halves, like mirror images of each other. The nerve tracts and structures found in one half will also be found in the other.

1.1 The spinal cord

1.1.1 Spinal nerves

The spinal cord acts like a cable that connects the brain with other parts of the body. It extends from the brain down the length of the back, protected by the bones that form the spinal column. The spinal cord is made up of columns of white matter, which are bundles of axons covered with myelin. Where these axons leave the spinal cord, they form nerves. There are 30 pairs of nerves on each side of the spinal cord. Each nerve divides into a motor and a sensory root (see Figure 1). The sensory root consists of nerve fibres that convey sensory information to the brain. This information is received from the sensory receptors in the skin; the skeletal muscles, tendons and joints; and the internal organs of the body. The information is conducted from the sensory receptors to the brain along the sensory root of the spinal nerve. The motor root consists of motor nerve fibres that convey information from the brain to the muscles and glands in the body (abdomen, arms and legs). The spinal nerves carry sensory and motor messages to and from the spinal cord and keep the body in communication with the brain.

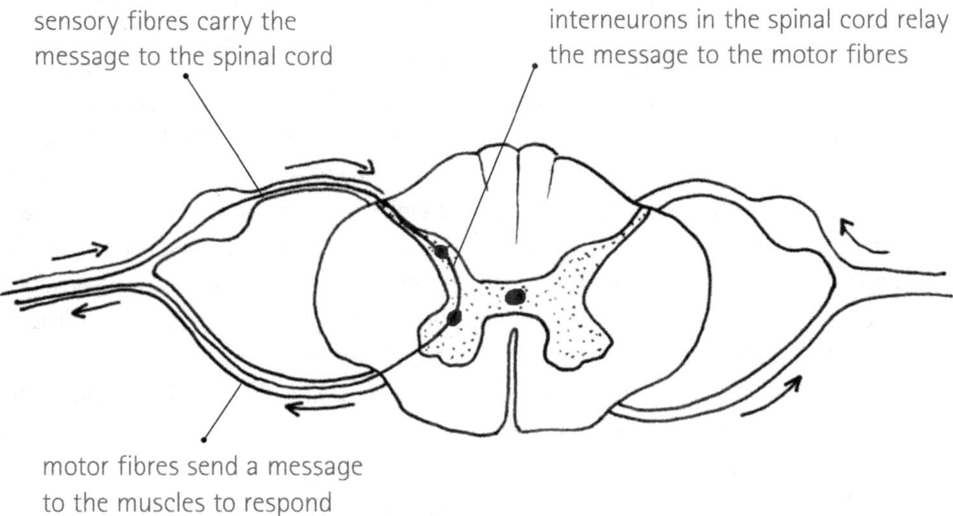
sensory fibres carry the message to the spinal cord
interneurons in the spinal cord relay the message to the motor fibres
motor fibres send a message to the muscles to respond

Figure 1 Cross-section of the spinal cord showing the path of a reflex action (looking from the front of the body)

1.1.2 Reflexes

Not only does the spinal cord carry information to and from the body, it also produces basic forms of behaviour, called reflexes. A reflex is a simple stereotyped response that follows immediately after a certain stimulus is received. For example, if you touch a hot stove (the heat is the stimulus), your hand jerks back without you thinking about it (a stereotyped response).

1.2 The brain

The brain is an extremely complex organ. It is estimated that there are 10 billion neurons in the brain and that any one of them may have thousands of connections with other neurons in the brain. The space between the skull and the brain is filled with fluid called cerebrospinal fluid, which is produced by the brain and surrounds it. By 'floating' in the fluid, the brain is protected from being bumped about and injured. The brain is also protected by the blood-brain barrier that keeps out certain harmful substances. The brain is richly supplied with blood vessels that carry important substances such as oxygen and glucose to the brain and transport waste products like carbon dioxide from the brain cells. In the brain, the passage of drugs is much more difficult than elsewhere in the body because the tiny blood vessels, called capillaries, are impermeable to many substances. This creates the blood-brain barrier.

The outer layer of the brain is called the cerebral cortex. It has a wrinkled appearance, like a pecan nut, because the surface of the cortex has bumps and grooves (also called fissures). The cerebral cortex is composed of tissue made up mostly of cell bodies that have a grey colour and this is why it is called grey matter. The brain consists of two halves, called cerebral hemispheres ('half rounds'). The two hemispheres are connected by a thick band of fibres called the corpus callosum, which allows the right and left cerebral hemispheres to communicate with each other. The left side of the brain controls mainly the right side of the body and likewise the right side of the brain controls mainly the left side of the body. This is called contralateral control (*contra* means 'opposite' and *lateral* means 'side'). For example, when an elderly person has a stroke or brain infarct in the left hemisphere of the brain, the result is often loss of sensation and motor control in the right arm and leg. Some parts of the body are controlled by the same side of the brain, which is called ipsilateral control.

There is also evidence that the two halves or hemispheres of the brain are specialised for different types of function. The left hemisphere is involved mainly with the logical organisation and analysis of information (or breaking it down into parts) and processing information sequentially (placing it in order or sequence). The left hemisphere is regarded as the language or verbal hemisphere. The right hemisphere, on the other hand, seems to process information holistically (as a big picture) and simultaneously (all at once). The right hemisphere is considered to be more creative (rather than logical) and is concerned with spatial or non-verbal abilities. There has been a tendency in the popular press to oversimplify the functions of the hemispheres, creating the impression that most of the time we use only one half of the brain and not the other. The fact is that most people use both hemispheres of the brain at all times. The two hemispheres work together to produce most behaviours – each hemisphere does the part of the task that it does best and shares the information with the other hemisphere. For example, language is processed mainly by the left hemisphere, but the right hemisphere also plays a role in the way language is used.

1.2.1 The lobes of the brain

The two hemispheres can be divided into smaller sections called lobes (see Figure 2). The lobes are marked out by certain fissures on the surface of the cortex and are also distinguished from one another by the fact that they have different main functions.

The occipital lobes

The occipital lobes lie at the back of the brain and are the primary visual area of the cortex – that is, the area where visual input is interpreted. If there is a tumour or cell growth that interferes with brain activity in the occipital lobe, vision will be affected. The occipital lobes are also responsible for combining visual stimuli into meaningful patterns. Examples of this are the ability to perceive that eyes, a nose and a mouth make up a recognisable face, or that a group of letters makes a word. In addition, the integration of sensory experiences takes place in the occipital lobes.

The parietal lobes

The parietal lobes are made up of somatosensory cortex. The word *somatosensory* refers to bodily sensations, such as touch, temperature, pressure and pain. The parietal lobes receive input about these sensations and also information from muscles and joints, which tells the brain about the body's position in space. Researchers have been able to map out which areas of the parietal lobes control which areas of the body. Those areas that are very sensitive, such as the lips and hands, have a larger area of representation in the parietal cortex than areas that are not as sensitive, such as the knees or back. The parietal lobes put together all the somatosensory information received and provide feedback based on that information, so that the individual knows, for example, what part of the body has been touched and where the feet and hands are in relation to the rest of the body and can co-ordinate movements in space.

The temporal lobes

One of the main functions of the temporal lobes is the perception of sound. Auditory information is projected to the temporal lobes, where it is registered and interpreted. For example, the temporal lobes allow us to understand spoken words and other sound patterns, such as music or rain on the roof. The left temporal lobe is regarded as the 'language centre' of the brain and damage to this area can negatively affect the ability to understand what is heard and to use language effectively. The right temporal lobe is concerned more with non-verbal sounds, but also plays some role in speech.

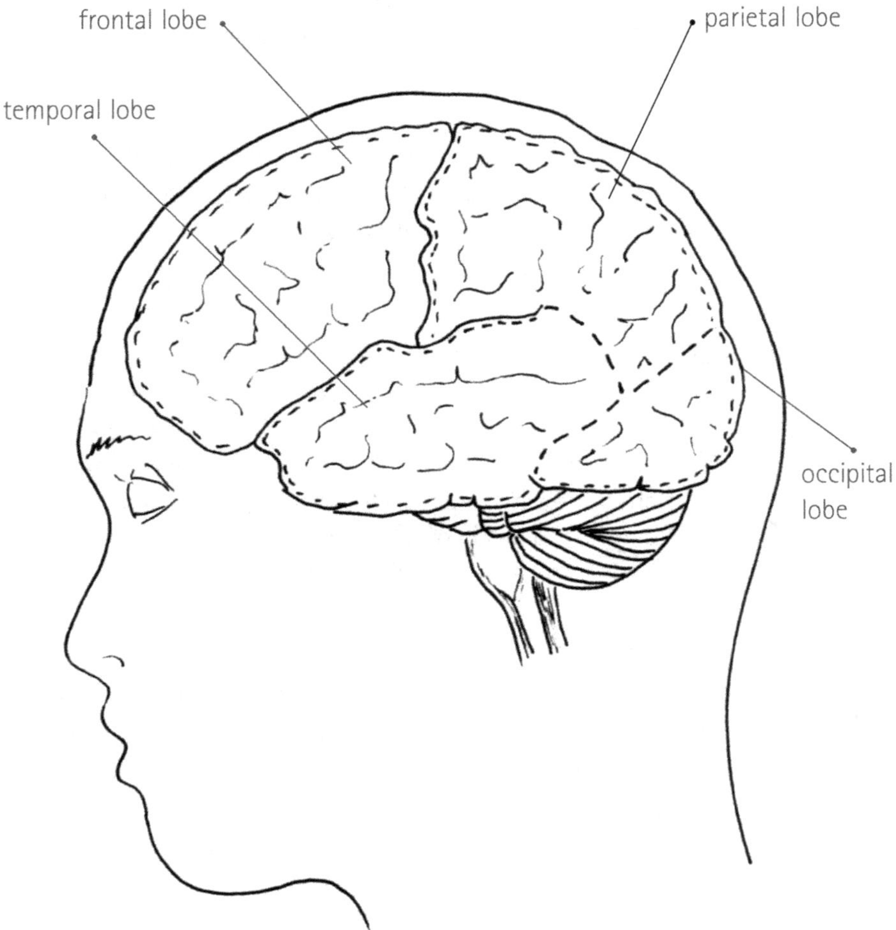

Figure 2 View of the outside surface of the left half of the brain

The frontal lobes

The frontal lobes represent the most recently evolved part of the brain. These regulate complex mental activities and behaviours. Whereas the other lobes have more specific functions, the frontal lobes function in a more generalised way to produce integrated behaviours. One of the main functions of the frontal lobes is the control of voluntary motor movement, including the production of speech. The motor area of the frontal lobes ensures smooth performance of a sequence of motor skills that make up complex actions like talking, typing or playing tennis. If this part of the frontal lobe is damaged, the person makes jerky, uncoordinated movements and may struggle to stop one movement and start another. Other important functions of the frontal lobe are to maintain attention and concentration through optimal arousal of the cortex; to apply abstract thinking, reasoning and planning; and to regulate emotions and behaviour.

Damage to certain areas of the frontal lobes can result in changed behaviour that is sometimes referred to as personality change, because the individual no longer behaves in the way he or she used to before the damage occurred. For example, the person may be over- or underactive, may lose interest in activities and may act inappropriately or become less inhibited. Much of what we call intelligent behaviour relates to the ability to effectively use functions regulated by the frontal lobe.

1.2.2 Major structures of the brain

The *neocortex* is the outer layer of the brain. Below the neocortex are a number of structures that make up the *subcortex* (sub means 'below'). The brain can also be divided into three sections – the hindbrain, the midbrain and the forebrain – which will be discussed separately. If you imagine cutting the brain in half, from front to back and taking away the left half, Figure 3 provides the view you would see of the right hemisphere, looking from the inside.

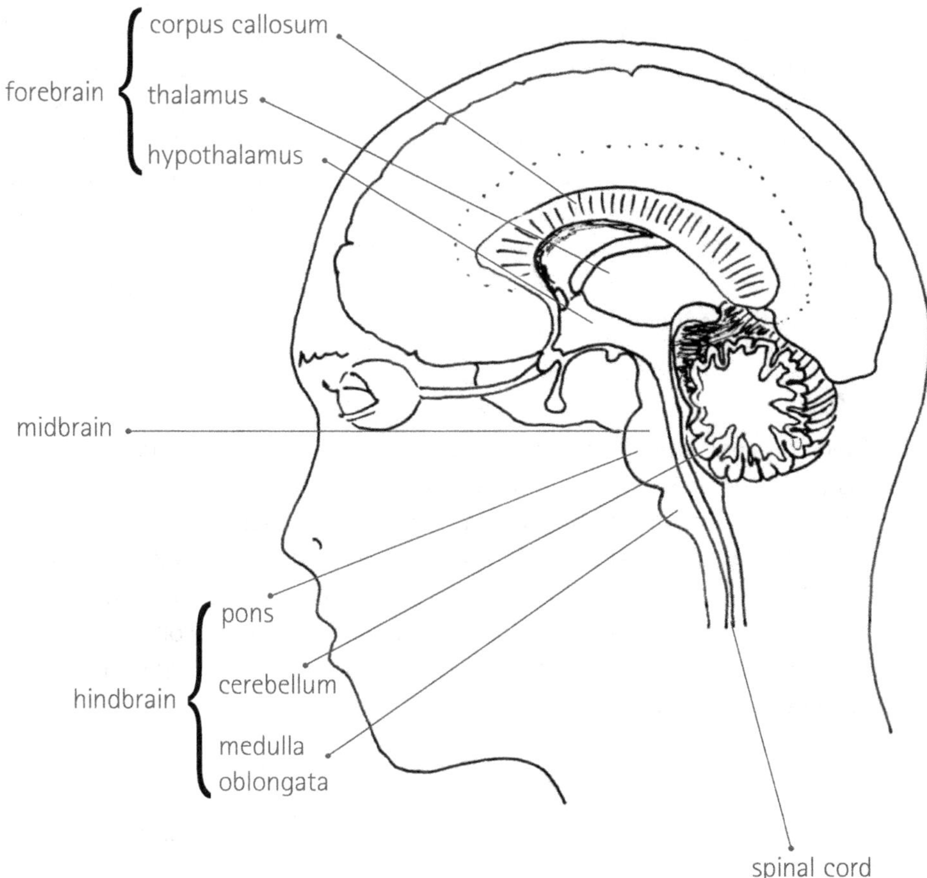

Figure 3 The main structures of the forebrain, midbrain and hindbrain

The hindbrain

The word 'hindbrain' indicates that this part of the brain is at the back of the brain (think of the word *behind).* This is the oldest part of the brain and the same structures are found in many animal species. There are three main structures of the hindbrain:

- The *medulla oblongata* is an extension of the spinal cord and consists of grey matter (cell bodies) surrounded by white matter (nerve fibres). Groups of neurons in the medulla oblongata act as reflex centres for processes that ensure survival, such as breathing and heart rate. On the front of the medulla oblongata there are two bumps, called pyramids, formed by the crossing of motor nerve tracts that maintain the brain's contralateral control of the muscles. Inside the medulla oblongata is a network of cell bodies, called the reticular formation, which extends upwards into the midbrain. The reticular formation stimulates the brain, keeping it active and alert but also preventing it from overstimulation by regulating input. In this way, it maintains an optimal arousal level so that the brain can function properly.
- The *pons* is the structure that acts as a bridge between the medulla and other brain structures. The pons also regulates sleep and wakefulness.
- The *cerebellum* is sometimes called the 'small brain' because it looks like a miniature cerebral cortex. The main function of the cerebellum is to co-ordinate motor movement. It does this by regulating posture, balancing muscle tone and muscle co-ordination. By integrating and comparing information received from the body, it allows the necessary adjustments to be made so that movements initiated by the brain are carried out in a co-ordinated sequence.

The midbrain

The midbrain is a very small part of the brain and is actually a continuation of the pons. It has two structures – the tectum and tegmentum:

- The *tectum* contains two structures: one is the reflex centre for vision (controlling eye blink and size of the pupil, for example) called the superior colliculus and the other is the reflex centre for hearing (controlling adjustment to volume and startle response to sound) called the inferior colliculus.
- The *tegmentum's* structures are mainly involved in the regulation of motor movement.

The forebrain

The major structures of the forebrain are the thalamus, hypothalamus, basal ganglia and limbic system:

- The *thalamus* consists of a collection of nerve nuclei and its main function is to act as a relay station for sensory information (that is, incoming sensory information is received by the thalamus and sent on to the appropriate structures or area of the cortex for integration and/or interpretation of the information).

- The *hypothalamus* lies below the thalamus and has many nerve nuclei that are involved in functions such as regulating (1) the internal environment of the body (such as temperature, water intake, sexual activity, heartbeat, blood pressure and digestion); (2) states of sleep and wakefulness; and (3) emotions.
- The *basal ganglia* are three large groups of neurons that regulate slow, smooth movements (like walking). Axons from some of the neurons project to the motor areas of the cerebral cortex and the midbrain.
- The *limbic system* is made up of several structures (hippocampus, amygdala, septum and limbic cortex) that regulate motivated behaviour, emotions and memory. For example, the limbic system evaluates experiences as positive (rewarding) or negative (disagreeable), links this with information in memory and helps the person to adapt to similar situations that arise. The hippocampus plays an important role in memory by comparing new incoming information with existing information in memory. The amygdala plays a role in the experience of fear and anger, as well as relaxation and is linked to the emotional aspects of memory. The septum is regarded as the brain's pleasure or reward centre. The limbic cortex regulates the subcortical structures mentioned here and plays an important part in the regulation of emotion.

1.2.3 General principles of brain functioning

Hierarchical functioning

The first principle is that brain functions are organised hierarchically – that is, more complex or higher structures control lower ones. Figure 4 illustrates the relation between the various brain structures. The functions of structures higher up the hierarchy are more complex than those lower down. Higher structures generally control lower ones, but the higher structures also depend on input from lower ones. For example, complex attention is a function of the frontal lobes, but in order to regulate attention, the frontal lobes are dependent on input from the reticular formation. This is an example of a feedback loop. Feedback loops are the basis for adjusting functions in response to demands from the environment. Even though the various structures have different functions, they need to work together in an integrated way for the brain to function effectively.

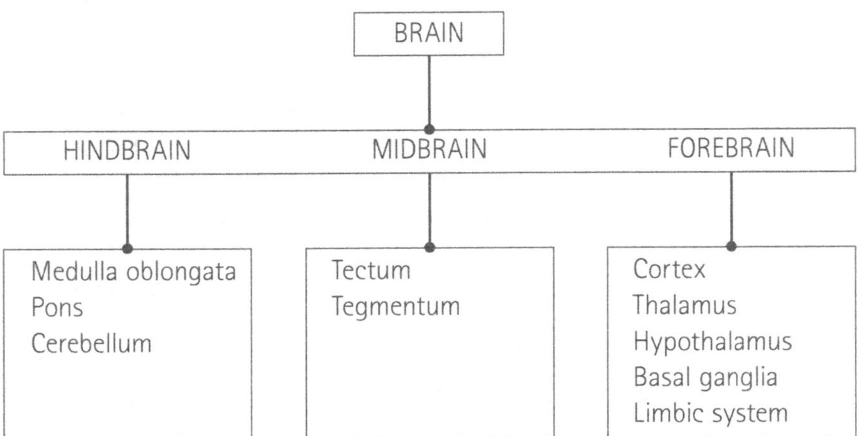

Figure 4 Organisation of the main structures of the brain

Specificity and plasticity

The second principle is that brain functioning is both specific and plastic. This seems contradictory, but what it means is that certain structures may be connected in specific ways (like the structures involved in memory, for example), but the brain is also capable of 'plasticity' or being changeable, in that new connections can be formed in the brain. For example, a child's brain has virtually the same number of neurons as an adult brain. However, during the child's development, the connections among neurons are formed in response to environmental stimulation and this is why a child's brain is regarded as more 'plastic' or adaptable than an adult's brain.

Lateralisation of functions

The third principle refers to the lateralisation of functions – that is, the location of functions more predominant in one hemisphere than the other. The higher up the hierarchy the structure is, the more lateralised its functioning is likely to be. Consider, for example, the different roles of the thalamus (a lower structure) and the cerebral cortex (a higher structure) in language. All sounds (auditory stimuli) are received by the thalamus, but only verbal sounds are projected to the left temporal cortex and non-verbal sounds to the right temporal cortex. This means that the cerebral cortex is more lateralised than the subcortical structures.

1.3 The peripheral nervous system

The peripheral nervous system is made up of two subsystems, the somatic (or bodily) nervous system and the autonomic nervous system.

1.3.1 The somatic nervous system

The *somatic nervous system* in turn has two components – one is sensory and the other motor. Remember that the word *soma* means 'body', therefore it makes sense that the somatic nervous system refers to the nerves that conduct information from the sensory receptors in the body to the central nervous system (sensory or afferent nerves) and from the central nervous system to the skeletal muscles in the body (motor or efferent nerves).

1.3.2 The autonomic nervous system

The *autonomic nervous system* controls the processes that regulate our internal organs and glands so that the body functions evenly. The autonomic nervous system also has two divisions, the *sympathetic* and the *parasympathetic* nervous systems. These systems have opposite effects, therefore the organs and glands are connected to both of them. The sympathetic system stimulates the organs and the parasympathetic system slows things down again so as to restore and sustain normal functioning. For example, the sympathetic nervous system increases heart rate when a person needs to flee from danger and the parasympathetic system restores the heart rate to normal when the danger is over. This example illustrates how the sympathetic nervous system prepares the body for action by activating processes to release energy from the body. The parasympathetic nervous system activates processes to restore the body's functioning again and build up the body's reserves. Other manifestations of the actions of the sympathetic and parasympathetic nervous systems are shown in Table 1.

Table 1 Effects of stimulation of the sympathetic and parasympathetic nervous systems

Sympathetic nervous system	Parasympathetic nervous system
Pupils of the eye dilate to let in more light	Pupils contract to limit the amount of light that enters the eye; optic muscles adjust
Structures in the lungs expand to absorb more oxygen	There is decreased lung action
The heart pumps faster and blood pressure rises	There is a reduction in blood pressure and heart rate
More blood reaches the muscles to increase the supply of oxygen and glucose	Some muscles relax
Less blood is available to the skin and digestive organs so that more is available for the brain and skeletal muscles	Blood supply to the skin is restored
Digestion is inhibited	Digestive processes increase

The autonomic nervous system is designed to bring about a state of balance, or homeostasis, in the body. The sympathetic and parasympathetic divisions work in relation to one another, constantly adjusting to bring about optimal functioning in the face of the demands placed on the person. However, it sometimes happens that one system may dominate the other. A person with sympathetic dominance is likely to be in a state of chronic tension, characterised by dilated pupils, sweaty hands, shallow breathing because of tension in the chest muscles, poor concentration (and distractibility), an inability to relax and sleep, overexcitement and emotional intensity. On the other hand, a person with parasympathetic dominance is likely to be under-aroused, appearing lethargic and poorly motivated. Such a person may have respiratory and digestive difficulties. A person who is autonomically balanced would have a moderate level of tension; reactions would be appropriate; and concentration, drive and motivation would be good.

It should be remembered that, although the autonomic nervous system is part of the peripheral nervous system, it is still controlled by structures in the central nervous system. For example, the hypothalamus, which is part of the central nervous system, controls some of the functions of the autonomic nervous system, like the release of hormones. The human nervous system works continually to respond and adapt to environmental demands in an integrated way.

Bibliography

Coon, D. 2004. *Introduction to psychology*. 10th edition. Belmont, CA: Wadsworth.

Jordaan, W. and Jordaan, J. 1998. *People in context.* 3rd edition. Johannesburg: Heinemann.

Morris, C.G. and Maisto, A.A. 2003. *Understanding psychology.* New Jersey: Prentice Hall.

Weiten, W. 2001. *Psychology: Themes and variations.* 5th edition. Belmont, CA: Wadsworth.

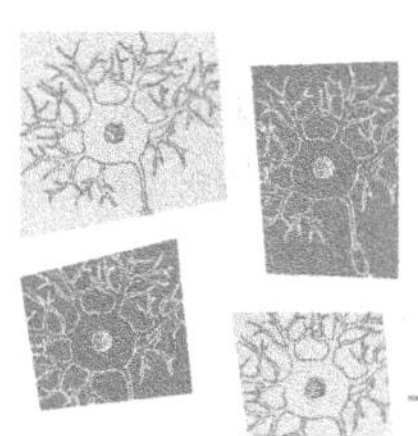

Human nervous system: The structure of the neuron

We have to begin by studying neurons when we want to understand how the nervous system works. A neuron (also called a nerve cell) is the basic building block in the structure of the nervous system. In other words, if we connect a number of neurons we build a nervous system. If we think of the nervous system as a complex network of electrical wires, a neuron is one of these wires.

The nervous system is a communication network. It carries messages throughout the body. The neurons are the basic elements of this communication network. The fact that there may be as many as 100 billion neurons in the human nervous system shows how complex this communication network really is.

In this section we will see what a typical neuron looks like and briefly consider different types.

1 The main parts of a neuron

All neurons are not exactly the same, but they do have similar parts. In other words, they are similar in structure. The main parts of a neuron are illustrated in Figure 1. These parts are the dendrites, the cell body, the axon and the axon terminals. From a structural point of view the cell body is the central part of the neuron and the dendrites and the axon are extensions of the cell body. A cell body has many dendrites, but only one axon.

The function of a neuron is to convey a message. From a functional point of view, the parts of a neuron is considered in terms of how the message is conveyed. The message is transmitted from the dendrites through the cell body and down the axon to the axon terminals. We portray the parts of the neuron in this order.

1.1 The dendrites

The neuron begins with a number of dendrites. The dendrites are extensions of the cell body. If we consider the neuron as a piece of electrical wire, we can think of the dendrites as a number of thin wires feeding into a thicker wire (the neuron). As each one of these thin wires (each dendrite) consists of even thinner wires, we can think of each dendrite as a number of very thin wires feeding into a dendrite wire and the dendrite wire feeding into the cell body. Another way to visualise this is to think of the neuron as a tree trunk and the dendrites as the branches. These branches (dendrites) keep on branching into thinner branches.

Thus a neuron has a number of dendrites and each one splits into finer and finer branches. All this branching has a significant effect – it allows the neuron to connect to a large number of other neurons.

1.2 The cell body (soma)

The dendrites are extensions of the body of the neuron cell, also called the soma, which is surrounded by the dendrites that extend from it. Although these dendrites are the main connections with the axons of other neurons, some of these axons may connect directly to the soma. The soma thus receives messages from other neurons through its dendrites and sometimes directly through itself.

Inside the cell body (soma) is the cell nucleus, which can be described as the control centre of the cell because it controls all metabolic activities in the cell. The metabolic activities are the processes that keep the cell alive and allow it to function properly.

Apart from its dendrites, the soma has one other extension, which is a thin fibre called the axon. A neuron has many dendrites, but it has only one axon extending from its soma. The axon extends from the soma in a specialised area of the soma called the axon hillock.

1.3 The axon

The stimulation (messages) received from the axons of other neurons (via the dendrites and the surface connections with the soma) accumulates in the soma and is summed in the axon hillock. When the stimulation reaches a particular level, the axon hillock initiates an impulse that runs along the axon.

Axons differ with regard to their thickness (diameter) and their length. Some axons are thin, while others are thick. Some are short and some are very long, connecting parts of the body that may be some distance away from each other (like from the base of the spine to the big toe). In many cases, axons are enclosed in a white fatty sheath called myelin, which insulates the axon.

The myelin sheaths are separated by small gaps, called nodes of Ranvier. The axon is not insulated at these gaps or nodes. When an axon is insulated with myelin, it can conduct impulses much faster than those that are un-myelinated (that is, not insulated with myelin) because the impulse jumps from node to node.

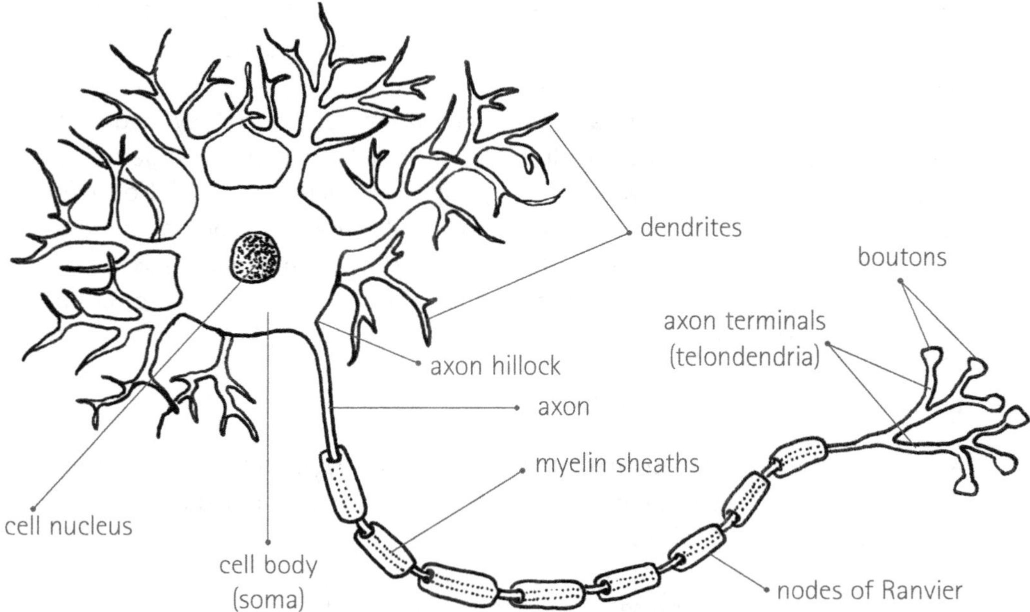

Figure 1 Schematic representation of a neuron in the human nervous system (enlarged millions of times)

The importance of myelin insulation becomes evident when axons that should be myelinated lose their myelin insulation. The effect of not having properly myelinated axons is seen in the disease multiple sclerosis, which attacks the myelin (Jordaan and Jordaan, 1998). The result is that messages are not transmitted properly and the person with multiple sclerosis ultimately becomes disabled. Dendrites and soma are not enclosed in myelin.

1.4 The axon terminals (telondendria)

Most axons end in axon terminals, also called telondendria. Each axon terminal (telondendron) ends in a small knob, called a bouton terminal. Each one of these bouton terminals connects to a dendrite branch from a following neuron. Because a neuron's axon may end in a number of telondendria, it may connect to a number of following neurons.

Inside the boutons are tiny containers, called vesicles, which are filled with neurotransmitters. These are chemical substances that play an important role in conducting a message from one neuron to the next.

1.5 The synapse

The bouton terminals of preceding neurons do not actually touch the dendrites of the following neurons. There is a small gap between a bouton terminal and a dendrite, which is called a synaptic cleft. A synapse is the place where a telondendron meets up with a dendrite. The bouton vesicles of the telondendron release their neurotransmitters into the synaptic cleft.

These neurotransmitters are very important because they regulate the communication between neurons. If one considers the immensely large number of synapses in the human nervous system (remember there are 100 billion neurons, each one forming a number of synapses with other neurons), one appreciates the fundamental role that neurotransmitters play. Most of the modern medicines used in the treatment of psychotic and mood disorders effect the levels of neurotransmitters in the nervous system.

2 Types of neuron

Neurons can be classified according to the functions they perform, the two main types being sensory and motor neurons. Sensory neurons are also called afferent neurons and motor neurons are also called efferent neurons:

- *Sensory (afferent) neurons.* These are the neurons that carry information detected by the senses (for example the eyes) from the environment to the spinal cord and brain. Information does not only come from the outside environment, but also from some of the organs inside the body. For example, messages come from changes in muscles or activities in organs such as the stomach.
- *Motor (efferent) neurons.* These neurons conduct messages from the spinal cord and brain to the muscles and glands. For example, if you want to run, your brain sends the necessary messages to the muscles involved.

There is another distinction to remember, namely the distinction between a nerve tract and a nerve. When axons are grouped together in a bundle, this bundle is referred to as either a nerve tract or a nerve:

- *Nerve tract.* The bundle is known as a nerve tract when it is in the spinal cord or the brain.
- *Nerve.* The bundle is called a nerve when it is in parts of the body that are not inside the brain and the spinal cord.

It is also important to keep in mind that neurons are well connected. The dendrites of a neuron connect it to a number of preceding neurons and its telondendria connect it to a number of following neurons. One should therefore not think of the nervous system as neurons that are connected to form single strings of neurons. In other words, the nervous system is not simply short pieces of electrical wire joined into longer pieces. Neurons form networks in which each neuron receives information from many neurons and in turn provides information to many other neurons. Each neuron is a node in a network of neurons.

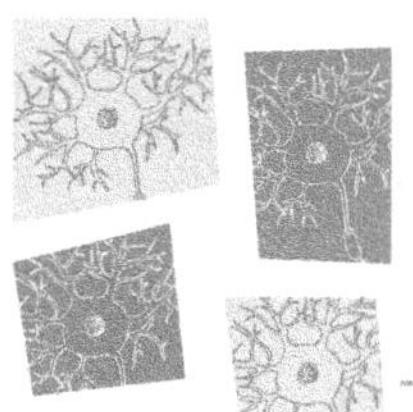

Individual differences in behaviour

Each person is unique. You have probably heard that many times, but have you ever really stopped to think why this is so? Why does one person get stressed by exams while another person stays cool and calm, without seeming to worry? There is seldom, if ever, only one reason for differences in people's behaviour. Behaviour is influenced by many factors. Some are within the person and some of them are outside the person in the environment, therefore we need to examine people from several perspectives, or on different levels, in order to understand why they behave in the way they do. We use the term 'context' for the different perspectives or levels. There are three main contexts: (1) the biological context; (2) the intra-psychic context; and (3) the social context. Each context contributes toward individual differences in behaviour and also gives us a different perspective or viewpoint for looking at and understanding behaviour.

1 The biological context

Human experience and behaviour cannot occur without bodily structures and functions. At the most basic level, the biological basis of behaviour is the conduction of impulses in neurons. Stimuli from the environment are conducted to the brain and other parts of the body to bring about various forms of behaviour. Various parts of the brain and body are responsible for different actions, for integrating different functions and for producing behaviour. Although we all have the same body parts, they are not necessarily of the same quality in all individuals. For example, people have ankles, calves, knees and thighs, but everyone's legs do not look the same. We also differ in strength and ability because of the way the parts are put together.

In the same way, we all have the same nervous system, but the way it functions is not the same for everyone. For example, if neurons and structures in the body and brain are damaged or unable to work properly, behaviour will be affected. Or if a person is malnourished, his or her body will function differently from that of a person who is well nourished. You have probably noticed too that you do not function so well when you are feeling sick. The way in which we receive sensory information from the environment also differs from one individual to another. For example, some people feel the cold easily and need to put on a jersey or blanket long before other people feel the cold. This means that our sensitivity to information is different. So we have to take a person's physical or biological functioning into account when we try to understand their behaviour.

2 The intra-psychic context

This context refers to the process that takes place within the individual (*intra* means 'within'). Intra-psychic processes refer to our experiences. Examples are the process of perception, including the organisation of information to make it meaningful, paying attention, thinking, reasoning, problem solving, intelligence, creativity, learning, memory, emotions and personality. Each person experiences things in a unique way, because each person processes information differently. Why is this so? The answer is that the processes of perceiving, thinking, learning or feeling do not occur separately. If you experience something, all these processes play a role together.

Let us look at various aspects of the intra-psychic context. The first one has to do with perception – that is, receiving and processing information. Perception gives our experiences meaning and people can have different perceptions of the same object or event. For example, most of us would perceive travelling at high speed as dangerous, but a trained racing driver would perceive it differently. In our everyday lives, we see how people's perceptions of things differ in terms of their likes and dislikes. If we all perceived everything the same way, life would be very boring! Unfortunately, differences in the way we perceive things can lead to conflict and problems. For example, differences in the way husbands and wives see or interpret behaviour can lead to marriage problems.

The second aspect refers to cognitive processes, or the way people know or understand things, for example through thinking, learning and remembering. These processes influence the way we understand and react to events, situations and things in our environment. Because our levels of ability differ, our experiences will be different too. What we learn influences the way we interpret our worlds and the way we cope with the demands of everyday life.

The third aspect concerns our emotions and personality. Our emotions indicate our sense of involvement with people and events. They give colour to our experiences. Our personalities and emotions also influence the way we see and think about our experiences. When you think about the variety of reactions of people you know to something like a television programme or a piece of music – some people may love it and others may hate it – you can see how people differ.

The biological and intra-psychic contexts are actually interdependent. This means that they influence one another. Your biological state can influence your perceptions (for example, a deaf person will experience the world differently from a person who can hear) or your emotions (for example, a person who has had a leg amputated may become depressed and see the world in a different way from other people). On the other hand, your emotions and personality can influence your physical health (for example, stress can contribute to becoming ill). Both biological and intra-psychic processes are the ingredients of a person's psychobiological makeup.

3 The social context

People do not live their psychobiological lives in a vacuum. They live amongst other people and in different situations. This is why it is necessary to consider the influence of the social context on people's behaviour. The social context refers not only to our interaction with other people around us, but also to the physical environment (at our workplace, for instance, or at home or in nature), as well as the culture and the society in which we live. For example, the socio-economic environment influences the school you go to, the kind of facilities you have access to and the social experiences you are exposed to. However, the environment alone does not determine your behaviour – you always have choices that will influence your experience of life.

Remember that it is not only the environment itself but also the way we perceive and experience it that influences our behaviour. Our actions are also influenced by the kind of decisions we make, no matter what kind of environment we find ourselves in. For example, having lots of money does not guarantee that you will be happy in life. What counts is what you do with it (and this refers to intra-psychic processes). So you can see that all the contexts are interrelated and all have to be taken into account to explain individual differences in experiences and human behaviour.

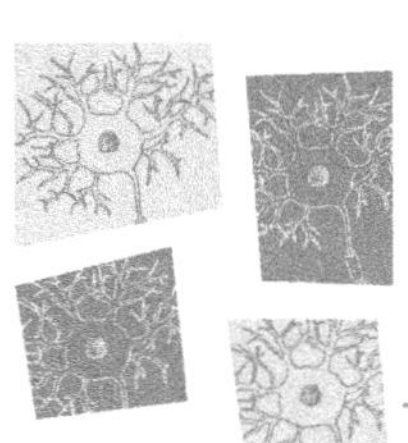

Information analysis: Correlation between variables

People have qualities. Somebody may be tall, have blue eyes, be good at mathematics, or be highly intelligent. Individuals differ in terms of these qualities, therefore these qualities are called variables. They vary for each individual. Psychologists are often interested in how these variables hang together. For example, they would like to know if being good at mathematics goes with being highly intelligent. In other words, they would like to know if there is a relationship between being good at mathematics and intelligence. We use a *correlation coefficient* to express the relationship between variables in a precise manner.

1 What is a correlation coefficient?

The way to express the relationship between variables in a precise manner is to calculate an *index of the relationship.* In this case, this index is called a correlation coefficient. The coefficient gives an indication of the degree (size or strength) of the relationship, as well as the direction of the relationship. The direction of the relationship can be direct or inverse. A *direct relationship* means that more of one thing goes with more of another. For example, if there is a direct or positive correlation between the motivation to study and examination results, it means that greater motivation goes with higher marks. An *inverse relationship* means that more of one thing goes with less of another. For example, if there is an inverse or negative relationship between height and atmospheric pressure, it means that greater height goes with lower pressure. This is quite easy to understand if we look at the numbers. The coefficient that we will calculate here is called the Pearson product moment correlation coefficient. The value of this coefficient always lies between –1 and +1 We can make a picture of this:

–1 ----------------------- 0 -------------------------- +1

A correlation coefficient of +1 means an absolute positive (direct) correlation and a correlation coefficient of –1 means an absolute negative (inverse) correlation. A correlation coefficient of 0 means no correlation.

Now see whether you can get the answer to the following question right: Which one of –1 and +1 indicates the larger correlation? Did you say +1? Wrong! Did you say –1? Wrong again! These two correlations are equal in size. The difference between –1 and +1 is the direction of the relationship, not its size, thus the inverse relationship of –1 is as strong as the direct relationship of +1. The strength of the relationship decreases as we approach zero. Going from –1 to +1 in the picture above means the strength of the relationship will first decrease (between –1 and 0) and then increase (between 0 and +1). The same things happen if we move in the opposite direction – that is, from +1 to –1.

2 How does one calculate a correlation coefficient?

There are a number of different ways to calculate correlation coefficients and they all give different kinds of values. Here we will calculate the Pearson product moment correlation coefficient – that is, a coefficient that always gives a value somewhere between –1 and +1.

First thing to remember: We will calculate the size and the direction of the relationship between two variables, called variable X and variable Y. If you want to apply this example of the calculation in other situations, you simply have to replace the X and the Y with the names of the variables in the other situation. For example, if you want to calculate the correlation between intelligence and academic performance, you simply have to replace the X with intelligence and the Y with academic performance.

Second thing to remember: The calculations look extremely complicated, but they are not. The only problem is there are quite a lot of them. Simply follow the recipe provided by this example closely and you should not have any problems.

Third thing to remember: In this example, we use a sample of five subjects. If you have more subjects, simply add those subjects in the table, as subjects F, G, H and so forth. If you run out of letters (after 26 subjects), simply continue by naming them AA, AB, AC and so on.

Let us work with an example. In this example, we have a sample consisting of five subjects called A, B, C, D and E. We want to calculate the relationship between variable X and variable Y based on the information provided by this sample. Note that we need more than one subject to calculate the relationship between two variables. A single subject cannot provide sufficient information to allow us to do the calculation. We need a sample consisting of more than one subject. In Table 1 below, it is clear that subject A has a score of 3 on variable X and a score of 3 on variable Y. Subject B's score for variable X is 2 and his or her score for variable Y is 3.

Table 1 A sample of five subjects with scores on variable X and variable Y

Subject	Variable X	Variable Y
A	3	3
B	2	3
C	3	2
D	5	2
E	1	5

The first thing you have to do is set up a table that contains the information of the X and Y variables for each subject in your sample. The values that appear in the same row as the subject are those that belong to the subject in question. The symbol X^2 means 'the value of X multiplied by itself' and the same for Y^2 – it means 'the value of Y multiplied by the value of Y'. For example, X^2 for subject C is $3 \times 3 = 9$. The symbol XY means the value of X multiplied by the value of Y. For example, for subject D, the value of XY is $5 \times 2 = 10$. The columns in the table are organised in a way that makes it easier to calculate the values. The Σ symbol is a mathematical symbol that means the sum of the values of a variable. For example, in this case the sum of the values of variable X is 14, therefore $\Sigma = 14$. The number of subjects in the sample is indicated by N. In this case $N = 5$.

You now have all the information you need to calculate the correlation coefficient. Follow the steps provided in Table 2 carefully. They are not as complicated as they may seem at first. The actions are described in words and are also represented in the form of symbols, which give a shorthand description. Note that you should not learn these steps by heart. The table provides a recipe that you can consult and apply when you need to calculate a correlation coefficient. Please do not try to memorise this information.

Table 2 A sample of five subjects with the information of their X and Y variables

Subject	X^2	Variable X	XY	Variable Y	Y^2
A	9	3	9	3	9
B	4	2	6	3	9
C	9	3	6	2	4
D	25	5	10	2	4
E	1	1	5	5	25
$N = 5$	$\Sigma X^2 = 48$	$\Sigma X = 14$	$\Sigma XY = 36$	$Y = 15$	$\Sigma Y^2 = 51$

Table 3 Steps to follow in calculating the correlation coefficient

Step	What to do: In words	What to do: In symbols	Example	Answer
1	Multiply the sample size with the sum of XY	$N\Sigma XY$	5×36	180
2	Multiply the sum of X with the sum of Y	$(\Sigma X)(\Sigma Y)$	14×15	210
3	Subtract the answer obtained in 2 from the answer obtained in 1	$N\Sigma XY - (\Sigma X)(\Sigma Y)$	$180 - 210$	–30
4	Multiply the sample size with the sum of X^2	$N\Sigma X^2$	5×48	240
5	Square the sum of X (multiply the sum of X with itself)	$(\Sigma X)^2$	14×14	196
6	Subtract the answer obtained in 5 from the answer obtained in 4	$N\Sigma X^2 - (\Sigma X)^2$	$240 - 196$	44
7	Multiply the sample size with the sum of Y^2	$N\Sigma Y^2$	5×51	255
8	Square the sum of Y (multiply the sum of Y with itself)	$(\Sigma Y)^2$	15×15	225
9	Subtract the answer obtained in 8 from the answer obtained in 7	$N\Sigma Y^2 - (\Sigma Y)^2$	$255 - 225$	30
10	Multiply the answer obtained in 6 with the answer obtained in 9	$[N\Sigma X^2 - (\Sigma X)^2)]\,[N\Sigma Y^2 - (\Sigma Y)^2]$	44×30	1 320
11	Take the square root of the answer obtained in 10		$\sqrt{(1\ 320)}$	36.33
12	Divide the answer obtained in 3 by the answer obtained in 11	$\frac{N\Sigma XY - (\Sigma X)(\Sigma Y)}{\sqrt{\{[N\Sigma X^2 - (\Sigma X)^2)]\,[N\Sigma Y^2 - (\Sigma Y)^2]\}}}$	$\frac{-30}{36.33}$	–0.83

The correlation coefficient (the strength and the direction of the relationship) is –0.83. In symbol form, one would write: rxy = –0.83 (This reads: The correlation coefficient for variables X and Y is –0.83).

Note that the negative sign indicates an inverse relationship. This means that more of variable X goes with less of variable Y. In other words, larger values in variable X tend to go with lower values in variable Y. For example, if X stands for height above sea level and Y stands for atmospheric density and the relationship between these variables is –0.83, it means that more height goes with lower density. The higher one goes up, the lower the density of the atmosphere.

3 How does one know whether the strength of the relationship is significant?

Once we have calculated the correlation between two variables, we have to determine whether the relationship is significant. This is so if it differs significantly from no relationship. In other words, the correlation coefficient we calculated needs to differ significantly from the value of 0. The easiest way to determine the significance of a correlation coefficient is to compare it to values listed in a table. For this purpose you can use Table 4.

Note that you also have to take the size of the sample into account when you determine the significance of the relationship between two variables. This is because the sample size is an indication of the number of people who provided information about the relationship between the variables in question. Obviously, if you consult more people (that is, if you use a larger sample) you can expect to get a more reliable and valid result, therefore the size of the sample plays a role in determining the significance of a particular correlation.

To check whether a correlation coefficient is significant, compare the coefficient you calculated for your sample with the one listed in Table 4. If your calculated coefficient is equal to or larger than the listed coefficient, it is statistically significant. This means the correlation (the value you calculated for the relationship between X and Y) is significantly more likely than no correlation (that is, a value of 0), therefore if your calculated coefficient is statistically significant, you can say there is a correlation between the variables in question.

If it is not statistically significant, you cannot say that the two variables are correlated. Then you have to state that there is no correlation between the two variables. Note that there are no negative values in the table. This is because *the table indicates the strength of the correlation, not the direction.* When you compare negative correlations (that is, inverse relationships), you simply ignore the negative sign, so the correlation coefficient calculated in the example above is not statistically significant. When we compare 0.83 to the correlation coefficient listed in Table 4 for a sample of 5, we see the value has to be 0.87 (or more) to be significantly different, therefore we cannot report a correlation between X and Y.

Table 4 Values of significant correlation coefficients for different sample sizes

Sample size (N)	Value of significant correlation coefficient
3	0.99
4	0.95
5	0.87
6	0.81
7	0.75
8	0.70
9	0.66
10	0.63
11	0.60
12	0.57
13	0.55
14	0.53
15–19	0.48
20–24	0.42
25–29	0.38
30–34	0.34
35–39	0.32
40–44	0.30
45–49	0.28
50–59	0.26
60–69	0.24
70–79	0.22
80–89	0.21
90–99	0.20
100+	0.19

We used the term 'significance of relationship' above without explaining what it means. It is easy to see that there is a relationship between two variables when it is expressed as a correlation coefficient, but it is not clear why the correlation coefficient needs to exceed a particular value before the correlation becomes significant.

The reason for this is that our measurements are never absolutely accurate. For example, when an individual obtains an intelligence score of 110, there is a possibility that his or her score is less than 110 (say 100), or that it is more than 110 (say 120). What we do know is that 110 is the most likely score for the individual. Although the individual's score may be 100 or 120, these scores are less likely for this individual. If one keeps in mind that intelligence is a variable (say variable X), it becomes clear that the scores obtained for a variable are not absolutely accurate. As this is true for all variables, the scores obtained for variable Y are also are not absolutely accurate, thus if we calculate the correlation coefficient between two variables (X and Y), we cannot expect the correlation coefficient to be absolutely accurate. For example, we may calculate a correlation coefficient and find that its value is 0.15. Based on this value, we think there is a positive (direct) correlation between the two variables, but due to the error in measurement the value may be 0. In other words, there may actually be no correlation between variables X and Y. Although we do not know the exact value of the correlation, we do know it is more likely that the correlation is 0.15 than 0. What we need to ask ourselves is: Is the value of 0.15 significantly more likely than the value of 0? In other words, we ask: Is the correlation we calculated (in this case 0.15) significantly more likely than 0 (which stands for no correlation). If the answer is 'yes', we say there is a correlation. If the answer is 'no', we say there is no correlation. The problem is how to find the answer!

It is easy to suggest that a particular value is more likely than a another value, but it is not easy to determine whether the fact that it is more likely is really significant. In other words, it is not easy to determine whether one value is *significantly* more likely than another value. One needs a computer to calculate the significance of the correlation coefficients we obtain. The computer calculations can be used to compile a table of significant correlation coefficients. All you have to do then is to compare the correlation you obtained with the correlations listed in the table.

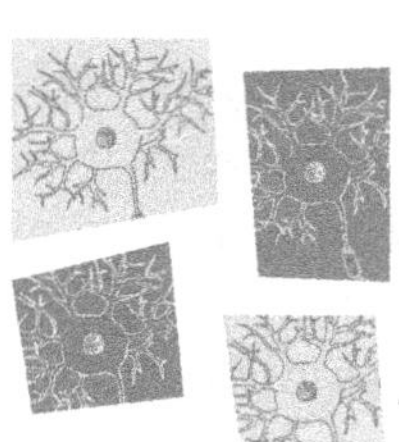

Information analysis: Difference between groups

Psychologists are often interested in the difference between groups. Groups can differ because they have different characteristics and the psychologist may be interested in the nature of these differences. Groups can also differ because one group was treated in a different manner from another. For example, one group may have used a particular learning technique and another group a different one. The psychologist would be interested in which learning technique worked best. To determine whether one group differs from another, we have to express the difference between them in a precise manner. One way to do this is to calculate a t-score.

1 What is a t-score?

A t-score is a precise expression of the difference between two groups. A t-score indicates how much the average of one group differs from the average of the other, therefore we have to calculate an average for each group and consider the difference between them. If there is a significant difference between the averages, we would indicate that the groups differ from each other.

Groups differ with regard to a particular aspect. The average that we calculate for a group is the group's average value for the particular aspect. Groups are compared in terms of this aspect. If we find a significant difference between the two averages, we indicate that the groups differ with regard to the aspect in question. For example, if we want to determine whether men and women differ with regard to language skills, we calculate the average language skills of a group of men and those of a group of women to see whether they differ. If the difference is significant, we could state that men and women differ with regard to their language skills.

The problem is, how does one determine whether the difference between the averages of two groups is significant? The core of the problem is the size of the numbers involved. The size of the difference between two averages is a function of the size of the numbers we use in our calculations. For example, the difference between an average of 100 and an average of 50 seems quite large (100 – 50 = 50) compared to the difference between 10 and 5 (10 – 5 = 5). The first difference is 50 and the second difference is a mere 5, yet in both cases the difference is half the value of the larger number. From this point of view, these two differences are equal. We have to circumvent this problem by calculating a *standard index* of difference, which is called a *t-score*. It expresses the difference between the averages of two groups in terms of their variances. The variance of a group is simply an indication of how much the individuals in the group differ from each other. In other words, the difference between two groups is expressed in terms of the differences inside each of the groups, thus a t-score is an index that expresses the difference between the two groups in terms of the variation inside them.

2 How do we calculate a t-score?

We first have to set up the two groups. Suppose we have a sample consisting of six subjects, called A, B, C, D and E. In Table 1, the size of the sample is indicated by the letter N. Variable X is the *independent variable* and variable Y is the *dependent variable*. The independent variable (X) is the variable in terms of which we will select the subjects to constitute two groups. The dependent variable (Y) is the variable in terms of which we will compare the two groups. We will calculate the average of variable Y for each group. Variable Y is the aspect in terms of which we want to compare the two groups.

Table 1 A sample with six subjects

Subject N = 6	Variable X	Variable Y
A	Male	3
B	Female	9
C	Female	8
D	Male	6
E	Female	6
F	Male	2

From Table 1, it is clear that subject A is a man who scored 3 on variable Y and subject C is a woman who scored 8 on variable Y. Table 2 shows how the sample was divided into two groups based on the two levels of variable X.

Table 2 The sample divided into two groups

Group A (men)				Group B (women)			
Subject	X	Y	Y^2	Subject	X	Y	Y^2
A	Male	3	9	B	Female	9	81
D	Male	6	36	C	Female	8	64
F	Male	2	4	E	Female	6	36
$n_A = 3$		$\Sigma Y_A = 11$	$\Sigma Y_A^2 = 49$	$n_B = 3$		$\Sigma Y_B = 23$	$\Sigma Y_B^2 = 181$

Note the following:

1. N indicates the total sample size and n the size of the subgroups of the sample (n_A is the size of group A and n_B the size of group B).
2. The square of Y indicated by Y^2 means Y multiplied by itself, in other words, $Y \times Y$.
3. The symbol Σ is a mathematical symbol that means 'the sum of the values of a variable'; thus ΣY indicates the sum of the values of variable Y and ΣY^2 means the sum of the squares of Y.
4. The subscripts A and B differentiate the information of the two group, thus ΣY_A is the sum of variable Y for group A and ΣY_B is the sum of variable Y for group B.

You now have all the information you need to calculate the t-score. Follow the steps provided in Table 3 carefully. These steps are not as complicated as they may seem at first. The actions are described in words and are also represented in the form of symbols. The symbols give a shorthand description. Note that you should not learn these steps by heart. The table provides a recipe that you can look up and apply when you need to calculate a t-score. Please do not try to memorise this information.

Table 3 Steps in calculating a t-score

Step	What to do: In words	What to do: In symbols	Example	Answer
1	Calculate the mean of Y for group A	ΣYn_A = mean of Y_A	11/3	3.66
2	Calculate the mean of Y for group B	$\Sigma Y_B/n_B$ = mean of Y_B	23/3	7.66
3	Subtract the answer obtained in 2 from the answer obtained in 1	$(\Sigma Y_A/n_A) - (\Sigma Y_B/n_B)$ = difference between mean	3.66−7.66	−4
4	Square the sum of Y for group A	$(\Sigma Y_A)^2$	$(11)^2 = 11 \times 11$	121
5	Square the sum of Y for group B	$(\Sigma Y_B)^2$	$(23)^2 = 23 \times 23$	529
6	Divide the square of the sum of Y for group A by the size of group A	$(\Sigma Y_A)^2/n_A$	121/3	40.33
7	Divide the square of the sum of Y for group B by the size of group B	$(\Sigma Y_B)^2/n_B$	529/3	176.33
8	Subtract answer in 6 from sum of Y^2 for group A	$\Sigma Y_A^2 - (\Sigma Y_A)^2/n_A$	49−40.33	8.67
9	Subtract answer in 7 from sum of Y^2 for group B	$\Sigma Y_B^2 - (\Sigma Y_B)^2/n_B$	181−176.33	4.67
10	Divide answer in 8 by the size of group A minus 1 = variance for group A (S_A^2)	$\frac{\Sigma Y_A^2 - (\Sigma Y_A)^2/n_A}{(n_A - 1)} = S_A^2$	8.67/2	4.33
11	Divide answer in 9 by the size of group B minus 1 = variance for group B (S_B^2)	$\frac{\Sigma Y_B^2 - (\Sigma Y_B)^2/n_B}{(n_B - 1)} = S_B^2$	4.67/2	2.33
12	Sum the variance for group A and variance for group B and divide by total sample size	$(S_A^2 + S_B^2)/N$ Note that $N = (n_A + n_B)$	$\frac{(4.33 + 2.33)}{6}$	1.11

13	Get square root of answer in 12 = standard error for difference between means (Sdiff mean)	sqrt $[s_A^2 + s_B^2)/N]$ = $(S_{diff\ mean})$	sqrt (1.11)	1.05
14	Divide the difference between the means (answer in 3) by the standard error for difference between means (answer in 13) = t-score	$\frac{(\Sigma Y_A/n_A) - (\Sigma Y_B/n_B)}{\text{sqrt } [(S_A^2 + S_B^2)/N]}$ = t-score	–4/1.05	–3.8

The t-score for the example indicated above is –3.8. Note the minus sign. Can you see where the minus comes from? It originates in step 3, where we subtract the mean of group B from the mean of group A. In this case, the mean of group B is larger than the mean of group A, which gives the minus value in subtraction. In practical terms, it means group B has more than group A of the aspect in terms of which we compare the two groups. For example, if we substitute variable Y with language skills, a t-score of –3.8 means the language skills of women are better than those of men. The value for language skills for women (group B) is larger than the value for language skills for men (group A).

3 How does one determine the significance of the difference between two groups?

It is easy to spot the difference between two group means. For example, in Table 3, step 3 shows that the average of group A and the average of group B have a difference of –4. The question is, how do we know whether this difference is significant? The solution is to express the difference as a t-score (divide the difference by the standard error of the difference) as we did in Table 3. The calculation obtained a t-score of –3.8. The next step is to determine the significance of the calculated t-score by comparing it to the t-scores listed in Table 4. Note that no negative values are listed in the table. This is because the table indicates the size and not the direction of difference. The sign of the index (positive or negative) indicates the direction of the difference. A positive sign means the average of group A is larger than the average of group B, whereas a negative sign means the average of group A is smaller than the average of group B.

The t-score calculated in the example above (–3.8) is significant when compared to the t-score listed in Table 4 at sample size 6 (2.77). The size of the difference between groups A and B (3.8) is larger than the size of a significant difference (2.77) for a total sample size of 6.

Table 4 The values of the t-scores for the sample sizes

Total sample size (N)	Value of significant t-score
3	12.70
4	4.30
5	3.18
6	2.77
7	2.57
8	2.44
9	2.36
10	2.30
11	2.26
12	2.22
13	2.20
14	2.17
15–19	2.13
20–24	2.08
25–29	2.06
30–34	2.04
35–39	2.03
40–44	2.02
45–49	2.01
50–69	2.00
70–99	1.98
100+	1.96

We used the term 'significance of difference' above without explaining what it means. It is easy to see that there is a difference between the mean scores of two groups and to express this difference as a t-value, but it is not clear why the t-value needs to exceed a particular value before the difference becomes significant. The reason for this is that our measurements are never absolutely accurate. For example, suppose an individual completes a questionnaire to determine his or her level of anxiety and he or she obtains a score of 65. Owing to the measurement error, the person's score may actually be 70 or it may be 60. All we know is that 65 is the most likely score for the individual. Although the individual's score may be 70 or 60, these scores are less likely for this individual.

This is true for all individuals who complete the anxiety questionnaire, therefore the average anxiety score for the group also varies somewhat. For example, we may calculate an average score of 55 for the group, but due to the measurement error, average scores of 60 or 50 may be possible. All we know is that average scores of 60 or 50 are less likely than the obtained score of 55. The same argument is true for a second group who completes the anxiety questionnaire. The second group's average score may be 60, but average scores of 55 or 65 may be possible for this group. Although we obtain a difference of 5 between the two groups (55 for the first group and 60 for the second group), it is possible to get a difference of 0 because their averages may overlap. All we know is that a difference of 5 is more likely than a difference of 0. The question is whether the difference of 5 is significantly more likely than the difference of 0. If the difference between the two groups is significantly more likely than no difference, we say there is a difference between the groups. However, if the difference between the groups is not significantly more likely than no difference, we say there is no difference between the groups. This is what the table gives us. The differences between two groups are expressed in terms of t-values and the t-values listed in the table correspond with differences that are significantly more likely than no difference.

Note that one also has to take the size of the sample into account when one determines the significance of the difference between the two groups. The size of the sample is the total number of people in the two groups, thus the sample size indicates the number of people who provided information that was used to determine the difference between the two groups. Obviously, if you consult more people (that is, if you use a larger sample), you can expect to get a more accurate result, therefore the size of the sample plays a role in determining the significance of the difference between the groups. If you have more people in a group, the average of the group becomes more (although not absolutely) accurate. If the averages of two groups are more accurate, the difference between the two averages will also be more accurate. Look at the table. The t-values decrease as the sample size increases. In other words, with larger sample sizes smaller differences between groups become significant. If you use a small sample (thus getting less accurate information) you need a large difference between the groups before you can see whether the difference between them is significant. However, if you use a large sample (thus getting information from more people and therefore being more accurate) significance shows up in a smaller difference between the two groups.

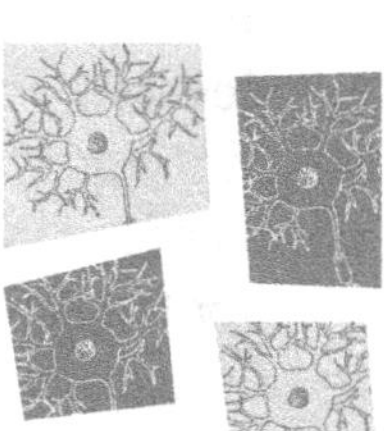

Information modelling: Expandable tree structures

The amount of information we are confronted with can be overwhelming. One way to handle large amounts of information is to build models to simplify and structure it. The expandable tree structure is a useful way to model the hierarchical structure of information.

1 What is a tree structure?

A tree structure is a diagram – that is, a picture – that looks like an upside-down tree. It has its root at the top and then branches out towards the bottom. The tree structure is used to organise information hierarchically. The root is the main idea and the *branches* are sub-ideas branching out from the root or main idea. Figure 1 indicates a tree structure. Note how much this looks like an upside-down tree.

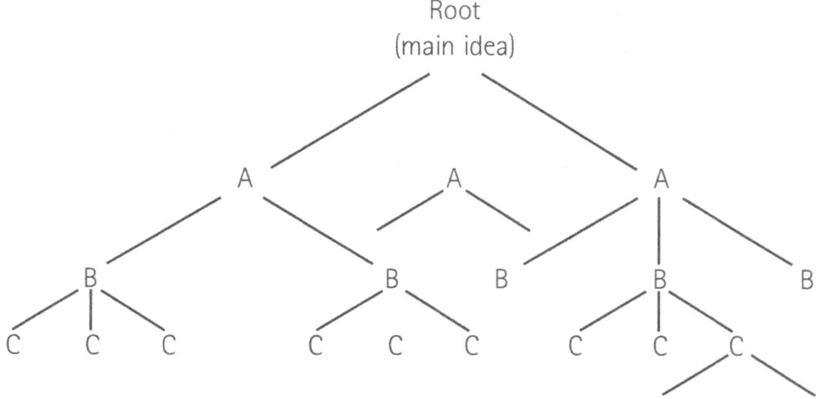

Figure 1 An example of a tree structure

Not all branching nodes are labelled in Figure 1, but you can see clearly how the tree branches into different levels – in this case, levels A, B and C. This is one of the interesting facets of a tree structure, namely that finer and finer details appear as you descend the structure. The main idea becomes more and more finely defined at lower levels of the tree. This characteristic of a tree structure represents the notion of resolution. At the top – that is, at the level of the main idea – the resolution of the concept is at its lowest. Level A represents a slightly increased resolution of the main idea or concept by suggesting that the main concept consists of three sub-concepts. At level B, the resolution increases further as the sub-concepts of level A are represented in more detail at level B.

For example, suppose the main concept is the concept of feelings. At level A, we may consider feelings in terms of four sub-concepts, namely sensory feelings, emotions, moods and social life feelings. At the next level (B), we can consider the sub-concepts of the sub-concepts of level A and discover that emotions consist of two further concepts, namely psycho-physiological arousal and cognitive content. Note how the resolution of the concept of feelings increases from a single notion into a constellation of much more finely defined ideas.

2 What is an expandable tree structure?

An expandable tree structure is one that expands or shrinks to show more or less detail. In other words, an expandable tree structure represents the hierarchical organisation of information in a dynamic manner by increasing or lowering the resolution of its display. It literally means that the structure closes or opens its levels as required so as to show just the right amount of information. This approach is often used in personal computers to show the user how information is organised in a folder structure. When the user clicks a particular folder, it expands to show the subfolders it contains. When it is clicked again, it hides them from view.

Although an expandable tree structure looks different from the traditional tree structure depicted in Figure 1, it is in fact the same kind. An expandable tree structure is the tree turned on its side. We can picture this as having the root on the left-hand side and the branches branching out towards the right. The difference is that instead of having the resolution levels as horizontal levels, they appear as vertical columns in the expandable tree structure. Also, the branching does not expand from the centre root outwards (towards both the left and the right) as in the traditional tree structure, but in one direction only, namely *downward.* Whereas the traditional tree structure grows downwards and branches outwards towards both the left and the right, the expandable tree structure grows from left to right and branches downwards. Figure 2 shows an expandable tree structure (top) next to a toppled or sideways traditional tree structure (bottom).

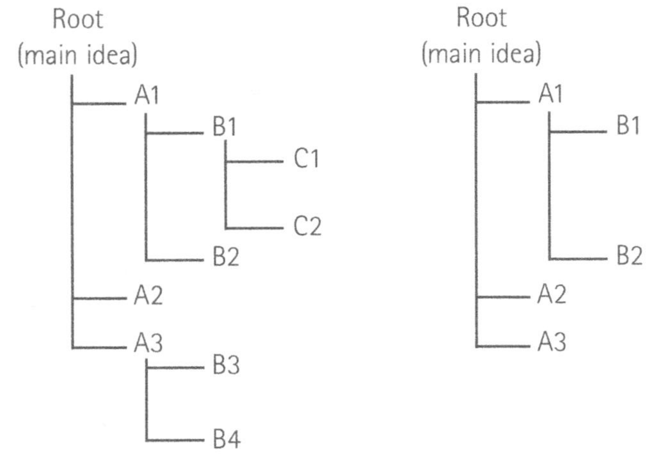

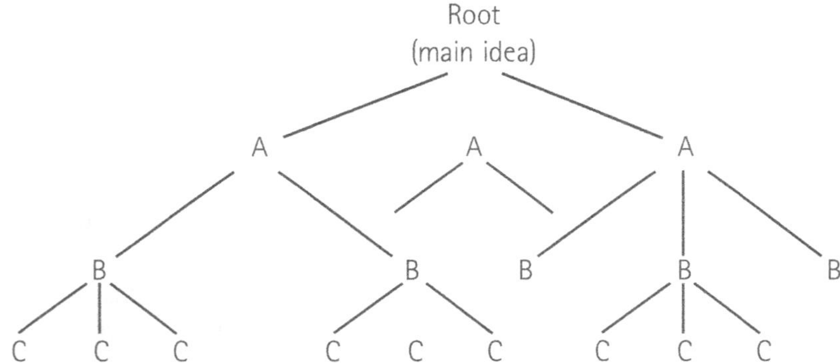

Figure 2 Comparison of a traditional tree structure and an expandable tree structure

The comparisons show how the vertical levels of the expandable tree structure correspond with the levels of the traditional tree structure. Also note the differences between the two expandable tree structures. They represent the same tree, but the one on the right has closed some of its nodes from view. On level B, nodes B3 and B4 are hidden and on level C, nodes C1 and C2 are hidden.

An expandable tree structure has predefined elements, which are the building blocks of expandable tree structures. You need them to build or assemble expandable tree structures. Expandable tree structures also have rules, which are used to combine elements correctly. In other words, when drawing an expandable tree structure, you use predefined elements which you combine according to particular rules. The elements and the rules of an expandable tree structure constitute a hierarchical *modelling language* and an expandable tree structure presents a hierarchical model of the event or phenomenon that is described by the modelling language.

3 A basic hierarchical modelling language

A hierarchical modelling language is made up of elements and rules, which we shall look at below.

3.1 Elements

3.1.1 The node

A node in a tree structure is where a branch *splits* into further branches. In other words, a node is a place where other nodes can be created. The *primary node,* the node at the beginning of the tree structure, is the *root* of the tree structure in question. The nodes at the end of *branches* (that is, the nodes that do not split into further branches) are the *leaves* of the tree structure. Consider a node, for example a node called A, somewhere in the middle of the tree structure. Then node A's *ancestors* are those nodes that are higher up in the tree structure (that is, between node A and the root node) and those nodes that are lower down in the tree structure (between node A and the leaves) are called *descendants* of node A. The node that comes immediately before node A is A's *parent* and the node immediately after node A is node A's *child.* Here is a list of node types:

- *Root node* – the top and left-most node of the tree
- *Leaf node* – a node with no descendants
- *Parent node* – the previous node higher up and to the left in the tree
- *Child node* – the next node lower down and to the right in the tree
- *Ancestor node* – any node higher up and to the left in the tree
- *Descendent node* – any node lower down and to the right in the tree

3.1.2 Elements of the node

A node consists of three elements, namely a *node name,* a *node label* and an *extension line.*

The node name

A node name is a word or a short phrase that describes the node. The word or short phrase is the text of the name. A node name is indicated by a short horizontal line followed by the name text. A node name may have or may not have an extension line that drops vertically from the node name. If a node name has an extension line, branching occurs at the node. If the node name does not have an extension line (that is, the node is not extended), the node is a leaf node.

The node label

There are two types of node label: the *root node label* and the *expansion node label:*

- *The root node label.* The label attached to the root of the tree is indicated by a small square. It indicates whether the tree is an expansion within a bigger tree. If the label is empty, the tree is not an expansion in a bigger tree. If the label is not empty, it contains an *address* that indicates where the bigger tree structure can be found. If the root node label is not empty, it means the root node appears in a bigger tree as a node that is expanded elsewhere.

- *The expansion node label.* This is a label that indicates whether the node is expanded elsewhere. The label is indicated by a small circle. If the label is empty, the node is not expanded elsewhere. If the label is not empty, it contains the *address* of the location where the node is expanded.

The extension line

An extension line is a vertical line in the expandable tree structure. It is shown as a broken line and it extends from a node label or a node name. An extension line that begins in a node label indicates the *scope* of the node. An extension line that begins in a node name indicates the *children* of the node. An extension line ends in another node label or in an extension line *foot.* An extension line foot is a short horizontal line at the bottom end of an extension line.

3.2 Rules

3.2.1 *Extension rules*

- Nodes on the *same extension line* cannot have similar names.
- Nodes on *different extension lines* can have similar names.
- An extension line that *begins in a node name* always ends in an expansion label.
- An extension line that *begins in an expansion label* ends in another expansion label or in an extension foot.

3.2.2 *Address rules*

- An expansion node label is shown but is left empty (that is, it does not contain an address) if the node in question is not expanded elsewhere.
- An expansion node label is shown and contains an address if the node in question is expanded elsewhere – that is, if the node hides its expansion. The *address* indicates where the node expansion can be found.
- The root node label is shown but is left empty if the tree is not contained in a bigger tree.
- The root node label is shown and contains the address of a bigger tree if the root node is contained in the bigger tree.

4 An example of an expandable tree structure

Figures 3a and 3b show how the elements and rules work in an expandable tree structure.

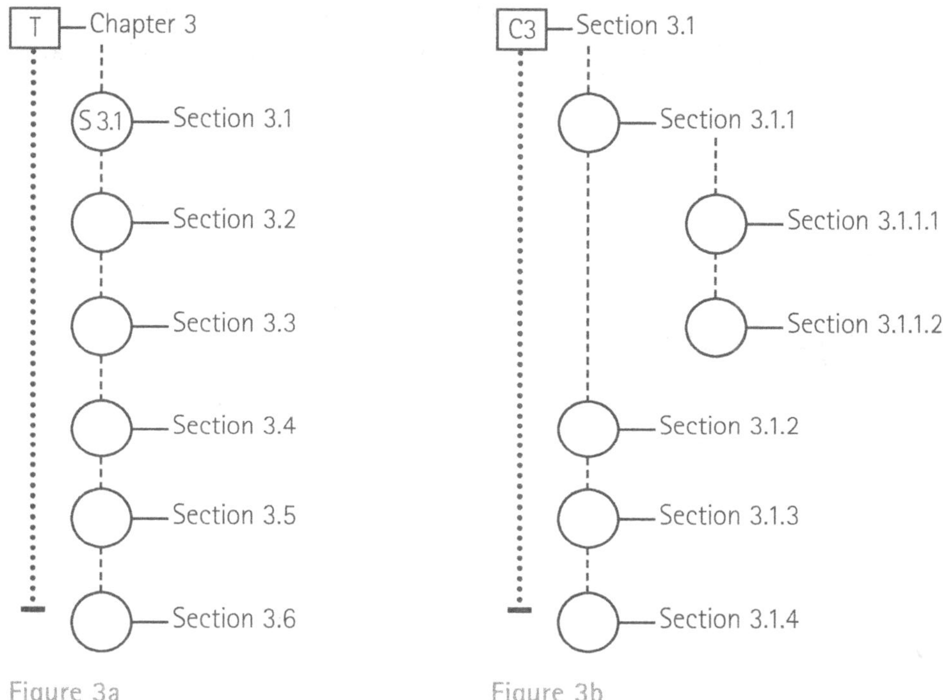

Figure 3a

Figure 3b

Figure 3 shows two expandable tree structures, namely Chapter 3 in Figure 3a and Section 3.1 in Figure 3b. The root node in Figure 3a indicates the *name* of the tree, namely Chapter 3. The node called Chapter 3 has six child nodes, named Section 3.1 up to Section 3.6. These nodes are recognised as the *children* of the node called Chapter 3 because they lie on the extension line that drops from this node name. It is also valid to say that Chapter 3 is the *parent* of sections 3.1 to 3.6. Chapter 3 is recognised as the parent of these nodes because their extension line begins at a node name, which is Chapter 3.

The extension line that drops from the root node label indicates the *scope* of this node, thus the scope of Chapter 3 is sections 3.1 to 3.6. In other words, Chapter 3 extends, or is *expanded,* across six sections. In this example, the six sections are leaf nodes, because they do not have extension lines dropping from their node names. Such an extension line indicates *branching.*

The root node label is not empty. It contains the address T. This means that Chapter 3 appears as a node in a bigger tree and the bigger tree is identified by T. For example, Chapter 3 may be a chapter in a bigger tree, called a textbook and the textbook is identified by the address T.

The expansion label of the node named Section 3.1 in Figure 3a is not empty. It contains the address S3.1. This means that Section 3.1 is expanded elsewhere and that the address of the expansion is S3.1 (see Figure 4).

The expansion of the node named Section 3.1 is shown in Figure 3b. The root node label is not empty and contains the address C3. This means Section 3.1 appears as a node in a bigger tree (Chapter 3) and the bigger tree (Chapter 3) is identified by the address, C3 (see Figure 4).

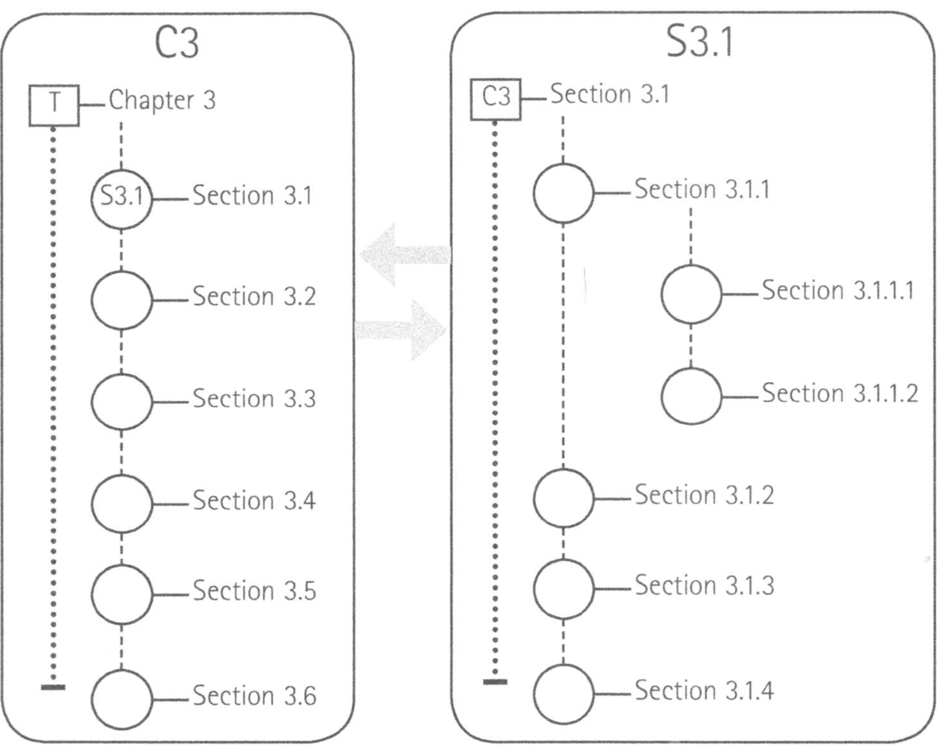

Figure 4 The relation between node addresses: A node address expanded into a root node

In Figure 4, the tree called Section 3.1 has a root node address, C3. This means that the tree called Section 3.1 is a node in another tree that can be found at C3. As expected, the tree at location C3 (namely Chapter 3) contains a node called Section 3.1. The expansion label of this node contains the address S3.1. This is the address where the expansion of Section 3.1 can be found.

The extension line from the root node label shows that Section 3.1 has a scope of four subsections (sections 3.1.1 to 3.1.4). Also note the extension line from the label of Section 3.1.1. This line shows that Section 3.1.1 has a scope of two subsections, namely sections 3.1.1.1 and 3.1.1.2.

Following the extension line from the node name, Section 3.1, it is clear that sections 3.1.1 to 3.1.4 are children nodes of Section 3.1. The extension line that drops from the node name Section 3.1.1 shows that sections 3.1.1.1 and 3.1.1.2 are children of Section 3.1.1. By following these extension lines in reverse, one can see that Section 3.1 is the parent of sections 3.1.1 to 3.1.4 and that Section 3.1.1 is the parent of sections 3.1.1.1 and 3.1.1.2. One can see that Section 3.1.1 and Section 3.1.1.1 form a descendant line of Section 3.1 and that Section 3.1 is an ancestor of Section 3.1.1.2. From these examples it should be clear that the extension lines form columns that represent layers or levels in an expandable tree structure. Each level is the child level of the level to its immediate left and each level is the parent level of the level to its immediate right.

5 How to use an expandable tree

Expandable trees structure information hierarchically. They are an excellent tool to guide you from a more general view to detailed perspectives of a situation. They manage information in a contextual manner, presenting each layer of concepts within the context of a former, more general layer of concepts. The top-down approach is an effective and efficient way to gather information and to gain insight. It allows you to explore a field of study from a general perspective and to gradually uncover more and more detail about it.

Expandable tree structures work very well on computers where you can click on the expansion label to hide or show additional expansions of a concept. In this way, it is easy to hide detail that may confuse you at more general levels of exploration. It is also easy to move quickly to levels of higher resolution where you can find the required detail if necessary. However, you can easily use expandable tree structures without a computer to organise your knowledge about a field of study. The technique is fairly simple:

1. Draw the most general outline on a single page or card. For example, suppose you want to explore the nature of societal issues (see Figure 5). The general outline would indicate that societal issues extend across violence, poverty, racism, multiculturalism, sexism and community development.
2. Draw each consecutive expansion of the tree on a separate page or card. For example, suppose you want to expand the concept of violence further (see Figure 6) and you discover that violence covers two issues, namely its nature and its effects. You also discover that the effects of violence in turn can be extended to a further two aspects, namely effects of alienation and effects on children.
3. Decide on a reference method to link your various pages of information. For example, you may decide to link the pages alphabetically according to the main concept (the root) of each page. This would mean that the page containing the further extension of violence belongs under V, because

> 'violence' is the root node on that page. You have to indicate this reference on the page that contains the 'societal issues' outline. Simply use V as the address label for 'violence'. In other words, the V indicates that 'violence' is further expanded and that the expansion of 'violence' can be found under V. These methods are illustrated in figures 5, 6 and 7.

The expandable tree shown in Figure 6 contains a root address label, S, to indicate that a node named 'violence' appears in a bigger tree structure ('societal issues') at location S. The same holds for the concept of racism (see Figure 5). The address label, R, is an address for the place where you will find an expansion of racism. The labels for poverty, multiculturalism, sexism and community development are empty, indicating that these concepts are not extended elsewhere. Note that the root concept, 'societal issues', has an address label, X. This means that 'societal issues' is a concept that appears in a larger schema somewhere else. The extension label, X, indicates the address of the larger schema (not depicted here).

The two expandable trees shown in figures 6 and 7 are expansions of 'violence' and 'racism'. Both have the same root address label, namely 5, indicating that these concepts fit into the schema of a bigger tree ('societal issues' – Figure 5) and that the tree structure of 'societal issues' can be found at location S.

A further aspect of the expandable trees illustrated here are the extension lines (vertical broken lines) that indicate the levels in a tree structure. The number of vertical lines indicates the number of levels. For example, the expandable tree structure for 'violence' has four levels or layers, with 'violence' at the first level, the 'effects of violence' at the second level, 'alienation' at the third level and 'fear' at the fourth level.

Tree structures show the hierarchical relationships among nodes. These hierarchies are expressed in terms of parent–children and ancestor–descendant relationships. For example, the node 'effects of violence' has two child nodes, namely 'alienation' and 'effects on children'. These child nodes are contained on the extension line that begins in the 'effects of violence' node name. Reading the extension line in reverse, it is clear that 'effects of violence' is the parent node of 'effects on children'. It is also clear that 'effects of violence' is an ancestor of 'avoidance'. You can also trace a clear line of descendants from 'violence' to 'avoidance', through the following chain of nodes: violence, effects of violence, alienation and avoidance.

Also note the scope of the various concepts. For example, the scope of 'modern racism' includes negative stereotypes, support with resistance, give and take, aloof distance and passive avoidance (see Figure 7). The scope of 'effects of violence' is alienation and the effects on children (see Figure 6).

A last point to note is that nodes on the same extension line cannot have similar names. For example, consider the extension line that expands 'alienation' as fear, avoidance and helplessness. It does not make sense to expand alienation in the following way: fear, avoidance, fear, helplessness and avoidance.

Expandable tree structures are useful because they provide a hierarchical modelling language which enables us to model the hierarchical relationships of events and phenomena. Hierarchical structures show how events and phenomena are organised in ever-increasing layers of complexity.

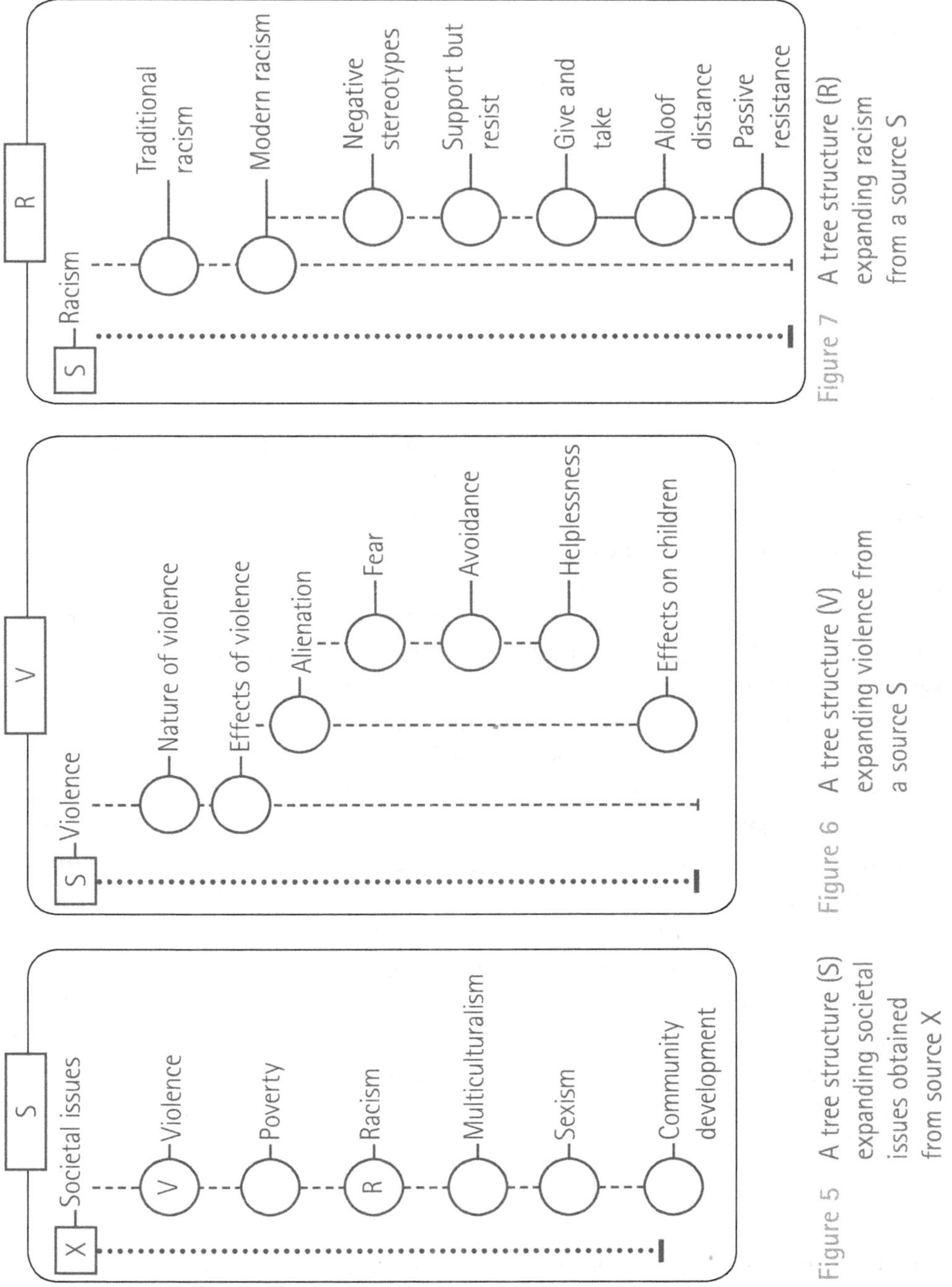

Figure 5 A tree structure (S) expanding societal issues obtained from source X

Figure 6 A tree structure (V) expanding violence from a source S

Figure 7 A tree structure (R) expanding racism from a source S

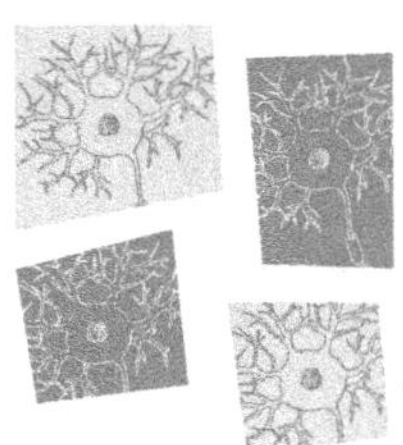

Information modelling: Flow charts

1 What is a flow chart?

A flow chart is a diagram in which information is organised spatially in a way that shows a flow (or stream) of information belonging to a central theme. A flow chart uses a set of elements (usually boxes) to represent the information. It also has a set of rules according to which the elements are connected and organised, using lines and arrows. Because a flow chart traces a process, it uses the elements (blocks, lines and arrows) to show you the route in which the information flows. It can also show you what happens when a particular route is blocked and can indicate alternative routes. When you read a flow chart, you follow the direction of the arrows, otherwise the information presented in the boxes is meaningless.

Flow charts can be very complex if they have large sets of elements and many rules. Normally you use complex flow charts when the aim is to represent or model complicated situations, especially if you want to represent more than one view of a situation. However, simple flow charts can also be very helpful. You can organise large volumes of information with just a few elements (boxes) and rules, provided you are not interested in too many views of the situation. For example, if you are interested in viewing the structure of something, you need a structural view. An example of a structural view would be a drawing indicating the different parts of a neuron. An example of a process view would be a description of the way in which impulses are conducted by the neuron. One can use visiograms to represent structure, or expandable tree structures if one wants a hierarchical description of structure. However, if you want to represent a process you have to use a flow chart.

2 A basic flow chart language

Let us start by defining a few elements and rules for drawing up flow charts.

2.1 Elements

The elements of a flow chart are the symbols we use to build it. The basic elements are rectangular- and diamond-shaped boxes, labels, connecting lines and arrows. The rectangular-shaped boxes represent objects and actions in the process that is being represented in the diagram. The diamond-shaped boxes are used to indicate decisions, the connecting lines are used to connect the boxes and the arrows are used to show the direction in which the process flows. Labels are used to name the boxes and can also be used to name the connecting lines. They consist of letters and/or numbers.

Figure 1 is a flow chart that represents the process of making tea. The kettle is switched on to boil water and a teabag is put into a teacup. The kettle is checked to see whether the water is boiling. If the water is not boiling, it is checked again. The process of rechecking whether or not the water is boiling is repeated until the water starts to boil, in which case the water is poured into the teacup. The process has three steps: (1) switch on the kettle to boil water; (2) put a teabag into a cup; and (3) pour boiling water into the cup. The steps or actions are linked via connecting lines with arrows showing how the process flows. The process also contains a decision, namely whether or not the water is boiling. The three object boxes and the decision box are labelled with appropriate names. Labels are also added to two of the arrowed connecting lines, naming them 'Yes' and 'No'.

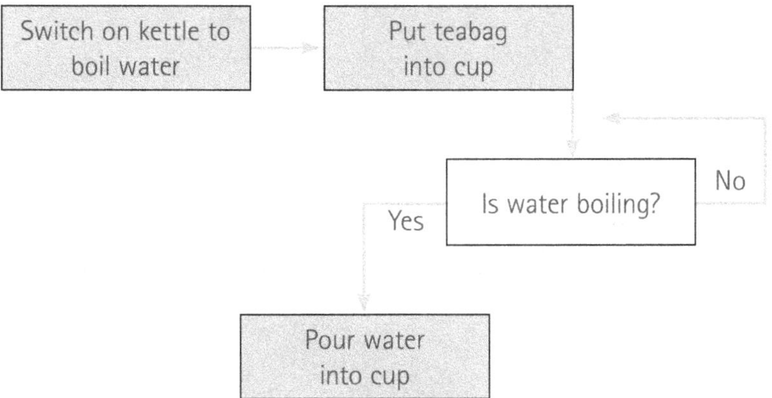

Figure 1 A flow chart describing the process of making a cup of tea

2.2 Rules

The rules of a flow chart are prescriptions for the ways in which the basic elements are used and combined. Here is the first simple rule: Labels should be attached in specific ways. When a label is attached to an object or action (rectangular) box, or to a decision (diamond) box, it should be placed inside the box. When a label is attached to a connecting line element it is placed next to the line. A connecting line joins an object or action (rectangular-shaped) box on any of the four sides of the box. In the case of a decision (diamond-shaped) box, a connecting line joins the box at any of the four corners of the box.

More than one connecting line may be joined to an action or object box and similarly more than one line may be joined to a decision box. Alternative processes are described when an action box is connected to more than box. Figure 2 shows an example of two alternative processes, one of making tea and the other of making soup. The difference between the two processes lies in what goes into the cup. In the case of tea, a teabag is placed into the cup and in the case of soup, soup extract goes into the cup.

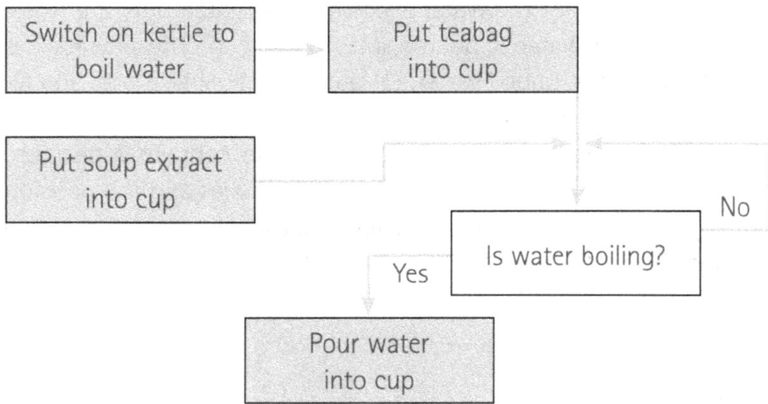

Figure 2 A flow chart describing the alternative processes of making a cup of tea and a cup of soup

3 Steps in drawing up a flow chart

Now that you have looked at the various elements, we are going to put them together to draw up a flow chart.

Step 1: Identify the starting point

The starting point of the flow chart is the point from which all the other steps flow. For example, if you are going to draw up a flow chart to show someone how to use a cellphone, the starting point would be to press the button that switches the phone on. The label for the first box would then be something like 'Switch on'.

Step 2: Identify the next point in the process

Because a flow chart represents a process, you have to show all the steps and elements involved in that process. Taking the example of the cellphone further, the next step would be prompted by the instruction to key in your personal PIN number.

The next box would have a label like 'Key in PIN'. Because it is a flow chart, we need to show the route and so we have to show the two steps connected by a line. Because step 2 follows step 1, we put an arrow at the end of the connecting line where it meets step 2 to show the direction of the flow of information.

Step 3: Identify the next point in the process

We have decided that the next step is to key in the number we want to call. So we put 'Call the number' in the next box and draw a connecting line from step 2 to step 3, again showing the direction with an arrow. However, it is not always so straightforward. What happens if the phone's battery is flat? We need to show an alternate route to indicate that there is another step – to recharge the battery – before it can be switched on.

Step 4: Complete the remaining points

Repeat steps 2 and 3 until you have completed the whole process that you want to represent in the flow chart.

Step 5: Create the connections and labels

Make sure that you have connected all the boxes correctly, that the route is clearly indicated with arrows and that alternative routes are shown. Also make sure that all the boxes are labelled clearly and that connecting lines have labels where necessary. When you look at your flow chart, you should immediately be able to get an overview of the process. If you cannot, you have to go back and check the steps carefully and make corrections until the process is clear and meaningful.

Step 6: Create a title

Give your flow chart a title so that the reader knows what it illustrates. Examples would be: 'A flow chart showing the steps involved in making tea', or 'A flow chart showing the process followed when legislation is passed by parliament'.

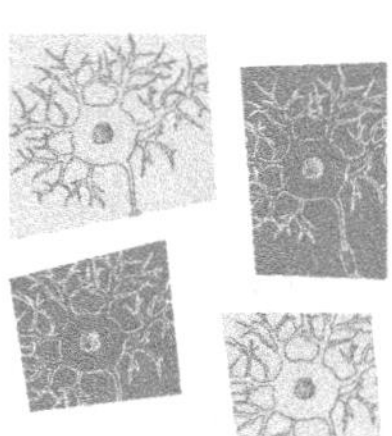

Information modelling: Graphs

1 What is a graph?

Graphs are used to display complex information in an easily understandable format. A graph combines spatial, textual and numerical information in a single image. This provides an overview that is easy to absorb in a glance, but it also allows a detailed view if one cares to look more closely.

A graph is a diagram in which information is presented in terms of one or more dimensions. Here we restrict ourselves to graphs in two dimensions. The general names for these dimensions are X and Y, but when one puts together a graph, X and Y are replaced with real names. For example, X could be called 'practise' and Y could be 'performance'.

A graph expresses the relationship between X and Y. For instance it can show how practise relates to performance. There may be no relationship between practise and performance, or perhaps more practise leads to better performance. To verify the nature of the relationship we have to observe practise and performance. In a graph that depicts this relationship, each observation of practise and performance is indicated by a dot. If we make a number of observations we create a series of dots. Each of these dots has a practise value as well a performance value, therefore when we put them together, the dots in the series show the relationship between practise and performance. They show how performance changes when practise changes.

In the previous example, the graph expresses change. There are many kinds of graphs, but here we consider only three. In addition to graphs depicting change, we also consider those that could be used to draw comparisons and those that show how things are distributed. These graphs can be drawn in different ways, but we restrict ourselves here to the basic two-dimensional graph.

2 A basic graph language

Let us start by defining a few elements and rules for drawing graphs.

2.1 Elements

A basic graph has only three elements, which are lines, dots and labels. Line elements are straight lines and are used to represent the dimensions of the graph. They can also be used to connect the dots in a graph. Dot elements are used to mark the observations that are made in terms of the dimensions of the graph. Label elements can be used to name dot elements. However, because dot elements are identified in terms of the dimensions of observation, they are not often labelled, but the dimensions are and labels are also used to describe the scales that are superimposed onto the dimensions.

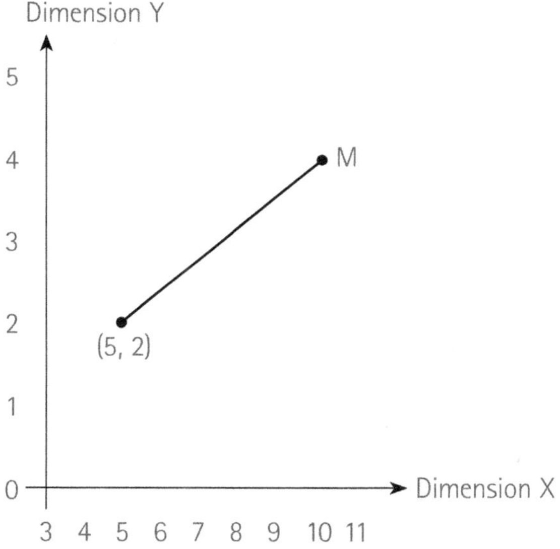

Figure 1 The various elements of a basic graph

A scale is the way in which a dimension is divided and each division has a label. In Figure 1, the scale that is superimposed on the Y dimension is labelled from 0 to 5. The scale on the X dimension is labelled from 3 to 11. In this case the labels represent numerical values, but a scale does not have to be numerical – it can also be categorical. For example, the X dimension could have been divided into sections called A, B, C and D. The graph in Figure 1 also contains two dot elements. These are named, but this is seldom done. The label M is just a name to distinguish the particular dot as observation M. The label (5,2) names the second dot in terms of its observation values. It indicates that the observation has a value of 5 on the X dimension and a value of 2 on the Y dimension. In this graph, a line element is used to connect dot M and dot (5,2), but dot elements are not always connected.

Let us revisit this graph in terms of the relationship between practise and performance. In Figure 2, 'practise' is assigned to the X dimension and 'performance' to the Y dimension. The scale used to measure practise is marked in hours and performance is scaled in terms of levels. The way in which the hour scale is positioned on the practise dimension tells us that the minimum number of hours that count as practise is 3 and the maximum time that can be spent on practise is 11. Similarly, performance is measured at 6 levels, ranging from level 0 to level 5.

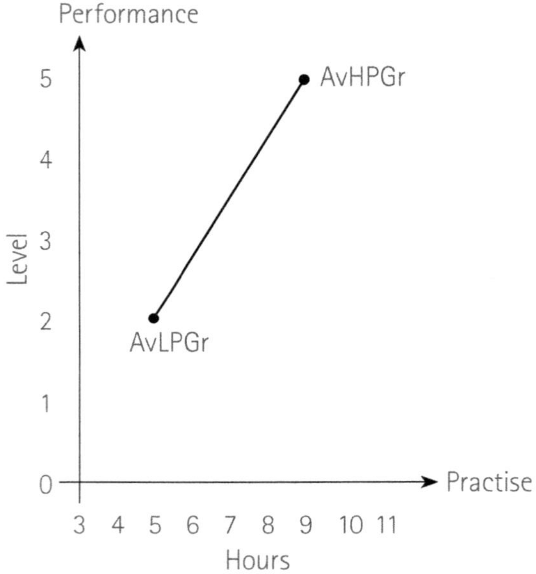

Figure 2 The relationship between practise and performance

Let us assume we have two groups: a low practise group (LPGr) and a high practise group (HPGr). On average, the low practise group practised for 5 hours, while the high practise group put an average of 9 hours into their practise. The average performance level for the low practise group was 2. The high practise group achieved an average performance level of 5. The observation of the low practise group is indicated by AvLPGr, which stands for average of low practise group. AvHPGr indicates the average of the high practise group.

The graph in Figure 3 represents the same information as the graph in Figure 2. The only difference is the way in which the practise dimension is scaled. Instead of using hours to measure practise, practise is divided into two categories, namely a low practise category (LoPr) and a high practise category (HiPr).

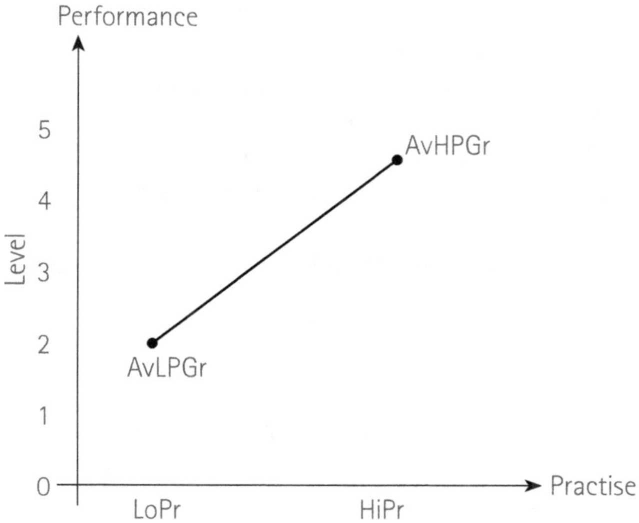

Figure 3 The relationship between practise and performance

2.2 Rules

The rules of the graph language determine how the elements of the graph are combined to obtain a well-formed graph. Let us have a look at these rules:

1. The X dimension is the primary dimension. The Y dimension is considered secondary to the X dimension, therefore the X dimension is mentioned first. For example, in Figure 1 the observation (5,2) reflects the value of the X dimension, followed by the value of the Y dimension.
2. The line elements representing the dimensions of the graph should intersect each other perpendicularly (at right angles). The X dimension is assigned to the horizontal line and the vertical line is called the Y dimension.
3. The point where the line elements representing the dimensions of the graph intersect is the origin of the graph. Although these lines extend beyond the origin (that is, below and to the left of the origin), the extensions are only required for more advanced graphs and are therefore not essential for the present discussion of the basic graph.
4. The labels that indicate the scale divisions on a dimension represent the midpoints of the division intervals. For example, if the scale divisions on a dimension are 0, 1, 2, etc, the division interval is –0,5 to 0,5 for 0; 0,5 to 1,5 for 1 and 1,5 to 2,5 for 2. Or, if the scale divisions are A, B and C, A would be the midpoint of the category represented by A; B the midpoint of the category represented by B; and likewise for C.
5. A numerical scale is superimposed on its corresponding dimension in such a manner that its lowest value matches up with the original of the graph. For example, the origin of the graph depicted in Figure 1 is scaled at (3,0).

This means values below 3 on the X dimension and below 0 on the Y dimension are not sensible or useful in this case.

6. A categorical scale is superimposed on its corresponding dimension in such a manner that the lowest limit of its first category matches up with the original of the graph. For example, if the categorical scale divisions are A, B and C, the lowest limit of the A category would be matched up with the origin of the graph.
7. The dot element that represents an observation is placed at the intersection of its X dimension value and its Y dimension value.

3 Graphs representing comparison

The graph in Figure 3 represents a comparison between two groups and therefore can be called a comparison graph. However, the way in which the graph is drawn makes it difficult to distinguish it from a graph showing change. The line element connecting the AvLPGr and AvHPGr observations shows how performance changes from low practise to high practise. When the graph is depicted as in Figure 4, the comparison becomes more clear.

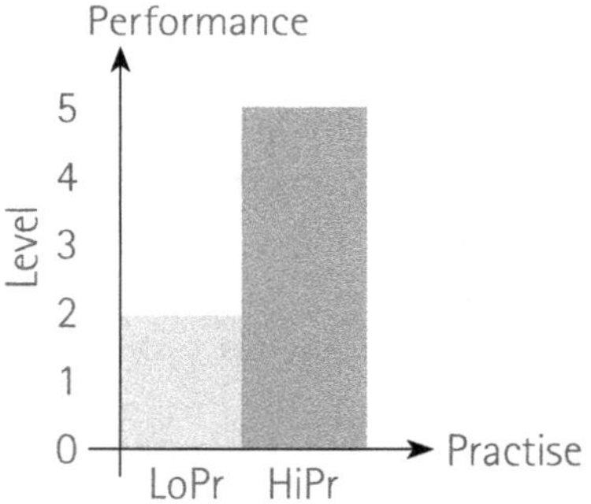

Figure 4 The performance difference between low and high practise groups

Here is another example (see Figure 5). This graphs shows the relationship between passenger satisfaction and the emotional intelligence of cabin crew. Cabin crew are divided into three groups: A group showing below average emotional intelligence (LoEQ), a group with average emotional intelligence (AvEQ) and a group who demonstrates above average emotional intelligence (HiEQ). However, note that passenger satisfaction is scaled in terms of the number of complaints. This means that higher scale values correspond to low satisfaction, whereas low scale values mean high satisfaction. The scale ranges from 0 complaints (0 × 10) to 50 complaints (5 × 10) per annum (p/a). The graph shows that cabin crew with below average emotional intelligence generate a large number of passenger complaints. Cabin crew with average emotional intelligence cause fewer complaints and cabin crew with above average emotional intelligence receive the lowest number of passenger complaints. Thus cabin crew with high emotional intelligence ensures passenger satisfaction.

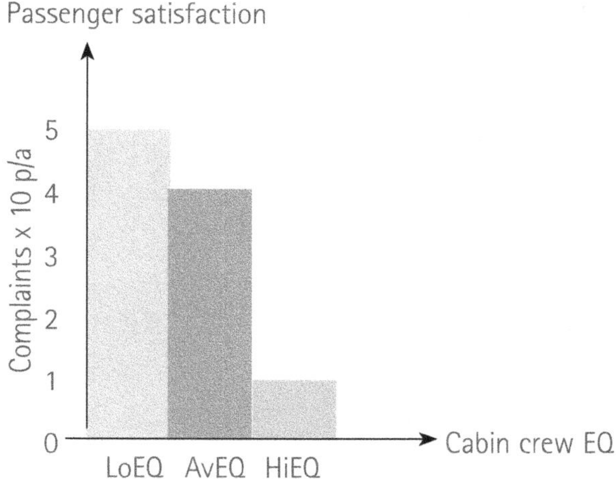

Figure 5 Passenger satisfaction and the emotional intelligence levels of cabin crew

4 Graphs representing change

Let us revisit the relationship between practise and performance, but now let us see how performance increases with practise.

The graph in Figure 6 clearly shows an increase in performance level as practise hours increase. At first the increase in performance is substantial. Performance rises sharply with every increase in practise hours. However, after 8 practise hours, the increase in performance becomes less substantial. As practise hours increase from 9 to 11, the corresponding increases in performance become less.

The graph in Figure 7 shows how performance changes as a function of stress. As stress increases from low to optimal levels, performance increases; however, when stress increases beyond the optimal level, performance starts to drop. In other words, stress is good to increase performance, but only up to a certain point. When people become overly stressed, their performance suffers. This is known as the Yerkes-Dodson law.

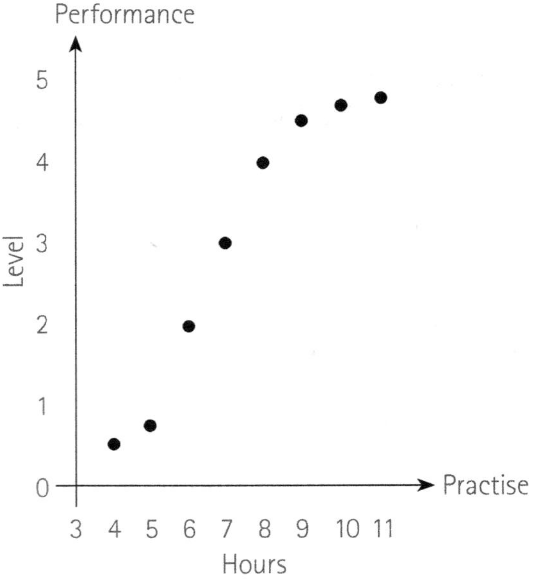

Figure 6 How performance increases with practise

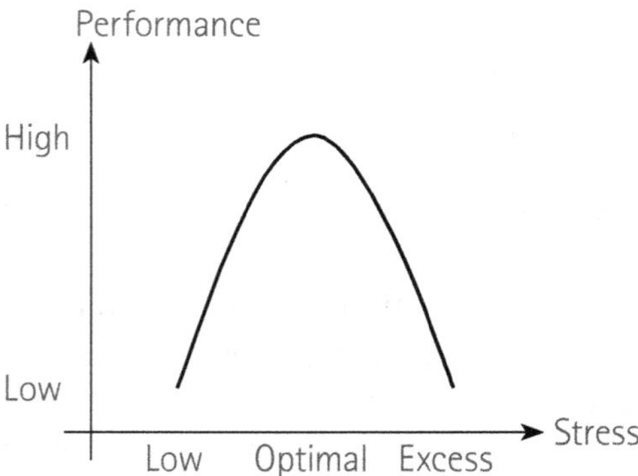

Figure 7 The relationship between stress and performance (Yerkes-Dodson law)

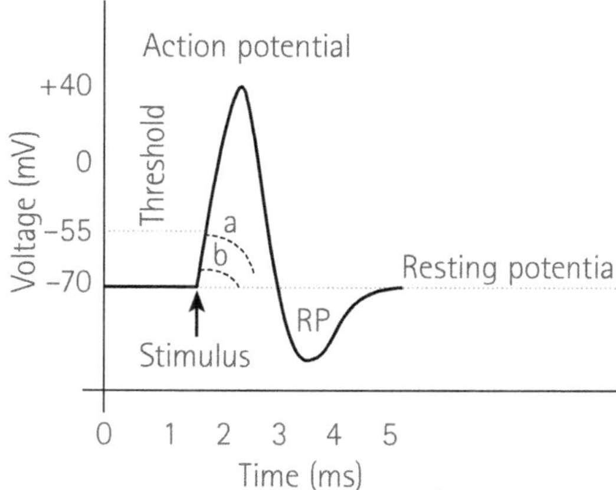

Figure 8 The relationship between time and change in membrane potential during impulse conduction

The graph in Figure 8 shows how the membrane potential changes during impulse conduction. The time dimension is measured in milliseconds (1 000th of a second) and the membrane potential in millivolts (1 000th of a volt). The graph shows a millisecond segment (the segment between 0 and 1 milliseconds) of the resting membrane potential at –70 millivolts. It indicates stimulus generation at a point just after 1 millisecond. The graphs shows two stimuli (a and b) not reaching the threshold, but stimuli that pass the threshold result in quick depolarisations of the membrane. When the membrane potential reaches +40 millivolts, the membrane begins to repolarise again. During repolarisation, the membrane potential drops below the resting potential before it returns to –70 mV at 5 milliseconds. The period it spends below –70 mV is the refractory period (labelled RP in the graph).

5 Graphs representing dispersion

Sometimes it is useful to see how observations are distributed spatially because distributions may reveal shapes, patterns and trends in observations. For example, suppose we plot the observations of a group of individuals' practise hours and performance levels. Let us call this group A (see Figure 9). The distribution shows a clear trend. Individuals with low practise hours tend to show low levels of performance and those with higher practise hours show higher levels of performance, but this is not so in the graph shown in Figure 10. Let us call this group B. The observations of group B seem to be distributed randomly. There is no obvious pattern, no clear relationship between practise hours and performance. People are as likely to demonstrate high performance as they are to demonstrate low performance regardless of their number of practise hours.

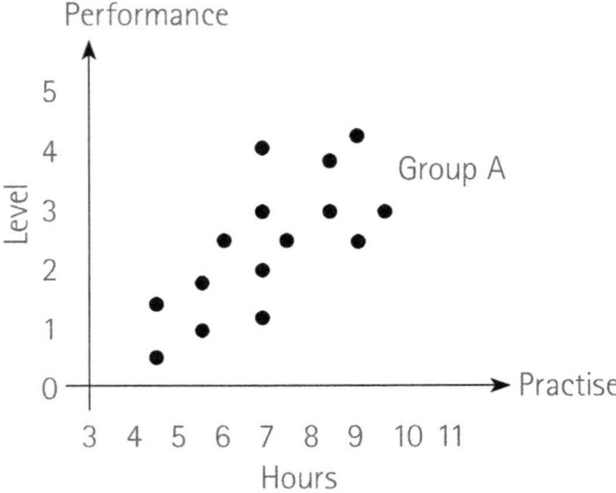

Figure 9 The dispersion of a group (A) of individuals' practise hours and performance levels

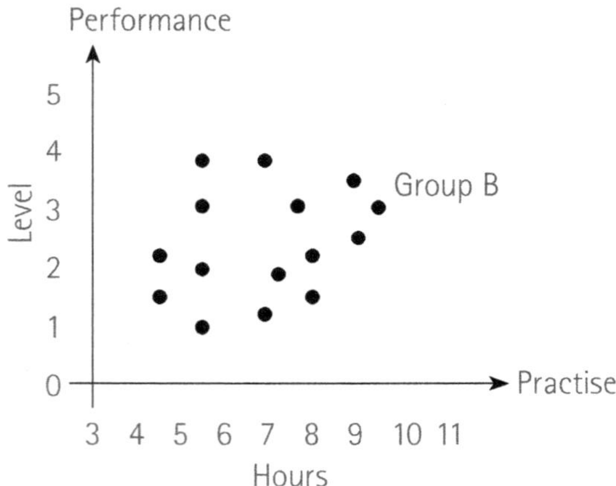

Figure 10 The dispersion of a group (B) of individuals' practise hours and performance levels

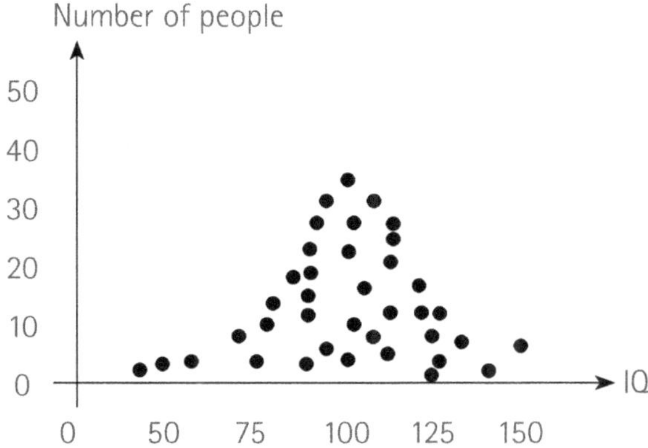

Figure 11 The dispersion of the IQ scores of a group of individuals

The graph depicted in Figure 11 shows the distribution of a number of individuals' IQ scores on a scale that ranges from 50 to 150. It is clear that most individuals obtained an IQ score of 100, whereas few obtained scores close to 50 and close to 150. As most people obtained a score of 100, this number becomes the norm. In other words, 100 is considered to be a normal IQ. People who score below 100 are below average and those above 100 are considered above average.

This is the famous bell-shaped distribution. In the general population, many psychological characteristics are distributed in this manner. Most people obtain an average score, but fewer people obtain scores that are further away from the average score, thus few people have a very high intelligence, but then also few people have a very low intelligence.

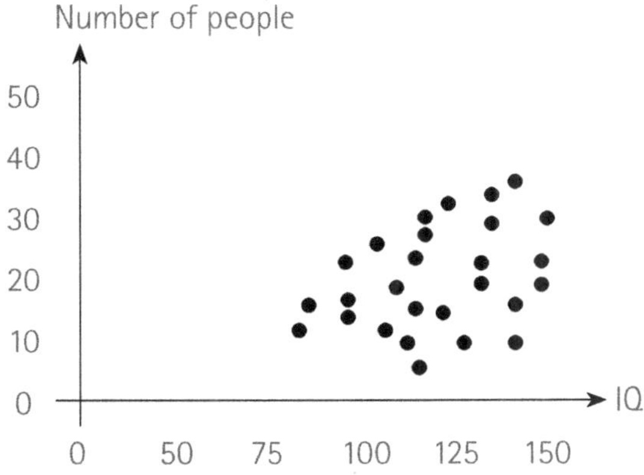

Figure 12 The skewed dispersion of a group of observations

The distribution shown in Figure 12 is skewed. It shows that most people obtained a score of 125 instead of 100. This can mean two things: The group may be more intelligent than the general population means, or the test that was used to measure the group's IQ scores was too easy. This group is more intelligent than the rest of the population. Figure 13 shows the reversed situation. In this case the group seems to be less intelligent than the population, or the test that was used to measure IQ was too difficult.

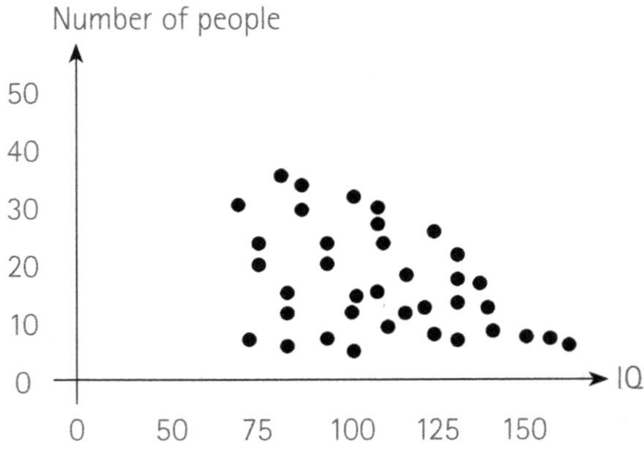

Figure 13 The skewed dispersion of a group of observations

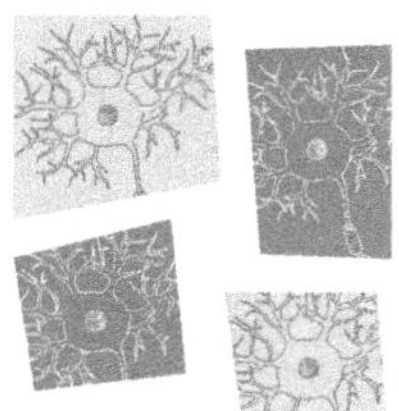

Information modelling: Visiograms

A written text is an inexpensive and elegant way to store information. People are used to written texts and understand how to read them. The problem is that the sentences and words that make up a text are sequential. A text has to be read from the beginning to the end. Sometimes, texts have headings that make it easier for readers to access relevant sections in the text without having to read the entire text, but the section that the reader is interested in still has to be read in a linear manner.

There are techniques to organise information in a non-sequential manner. This is useful to show the relationships among various ideas. It is quicker and easier to understand material if one can see the relationships among ideas as they really exist instead of having to read the information in a sequential manner and then form a picture of the various relationships in one's mind. The *unified modelling language* (also known as UML) is a standardised visual language that is used to present information in a manner that makes it easier to grasp the relationships among ideas and to describe the processes as they unfold in time. In the next section, we describe a technique for producing a description that we call a *visiogram*. The visiogram demonstrates certain UML principles at a very basic level, but it is important to remember that the visiogram is not a mini UML.

1 What is a visiogram?

A visiogram is a diagram – in other words, a kind of drawing. A visiogram is used to describe matters visually. Visiograms are useful because a visual representation is easier to understand than an ordinary verbal or written description, especially if the description is complicated. Descriptions easily become complicated and difficult to understand when they contain numerous new facts and refer to the interrelationships among these facts.

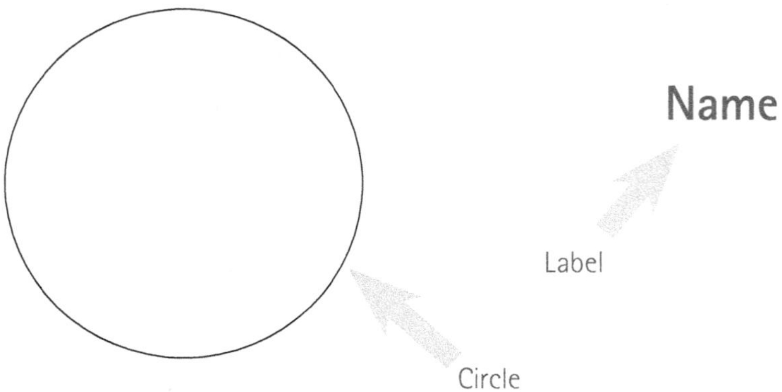

Figure 1 The circle and the label are elements of the visiogram

You can absorb more information and grasp the information more quickly if you have a visual image of the matter being described.

A visiogram has predefined *elements,* which are its building blocks and are needed to build or assemble it. Visiograms also have rules, which are used to combine elements. In other words, when we draw a visiogram, we use pre-defined elements, which we combine according to particular rules. The elements and the rules of a visiogram constitute a *modelling language* and a visiogram presents a *model* of the event or phenomenon that is described by the modelling language.

Suppose you use circles to represent things. Then a circle is an element of the visiogram. If, in addition, you use labels to indicate the names of things, then a label is another kind of element of the visiogram (see Figure 1).

However, we cannot assemble a visiogram correctly if we do not know how to combine its elements. In other words, we need to know the rules of the visiogram. Suppose the following rule exists for our visiogram: Circles are labelled by placing the label on the inside and towards the bottom of the circle. Applying this rule, we have to place the name of a circle the inside it and close to the bottom of it (see Figure 2).

We now have a very basic modelling language. This language has a vocabulary and a syntax and it is able to indicate events or phenomena. The language has two words in its vocabulary, namely a circle and a label. According to the syntax (which means the rules) of this language, the label has to be placed inside the circle and toward the bottom of it. The language can be used to indicate and name an event or a phenomenon. For example, the language can be used to indicate a person (a circle with the word 'person' inside, placed towards the bottom of the circle), the field of psychology (a circle with the word 'psychology' inside), or an accident (a circle with the word 'accident' inside).

A modelling language can become complex when a large number of elements and rules are used. We may need numerous elements and rules if we have to model very complex situations. However, we do not always need a complex modelling language. Many situations can be modelled using just a few elements and a few rules. Next, we will define a basic modelling language that is very simple but is sufficient to model basic events and phenomena in psychology.

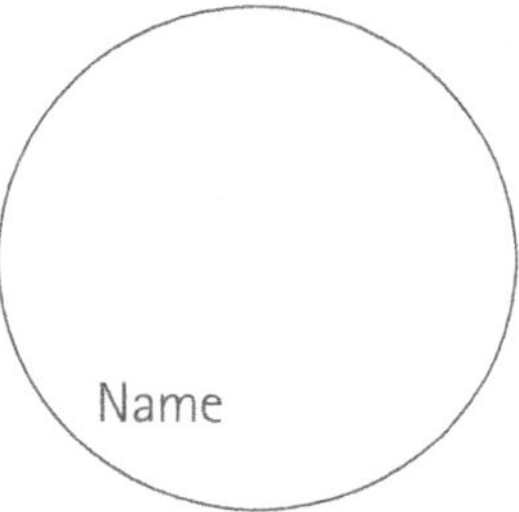

Figure 2 The circle is labelled on the inside and towards the bottom of the circle

2 A basic modelling language

A modelling language has elements and rules.

2.1 Elements

The elements of a modelling language are the building blocks of the visiogram. Our basic modelling language has three elements, which are as follows:

2.1.1 The circle element

The circle element is a circle. The circle represents things and usually corresponds to nouns in ordinary language. Examples of things are person, group, society, emotion, personality, brain and so forth.

2.1.2 The line element

The line element is a line that connects circles. The line represents the association between things. Label elements can be attached to a line element to describe an association – that is, to describe how two things are related. The relationship between two things may be *unidirectional* (pointing in one direction only) or *bidirectional* (working in both directions). Unidirectional relationships are indicated by adding an arrowhead to the name of an association (see label element). Bidirectional relationships do not have arrowheads in their names.

2.1.3 The label element

The label element is a word or a phrase. A label is used to indicate the names of things and the names of the associations among things. It is also used to indicate the number of *instances* of a thing in an association and to name the roles that things play in an association. Label elements that are attached to unidirectional relationships use arrows to indicate the direction of these associations.

2.2 Rules

The rules of a modelling language determine how the elements of the language are combined to obtain a well-formed visiogram. Our basic modelling language has three kinds of rules:

2.2.1 Containment rules

1. A circle element is external to another circle element if it does not contain, or is not contained by, the other circle element.
2. A circle element fully contains another circle element if it encloses the other circle element.
3. A circle element partially contains another circle element if it overlaps with, but does not enclose, the other circle element.
4. A circle element contains none, one or more than one circle element.

2.2.2 Connecting rules

1. A line element connects two circle elements to each other.
2. A line element is joined (attached) to the perimeter of a circle. The line element can join the circle element anywhere on the perimeter of the circle element.
3. A circle element has none, one or more than one line element attached to it.

2.2.3 Labelling rules

1. A circle element is labelled on the inside and towards the bottom of the circle.
2. The name of a line element is indicated just above and towards the middle of the line.
3. If the association is unidirectional, an arrowhead is added to the name of the line element to indicate the direction of the relationship.
4. The role that a thing plays in an association is indicated where the circle element representing the thing connects with the line element representing the association and just below the line element in question.
5. The number of instances of a thing in an association is indicated where the circle element representing the thing connects with the line element representing the association and just above the line element in question.

2.3 Examples of elements and rules

Figures 3 to 6 show you how these rules of containment, connecting and labelling are applied. We will look at Figure 6 in detail.

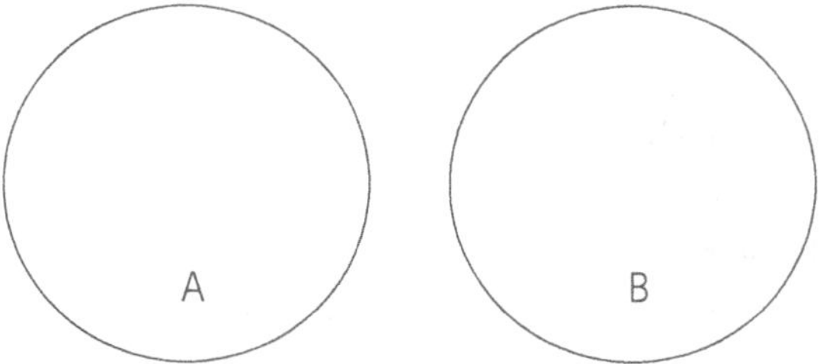

Figure 3 Circle element B is external to circle element A

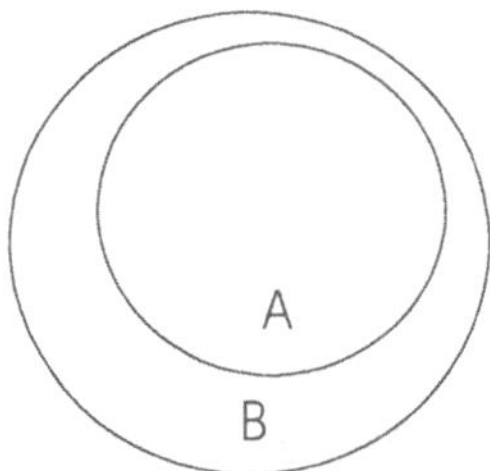

Figure 4 Circle element B fully contains circle element A

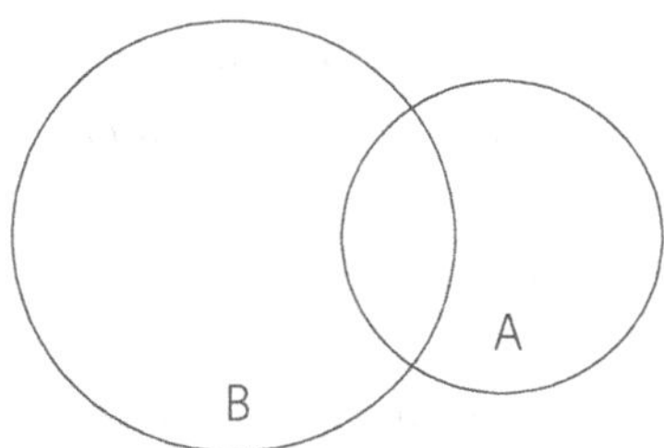

Figure 5 Circle element B partially contains circle element A and circle A partially contains circle element B

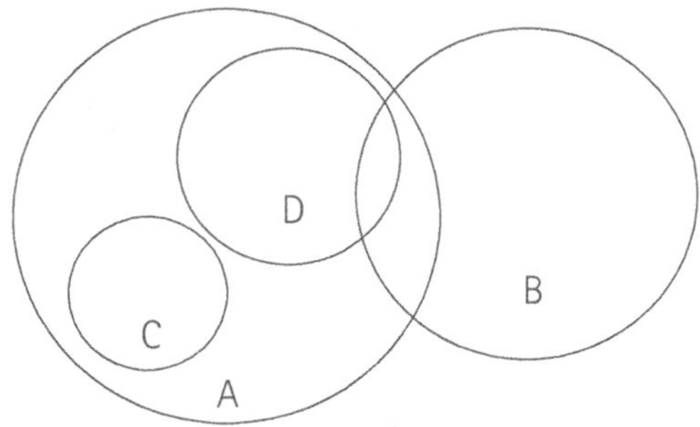

Figure 6 Multiple containment

In Figure 6 (multiple containment), the following statements are true:

- Circle element A contains more than one circle element.
- Circle element A contains circle elements B, D and C.
- Circle element A fully contains circle elements C and D.
- Circle element A partially contains circle element B.
- Circle element B contains more than one circle element.
- Circle element B partially contains circle elements A and D.
- Circle element D contains one circle element.
- Circle element D contains circle element B.
- Circle element D is contained by two circle elements, namely A and B.
- Circle element D is fully contained by one circle element, namely A.
- Circle element D is partially contained by one circle element, B.
- Circle element D is external to circle element C.
- Circle element C is external to circle element D.
- Circle element C contains no circle elements.
- Circle element C is contained by one circle element, namely A.

Note the following about the elements in Figure 7:

- Circle element A has two associations, namely association X with circle element C and association Y with circle element B.
- Circle element C has two associations, namely association X with A and Z with B.
- Circle element B has two associations, namely Y with A and Z with C.
- The name of the association between A and C contains an arrowhead (X>). It is unidirectional and points from A to C.
- One instance of circle element A is associated with three instances of circle element C.
- In association Y, circle element A plays role M and circle element B plays role N.

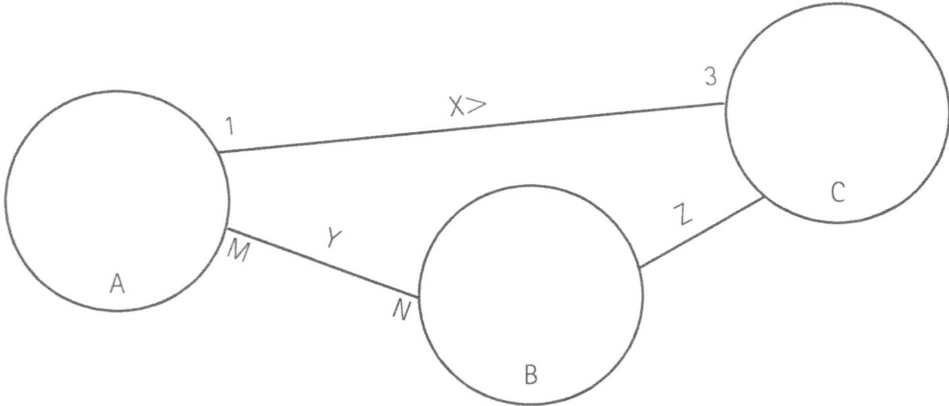

Figure 7 Line elements connect circle elements that are external to each other

Suppose the following:

- Label A is replaced by 'Woman'
- Label B is replaced by 'Man'
- Label C is replaced by 'Child'
- Label X> is replaced by 'Mother'
- Label Y is replaced by 'Married'
- Label Z is replaced by 'Father'
- Label M is replaced by 'Widow'
- Label N is replaced by 'Late husband'

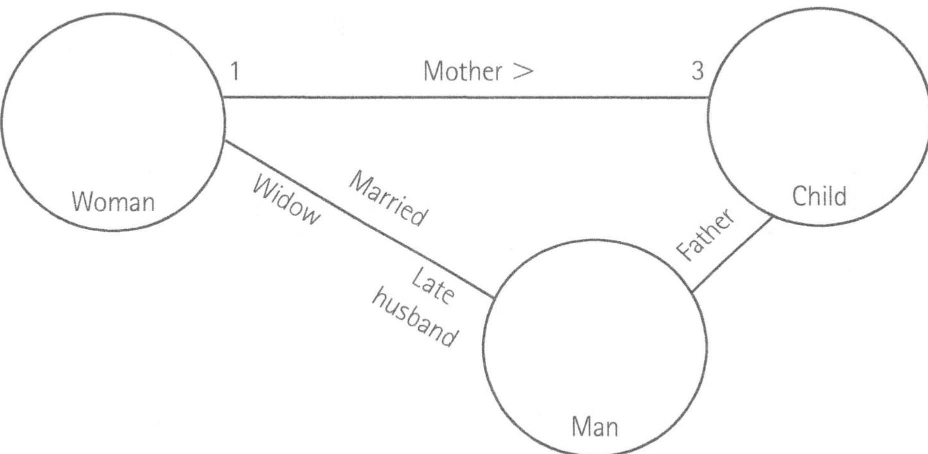

Figure 8 A model of a family

The visiogram in Figure 8 presents a model of a family. The family consists of a mother, three children and a late husband. Note that this is not the only way in which the family could be modelled. You may choose to structure the model differently. For example, instead of labelling the association between woman and child as 'mother', you may describe the association by indicating the roles that woman and child play in the association. For example, you may indicate the role of woman as 'mother' and the role of child as 'child'. Also note that a model can provide too much information (the model is superfluous) or too little information (the model is lacking). For example, in this model it is not really necessary to indicate the direction of the mother relationship between woman and child. The name of the association (that is, 'mother') is sufficient to indicate the direction from mother to child. It is highly unlikely that the child will be the mother of the woman. However, a model can also be lacking. For example, the number of instances of child is not indicated in the father association. By implication of the other two associations (man married to woman and woman having three children), one could expect 'man' to be associated with three instances of 'child' (that is, the man being the father of the woman's three children). However, the model does not indicate directly that the father has three children. In this case, the lacking information is not too serious because the model makes sense by implication (that is, the model allows you to deduce logically that 'man' is associated with three instances of 'child' and that 'child' is associated with one instance of 'man'). Information is sometimes left out to make a model appear less cluttered; however, you should always make sure that a model does not lack vital information. This occurs if the model is ambiguous and cannot be interpreted.

3 Well-formed visiograms and valid visiograms

A visiogram has to be both *well formed* and *valid.* A visiogram is well formed if the elements and the rules of the visiogram's modelling language are used correctly. A visiogram is valid if the model presented by it is correct. If the elements and the rules of a visiogram's modelling language are not used correctly, the resulting visiogram is ill formed and it is invalid if the model presented by it is not correct.

Suppose the visiogram in Figure 9 models the idea that each individual human being has a body and a mind. Then the visiogram is ill formed and invalid. The visiogram is ill formed because: (1) the label indicating the number of instances of the circle element named 'body' (that is, that the number of bodies is one) is placed incorrectly below the line element that indicates the association between body and individual (it should be placed above the line element); and (2) the label that names one of the circle elements as 'mind' is placed incorrectly outside the circle element in question (it should be placed inside, towards the bottom of the circle). The model is also invalid because it suggests that two individuals are associated with part of a single body.

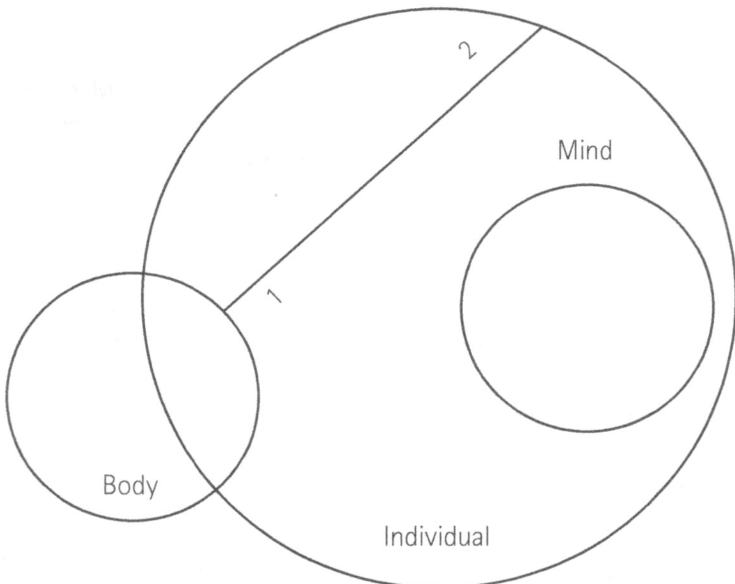

Figure 9 An ill-formed and invalid model

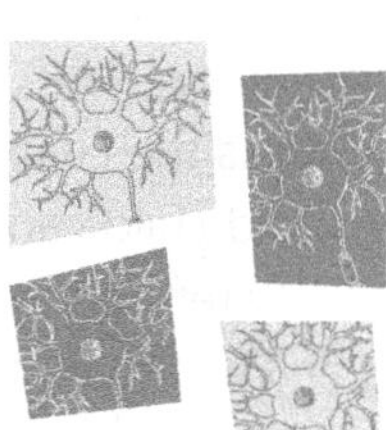

Intelligence: Concept and measurement of

Intelligence is a complex concept and there are many different definitions of it. David Wechsler, the man who developed many of the intelligence tests we use today, defined intelligence as the ability to act purposefully, to think rationally and to deal effectively with the environment. Many experts agree that intelligence reflects memory, the ability to reason and solve problems and the capacity to learn and to adapt to the environment (Coon, 2004). Intelligence also refers to the ability to perform complex tasks and the speed at which tasks can be performed (Jordaan and Jordaan, 1998).

The word 'intelligence' refers to a concept that describes certain types of behaviour. Intelligence is not a 'thing' in itself. Some people are regarded as 'more intelligent' than others, but it is difficult to determine what the criteria are for being more intelligent. Certain behaviours may be regarded as demonstrating intelligence in one context and not in another. For example, in one situation it may be considered intelligent to complete a task very rapidly and in another context it may be more intelligent to complete the task slowly and pay more attention to accuracy.

One way to understand the concept of intelligence is to look at how it is measured. Intelligence is measured using psychological tests, which provide standardised measures of a person's behaviour. This means that the person's behaviour is compared to predetermined norms, which indicate how well a person scores relative to other people. Norms are based on the performance of a large group of people who are representative of the general population.

Psychologists use intelligence tests in an attempt to measure behaviours that are regarded as demonstrating intelligence. You can imagine that there may be millions of possible tasks that tap intelligence, but it is just not possible to include them all in one test. An intelligence test is made up of only a sample of all the possible tasks that may measure intelligent behaviour. In the case of children, tests of intelligence are based on the tasks that children are able to perform at certain ages. We know that older children can perform some tasks that younger children cannot do. As a child increases in age, he or she is capable of performing more complex tasks and doing so more efficiently than a younger child.

1 Mental age

Performance on an intelligence test can give us an idea of a child's mental age (MA). This is based on the age-related questions that the child can answer or tasks the child can perform on a test of intelligence. For example, the average 13-year-old child can define the word 'democracy' but most eight-year-old children cannot, therefore the ability to define the word 'democracy' may be regarded as indicating ability equal to that of a 13-year-old child. This is just one aspect or item for estimating MA. When several items on a test are taken into account, an overall MA can be estimated. For example, if Jan can perform all the tasks expected of a 10-year-old child on a certain test, then Jan's MA is 10 years. Sometimes children cannot perform tasks expected of children of their own age, but they can perform other tasks expected of younger or older children. We can still work out their MA, based on age-related task expectations.

Consider the following example: Dineo is 12 years old. She can perform all the tasks designed for children 12 years and younger and she can also perform half of the tasks for 13-year-old children and a quarter of the tasks for 14-year-old children. We can write down Dineo's MA as 12 years + (half of a year = six months) + (quarter of a year = three months). If we add up the years and months, Dineo's MA is 12 years and nine months.

Here is another example: Simon is eight years old and he is in a school for children with learning difficulties. Simon can do all the tasks expected of a six-year-old child, one quarter of the tasks expected of a seven-year-old child and none of the tasks expected of an eight-year-old child. What is Simon's MA? We start with the year that Simon can do all the tasks, which is six years. We add on one quarter of a year (one quarter of what is expected of a seven-year-old child), which is three months. We cannot add on any more because he was not able to do the tasks for eight-year-old children. Your answer should therefore be that Simon's MA is six years and three months.

2 Intelligence quotients

MA can give a good indication of the child's level of ability, but it does not tell us much about the level of the child's functioning in relation to other children of the same chronological age (CA), which is the child's age in years and months. In order to estimate a child's intelligence, we therefore need to know the child's CA as well as the child's MA (average performance on intellectual tasks). On the basis of CA and MA, we can work out a child's intelligence quotient (abbreviated as IQ) by multiplying the ratio between MA and CA by 100.

Intelligence quotient (IQ) = MA/CA × 100

If a 10-year-old child has a mental age of eight years, the IQ would be 80 (IQ = 8/10 × 100 = 80). Because tests are based on age-related tasks, the average MA of children in one age group should be the same as their CA. The average IQ for children at any age is 100. We can work this out as follows: a 10-year-old child with a mental age of 10 years has an IQ of 100 (10/10 × 100 = 100).

IQs allow us to compare the test performance of children of different ages. Because we know an IQ of 100 is average, anything above 100 is above average measured intelligence and an IQ below 100 is below average measured intelligence. Why do we talk about measured intelligence and not just intelligence? Remember we said that intelligence tests are made up of a sample of all the possible tasks that could reflect intelligent behaviour. A test comprises some but not all of these tasks and therefore the test taps only some aspects of intelligence. There are different ways of defining intelligence that influence the kinds of task to be included in a particular test of intelligence. This is why an IQ score can never be a total reflection of a person's intellectual ability. We therefore refer to measured intelligence because the IQ is an indication of the child's performance on that particular test or measure of intelligence.

The expression of IQ as the relation between CA and MA applies only to children. MA generally increases until the age of about 16 and then it remains on the same level. If we tried to work out adults' IQ based on the relation of CA to MA, we would find that adults' IQ would decrease with age, which is generally not the case. For example, a person who is 16 years old may have an IQ of 100 but when the same person is 32 years old, the IQ based on MA would be 16/32 × 100 = 50! Test developers have found other ways of working out adult IQs based on the average number of tasks that certain age groups can perform.

A child's IQ becomes quite stable by the age of six years. This can then be used as a reasonably reliable predictor of the child's later ability. IQ remains fairly constant throughout adulthood and starts to decline when people are very old. This is a general trend. There are other factors in addition to intelligence that can affect people's performance on intelligence tests, such as anxiety, ill health, language difficulties, exposure to a stimulating environment and so on. A test score alone can be misleading – it has to be interpreted in the light of all these factors. Psychologists are trained in the correct interpretation of test results and this is why only trained psychologists can administer and interpret intelligence tests. An incorrect interpretation of a score on an intelligence test can have a very negative impact on a person's life.

Bibliography

Coon, D. 2004. *Introduction to psychology.* 10th edition. Belmont, CA: Wadsworth.

Jordaan, W. and Jordaan, J. 1998. *People in context.* 3rd edition. Johannesburg: Heinemann.

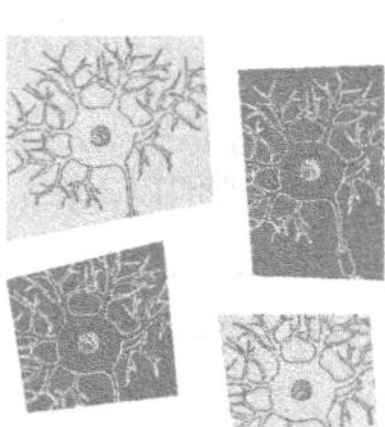

Intelligence: Theories of

Originally it was thought that intelligence was a specific ability, but it is increasingly being realised that intelligence has different manifestations. Some of the important theoretical frameworks of intelligence are described here.

1 Biological intelligence

More than 100 years ago, a British scholar, Sir Francis Galton, made a study of families. He concluded that success runs in families because intelligence is passed from generation to generation through genetic inheritance. He thought that the contents of the mind were based on sensations and that people differed in terms of their sensory, perceptual and motor processes. He tried to assess mental ability by measuring simple sensory processes, like reaction time or sensitivity to sounds. Later it was found that these sensory processes were not related to other criteria of mental ability, such as success at school.

It is interesting to note that, since the 1980s, there has been renewed interest in reaction times as a measure of intelligence. There is strong evidence of a relation between biological measures and performance on intelligence tests. The reason for this is thought to be that speed of information processing is an integral part of general intelligence (Perkins, 1995).

Galton coined the phrase 'nature versus nurture', referring to the debate about the contributions of heredity and environment to intelligence. 'Nature' refers to the inherited component of intelligence and 'nurture' refers to the effects of the environment.

2 Intelligence as one general factor (g) or multiple factors

There is a view that intelligence is based on one single component or factor. A British psychologist, Charles Spearman (1927), was the first person to suggest that differences between individuals' intellectual ability could be explained by this one factor. He based his theory on research findings that there was a strong relation between performances on different intellectual tasks. Spearman called this underlying factor 'general intelligence' or 'general intellectual ability', abbreviated as 'g'. Spearman acknowledged that other factors played a role in specific abilities or tasks and he called these 'specific factors', abbreviated as S-factors. For example, doing well on arithmetic tasks would be an indication of arithmetic ability as an S-factor.

In contrast to Spearman's theory, Thurston (1947) suggested a multiple factor theory of intelligence. He identified seven factors that he thought represented primary mental abilities, which are the following:

- *Verbal comprehension,* or the ability to understand concepts in verbal form
- *General reasoning,* or the ability to solve complex problems or plan something new by drawing on experience
- *Word fluency,* or the ability to speak and write fluently
- *Memory,* or the ability to learn and remember information
- *Number ability,* or the ability to work with numbers
- *Spatial ability,* or the ability to represent things visually in space and to manipulate them mentally
- *Perceptual speed,* or the ability to recognise objects and identify similarities and differences.

Thurston believed that these factors were independent of each other; however, research has shown that they are related. Thurston later acknowledged that the primary mental abilities were related to a general factor, based on 'g'.

Guilford (1967) also rejected the idea of one general factor of intelligence. According to his theory, intellectual activity has three components: *operations, content* and *products:*

- *Operations* are the ways that the brain deals with tasks. Examples of operations are processes such as evaluation and memory.
- *Content* refers to the different forms of mental representation, such as visual, auditory or behavioural.
- *Products* are the results of operations. For example, a product could be the identification of relationships between things, resulting from mental operations.

3 Multiple intelligences

Gardner's (1999) opinion is that IQ tests generally focus on verbal and mathematical skills and overlook other important skills. He therefore developed a theory of multiple intelligences. This is an example of an approach that defines intelligence in terms of mental skills or abilities. Gardner (1999) does not view intelligence as the collaboration of independent abilities but suggests that there are eight autonomous or separate kinds of intelligence as follows:

- *Musical intelligence* – for composing, appreciating and performing music
- *Bodily-kinaesthetic intelligence* – for the movement of the body or body parts (like dancing or playing football)
- *Logical-mathematical intelligence* – for logical reasoning, solving problems and numerical calculation
- *Linguistic intelligence* – related to the expression and understanding of words (language)
- *Spatial intelligence* – for organising things in space (like drawing or navigating a ship)
- *Interpersonal intelligence* – for getting on with people
- *Intrapersonal intelligence* – for understanding ourselves and being in touch with our feelings
- *Naturalist intelligence* – for recognising, understanding and organising patterns and relationships in the natural environment

Gardner is still investigating whether these various intelligences are independent. He believes that some are predominant in certain situations and cultures, but that people should try to develop all of them. Interpersonal intelligence is similar to the concept of *emotional intelligence* (Goleman, 1995), which refers to the skills of understanding and evaluating one's own and other people's emotions and using them constructively to attain goals.

4 Information-processing approach

The information-processing approach, also called the cognitive processing approach, is based on the idea that intelligence is based on three components – attentional processes, information processes and planning processes. These are believed to be the information-processing strategies that underlie intelligence. The cognitive perspective focuses on how people *use* their intelligence, rather than on how much or the amount of intellectual ability they have.

An application of the cognitive perspective is found in Robert Sternberg's (1995) theory that intelligent behaviour should be viewed as part of the situation or context it occurs in and not seen as something we can infer from a test result. Sternberg's theory is called a triarchic theory of intelligence because, in his view, intelligence is based on three aspects: componential intelligence, experiential intelligence and contextual intelligence:

- *Componential intelligence* refers to the ways in which people process information. Examples are processes used for planning and problem solving, or obtaining new information. These are the types of mental process that intelligent thought depends on.
- *Experiential intelligence* refers to the way a person's past experience contributes to knowledge and skills that are applied in life situations or tasks.

This means that experiential intelligence allows a person to meet the demands of different situations, based on that person's experience. The idea is that the more experience you have, the better equipped you are to cope with the demands of unfamiliar situations. With experience you can also learn to process information or perform a certain task automatically. In this way, experiential intelligence allows you to deal with different tasks at the same time. If your experience allows you to deal with one thing automatically, you are able to give conscious attention to something else at the same time. For example, when you have learned to drive a car, you can change gears automatically and give more attention to what is happening on the road.

- *Contextual intelligence* refers to the ability to adapt to real-world situations and various contexts. Sternberg's (1997) view is that intelligence is a culturally defined concept. Certain acts may seem simple, but in a particular context they may represent highly adaptive behaviour. Different forms of intelligent behaviour are valued in different contexts. For example, being able to walk for long distances in the heat is not generally regarded by Westernised cultures as an indication of intelligent behaviour. However, for nomadic tribes in Somalia, this is an important adaptive ability that allows their survival and can therefore be regarded as intelligent behaviour.

5 Heredity versus environment

A theme common to many theories of intelligence is the question of whether intelligence is determined by innate skills and/or abilities, or whether it is the result of environmental experiences. This is the so-called 'nature versus nurture' debate. Nature refers to our genetic inheritance and nurture refers to environmental influences. A great deal of research has been done on the contribution of hereditary and environmental factors to intellectual ability.

In general, studies on heredity and environment have shown the following:

- People who are closely related (in terms of genetics) obtain similar scores on intelligence tests. The closer the relationship, the more similar the scores are likely to be. For example, it has been found that the test scores of identical twins are more similar than those of fraternal twins (Bouchard et al., 1990). This finding seems to confirm the notion that intelligence is hereditary.
- People who are raised in similar environments obtain similar scores on intelligence tests. In general, this means that people who share the same environment are exposed to the same kinds of stimulation and support for the development of skills and abilities that influence performance on intelligence tests. Studies (Flynn, 1987) have shown that when children are removed from a disadvantaged home with poorly educated parents and placed in a better socio-economic environment, their test scores are better than those of their siblings who remained in the disadvantaged home environment.

> These findings suggest that environment has an important influence on performance in intelligence tests.

What can we conclude from this? Most psychologists believe that heredity makes a major contribution to intelligence and they also agree that the environment affects intelligence. This means that both nature and nurture influence our intellectual ability. Genetic potential is present at birth and there is a wide variation in people's genetic potential. Variations in environmental conditions can determine whether the person develops that potential or not. We can say, therefore, that genetic factors determine a person's potential and environmental factors activate it. This means that heredity imposes an upper limit or ceiling on intelligence, even under ideal conditions. For example, if a child is born with a genetic condition that causes mental retardation, that child's intellectual functioning will always be below average even if the child's environmental conditions are optimal. On the other hand, a child with average genetic potential who lives in a disadvantaged environment may be unable to attain an average level of functioning. Impoverished and unstimulating environments can severely limit the development of intellectual ability in childhood (Dawes and Donald, 1994). Children are best able to develop their potential in a stable environment where caring adults spend time with them, answer their questions and encourage discussion and intellectual exploration. We can conclude that intelligence reflects the combined effects of both heredity and environment.

What are the implications for scores on intelligence tests? Intelligence tests rely heavily on the skills and knowledge that people have learnt at school and from formal instruction. Scores obtained from intelligence tests give an indication of how well people are able to apply their knowledge and skills to the tests. This means that intelligence tests cannot directly measure genetic potential. Test performance is largely a reflection of a person's education and environment because IQ tests unavoidably contain items that are influenced by a person's previous learning. This is why it is sometimes difficult and unfair to compare the abilities of people from different socio-economic and cultural backgrounds in terms of scores on a particular intelligence test. In South Africa, attempts have been made to develop culturally fair tests of learning potential in an effort to determine different individual levels of ability (Foxcroft and Roodt, 2001).

Bibliography

Bouchard, I., Lykken, D., McGue, M., Segal, N. and Tellegren, A. 1990. Sources of human psychological differences: The Minnesota twins reared apart. *Science,* 250, 223–228.

Coon, D. 2004. *Introduction to psychology.* 10th edition. Belmont, CA: Wadsworth.

Dawes, A. and Donald, D. (Eds). 1994. *Childhood and adversity. Psychological perspectives from South African research.* Cape Town, South Africa: David Philip.

Flynn, J.R. 1987. Massive IQ gains in 14 nations: What IQ tests really measure. *Psychological Bulletin*, 101, 171–191.

Foxcroft, C. and Roodt, G. 2001. *An introduction to psychological assessment in the South African context.* Cape Town: Oxford University Press.

Gardner, H. 1999. *Intelligence renamed. Multiple intelligences for the 21st century.* New York: Basic Books.

Goleman, D. 1995. *Emotional Intelligence.* London: Bloomsbury.

Guilford, J.P. 1967. *The Nature of human intelligence.* New York: McGraw-Hill.

Perkins, D. 1995. *Outsmarting 10: The emerging science of learnable intelligence.* New York: Free Press.

Spearman, C. 1927. *The abilities of man.* London: Macmillan.

Sternberg, R. 1995. *In search of the human mind.* 2nd edition. Fort Worth, TX: Harcourt Brace.

Thurston, L. 1947. *Multiple factor analysis.* Chicago: University of Chicago Press

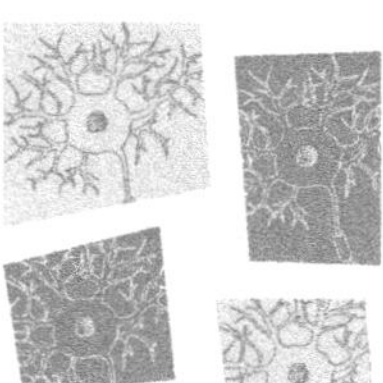

Intelligence and creativity

Creative thought involves the generation of original, novel and useful ideas (Weiten, 2001). Creative thinking is related to intelligent thinking, but it is not the same as intelligence. Creative thought differs from routine problem solving because it is inventive and includes originality. In addition, creative thinking is adaptive in the sense that it must be appropriate to the situation and problem. Examples of creative and original thinking can be found in many breakthroughs in science, technology, literature and the arts that were previously considered unthinkable.

Many people believe that creativity involves sudden flashes of insight or 'Aha!' experiences. Although people do have creative bursts, creative achievements are generally the result of long, hard work based on years of experience and/or study. Creative breakthroughs are not related to unconscious thought processes, such as dreams. Most cognitive psychologists agree that creative thoughts emerge from conscious problem-solving efforts.

Certain types of thought process are associated with creative thinking. The first of these is *divergent thinking.* This refers to the ability to produce unusual and unconventional thoughts or solutions to problems. Guilford described divergent thinking as thinking 'that goes off in different directions'. It is characterised by expanding the range of alternatives by generating many possible solutions. For example, if you work for an advertising agency, you would need to use divergent thinking to come up with a range of possible slogans for a particular product. Divergent thinking contrasts with convergent thinking. Convergent thinking describes the thought process that produces conventional or correct answers to problems. By using convergent thinking, you try to narrow down a list of alternatives to reach a single correct answer. Convergent thinking generally relies on existing knowledge and logical solutions. For example, finding the right answer to multiple-choice questions involves convergent thinking.

The second component of creative thinking is *cognitive complexity.* This refers to the ability to think beyond what is presented to you and to use complex thought patterns. For example, if you have to make a picture using a shape like this – < – you could merely close up the open side to make a triangle (convergent thinking), or you could turn the < into a light shining from a torch (divergent thinking).

1 Measuring creativity

Psychologists have attempted to measure creativity with tests that rely on creative thinking. For example, a typical test item may be to list various uses for a paper clip. The score would depend on the number of alternatives and their originality (the alternatives over and above conventional uses). Tests of creativity are based on the assumption that creative people can see unusual relations between concepts, which go beyond the obvious everyday connections. For example, making an earring out of a paper clip would be an unconventional and creative use for it. Unfortunately, tests of creativity are limited because they measure creativity out of context. People may be creative when they are working in a particular context but may not be able to come up with creative ideas in a test. It is difficult to predict creative achievement because it depends on other factors besides creativity, such as motivation, personality and intelligence.

Although there is no such thing as a creative personality, very creative people are generally imaginative, flexible and non-conforming. They tend to think for themselves and are not easily influenced by the opinions of others. They are also willing to take risks and attempt changes.

Creativity and intelligence are related, but they represent different kinds of mental ability. Most highly creative people have above average intellectual ability (Ochse, 1990). However, there is a weak relation between creativity and IQ scores. The most likely reason for this is that IQ tests force the creative person, who usually is a divergent thinker, to use convergent thinking to work out the answers. The creative person may therefore not perform well on a conventional test of intelligence. Measured intelligence does not guarantee creativity. Creative ability is associated with flexibility and spontaneity.

Bibliography

Ochse, R. 1990. *Before the gates of excellence.* Cambridge and New York: Cambridge University Press.

Weiten, W. 2001. *Psychology: Themes and variations.* 5th edition. Belmont, CA: Wadsworth.

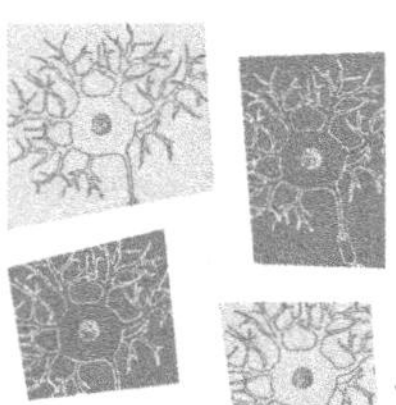

Interpersonal communication

Humans are inherently social beings. Most of our activities involve interaction with other individuals, or are conducted in the context of one or another group. The ability to communicate is essential in our daily existence. It is the social glue that keeps us together (Abrahams and Ruiters, 2003), so intuitively we know what it means to say that people communicate, but on closer inspection the complexity of the notion of communication quickly becomes apparent.

1 The basic elements of communication

Technically speaking, communication is the process of sending a message and receiving feedback (Aleksander, 2003). In social contexts, this statement translates into a more comprehensive consideration: Who communicates what to whom, in what context, in what manner and according to what rules? (Jordaan, 1998). If we consider these statements carefully, we can identify six elements that are basic to all forms of communication. These are a sender, an encoder, a channel, a decoder, a receiver and a signal (Aleksander, 2003).

In interpersonal communication, the *sender* and the *encoder* are bundled together in the person who communicates and the *decoder* and *receiver* are embodied in the person on the receiving side of the communication. The *signals* are the verbal and non-verbal signs that convey the content of the message and the *channel* consists of the human senses (visual, auditory, smell, touch and taste) that carry the verbal and non-verbal signs of the message.

2 The basic process of communication

Communication requires rules. The decoder cannot decode the message if it does not know how the message was encoded in the first place. In interpersonal communication, these rules can be quite complex because they include linguistic and cultural as well as personal aspects. The ways in which people express themselves verbally and non-verbally regulate their communication. Individuals' verbal and non-verbal expressions are determined by their language, culture and personal style. If somebody speaks a particular language badly, using incorrect words, faulty grammar and poor pronunciation (poor encoding of the message), the listener may find it difficult to understand the person because he or she cannot apply the language's decoding rules.

Cultural differences may also cause encoding–decoding difficulties when the rules are not clear. In my culture, it may be required of me to position myself at a lower level than you if you are senior to me, so when we meet I will seek to sit down as soon as possible to convey the message of respect. However, according to your culture, things may be different and people may not be supposed to sit down unless invited to do so, thus if you do not know the cultural rules I apply, you may decode my signal of respect as rude behaviour.

However, from a psychological point of view, the most interesting difficulties with encoding and decoding lie in the field of personal style. Some psychological theories suggest that people encode needs and intentions into their verbal and non-verbal behaviour without being aware that they do so. These needs and intentions remain unfulfilled if other people cannot decode them correctly and the person may become unhappy and seek the help of a psychologist. The role of psychologists is to decode the unconscious needs and intentions and to help people express these in such a manner that others can understand them.

Communication requires clear transmission. Even if the rules of encoding and decoding are perfectly clear, it may sometimes be difficult to decode a message because it is drowned in too much *noise*. 'Noise' is a technical term that is used to describe the quality of transmission. The clarity with which a message is conveyed depends on how much noise there is during the conveyance of the message. It is much harder to have a conversation with somebody in a room full of talking people than in a quiet place. It is also much harder to read an essay presented in illegible handwriting than in a neatly typed format.

Communication occurs in particular *contexts*. A message may take on different meanings depending on the context in which the sender and the receiver find themselves. For example, the meaning of the message: 'She is beating him' depends on whether the message is conveyed in the context of a game or a fight. However, contexts do not only define the meaning of a message, they also determine its relevance and the appropriateness.

We often see in ordinary conversations how people ignore the context of a communication by making irrelevant remarks. For example, a group of friends may be busy discussing whom to invite to a social function when one of the group members starts to talk about the catering requirements. Although catering is not an unrelated issue, the context of the conversation is the guest list. The person's remarks are irrelevant, not because catering is an irrelevant issue, but because he or she ignored the specific context of the conversation.

3 The dynamics of interpersonal communication

The communication between humans is a dynamic process that occurs continuously. Even when we are not intentionally communicating, we still send signals. On other occasions, the messages we send are complex and are communicated on more than one level (Jordaan, 1998).

It is *impossible not to communicate.* Two people may sit together in silence, apparently not communicating, but their body language still conveys a message. They may both appear relaxed, conveying the pleasure of being in each other's company, or one may be watching the other in a threatening manner, conveying displeasure. The other person may have a facial expression of disbelief, conveying surprise at the first person's reaction. The principle that it is impossible not to communicate has implications for the course and outcome of our day-to-day interpersonal communications and for the relationships in which they occur (Jordaan, 1998). We sometimes send messages without intending to do so. On other occasions, the messages we send are misunderstood, or not understood at all.

Communication is a *pattern within an ongoing process.* The knowledge we have and the way in which we think about things determine how we understand and react to the messages we receive from others, therefore there are consistencies in what we say and how we react physically. Because this is true for everybody, there are patterns in the verbal and non-verbal messages we convey to each other. For example, I may be an extremely logical person, while you are much more emotional in your approach. In our conversations, regardless of what we talk about, I will tend to emphasise the logical sequence of events, while you may focus on their emotional impact. This can be a complementary situation in which we contribute to one another's knowledge and understanding of things, but it can also be a source of conflict. We may disagree because we look at things so differently, thus there are patterns of agreement or disagreement in our communication that do not start or end with a particular conversation. These patterns constitute a communication that carries on through many conversations.

Communication happens on *different levels.* The human channel of communication consists of five senses and therefore it can simultaneously convey various modalities of a message. This enables humans to distinguish between *what* is said and *how* it is said. What we say occurs on the *informative content* level; how we say something concerns the *meta-communicative* level. The informative content of a message is the meaning that the words or symbols have. The meta-communicative content is additional information that qualifies the meaning of the words or symbols. This refers to the tone in which words are uttered, as well as non-verbal cues such as facial expressions and other bodily gestures. For example, you may tell me that you like me (informative content) and then smile and touch my arm lightly (meta-communicative content). In this example, the meta-communicative content corroborates and confirms the informative content. Your smile and touch confirm the verbal statement you made. The communication is therefore *congruent.* Communication is *incongruent* when the informative content is not supported by the meta-communicative content. For example, I may say I like your dog, while, with an expression of disgust, I am fiercely trying to wipe his little paw marks off my clothes.

Bibliography

Abrahams, F. and Ruiters, R.R. 2003. Industrial psychology: Selected topics. In L. Nicholas, *Introduction to psychology.* Cape Town: UCT Press.

Aleksander, I. 2003. Understanding information bit by bit: Shannon's equations. In G. Farmelo (Ed), *It must be beautiful: Great equations of modern science.* London: Granta.

Jordaan, W. 1998. Interpersonal relationships. In W. Jordaan and J. Jordaan, *People in context.* 3rd edition. Johannesburg: Heinemann.

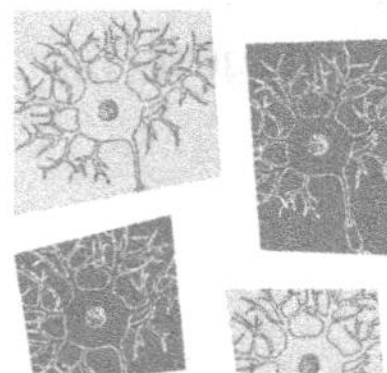

Interpersonal dynamics

Human beings are fundamentally social. The basic need that drives social affiliation is the need to belong (Baumeister and Leary, 1995). There are reasons for this need. We evolved the ability to affiliate with others for survival purposes. Living with others increases our chances of survival and provides opportunities for reproduction. We become anxious if we are isolated from others and our need for affiliation further increases under such circumstances (Gazzaniga and Heatherton, 2003:453). So strong is the need for affiliation that people have special mechanisms to detect and reject cheaters in order to protect the existence of the group. People who violate group rules are stigmatised and socially excluded (Gazzaniga and Heatherton, 2003:455), therefore we are prepared to go to great lengths to remain part of a group. We are willing to accept group norms, to act compliantly and to obey authority (Gazzaniga and Heatherton, 2003:465–469).

1 Overt and covert behaviour

Because of the deep-seated need for social affiliation, people are exceptionally good in the ways in which they interact with each other. Psychologists distinguish between overt and covert interactions. Overt interactions refer to people's visible behaviour, whereas covert interactions refer to the patterns in overt behaviour. Personality theorists see covert behaviour patterns as expressions of people's characters. This is the kind of behaviour that interests psychologists when they try to explain why people behave in the ways they do. For example, the personologist, Karen Homey (in Naidoo, 2004), identified three covert patterns underlying individual interactions. These are (1) moving towards people; (2) moving against people; and (3) moving away from people. Psychologists who work according to Homey's theory will try to detect these underlying patterns in people's overt behaviour, therefore when somebody says: 'I do not agree with you', the psychologist may identify this statement (overt behaviour) as a movement against others. If the person has a habit of being disagreeable and resisting working with others, the psychologist may identify the tendency to move against others as a behaviour pattern of the person.

In the following sections, we concentrate on overt behaviour, because this is the most visible form of interpersonal dynamics.

2 Prosocial and aggressive behaviour

One way to look at overt behaviour is to describe it in terms of an interpersonal behaviour continuum. The one end of this continuum represents prosocial behaviour and the other end aggressive behaviour. Behaviour in the middle of this continuum is neutral – it reflects socialising that is neither prosocial nor aggressive.

Prosocial behaviour is behaviour in which one person benefits from another's actions. Aggressive behaviour is behaviour that has the intention to harm somebody else. Human behaviour moves between these two extremes and psychologists have for a long time been interested in the circumstances that surround prosocial and aggressive interaction.

2.1 Prosocial behaviour

Prosocial behaviour includes doing favours, offering assistance, paying compliments, or simply being pleasant and co-operative (Gazzaniga and Heatherton, 2003:472). There are a variety of theories about the reasons why people act prosocially. Some theories assume that people are altruistic; in other words, that they offer help without expecting anything in return. Other theories see prosocial behaviour as a more selfish act, namely an investment for a future benefit (I help you now, because I may need your help in future). The payoffs may also be personal (I feel better about myself when I help others) or social (I help you because it improves my social image). Helping others may also be a tendency that we have been born with. We know that infants become distressed and offer comfort when they see other infants cry (Gazzaniga and Heatherton, 2003:473). The innate tendency to help others may be a survival mechanism in the sense that we need to work together to ensure the survival of our group or our next of kin.

We may have an inborn tendency to help others, but there is also a social component to helping behaviour. The murder of a young woman in New York City in 1964 spurred intense research into the circumstances under which people are likely to offer help. The most shocking aspect of the murder was that 38 people witnessed the event but nobody offered help. A large body of research findings suggests that there are four major factors that determine prosocial behaviour (Gazzaniga and Heatherton, 2003:474):

- The first of these is *diffusion of responsibility.* When people find themselves

in a group, they are less likely to take personal responsibility. People can hide in a group because they are less identifiable.
- *Identifiability* is the second factor that plays a role in prosocial behaviour. People who are not anonymous are more likely to offer help.
- The third factor concerns people's fear of making a fool of themselves. When a situation is *socially ambiguous*, people are less likely to offer help.
- The fourth factor is the *cost versus benefit* trade-off in a helping situation. People are less likely to help if there is a possibility that they can suffer harm themselves, or if they could actually benefit from doing nothing.

In addition to innate and social factors, there may also be personality characteristics that determine prosocial behaviour. Some research suggests that people who display helping behaviour are more self-assured, sympathetic and emotionally understanding and have greater empathy (Feldman, 2003:464).

How do people engage in prosocial behaviour? According to a model developed by Latané and Darley (in Feldman, 2003:464), the process of helping behaviour involves four basic steps:
- Noting a person, event or situation that may require help
- Interpreting the event as one that requires help
- Assuming responsibility for taking action
- Deciding on and implementing the form of assistance

2.2 Aggressive behaviour

Physical aggression is common in animal and child behaviour, but is relatively rare among human adults (Gazzaniga and Heatherton, 2003:469). Adult aggression normally involves words or actions meant to threaten, intimidate or hurt others. However, regardless of the form of aggressive behaviour, the question still remains as to whether aggression is innate or the product of psychosocial circumstances.

There are three main approaches to understanding aggression. These are (1) instinct approaches; (2) frustration–aggression approaches; and (3) observational learning approaches (Feldman, 2003:462–463).

Konrad Lorenz is one of the major proponents of the *instinct approach* to aggression. Like Sigmund Freud, Lorenz considered aggression as the primary instinct to fight off threats. He viewed it as an energy that builds up and that has to be discharged at some point and he described the discharge of aggressive energy as a process of catharsis (Lorenz, 1966). According to Lorenz, people need opportunities for catharsis. In older times, people could discharge their aggressive energies through acts of war, but modern-day living requires more acceptable means of catharsis, such as games and sports activities.

Frustration–aggression approaches explain aggressive behaviour as the outcome of frustration. We become frustrated when we are blocked from doing something that we really want or desperately need to do. Early frustration–aggression theories suggested that frustration always leads to aggression, but more recent formulations suggest that frustration produces anger, which leads to a readiness to act aggressively. Whether or not aggression actually occurs depends on two things: (1) whether the feelings produced by frustration are negative; and (2) whether aggressive cues are present in the situation (Feldman, 2003:462). Aggressive cues are things (for example a gun) or ideas (for example the name of an aggressive person) that have previously been associated with actual aggression, thus frustration leads to aggressive behaviour, but only if the frustration is associated with negative feelings and if aggressive cues are present.

However, there are also theories suggesting that we learn to be aggressive. These are referred to as the *observational learning* approaches. Social and environmental conditions can teach individuals to be aggressive. In social situations, people learn through imitation. When I see somebody getting his way through acting aggressively, I am likely to imitate his behaviour when I find myself in a similar situation. However, when I see the opposite happening, namely that somebody is punished for displaying aggressive behaviour, I am unlikely to imitate his behaviour (Feldman, 2003:463).

3 Interpersonal attraction

So far we have looked at overt behaviour in terms of a continuum of prosocial and aggressive behaviour. A second dimension of overt interpersonal behaviour is the continuum that describes attraction and repulsion between individuals. How do people choose with whom they want to affiliate and how do they establish *affiliative* relationships?

There are several factors that determine whom people choose to affiliate with. Considerations such as proximity, similarity and complementarity and personal attraction contribute to people's affiliative choices (Gazzaniga and Heatherton, 2003:475–477). A fourth factor is communication. These factors explained are:

- *Proximity.* This refers to the frequency with which individuals come into contact. Researchers have found that the more often individuals come into contact, the more likely they are to become friends (Gazzaniga and Heatherton, 2003:475). The positive effect that proximity has on the development of friendship may be due to another phenomenon, namely familiarity. People like things that are familiar and tend to fear those that are novel to them. Simply being exposed to something repeatedly and thus getting more familiar with it, leads to increased liking. This phenomenon is known as the exposure effect.
- *Similarity and complementarity.* People who have similar attitudes, personality traits and demographics (for example age and level of education) tend to like each other because they find one another familiar and they share interests and activities, but this does not mean that we only affiliate with those who

are similar to ourselves. People may seek out the company of others exactly because their attitudes, personality traits and demographics are different to their own. This happens when they feel a need to complement their own characteristics with what they experience to be lacking in themselves. For example, an introvert may need the energy and social involvement that an extrovert friend can offer and the extrovert may need the reflexive contemplations of an introvert.

- *Personal attraction.* People are attracted to others for physical and psychological reasons. They tend to like those who have admirable personality characteristics, such as kindness, dependability and trustworthiness, but dishonesty, insincerity and lack of personal warmth are disliked. Competence is a likeable characteristic, provided the individual is not too competent or perfect, because this makes others feel uncomfortable (Gazzaniga and Heatherton, 2003:476). There is also strong evidence that people like others because of their perceived physical attractiveness (Jordaan, 1998). There are various reasons for this. There is a stereotypical perception that beauty equals goodness. Attractive people are considered to be good people on face value. There are also other reasons, like the aesthetic pleasure of looking at a beautiful person, the idea that good-looking people are socially acceptable and the desire to benefit from associating with good-looking people.
- *Communication.* This is an additional factor in establishing an affiliative relationship. The process of interpersonal affiliation is mediated by verbal and non-verbal communication. People discover each other by talking to each other. They learn about one another through what they say. In the process of talking, they send and receive verbal messages that convey information about themselves. However, non-verbal communication is equally important. People use eye contact, facial expressions, body gestures such as touching and tone of voice to convey non-verbal messages about what they feel and think (Jordaan, 1998).

So how do people establish affiliative relationships? There are three phases in the development of an interpersonal relationship (Jordaan, 1998). During the first phase, the two individuals notice each other and evaluate one another's attributes at face value. The second phase begins when the two individuals start to interact. Initially, the interaction is regulated by cultural rules and social etiquette. The individuals exchange normal socially acceptable pleasantries about everyday events. This gives them the opportunity to observe and analyse one another's characteristics and – depending on how they feel about each other – they may begin to explore mutual interests. As this phase continues, the two individuals may seek out one another's company more frequently. Towards the end of the second phase, they begin to understand each other, know about one another's points of view and are prepared to criticise and praise one another. The third phase begins when they make a commitment to each other. The commitment may be explicit (as when two people verbally agree to become lovers to the exclusion of others) or it may be implicit (as when two people become very good friends). In this phase, they feel responsible for one another and for the kind of relationship they have. Their behaviour and their interactions are aimed at moulding the relationship and they foster it by disclosing information about themselves that they would not easily share with others (Jordaan, 1998).

In their interactions with each other, humans display complex interpersonal dynamics. Their overt actions hide covert patterns of interaction. Psychologists identify these covert patterns to explain why people display prosocial and aggressive behaviour and to explain how they go about choosing and establishing affiliations with others.

Bibliography

Baumeister, R.F. and Leary, M.R. 1995. The need to belong: Desire for interpersonal attachments as a fundamental human motivation. *Psychological Bulletin,* 117, 497–529.

Feldman, R.S. 2003. *Essentials of understanding psychology.* 5th edition. New York: McGraw Hill.

Gazzaniga, M.S. and Heatherton, T.F. 2003. *Psychological science: Mind, brain and behaviour.* New York: Norton.

Jordaan, W. 1998. Interpersonal relationships. In W. Jordaan and J. Jordaan, *People in context.* 3rd edition. Johannesburg: Heinemann.

Lorenz, K. 1966. *On aggression.* New York: Harcourt Brace Jovanovich.

Naidoo, P. 2004. Personality theories. In L. Swartz, C. de la Rey and N. Duncan (Eds), *Psychology: An introduction.* Cape Town: Oxford University Press.

Interpersonal relationships

We maintain a variety of interpersonal relationships in our daily lives. Strictly speaking, we have an interpersonal relationship with every person we come in contact with. However, many of these relationships are fleeting – for example a once-off interaction with a cashier at the supermarket till. Other relationships are more substantial, but are casual – for example the guy on the street corner you buy the newspaper from each morning. It is only when we consider our interpersonal relationships with work colleagues, friends, family members and life partners that we can talk about prolonged and substantial (close) interpersonal relationships.

In this section, we consider the nature of interpersonal relationships in four contexts:

- Casual interaction
- Friendship
- Family
- Love

We will not consider work relationships in this section, because the contexts of casual interaction and friendship already capture those aspects of work relationships that we are interested in here.

Casual relationships are substantial, but are distant and contractual in nature. These relationships normally occur because people need to interact for the benefit of one or more of the individuals involved in the relationship. They are based on equity principles. Close relationships are characterised by interdependence, emotional attachment and psychological need (Jordaan, 1998), thus people are closely involved with those they have a close relationship with (interdependence), they experience feelings of care and affection (emotional attachment) and they experience fulfilment (psychological need) in their interactions with others in the relationship.

People experience loneliness when they do not encounter these attributes in their interpersonal relationships (Jordaan, 1998).

1 Casual relationships

Casual relationships are based on *contracted interactions*. In other words, the people involved in a casual relationship interact for a purpose and they follow a sociocultural protocol in their interaction. The purpose could vary from a friendly exchange that happens simply for the purpose of goodwill (greeting the person who cleans your office every day) to a substantial and important outcome (finalising a contract with the builder of your house). In any of these circumstances, those involved in the interaction act according to established social and cultural norms.

The entire relationship is characterised by principles of *equity*. This means that a casual relationship between two individuals is satisfactory if one individual's inputs into and benefits from the relationship equal those of the other individual (Jordaan, 1998). For example, I buy a newspaper from you every day at the traffic light. For me, it is convenient that you bring the paper to the street. You gain as well, because I buy the paper every day. However, you can expect me to become dissatisfied with the relationship if I feel I have to contribute a lot for a low return, while you gain a lot for little input. For example, I may feel that I have to put in too much if you ask me to pay double the normal price of the newspaper. A casual relationship comes to an end when one or both of the individuals involved in it have nothing more to bring to it, thus our relationship ends if you do not have any more papers to sell, or if I do not have the money to pay for them.

2 Friendship relationships

Friendship relationships are based on *communality*. This kind of relationship is characterised by the individuals' sensitivity and responsiveness to one another's needs, with no calculation of cost (Jordaan, 1998). The difference between casual and friendship relationships is what Jacques Derrida, the French philosopher, referred to as the economy of the gift (Derrida, 1995). According to Derrida, a gift is only a true gift if both the giver and the receiver forget the giving of the gift. In other words, when the receiver receives the gift, he or she should not feel that something must now be given in return and the giver should not expect anything in return either. Both should forget that a gift has exchanged hands. True friendship works on this principle. Gifts are exchanged, but nobody ever owes anybody anything. Casual relationships, on the other hand, are based on the principle that the giving of the gift should not be forgotten. Each time I give you something, I expect something in return.

How does this work in practice? Jordaan (1998) lists the following examples: When you collaborate with somebody else, a relationship based on equity requires that all contributions are recorded to make sure that both contribute equally.

However, for a relationship based on communality, the end result is more important than the individual contributions, therefore no contribution records are kept. A second example: When somebody needs your help badly in a relationship based on equity, you will respond to the person's needs in as much as you believe that he or she will be able to return the favour sometime. However, in a relationship based on communality, you will be keenly aware of the person's needs and you will gladly help even if the person is not likely ever to respond to your needs in a similar fashion.

3 Family relationships

The family is a complex system. Its members represent at least two generations and sometimes three when grandparents are included in the system. In some societies, the family system is an extended group, which includes cousins, aunts and uncles. The family is an important structure. It lays the foundation for a child's development even before the child is born and it prepares the child to acquire skills in interpersonal processes and communication (Nsamenang, 2004).

The relationships that children form with their parents depend on the nature of the attraction between the child and the parent, as well as the personal characteristics of the child. Research studies have revealed five elements of the parent–child relationship (Jordaan, 1998):

- Admiration
- Comradeship
- Trust
- Intimacy
- Emotional closeness

The degree to which these elements are present in the interaction between the parent and the child is an indication of the quality of their relationship. Admiration is expressed through the degree of respect and appreciation that the child shows towards the parent, comradeship through the degree of enjoyment of parental company, trust through the degree to which the child relies on parental integrity, intimacy through the degree to which things are shared with the parent and emotional closeness through the degree to which the child identifies with the parent's joys and sorrows.

Children's personal characteristics determine to what degree they are able to display these qualities in the relationships with their parents. Children should be able to help, forgive and tolerate their parents (demonstrate goodwill); be reasonable and understandable (demonstrate common sense); respect parents' rights; commit themselves and meet obligations (demonstrate fairness); endure hardships for their parents' sake (demonstrate resolution); curb disruptive emotions; and exercise self-discipline (demonstrate moderation) (Jordaan, 1998).

The family is the secure base on which children build the confidence needed to relate to others and the world beyond the family (Nsamenang, 2004). Children learn how to function outside the family by learning how to achieve their social needs within the contexts of their families. These are needs such as: (1) the need for *inclusion;* (2) the need for *control;* and (3) the need for *affection* (Jordaan, 1998).

Humans are inherently social beings and children have to learn how to become part of groups (achieving the need for inclusion), when to lead and when to follow (achieving the need for control) and how to handle emotions in interpersonal interactions (achieving the need for affection). In families with healthy interaction patterns, the child learns how to connect interpersonally, but also learns how to balance being socially dependent on others against being socially independent from them. The child who has learned to achieve the need for inclusion in a healthy manner is likely to grow up to be an individual who shows appropriate social behaviour. He or she would not find it difficult to form interpersonal relationships, but would also be able to distance him- or herself from others and be happy to be left alone. The child who comes from a family in which he or she has been carefully guided to take decisions and to accept responsibility (achieving the need for control in a healthy manner) is likely to grow up to be an individual who functions in a democratic fashion, taking the lead or following the suggestions of others, depending on the situation. The child whose emotions have been handled in a rational manner (achieving the need for affection in a healthy way) is likely to grow up to be an individual who understands the emotional needs of others and who knows when to conduct a relationship on an emotional level and when to distance him- or herself emotionally (Jordaan, 1998).

The fact that children grow up and leave their family of origin does not mean that their relationship with their family comes to an end. The basic qualities of the parent–child relationship are still maintained even when children start their own families, but as family structures change, the interpersonal relationships in the family evolve. New relationships develop as new family members arrive (for example, grandparent–grandchild relationships, or a new partner after divorce or the death of a spouse). Other changes are more subtle. For example, in late adulthood family roles become more androgynous, with males appearing more nurturing and females becoming more assertive, which may be especially apparent in grandparenting roles (Duncan, Van Niekerk and Mufamadi, 2003).

4 Love relationships

Although we know quite a lot about what makes people like each other, our understanding of love is more limited. Love is difficult to observe and study scientifically, yet it is a central issue in most people's lives. We know that being in love differs from merely liking somebody in that it includes feelings of passion, sexual desire, closeness, fascination and caring (Feldman, 2003:460). We also know that love is not a static relationship but that it evolves over time. When people fall in love, their feelings are consumed by passion and an encompassing desire to know more about the other person, but as the relationship develops, it loses some of its passion and gains in care and commitment. Based on these understandings, most researchers distinguish two kinds of love, namely romantic love and companionate love. Romantic love has strong components of sexuality and infatuation and often predominates in the early part of a love relationship. Companionate love occurs when one desires to have the other person near and when one has a deep, caring affection for the person (Santrock, 2003:688). However, the most comprehensive description of love is provided by the psychologist Robert Sternberg.

According to Sternberg (1986), love has three components, namely passion, intimacy and commitment. Passion is the component people most strongly associate with being in love. It includes strong emotions, sexual attraction and an encompassing interest in the other person. Intimacy refers to individuals' desire to touch each other physically and to be emotionally close to each other. They share things, learn to trust each other and become committed to each other. Commitment is a voluntary decision to maintain the relationship on a long-term basis.

The kind of love one experiences depends on the mixture of components it consists of. The most complete form of love is consummate love, which contains all three of the components. Romantic love includes intimacy and passion, but lacks commitment. Companionate love has intimacy and commitment, but less passion. Being infatuated with somebody (fatuous love) is love from a distance. There is no intimacy, but you experience passion and commitment.

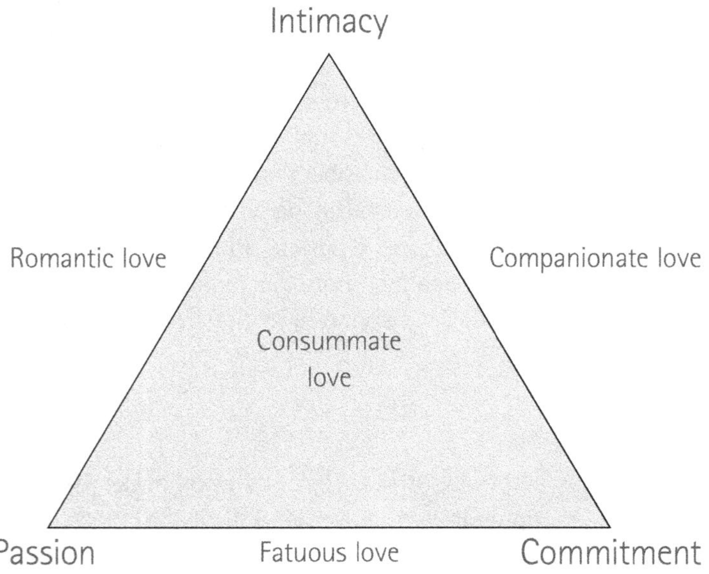

Figure 1 Robert Sternberg's triangle of love

Love relationships are often institutionalised. Marriage is the most common example of this, but not the only one. Any process that two individuals go through to confirm their commitment to one another is in fact a form of institutionalisation, thus the institutionalisation of a love relationship can vary from a private informal agreement between two individuals to a formal public declaration of commitment.

Institutionalisation often assumes a model for the relationship. Such a model is not only an example of how the relationship should be structured and conducted, but is often meant to provide a norm for the relationship (Jordaan, 1998). In other words, the success or failure of the relationship is judged in terms of the criteria provided by the model. The institution of marriage, for example, has assumed three models over the years. These are the patriarchal, the partnership and the egalitarian models of marriage (Jordaan, 1998).

According to the *patriarchal model*, husband and wife are not considered to be equal in the relationship. The husband is sovereign, possesses power and exercises control. He is expected to be strong, rational and restrained. The wife is supposed to be dependent, loving and emotional and a full-time homemaker. Her only means of exercising control is through subtle manipulation. The *partnership model* sees the husband and wife as companions and friends, with the tacit understanding that the husband's interests are decisive. He provides leadership and is rational, but also approachable and emotional in his dealings with his wife and children. The wife may be a part-time breadwinner or engage in activities outside the house, but her main task remains that of homemaker. Although she is expected to show some intellectual ability and display a measure of independence, she is also expected to be motherly, loving and emotional. The *egalitarian model* sees husbands and wives as equals. There is a respected symmetry in the way in which they regard and treat each other as equals. Both parties are breadwinners in their own right – both have careers and they adapt their role divisions in and around the house accordingly. Although the husband is still expected to be rational, he should also be able to express his emotions more freely and, in addition to her emotionality, the wife is expected to be as rational and self-actualising as her husband (Jordaan, 1998).

Bibliography

Derrida, J. 1995. *The gift of death.* Chicago: University of Chicago Press.

Duncan, N., Van Niekerk, A. and Mufamadi, J. 2003. Developmental psychology: A life-span perspective. In L. Nicholas (Ed), *Introduction to psychology.* Cape Town: UCT Press.

Feldman, R.S. 2003. *Essentials of understanding psychology.* 5th edition. New York: McGraw Hill.

Jordaan, W. 1998. Interpersonal relationships. In W. Jordaan and J. Jordaan, *People in context.* 3rd edition. Johannesburg: Heinemann.

Nsamenang, B. 2004. The intersection of traditional African education with school learning. In L. Swartz, C. de la Rey and N. Duncan (Eds), *Psychology: An introduction.* Cape Town: Oxford University Press.

Santrock, J.W. 2003. *Psychology.* 7th edition. New York: McGraw-Hill.

Sternberg, R.J. 1986. A triangular theory of love. *Psychological Review,* 93, 119–135.

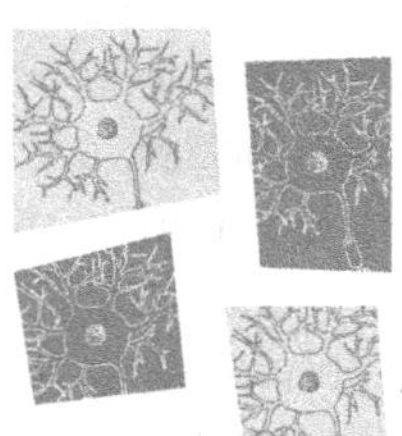

Learning: Associative learning

You may have heard someone say: 'I do not mind the heat; I have become conditioned to it'. This means that the person's body has learned to adjust successfully to hot weather. *Conditioning* is the kind of learning that happens on an automatic level. We do not deliberately learn a conditioned response. The response occurs because of the spontaneous or automatic association of one event or stimulus with another. The essence of associative learning is the pairing or association of stimulus and response.

1 Classical conditioning

Classical conditioning refers to the type of learning that takes place when a response usually elicited by one stimulus is then associated with a different stimulus that normally would not lead to that response. This sounds complicated, so let's examine it further.

The first person to provide experimental proof of classical conditioning was Ivan Pavlov, a Russian scientist, who was studying digestion in dogs. He noticed that not only did dogs produce saliva when they saw or smelt food, but they also did so when they heard sounds associated with food (such as the footsteps of the person coming to feed them) before the food was produced. Pavlov then developed an experiment to investigate this phenomenon. He rang a bell just before he gave food to the dogs. A ringing bell is a stimulus that does not normally lead to salivation, but the dogs learned to associate the bell with food and so the bell triggered the response that normally appeared with food. In other words, the dogs became conditioned to salivate in response to a new stimulus (the bell). This is an illustration of *classical conditioning.*

We can break down the elements of classical conditioning as follows:

- *An unconditioned stimulus* (unconditioned = not conditioned or not associated with something). This is a stimulus that causes the subject to respond in a specific way before any learning has taken place. In the example of Pavlov's experiment, the food is the unconditioned stimulus. Right from the beginning, the food caused the dogs to salivate.

- *An unconditioned response.* This is the response to an unconditioned stimulus. Dogs automatically produce saliva (to aid digestion) when they see or smell food. Salivation is not a conditioned or learned response.
- *A conditioned stimulus.* This is a stimulus that initially is neutral, but through association (that is, being paired with an unconditioned stimulus), it may produce the desired response when presented without the unconditioned stimulus. In Pavlov's experiment, the bell is the conditioned stimulus. At first the bell would not have produced salivation in the dogs. However, when it was rung just before the food was presented, the dogs became conditioned to the fact that the bell signalled that the food was coming. After they had made this association, the dogs salivated when they heard the bell, even if they could not see or smell food. The bell became the conditioned stimulus – the dogs learned that it was associated with food (the unconditioned stimulus).
- *A conditioned response.* This is the response that follows the conditioned stimulus. At first, salivation was the unconditioned response to food (it happened automatically). After the bell was paired or associated with food, the bell became the conditioned stimulus. The dogs' salivation after hearing the bell therefore became the conditioned response to the conditioned stimulus (the bell). In this way, the salivation became a learned or conditioned response because a bell would not normally trigger salivation.

Classical conditioning can take place in humans as well. Certain phobias or irrational fears are the result of classical conditioning. For example, if a very young child hears a terrible noise every time he or she tries to play with a puppy, the child may acquire a fear of puppies. A puppy does not normally trigger feelings of fear, but in this example the puppy becomes the conditioned stimulus (because it is paired with a frightening noise) for the fear response.

1.1 Principles of classical conditioning

Learning a conditioned response depends on reinforcement. *Reinforcement* means strengthening the likelihood of a response. Classical conditioning is reinforced when the conditioned stimulus is followed immediately by the unconditioned stimulus. For example, the dogs are likely to continue salivating when they hear the bell if food is presented shortly after it is rung. If the food is never presented after the bell, the dogs will soon stop salivating when they hear the bell and the conditioned response will fade away. The disappearance of a previously learned response is called *extinction.* However, if the bell is rung the next day after the response has disappeared, the dogs may again expect food and may salivate again. This is called *spontaneous recovery* and refers to the reappearance of a response which seems to have been extinguished.

Once a response to a conditioned stimulus is learned, the conditioning paradigm can be extended to include other stimuli as well. If a new neutral (unconditioned) stimulus is paired with the conditioned stimulus, the new stimulus can become a conditioned stimulus as well. For example, if a bright red light is flashed and then the bell is rung (just before the food is presented), the dogs will learn to associate the red light with the bell and soon the red light alone will cause an increase in saliva production. This is called *higher order conditioning.* Higher order conditioning means that conditioning goes one or more steps further than the original conditioning.

The effect of a conditioned stimulus can also be extended to include other similar stimuli. This means that, after conditioning, stimuli that are similar to the conditioned stimulus may also trigger the same response. This is called *stimulus generalisation,* which refers to the tendency to respond to similar but not identical stimuli. The response to the conditioned stimulus becomes 'generalised' to other stimuli. For example, a boy who burned his fingers with matches may not only be afraid of matches but also of other kinds of flame, such as candles, fires and lighters. In effect, the boy's response to matches has become extended or generalised to similar stimuli. Stimulus generalisation can also serve an adaptive function, because in everyday life we have to cope with a variety of stimuli. We cannot learn how to respond to each and every stimulus we encounter, but if we have learned to cope with one kind of stimulus, we are then better able to cope with similar stimulus situations.

In contrast, stimulus discrimination can also occur. This means that the animal or person can discriminate or detect differences among similar stimuli and only respond to a specific stimulus. When stimulus discrimination occurs, the animal or person that has learned a response to a particular stimulus does not respond with the same response to new and similar stimuli. For example, a dog can be conditioned to discriminate between the sounds of different bells (similar stimuli). In this instance, the dog would learn that the sound of only one kind of bell is followed by food and that other bells do not signify food.

2 Operant conditioning

Operant conditioning is another form of learning by association. In *operant conditioning,* the learning that takes place depends on the *consequences* of the response that the person makes. For example, learning may take place because a certain type of response is rewarded or punished. We know, for example, that if we break the speed limit we are likely to get a fine. Having to pay a fine is a consequence of a certain type of behaviour (travelling too fast) and a fine is a form of punishment. We have learned that we have to drive within the speed limit in order to avoid the punishment. This is not an automatic response; it is something we have to actively do. Another term for 'doing' something is 'operating on' the environment. This is why this form of learning is called operant conditioning.

Learning usually takes place because of the consequences of the action or operation. In operant conditioning, responses are most often voluntary. For example, if you want to use your computer, you know that you have to switch it on first. When you push the right button, the computer comes on. Your action is reinforced by the fact that the computer starts working. In other words, you have learned through operant conditioning that the computer will work when you switch it on. However, if you pushed the wrong button and the computer did not switch on, your action would not be reinforced. You would then learn through operant conditioning that pushing that particular button does not lead to the desired result.

Operant conditioning does not always involve producing an action; it sometimes involves withholding an action or not responding. For example, if you get an electric shock each time you touch an electric fence, you will learn not to touch the fence (that is, to stop responding). This is also a form of operant conditioning.

An American psychologist, Skinner, became well known for the experimental procedure he developed to demonstrate the principles of operant conditioning. The following is a typical experiment: A hungry rat is placed in a small box. There is nothing in the box except a small handle and an empty food tray. The rat is motivated to look for food because it is hungry. While the rat is exploring the box, it accidentally steps on the handle and a food pellet drops onto the tray. At this stage, the rat does not associate stepping on the handle with the food. However, while exploring the box further, it again accidentally steps on the handle and the food appears. The rat soon learns that every time it steps on the handle, food appears. The rat has learned this through the process of operant conditioning.

Operant conditioning explains most of our everyday behaviour. It is often used by parents and teachers to shape children's behaviour. For example, children are rewarded for good behaviour with praise, or a star, in order to reinforce the occurrence of good behaviour. In psychology, operant conditioning can be used to change other adults' or children's behaviour as well as our own. Operant conditioning is based on the notion that behaviours that are reinforced or rewarded are likely to be repeated and behaviours that are punished are not. Remember also that rewards do not mean the same thing to everyone. For example, if a child does not like green sweets and you try to offer one as a reward for good behaviour, you may find that the 'reward' does not work. This is why it is better to talk about a 'reinforcer' rather than a reward. A reinforcer is anything that follows a response and increases the likelihood that the desired response will occur again. The differences between classical and operant conditioning are summarised in Table 1.

Table 1 A comparison of classical and operant conditioning (adapted from Coon, 2005)

	Classical conditioning	Operant conditioning
Type of response	Automatic, reflex	Voluntary
Reinforcement	A conditioned stimulus is associated with an unconditioned stimulus and the reinforcement occurs before the response	Reinforcement occurs after the response
Activity of learner	Passive	Active
Nature of learning	A neutral stimulus becomes a conditioned stimulus through association with an unconditioned stimulus	The likelihood of a response is influenced by the consequences or reinforcement that follows

2.1 Principles of operant conditioning

In operant conditioning, new behaviours are learned because they are reinforced. Reinforcement is most effective when it occurs immediately after the desired response is produced. For example, in the experiment with the rat, if the food pellet appeared some time after the rat stepped on the handle, the rat would not associate the action (stepping on the handle) with the food. Here is another example: Imagine you are trying to teach your daughter to be more polite. If you praise her immediately after she says 'please' or 'thank you', she is likely to feel good and to say 'please' or 'thank you' again when the situation demands it. If, however, you praise her some time later, the praise (reinforcement) is not likely to be as effective. The rule is that the shorter the time between response and reinforcement, the better. Responses that are not reinforced gradually fade away or are extinguished.

The two examples given here illustrate positive reinforcement. Positive reinforcement occurs when a pleasant or desirable reinforcer follows a response. Operant conditioning can also be reinforced by negative reinforcement, which occurs when making a response removes an unpleasant event. For example, if you take a pill that relieves a headache, you learn through operant conditioning that your action (taking the pill) removes an unpleasant event (the headache). A negative reinforcer increases the likelihood of a response but does so because the response ends the unpleasant event.

Negative reinforcement is different to punishment. Punishment refers to an unpleasant consequence of a response. If you had to pay a fine every time you said a swear word, the fine would be the punishment. By realising that you will be punished when you swear, you would learn (through operant conditioning) to stop swearing.

Punishment decreases the likelihood that the response (swearing) will occur again, whereas negative reinforcement increases the likelihood of a response. Let's look at an example from Coon (2005): Imagine that you live in a flat next door to a group of young people who play music very loud late at night. You decide to bang on the wall between you to indicate that you are unhappy about the noise. If the volume of the music decreases, you have obtained the desired response (negative reinforcement) and you are likely to bang on the wall again in future if you are bothered by the loud music. However, if the young people do not turn down the music when you bang on the wall, but actually turn it up louder (punishment), you will not bang on the wall again.

Operant conditioning can also take place if reinforcement is not continuous (that is, if every response is not reinforced). We call this *partial reinforcement,* which means that reinforcement does not follow every response and only some are reinforced. For example, when you play the slot machines at a casino, you do not win money (reinforcement) each time you pull the handle. You may win money every now and then at intervals just frequent enough to encourage you to keep on trying. The different schedules of reinforcement are fixed-ratio, variable-ratio, fixed-interval and variable-interval reinforcement schedules:

- *Fixed-ratio schedule.* This means that a fixed number of responses must be made in order to obtain reinforcement. An example of a fixed-ratio schedule of reinforcement would be if the rat is rewarded with a food pellet only after the fifth time that it steps on the handle. The rat soon learns that it has to press the handle five times before it gets the food pellet. Fixed-ratio schedules generally produce good response rates because the reinforcement is predictable. You could use a fixed-ratio schedule of reinforcement to change everyday behaviour. For example, if you wanted to encourage teenagers to help with the housework, you could reward them with extra pocket money after every fifth time they wash the dishes.
- *Variable-ratio schedule.* In this case, the number of responses that the rat must make before it is reinforced is varied. Referring to the previous example, with a variable-ratio schedule, the rat would get the food pellet after an average of five responses. Variable-ratio schedules also produce good response rates. In everyday life, payouts from a slot machine are an example of variable-ratio schedule reinforcement. Because the reinforcement is less predictable, there is greater resistance to extinction (people are tempted to play again 'just in case' they may win).
- *Fixed-interval schedule.* The word 'interval' refers to the passage of time, so reinforcement according to a fixed-interval schedule is reinforcement that is produced for the first correct response after a certain amount of time has passed. In the example of the rat, if the fixed interval for reinforcement is two minutes, it does not matter how many times the rat steps on the handle, it will only get a food pellet for the first time after a period of two minutes.

Fixed-interval schedules produce a moderately good rate of responding, but responses generally occur in spurts. For example, if you have to submit assignments every two months, you are unlikely to work every day (even if you should!). You will probably do very little just after you have submitted one assignment and then work frantically just before the next one is due.

- *Variable-interval schedule.* This is a variation of the fixed-interval schedule – reinforcement is given for the first correct response after different intervals of time. For example, the rat may get a food pellet for correct responses after different time intervals that work out as an average of two minutes. Variable-interval schedules produce a slow, steady response rate that is strongly resistant to extinction. An example of variable-interval reinforcement is trying to get through to a telephone number that is engaged (Coon, 2005). You try repeatedly at different intervals of time, even though you do not know how often you will have to try until you get through (the reinforcement).

Schedules of reinforcement do not work in the same way with punishment. In order to be effective, punishment should occur only after the undesired response. For example, if you want to stop your son throwing stones at an animal, you should punish him each time he does it. If he is punished sometimes and not at other times, he will think it doesn't matter and will not stop the undesirable behaviour. The effectiveness of punishment depends on *timing, consistency* and *intensity.* This means that punishment is effective if it occurs each time the undesirable response occurs (consistency), immediately after the undesirable response occurs (timing) and if it is severe enough (intensity). However, it is important that the severity of the punishment fits the seriousness of the action, or the punishment may not have the desired effect.

In everyday life, punishment is not the only way to control behaviour. If you want to change behaviour, it is best to use a combination of punishment, reinforcement of the desired responses and non-reinforcement of undesirable behaviour. If you have to use punishment, here are some guidelines to bear in mind (Coon, 2005; Sdorow and Rickabaugh, 2002):

1. Do not use punishment if you can stop bad behaviour in other ways (such as praising good behaviour).
2. Punish during or immediately after the bad behaviour. For example, if a child does something wrong, point it out immediately and do not threaten to tell someone (such as the child's father) about it later on.
3. Use the least possible amount of punishment that will change the behaviour. Punishment should be strong enough to stop the bad behaviour, but not excessive. For example, verbal scolding or taking away privileges is preferable to physical punishment.
4. Be consistent. Every incidence of the bad behaviour should be punished. In the case of parents, both parents should agree on the punishment.

5. Expect the punished person to feel angry.
6. Punishment should be aimed at the bad behaviour and not at the child. Try to be kind and respectful. The aim of punishment should be to help the person concerned and not to give vent to your own feelings.
7. Make the effort to reinforce good or desirable behaviour. It is easier and more effective to strengthen and encourage desired behaviour than to punish undesired behaviour.

In the same way that stimulus generalisation occurs in classical conditioning, it also occurs in operant conditioning. In operant conditioning, there is a tendency to respond in a certain way to similar stimulus situations. For example, if you find that a friendly smile results in good service (reinforcement) at the bank, you are likely to use it to get service at the post office and garage too. However, we also learn that there are certain situations in which a smile is inappropriate and would not elicit the desired response (for example in a hijack situation) and this refers to the process of stimulus discrimination.

Bibliography

Coon, D. 2005. *Psychology: A journey.* Belmont, CA: Wadsworth.

Sdorow, L. and Rickabaugh, C. 2002. *Psychology.* 5th edition. New York: McGraw-Hill.

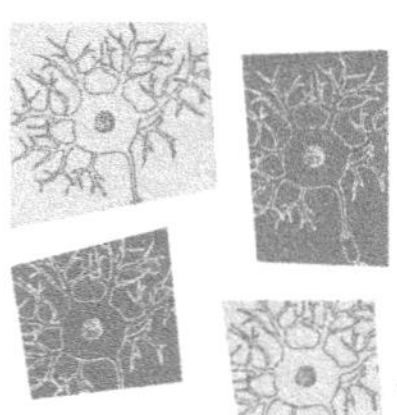

Learning: Cognitive learning

In contrast to the idea that learning takes place through the association of a stimulus with a response (for example as in classical and operant conditioning), cognitive theorists have paid more attention to the cognitive factors that influence the process of learning. Even though classical and operant conditioning rest firmly on the basis of the association between stimulus and response, some cognitive theorists believe that cognitive factors play a role in associative learning because of expectancies – that is, the expectations of how things are associated or connected. In Pavlov's study, we can say that the dogs learned to expect that food would follow the bell. We can see this effect in everyday life. For example, you may find that when you are about to get an injection, your muscles tense up and you hold your breath. This is because you have learned to expect that an injection will hurt and, as a result, your body prepares for pain (Coon, 2005). In classical and operant conditioning, thinking (a cognitive process) plays a role on a low level of awareness. There are other forms of learning that involve thinking at a higher level.

In general terms, *cognitive learning* refers to 'understanding, knowing, anticipating or otherwise making use of information-rich higher mental processes' (Coon, 2005) to facilitate learning. This implies that for learning to occur, the relationship between stimuli or between behaviours (responses) and consequences has to be assessed. This means that cognitive learning is the result of thinking and other cognitive processes.

1 Cognitive maps

One example of cognitive learning is our use of cognitive maps to represent the environments in which we live. A cognitive map is a mental representation of the spatial features of an area, a building, or even the contents of a book. Cognitive maps generally refer to geographical areas, such as a mental map of the route to your home or the environment in which you live. However, there are different kinds of cognitive maps.

When studying, many students find it useful to draw diagrams showing how concepts fit together and this is one form of a cognitive map.

2 Perceptual–motor skills

One form of cognitive learning is seen in the acquisition of perceptual–motor or sensory–motor skills (Jordaan and Jordaan, 1998). Perceptual–motor skills are based on motor movements that are guided by perception. For example, professional tennis players have highly developed perceptual–motor skills. Their actions on the tennis court depend on accurate perception of what other players are doing, the direction and way the ball is moving and the movement of their own body (including balance, co-ordination and speed) in response. There is continual feedback from the external and internal environment that influences their responses.

When you learn a perceptual–motor skill, the first phase involves cognitive processes. You may have a verbal plan to guide you. For example, when you learn to drive, your efforts are often guided by being told what to do, such as 'first check the mirrors, then turn the key to start the motor, then put on the indicator' and so on. The verbal plan also helps you to break down a complex task into smaller and more manageable components so that you can concentrate on one thing at a time. At first you have to think consciously about each step in the process. However, you soon learn to associate some of the skills, such as working the clutch and accelerator together to change gears. If you practise often enough, these sequences of skills become more fluent and fewer mistakes are made. You do not have to concentrate hard on each separate action. With time and practise, the skills become combined in a pattern and you no longer have to think consciously about what you are doing. Driving skills become almost automatic. Your perceptions of all the components of the task become integrated into a learned perceptual–motor skill.

3 Intellectual skills

Intellectual skills are learned – and we never stop learning. We learn by associating one thing with another, or by discriminating between different things. We form concepts to represent things and we learn rules for using the concepts to think and reason. On the highest level, we can think about our own thinking. For example, when you have had an argument with someone, it is good to think about the interaction afterwards and consider what you said, why you said it, the reasons for reacting the way you did and the possibility of other ways of dealing with the situation. This is an example of *metacognition,* which means knowledge of your own cognitive or mental processes.

The acquisition of verbal skills is an example of learning intellectual skills. As children grow older, they are able to use their developing verbal (or language) skills more efficiently and to apply the information they have acquired. For example, Grade 1 learners can name the letters of the alphabet and by Grade 2 can write letters on paper and form words with them. Not only do these children have the information they need (that is, know what letters are), they know how to use them, which is an *intellectual skill.*

Much of cognitive learning takes place through understanding. Formal study at university is a form of cognitive learning. At times, we have all learned things by repetition and memorisation, but learning is more lasting and effective when we discover information on our own. *Discovery learning* refers to skills gained by insight and understanding, through trying new strategies and discovering new solutions (Coon, 2005). The first-year course in psychology is based on guided discovery – students are given guidance and encouragement while also having the freedom to think actively about solving problems and thereby to gain useful knowledge.

Bibliography

Coon, D. 2005. *Psychology: A journey.* Belmont, CA: Wadsworth.

Jordaan, W. and Jordaan, J. 1998. *People in context.* 3rd edition. Johannesburg: Heinemann.

Sdorow, L. and Rickabaugh, C. 2002. *Psychology.* 5th edition. New York: McGraw-Hill.

Learning: Concept of

We all have a general idea of what learning is, even though we may find it difficult to define. *Learning* is formally defined as 'a relatively permanent change in behaviour due to experience' (Coon, 2005:217). This implies that we can see that learning has taken place when there is a change in behaviour. Look at the following example: Nomsa submitted her first assignment late and therefore it was not marked. After that, Nomsa made sure that all her other assignments were submitted before the closing date so that they would be marked and she would receive the credits she needed for admission to the examination. Nomsa learned that late assignments do not get marked (a specific experience) and therefore changed her behaviour so that she submitted all the assignments before the closing date (a relatively permanent change in behaviour). This indicates that learning took place.

Do changes in behaviour always mean that learning has taken place? Not always. Look at the definition of learning again. The change in behaviour has to be 'relatively permanent', which means that it must be long lasting and it must be the result of experience. Our behaviour may change because of temporary conditions such as illness, tiredness or decreased motivation, but this kind of behaviour change is not the result of learning. Consider this example: Anna is usually a very kind and patient person who is prepared to spend time helping others. One day when she was not feeling well and had a bad headache, she got very impatient and irritable with the children who were making a noise. The next day, when she felt better, she was again patient and caring. This change in behaviour does not reflect learning – it merely shows that there are many factors (apart from learning) that can affect behaviour. The change in Anna's behaviour was temporary and was the result of not feeling well. The change was not the result of learning through experience. When learning has taken place, the change in behaviour is long lasting and is caused by certain experiences.

Most human behaviour is learned behaviour. It would be hard to imagine what life would be like if we lost everything we had learned. We would not know how to speak, to interact with others, to write and to do the things we enjoy.

Generally speaking, there are three types of learning. The first is called *associative learning,* because learning takes place by associating one thing or event with another. Classical and operant conditioning are forms of associative learning. The second type of learning is called *cognitive learning,* because learning involves thinking. The third type of learning is *social learning,* which refers to the way we acquire social behaviours.

Bibliography

Coon, D. 2005. *Psychology: A journey.* Belmont, CA: Wadsworth.

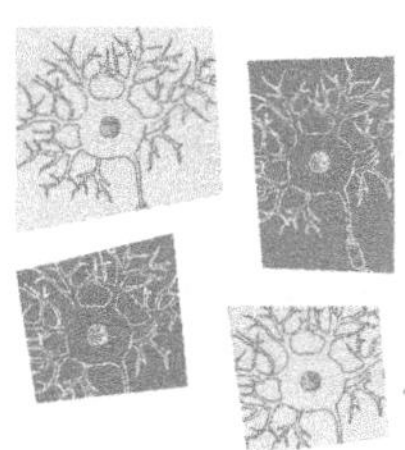

Learning: Social learning

Social learning refers to the way we learn through interacting with other people. It illustrates the fact that not all learning is formal but also happens informally in everyday life.

One of the ways in which social learning takes place is through *operant* social learning. Many parents and teachers use operant social learning to encourage good behaviour in children. For example, young children may be given stars at school to encourage their efforts. In other words, we learn socially acceptable or desirable behaviour through being rewarded for appropriate behaviour and being punished for bad behaviour. For example, getting a fine for speeding is punishment in terms of operant social learning. Being praised for doing well is a reinforcer in terms of operant social learning.

Whether or not social acts reinforce behaviour depends a lot on social needs. For example, there is a basic human need for security, therefore we try, through our behaviour, to gain social acceptance and approval from others in order to meet our need for security (Jordaan and Jordaan, 1998). The effectiveness of social reinforcement also depends on other factors, such as the type of reinforcement that is offered and the strength of motivation to produce the socially desired behaviour.

Another way that social learning occurs is through observation. *Observational learning* means learning by watching and imitating the behaviour of others and observing the consequences of those actions. Observational learning occurs when the way we behave or respond is influenced by observing others, who are called *models* (Weiten, 2001). The model serves as an example and, through observation, the observer may learn new responses, learn when those responses are appropriate (on the basis of their consequences) and learn general rules that can be applied to different situations (Coon, 2005).

Albert Bandura (1986) studied observational learning extensively. According to Bandura, there are four essential components to observational learning:

1. *Attention.* You must pay attention to the model's behaviour and the consequences of that behaviour.
2. *Retention.* Another word for retention is 'keeping' or 'saving'. You must save a mental representation of what you have observed, in order to be able to use it at a later stage.
3. *Reproduction.* You must be able to reproduce the observed behaviour that you have stored in your memory.
4. *Motivation.* You will only reproduce behaviour you have observed if you are motivated to do so (that is, if the response to your behaviour will be worthwhile).

For example, you may be lonely and want to make friends, but you may feel unsure about yourself in social situations. You want people to see you as pleasant, not as loud and over-assertive. You have a friend who is well liked by others and is very comfortable at social gatherings. At a party, you observe how your friend introduces himself to others and you pay attention to what he does to make people feel comfortable. You make a mental picture in your memory (retention) so that you can use it (reproduction) at the next opportunity. You are motivated to apply what you have learned through observation because you do not want to be lonely. If you can make friends as a result of applying what you have learned through observation, you have obtained reinforcement for using the responses that you learned.

You can see from the components of social learning that *cognitive processes* also play an important role in social and observational learning. Attending, remembering, recalling and deciding on a course of action are all cognitive processes and are components of the learning process.

The cognitive theorists also promote the idea that learning can take place without observable changes in behaviour. Their focus is more on the acquisition of knowledge than on observable behaviour change as an indicator of learning. For example, if you study for hours and hours yet still fail an exam, this does not mean that learning has not taken place. It may mean that other factors (such as anxiety or misunderstanding the questions) affected your performance so that your marks did not provide an accurate indication of how well you had learned. Learning that is not apparent because it is not yet demonstrated is called *latent learning* (Coon, 2005) or hidden learning. Performance on a test is an indication of only some of your information or knowledge. A great deal of what we have learned is never used, mostly because we have not had the occasion to do so. This points to the idea that learning and performance are not necessarily the same thing. In addition, whether or not we act (perform) on what we have learned depends on our motivation. We do not necessarily imitate everything that we observe; we are selective in what we decide to reproduce. What we do depends not only on motivation but also on the consequences of that behaviour (in terms of reinforcement and punishment). We do not even have to experience the consequences ourselves in order to decide whether to imitate a behaviour or not. We can learn from what happens to others. For example, a teenager may decide to try drinking alcohol after seeing an adult drinking and having fun at a party. Having fun is the reinforcement for drinking. However, the teenager may decide not to drink after seeing someone become very ill after drinking or ruining a life through it (punishment).

Although the different types of learning are discussed separately here, it is clear that there are many overlaps. For example, there is an element of cognitive learning in conditioning. In addition, social learning may be regarded as a form of cognitive learning. At times, social learning also rests on operant conditioning principles.

Bibliography

Bandura, A. 1986. *Social foundations of thought and action.* Englewood Cliffs, NJ: Prentice Hall.

Coon, D. 2005. *Psychology: A journey.* Belmont, CA: Wadsworth.

Jordaan, W. and Jordaan, J. 1998. *People in context.* 3rd edition. Johannesburg: Heinemann.

Sdorow, L. and Rickabaugh, C. 2002. *Psychology.* 5th edition. New York: McGraw-Hill.

Weiten, W. 2001. *Psychology: Themes and variations.* 5th edition. Belmont, CA: Wadsworth.

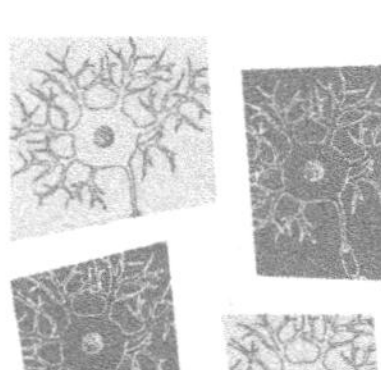

Memory

Our memories are an essential part of who we are. We rely on information in memory for almost everything we do, without realising how much we depend on it. Without our memories, we would struggle to establish our identity and we would have a great deal of difficulty functioning in everyday life. Memory is affected by many factors, such as age, physical health and the kind of activities we do. There is a wide range of what is considered normal memory. Some of us remember things well and others have difficulty.

There are many events that take place before we can remember something and this is why it is important to see memory as a process. There are different aspects of memory that have different functions. We cannot remember everything, but select and organise information that we remember. Memory is an active process that stores, organises and retrieves information.

Memory involves three important phases: (1) encoding, or getting information into memory; (2) storage, or keeping things in our memory; and (3) retrieval, or drawing information from the memory store.

1 Encoding

Before information can be processed in memory, the brain has to encode the information in order to work with it. Encoding refers to the process of forming a memory code. If we compare memory to working with a computer, encoding is similar to transforming information into a code of numbers and letters by entering data using the keyboard.

When you form a memory code of something or some event, you remember what things looked like or what they meant, the associated sounds and so on. We can only encode information in memory if we pay attention to the information we wish to remember. There is so much information in our environment that we are unable to process or remember all of it. By paying attention to and disregarding some information, you decrease the amount of information so that it is more manageable. Attention is a very important aspect of remembering. For example, if you sit through a meeting or class and do not pay attention, you are unlikely to remember what was said. When you pay attention, you focus on certain stimuli and events and filter out the things that are not important. In this way, you select what is relevant and you are more likely to remember it.

There are different strategies to improve our memory by making encoding more effective. The first of these is elaboration, or linking one fact to other bits of information. You can do this by thinking of examples that illustrate an idea. For example, you may have difficulty remembering the meaning of the word 'hypothesise', but you will remember it immediately if you use it in an everyday personal context, such as: 'There are heavy clouds about and I hypothesise that it may rain, so I must take my umbrella to work'.

Secondly, another way of improving encoding is through using visual imagery. You can create pictures or visual images of things you want to remember. For example, if you want to remember to post a letter, buy bread and get a book from the library after work, it would help you remember all three if you make a mental picture of a letter, a loaf of bread and a book. You could use other forms of mental imagery as well, such as forming a semantic code based on word meanings. For example, if you want to remember someone's name, it may help to link the name with a recognisable feature of that person. If you meet someone called Nonnie who has very attractive eyes, you could link 'Nonnie' and 'nice eyes' to remember her name.

Thirdly, encoding is easier when you can make the information personally meaningful. For example, you read that fears can develop through classical conditioning and you apply this to your own fear of snakes. By applying the information to your own experience, you are likely to remember what classical conditioning is.

When the information is encoded, it is available for further processing in the brain. If information is not encoded, it will not be remembered in future.

2 Storage

Encoded information is ready for storage in memory. Storage involves holding or maintaining information in the memory store. If we think about computers again, storage is similar to saving information in a file on the computer's hard disk. Storage is usually seen as involving different stages.

2.1 Sensory memory

Information is kept in its original sensory form for a very brief time (a fraction of a second). It is so brief that you are often only aware of an after image rather than the stimulus itself. For example, if you are standing in the dark and move a torch quickly in a circle, you will not see one point of light from the torch. You will see a continuous circle, which is the after image of the torchlight. We do not remember everything we see and hear (sensory information). Information is held in sensory memory just long enough for part of it to be selected for longer storage.

2.2 Short-term memory

Short-term memory is a temporary store for small amounts of information. Short-term memories are encoded as images or as sounds. We keep information in short-term memory for approximately 20 seconds. However, you can keep information in short-term memory for much longer if you keep rehearsing it. Rehearsal is repeatedly verbalising or thinking about the information. For example, imagine that you look up a new telephone number in the book and dial it straight away. About half an hour later, you need that telephone number again, but you cannot remember it and have to look it up again. However, if you do not get through the first time and keep repeating the number every time you try, you are likely to remember the number for much longer. Rehearsal helps us to remember and keeps the information in memory. We forget information in short-term memory when other events or information interfere with the storage process or compete for our attention.

Unfortunately, the capacity of short-term memory is limited. We can only keep a certain amount of information in our heads. Research has shown that we can process approximately seven bits of information efficiently at any one time. The golden rule is seven plus or minus two. This means that we can deal most efficiently with between five (7 – 2 = 5) and nine (7 + 2 = 9) bits of information at a time, so if you want to learn lots of facts, organise them in groups of approximately seven keywords in a group and you are more likely to remember them.

Short-term memory capacity can be increased by breaking down large amounts of information into smaller chunks. For example, it is difficult to remember a 10-digit cell number such as 0956380271, but if you break it down into 'zero nine five – six three eight – zero two – seven one', you are more likely to remember it.

Short-term memory is not just a temporary storage place where information that is rehearsed is passed on to long-term memory and information that is not rehearsed is lost. Recent research has revealed that there is a kind of short-term memory called *working memory* (Baddeley, 1990) that helps us cope with new situations and to solve problems. Working memory allows us to draw on and work with all kinds of information from memory, as well the information that is present, to apply to new situations. Working memory is described as the 'desktop' of memory, or a mental notebook. Baddeley suggested that there are various components of working memory:

- *A phonological loop.* This allows access to verbal information or sounds. For example, if you wanted to recall a telephone number, it would be accessed by the phonological loop.

- *A visuospatial sketchpad.* This allows you to manipulate visual images. For example, if you want to work out another route home to avoid traffic, you would use your visuospatial sketchpad.
- *The executive control system.* This controls, monitors and regulates the information needed for reasoning and problem solving.
- *Long-term knowledge store.* Sometimes you need to draw information from long-term memory for use in solving a particular problem. For example, you may be struggling to operate a new cellphone and you draw on information in your long-term memory where the knowledge of how you operated a previous phone was stored in order to solve the problem with your new phone.

2.3 Long-term memory

Long-term memory is the store where information is held for long periods of time. The capacity of long-term memory is believed to be unlimited and we can remember an astounding amount of information. The more you know, the easier it is to add to the long-term memory store. We select information to store in long-term memory on the basis of the meaning and importance of that information. The more meaningful and important it is, the more likely it is to be stored.

We do not store every single experience in long-term memory, but it is generally believed that information held in long-term memory is permanent. You may wonder whether this is true when you struggle to remember something. When we cannot remember something, this is because we cannot retrieve or find it – not because it is not there. For example, you meet up with a school friend whom you have not seen for some time and she asks you about an event at the matric dance. You initially do not remember the event. However, when she starts talking about it, you suddenly remember it. You thought you did not remember, but the information was there. Your friend provided *cues* to help you retrieve the information that you did not remember on your own.

There are different types of long-term memory. The main division is between declarative and non-declarative or procedural memory.

2.3.1 Declarative memory

The declarative memory system refers to the store of explicit, factual information. For example, information about names, places, facts and events is stored in declarative memory. If you ask the question: 'What … ?', the answer should be in declarative memory. For example, the answer to the question: 'What did you learn today?' lies in the declarative memory system. We consciously think about facts in declarative memory and for this reason it is also called explicit memory.

There are two types of declarative memory: semantic memory and episodic memory. Semantic memory refers to the store of general knowledge, such as who is the president of the country, as well as the meaning of words and the relation between words and concepts. Semantic memory is not related to the specific time when the information was learned. However, episodic memory refers to remembering events and personal experiences that are related to specific times, such as what you were doing when Nelson Mandela was released from prison.

2.3.2 Non-declarative memory

The non-declarative memory system deals with actions, perceptual-motor skills, conditioned responses and implicit memories. It is also called the procedural memory system and it answers the question: 'How … ?' For example, the answer to the question: 'How did you do that?' would be found in the procedural memory system. Memory for procedural or perceptual–motor skills is mostly unconscious in the sense that we are not consciously aware of it. For this reason, it is also called implicit memory.

This example should help you remember the difference between declarative and non-declarative memory: You may know the rules of the road and these are stored in declarative memory, but your memory of how to change gears smoothly while you are driving is stored in non-declarative or procedural memory.

Although there are many theories to explain long-term memory, there is still no conclusive evidence for explaining the way in which the brain holds the enormous amount of information you have so that you can retrieve it when you need it.

3 Retrieval

Retrieval describes the process of getting stored information out of memory. A similar process in working with a computer would be finding and opening files to access information that is stored on the disk.

Retrieval is made easier when we have cues or stimuli that help us to access our memories. For example, imagine that you cannot remember the name of the structure that links the left and right hemispheres of the brain. If I said the word 'corpus', you would probably find it easy to remember the word 'collosum' and complete the name of the structure. Many of us have experienced the 'tip-of-the-tongue phenomenon', which refers to the temporary inability to remember something, although we are sure we know the information. For example, you may be unable to recall the name of a street in the area where you grew up, yet you are sure that you do know the name. This phenomenon is an example of a failure in retrieval of stored information.

When we have difficulty remembering, it also helps if we re-create the context of whatever it is we are trying to remember. For example, you may remember that you have to telephone someone but you are not sure who, so you imagine yourself in the place where you were standing when you received the message to phone, to whom you were talking and what you were talking about. When you recreate the context, it provides cues to help you remember whom you had to call. These are called context cues. Many of us have the experience of walking into a room to get something and then not remembering what it is we have to get. If we go back to what we were doing before we walked into the room, we are likely to remember what it is we were supposed to do.

There are cultural influences on the ways in which we encode information and events and how easily they are remembered. For example, many traditional African cultures have a strong oral tradition, which means that people learn predominantly through the spoken (rather than the written) word by speaking and telling stories. People from these cultures find it easier to encode information after hearing it than reading it (Plotnik, 2002).

4 Forgetting

Forgetting refers to the process of being unable to retrieve the information we have stored in memory. Because memory is such a complex process, there is no easy explanation of why we forget. It could be the result of faulty coding, problems with storage or retrieval, or a combination of any of these. Here are some reasons for forgetting (from Weiten, 2001):

4.1 Ineffective coding

Sometimes we think we have forgotten something when in fact we have actually never remembered it. This happens when we have not paid sufficient attention. The material is then not *coded,* or it is not coded effectively. When you cannot remember what you read in your book, it is probably the result of ineffective coding.

4.2 Decay

Some theorists suggest that we forget things after a time because the physiological mechanisms that are responsible for memories (called memory traces) fade away or decay. However, forgetting does not only depend on the amount of time that passes since learning, but also on the amount, complexity and type of information that you have to remember during that time (Weiten, 2001). The greater the amount and complexity of the information, the more likely you are to forget. In addition, memories that are not retrieved or used become weaker over time. We are more likely to remember the things that are important to us or have personal meaning.

4.3 Interference

One reason why we forget information is that there is competition from other material that interferes with the memory process. For example, if you learn a shopping list and then you have to complete a complex arithmetic task, you are likely to have difficulty remembering the shopping list later on. Some people find that when they are on their way to do something and get interrupted by a phone call, they forget what it is that they have to do. The phone call competes for their attention and serves as interference.

4.4 Retrieval failure

Sometimes you remember things that you could not remember before. This may be because the situation you are in provides a good cue for what you want to remember. The more similar the cue is to the memory code, the easier it is to remember.

4.5 Motivated forgetting

Sometimes we want or need to forget something; in other words, we have internal motivation to forget something. For example, you may want to forget an incident in the past, such as when you behaved badly at a friend's party, because it embarrasses you and you feel bad when you remember it.

Memory is another process that helps to explain why our experience of the world is subjective. Your memory of a particular event can be influenced by how much attention you have given it, the meaning you ascribe to it, how you link your experience to existing knowledge, how you search your memory store and so on. No two people perceive, interpret and remember events in exactly the same way.

5 Improve your memory

If you need to memorise information, here are some ways to improve your memory skills (adapted from Coon, 2005; and Weiten, 2001):

1. *Recitation.* By summarising aloud while you are learning, you not only provide instant feedback, but you also practise retrieving the information you are learning.
2. *Rehearsal.* The more you rehearse, the better you will remember. When you rehearse, look for links to existing knowledge to help you remember.
3. *Selection.* Select key words or important facts to provide cues for the information you need to remember.
4. *Organisation.* Organise information into smaller and more manageable chunks.
5. *Whole learning.* Try to learn an overall scheme of what you need to learn rather than concentrate on separate parts. If there is a lot of information, you can learn the parts separately and then learn to link them.
6. *Serial position.* When you have to learn bits of information in a sequence, remember that you are likely to make mistakes in the middle of the sequence

or list and so you have to pay particular attention to the bits in the middle. We tend to remember the things that come first and last better than those in the middle.

7. *Cues and strategies.* Try to add cues to what you are learning. If you cannot remember a fact, use a strategy such as working through the alphabet to prompt retrieval of the information you need.
8. *Over-learning and review.* When you have acquired the information, learn it again to make sure you have it. Review the information again shortly before you have a test.
9. *Spaced practise.* Alternate your study sessions with brief rest periods to make sure that you are paying attention to what you are learning.
10. *Sleeping and eating.* Sleeping after learning helps to consolidate the remembered material. You are not likely to perform well if you are hungry.

Bibliography

Baddeley, A. 1990. *Human memory.* Needham Heights, MA: Allyn & Bacon.

Coon, D. 2005. Psychology: A *journey.* Belmont, CA: Wadsworth.

Jordaan, W. and Jordaan, J. 1998. *People in context.* 3rd edition. Johannesburg: Heinemann.

Plotnik, R. 2002. *Introduction to* psychology. 6th edition. Belmont, CA: Wadsworth.

Sdorow, L. and Rickabaugh, C. 2002. *Psychology*. 5th edition. New York: McGraw-Hill.

Weiten, W. 2001. *Psychology: Themes and variations.* 5th edition. Belmont, CA: Wadsworth.

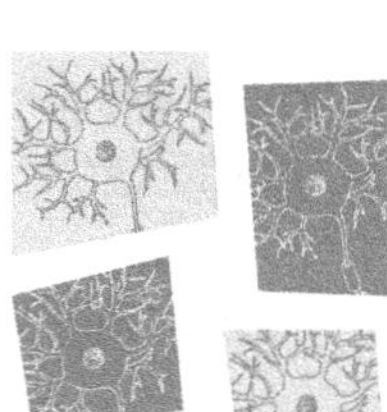

Motivation: The nature of motivated behaviour

The concept of motivation relates to other concepts in psychology, such as emotions, consciousness and free will. It is a multidimensional concept that covers a diverse set of brain-mind processes, but, broadly speaking, motivation refers to all the mental activities that compel organisms into action (Panksepp, 2004). Machines do not display motivated behaviour. There is no motivation linked in somewhere between the input a machine receives and the output it produces. The ability to choose plays a role in this. We do not think of the acceleration of a car as motivated behaviour because the car cannot choose whether or not it wants to accelerate. We only describe actions as motivated behaviour when an organism decides for itself what course of action it should take. However, the choice does not happen randomly. There is always a reason for choosing one option rather than another, thus motivated behaviour is action that is chosen deliberately.

1 Dimensions of motivation

There are two things one should note about a deliberately chosen action. First, we are not necessarily aware of the reasons for our actions. In everyday behaviour, we sometimes know precisely why we choose to act in a particular way. We may sometimes act without thinking, but afterwards we are still able to trace back the reasons for the action. However, according to psychoanalytic theory, we may also be motivated by unconscious factors. In other words, sometimes the reasons for our actions remain hidden from ourselves, even when we try to explain them.

The second point we should note about a deliberately chosen action is that the reasons for our actions may be *intrinsic* or *extrinsic* to ourselves. We may be motivated by our internal psycho-physiological states (by being hungry or angry, for instance), or by external factors in the environment (such as finding a shady spot on a hot day or owning a beautiful house).

These characteristics of the reasons for our actions indicate the basic dimensions of motivated behaviour, namely the *conscious versus unconscious* nature of motivation and the *intrinsic versus extrinsic* nature of motivation.

2 The sources of motivation

There are many theories of motivation, but they can be categorised in terms of what they consider to be the basis of motivated behaviour. There are at least four sources of motivation:

- Biological patterns of behaviour
- Bodily homeostasis
- Optimum arousal
- Cognition (Santrock, 2003:315–316)

2.1 Biological patterns of behaviour

Biological patterns of behaviour are called *instincts.* An instinct is an inherited (innate) tendency to carry out a particular pattern of behaviour in specific circumstances. Early psychologists like William McDougall and Sigmund Freud were influenced strongly by Charles Darwin's theory of evolution and attributed human motivation to instincts (Sdorow and Rickabaugh, 2002:328). Freud (1925) considered the instincts that motivate sex and aggression as major factors in human personality. For Freud, all instincts have a source, a goal, an object and an impetus. The source of an instinct is the part of the body where biological stimulation occurs. The goal of an instinct is the experience of satisfaction (psychological gratification) that results from the reduction or removal of the biological stimulation. The object of an instinct is anything that mediates the reduction or removal of the biological stimulation, thus the object offers psychological gratification. The impetus of an instinct is its intensity or driving force. The stronger the biological stimulation, the more energy required to reduce or remove the stimulation. This implies greater intensity (impetus) of the instinct.

Our instinctive behaviours are based on core emotional systems in the brain and all mammals, including humans, have brain systems for the following:

- Becoming angry if access to resources is thwarted (a rage system)
- Becoming scared when bodily well-being is threatened (a fear system)
- Sexual desires (a lust system)
- Urges to exhibit loving attention toward our offspring (a care system)
- Feelings of separation distress when we have lost contact with loved ones (a panic system)
- The boisterous joyousness of rough-and-tumble playfulness (a play system)
- Exploratory activity directed at searching and foraging for resources (a seeking system)

These brain processes help us adapt and survive in our environments (Panksepp, 2004).

2.2 Homeostasis

The body maintains a steady state of physiological equilibrium. This is known as *bodily homeostasis.* Any deviation from equilibrium that is caused by physiological deprivation results in a *need,* which is characterised by a state of tension called a *drive.* A drive is a motivational force that compels individuals to act in a manner that would counter the state of deprivation, fulfil the need and reduce the tension (Sdorow and Rickabaugh, 2002:328).

The drive model of homeostasis defines a motivational cycle (Jordaan, 1998). A drive condition emerges as a result of deprivation. For example, when the body loses water through perspiration, receptor cells in the hypothalamus signal a need that one experiences as thirst. This leads to goal-oriented, preparatory activities (looking for water), which help one to locate an object (reinforcer) that will reduce the intensity of the need (a tap or a place to buy a bottle of water). The reinforcer enables a consummation response (drinking the water), which restores the homeostasis, lowering the need (thirst) and reducing the intensity of the drive (to look for water).

Theories that try to explain motivation as maintenance of homeostasis are referred to as *drive-reduction* theories.

2.3 Optimum arousal

Individuals have characteristic *levels of physical arousal.* Our characteristic level of arousal is determined by the characteristic ratio between the levels of sympathic and parasympathic activity of our autonomic nervous system. Our level of arousal varies in response to sensory input. When we are under-stimulated, the level of arousal drops below our characteristic level of arousal and when we are overstimulated it rises above it. People differ with regard to their characteristic levels of arousal. Some need highly stimulating environments (high sensation seekers), while others prefer serene and calm circumstances (low sensation seekers). However, regardless of the kind of sensation seeker one is, if one's levels of stimulation and activity are too low, one will try to increase them by seeking stimulation.

The arousal approaches to motivation go beyond the drive reduction theories of motivation in the sense that motivation is not simply a matter of trying to maintain homeostasis, but rather a matter of actively seeking stimulation to maintain levels of arousal that are particular to each of us (Feldman, 2003:252; Santrock, 2003:316).

2.4 Cognition

Motivated behaviour cannot be fully understood in terms of the instincts, drives and arousal approaches to motivation. We are also motivated by what we value in the world around us. A wide range of social and cultural factors play a role in motivating people, even where the behaviour is related to biological drives like hunger or thirst. For example, people are motivated not only to eat but to obtain particular kinds of food, or to go to places where they prefer to eat (Jordaan, 1998). These are personally, socially and culturally valued incentives that 'pull' people towards a goal. This is in contrast to instincts, drives and excitement seeking, which are internal states that 'push' people towards goals (Sdorow and Rickabaugh, 2002:329), but the desire to obtain valued external goals is not sufficient to explain motivated behaviour. Internal instincts, drives and arousal work in tandem with external incentives to 'push' and 'pull' behaviour. For example, at the same time that we seek to eat because we feel hungry (pushed behaviour), we are drawn to food that looks appetising (pulled behaviour). Behaviour is motivated from inside (intrinsically) as well as from the outside (extrinsically).

However, not all intrinsic motivation comes from instincts, drives and excitement seeking. Personal cognitive factors such as self-determination, curiosity and challenge also motivate behaviour intrinsically. Some students study hard because they are internally motivated by the challenge of providing high-quality work, while others do so because they want to get high marks or please their parents (external motivation). Although internal motivation often results in improved performance, creativity and self-esteem, highly successful individuals seem to be both intrinsically motivated (they emphasise personal effort and maintain high personal standards) and extrinsically motivated (they are often highly competitive) (Santrock, 2003:316).

Bibliography

Feldman, R.S. 2003. *Essentials of understanding psychology.* 5th edition. New York: McGraw Hill.

Freud, S. 1925. Instincts and their vicissitudes. In *Collected papers, volume 4.* London: Hogarth Press.

Jordaan, W. 1998. Basic motivation concepts. In W. Jordaan and J. Jordaan, *People in context.* 3rd edition. Johannesburg: Heinemann.

Panksepp, J. 2004. Motivation: From intrinsic psychobiological to extrinsic cognitive-cultural approaches. In L. Swartz, C. de la Rey and N. Duncan (Eds), *Psychology: An introduction.* Cape Town: Oxford University Press.

Santrock, J.W. 2003. *Psychology: Essentials.* 2nd edition. New York: McGraw-Hill.

Sdorow, L.M. and Rickabaugh, C.A. 2002. *Psychology.* 5th edition. New York: McGraw-Hill.

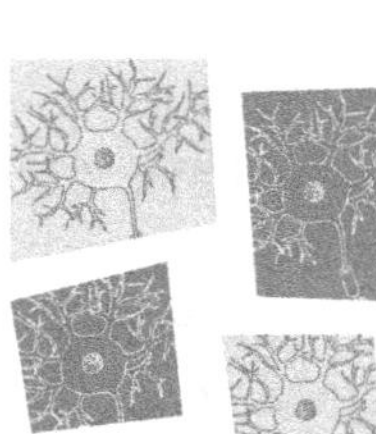

Motivation: The process of motivated behaviour

Motivated behaviour occurs when an individual decides deliberately on a course of action. Such actions are not executed randomly. Motivated behaviour consists of a sequence of related actions that are initiated and guided by a combination of instincts, drives and rational conceptions. It involves a process rather than a series of distinct and discrete motivational events. During the course of a normal day, we may eat, complete certain tasks and spend time in the company of other people. Various needs are fulfilled through these activities, but we do not experience and react to these needs individually and discretely. We do not suddenly stop doing a task because we feel hungry. Our behaviour flows from one situation to the next. We prioritise and react to our needs in the course of events.

However, we do not have full control over the process of motivated behaviour. Our ability to override and prioritise needs is limited. If we are really hungry and forced to make a choice between eating and socialising with friends, most of us would probably opt for eating. It looks as though some needs are more fundamental than others.

1 A hierarchy of needs

What does it mean if some needs are more fundamental than others? The person who is most famous for trying to find an answer to this question is Abraham Maslow. According to Maslow (1970), humans have an inherent need to actualise themselves. This is true for everybody. Regardless of who or what we are, we all have the need to realise our highest potential in our own unique ways. We want to feel satisfied with ourselves and to know that we are using our talents to the fullest.

However, to achieve a state of self-actualisation a number of other needs have to be fulfilled. Maslow envisaged a *hierarchy of needs.* We start at the bottom of this hierarchy and work our way up till we get to the ultimate need of self-actualisation. As we progress up the hierarchy of needs, we have to satisfy the current layer of needs at least partially before we become aware of the next layer of needs.

Physiological needs are the lowest layer in Maslow's (1970) hierarchy. These are primary drives, such as the needs for water, food, sleep and sex. The next layer of needs consists of the needs for a safe and secure environment (safety needs). Then comes the *need for love and belongingness.* This layer of needs concerns our desire to obtain and give affection and to feel that we contribute to the groups and the society that we belong to. The fourth layer is the *need for esteem* – the desire to develop a sense of self-worth – and finally there is the need for *self-actualisation.*

Maslow's hierarchy of needs has been criticised because researchers have been unable to validate the specific ordering of the layers of needs (Feldman, 2003:255). There are also ordinary phenomena that demonstrate inversions in the ordering of the layers. For example, an artist may be willing to live under very poor conditions in order to actualise himself as an artist, or a revolutionary may be willing to starve herself to death in an act of political opposition. Maslow's theory also focuses on the individual in isolation from the context in which the individual finds him- or herself. The theory does not allow for the socio-political context in which humans try to actualise themselves (Jordaan, 1998).

2 Needs in a socio-political context

Despite the criticism expressed against it, Maslow's hierarchy of needs remains an important conceptual contribution to understanding motivated behaviour. It highlights the fact that behaviour is not motivated by a set of discretely individual needs, but is founded rather in a set of hierarchically interlinked needs. The hierarchy also explains that people who are motivated by lower-level needs will be relatively unconcerned by higher-level ones (Feldman, 2003:255). In other words, when people are not sufficiently fed and do not have proper housing, one cannot expect them to be concerned with developing a sense of self-worth. Furthermore, because Maslow's hierarchy focuses on individual behaviour divorced from context, it can be imported into a more encompassing frame of reference, such as a socio-political context. This is exactly what Davies (1991) did. He accepted Maslow's basic principle, namely that needs are hierarchically organised and reinterpreted them in a socio-political context (Jordaan, 1998).

Davies (1991) distinguishes four kinds of needs that people work through in their attempts at self-actualisation:

- Physical needs
- Socio-affective needs
- The need for self-esteem (dignity)
- The need for self-actualisation

He calls these needs *substantive needs.* However, people experience additional needs, called *instrumental needs,* that help them satisfy their substantive needs. These are the needs for security, knowledge and power. In addition to these needs, there are two kinds of barriers that people may encounter in their attempts to satisfy their needs, namely personal barriers (internal barriers) and socio-political barriers (external barriers). When people encounter these barriers, this leads to experiences of being challenged or frustrated, and, in their attempts to work around these barriers, people display various kinds of co-operative as well as aggressive behaviours.

So Davies's hierarchy of substantive needs puts people's lives in a socio-psychological perspective. Individuals' first priority is to fulfil their physical needs, such as having sufficient food and water and a place to stay. If people do not have easy access to these basic necessities, they spend most of their time finding food and water and building shelters to protect themselves against the elements. Only when these physical needs have been satisfied can one expect people to become aware of the need to belong. In other words, unless their physical needs have been taken care of, one cannot expect people to organise themselves into communities in which they identify with their place of living and where they feel part of and want to protect, the group who stays and works there. Slum areas are characterised by poorly kept buildings, the absence of gardens and the presence of gangs and crime, because people there are too busy with physical survival to care about community. However, when people begin to affiliate themselves with those around them (satisfying socio-affective needs), the physical signs of community appear. Small gardens, corner shops and places to meet and socialise are signs of a stable and nurturing environment in which people feel they can participate and in which they can develop an economy of receiving and contributing. They find their places in the community, based on mutual respect for one another, which leaves them feeling good about themselves (satisfying the need for self-esteem or dignity) and which creates the opportunities for actualising their true potentialities. A community need not be economically powerful and well developed to offer opportunities for self-actualisation. Think of the seamstress, the handyman, the plumber and the carpenter who practise their trades in small corner shops or from their own houses.

However, the fulfilment of substantive needs depends on the fulfilment of instrumental needs. For Davies (1991) the needs for security, knowledge and power are the means to an end. They are the means to the fulfilment of people's substantive needs. In other words, none of the substantive needs can be satisfied in the absence of security, knowledge and power.

The need for security is a need for stability and safety. People want environments in which they are not likely to suffer bodily harm and they want the assurance that these circumstances are likely to continue. The second instrumental need is the need for knowledge. People need knowledge, not only in the sense of understanding their current circumstances, but also in the sense of knowing how to create and manage knowledge. The third need is the need for power. Basically, the need for power is a need for personal agency, which means the freedom to act and to exercise control in a situation.

People cannot fulfil their substantive needs and build a community in the absence of these instrumental needs. For example, people cannot satisfy their physical need for shelter if their environment is pounded by natural disasters that destroy their housing (absence of security), or if they do not have the knowledge to build shelters that can withstand the weather (absence of knowledge), or if they are prohibited from owning land where they can build shelters (lack of power). The instrumental needs are operative on all levels of the hierarchy of substantive needs. The following are some examples:

- Elderly people often become lonely and cannot satisfy their socio-affective needs because they do not have the means to get to friends and family (lack of power).
- Employees may fail to develop self-esteem and dignity at work because they may be constantly reminded by the company that they could lose their job if they make a mistake (absence of security).
- A community may fail to adopt new farming techniques and become self-sufficient because the members cannot write or read (lack of knowledge management).

How do people react when they are kept from satisfying their needs? According to Davies (1991), they try to work around obstructions. There are two kinds of obstruction, namely internal barriers and external barriers. *Internal barriers* are personal factors that limit an individual's ability to satisfy his or her needs, such as intellectual ability, interests, aptitudes, motivation and education. *External barriers* are societal issues such as prejudice (racism, sexism), violence and economics (poverty, unemployment). People employ both co-operative and aggressive forms of behaviour in their attempts to overcome the barriers that prevent them from satisfying their needs. For example, when I suspect I did not get a promotion because of my style of interpersonal interaction, I can accuse the company of unfair labour practice (aggressive behaviour), or I can enrol for an interpersonal skills development course (co-operative behaviour). However, the behaviour that people display is often a complex combination of co-operative and aggressive forms of behaviour and the result of an interaction between internal and external barriers to behaviour. For example, a student may fail to proceed in his or her studies due to a combination of a poor education system (external barrier) and low motivation (internal barrier). This student may enrol for a course in learning skills (co-operative behaviour), but may also accuse the institution of unfair discrimination (aggressive behaviour).

So, to sum up, human behaviour is motivated. We do not react like machines in a fixed and predetermined manner, but our actions are also not executed randomly. Motivated behaviour is somewhere between these two extremes, always filled with purpose.

Bibliography

Davies, J.C. 1991. Maslow and theory of political development: Getting to fundamentals. *Political Psychology,* 12(3), 289–420.

Feldman, R.S. 2003. *Essentials of understanding psychology.* 5th edition. New York: McGraw Hill.

Jordaan, W. 1998. Motivation as a life process. In W. Jordaan and J. Jordaan, *People in context.* 3rd edition. Johannesburg: Heinemann.

Maslow, A.H. 1970. *Motivation and personality.* New York: Harper & Row.

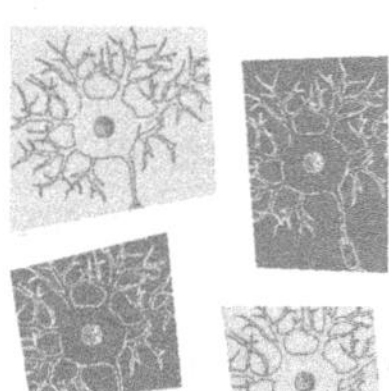

Personality and health

1 Personality and stress

Stress is part of modern life and most people cope fairly well with the demands posed by daily living. However, some people find it less easy to cope than others. When you cannot cope with stress, you develop various ways of reacting, one of which is in the form of physical illnesses when your body shows the symptoms of stress.

There are many factors that affect our ability to cope and personality is one of them. It is generally recognised that people with a particular personality type tend to have more illnesses than others. Personality alone is not the cause of the disease or disorder, but personality type contributes to the risk of getting the disease. Prolonged or chronic stress is often associated with psychosomatic diseases, such as ulcers and heart problems. These psychosomatic diseases result from problems in body functions in the presence of chronic stress. The kind of psychosomatic disease that develops is associated with weakness or poor functioning of a part of the body, which may be inherited. In the presence of chronic stress, the weak part of the body is the most vulnerable. This is why people tend to respond to stress with a particular type of bodily reaction. For example, one person may respond by always getting headaches, whereas another person may frequently get stomach upsets. This is called response specificity, referring to the tendency to respond to stressors with a specific type of physiological reaction. In this section, we look at an example of one type of behaviour pattern that has been well documented, the so-called cardiac personality, referring to people at high risk for heart disease.

Two well-known cardiologists in the United States have developed a classification system of people's risk for heart disease on the basis of their personalities (Friedman and Rosenman, 1974). Those who have a high risk are called type-A personalities and those who are unlikely to have a heart attack are called type-B personalities.

Type-A individuals strive hard for success in everything they do. Obvious signs of a type-A personality are time urgency and chronic anger or hostility. Type-A people are very competitive and achievement oriented. They generally believe that, with enough effort, they can do anything and they push themselves very hard. They generally do not trust other people. They hurry everywhere, do several things at once, see everything as urgent and get impatient, frustrated and angry with people who do things slowly or stand in their way. They also tend to bottle up their emotions and do not express them outwardly. This increases the heart rate and blood pressure, which places tremendous strain on the heart. In this way, feelings of anger and hostility are strongly related to an increased risk of heart attack.

After the identification of such personalities, it became apparent that there are some type-A people who do not develop heart disease. Psychologists then became interested in finding out why. They discovered that there are some people who seem to be unusually resistant to stress, the so-called *hardy personality.* A study of hardiness examined managers in highly stressful positions and found that some of the managers tended to get sick after stressful events, while others were very seldom ill (Kobasa, 1979). Both groups were typical type-A personalities, but the main difference was in their approach to life. The hardy group had (1) a sense of *personal commitment* to themselves, their work and their families and other stable values; (2) a sense of *control* over their lives and their work; and (3) they tended to see life as a series of *challenges* rather than as threats or problems. When you feel a sense of commitment, you find ways of turning something that seems uninteresting into something of importance by getting involved. When you feel in control of a situation, it is less stressful because you feel that you can influence things that happen in your situation and you do not see yourself as a passive victim. Seeing events as challenges rather than problems allows for continual growth through learning from experience. From this, you can see that viewing your life in more positive terms is one way of combating stress. Happy people tend to view things positively and happiness is related to hardiness. It is not just a reaction to circumstances but is a general personality characteristic.

It is important to realise that one can succeed in life without sacrificing one's health and happiness in the process. If you recognise some of these characteristics in yourself, you may want to look at the following suggestions for reducing hostility.

2 Strategies for reducing hostility

1. Be aware of your angry, hostile and cynical thoughts by recording them in a journal or diary. Note what happened when you felt this way and what actions you took and review this at the end of each week.
2. Admit to someone that you have a problem with excessive anger and hostility.
3. Interrupt the hostile thoughts whenever they occur.
4. When you have these thoughts, try to work out for yourself why they are irrational or unreasonable.

5. When you are angry, try to put yourself mentally in the other person's shoes.
6. Learn to laugh at yourself. Humour can defuse anger.
7. Learn how to relax (for example by sitting quietly and listening to music, or going for a walk).
8. Practise trusting other people.
9. Make an effort to listen carefully to other people.
10. Learn to make your point without being aggressive.
11. Do not let small irritations get in your way and pretend that today is the last day of your life.
12. Try to forgive people rather than blame them. We all have shortcomings.

(Adapted from Coon, 2004.)

Bibliography

Coon, D. 2004. *Introduction to psychology.* 10th edition. Belmont, CA: Wadsworth.

Friedman, M. and Rosenman, R. 1974. *Type-A behaviour and your heart.* New York: Knopf.

Kobasa, S. 1979. Stressful life events, personality and health: An enquiry into hardiness. *Journal of Personality and Social Psychology,* 37, 1–11.

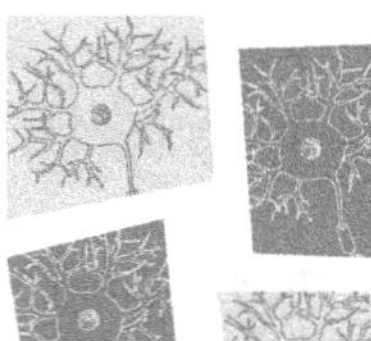

Personality concepts

1 Personology

To gain a better understanding of human behaviour, we need to turn to the field of study called personality psychology or personology. We use our common sense or everyday knowledge of human nature to try to understand one another, but this is generally not quite enough and therefore we need to look at formal theories.

Personality theories provide a way of describing, explaining and predicting human behaviour. Many personality theories have been developed by psychotherapists and are based on their experience in working with people. Before developing a theory, psychologists generally make an extensive study of theories and research findings and then try to improve on the shortcomings of existing theories and knowledge. They need to evaluate their own observations in the light of existing knowledge and improve on their theories as they work. On the basis of this, you can see that a personality theory should provide a better explanation of human behaviour than everyday knowledge or common sense does.

There are more than 30 different personality theories (Meyer, Moore and Viljoen, 2002). This is an indication that there is no single correct explanation of human functioning. One of the reasons lies in the complexity of human behaviour. Our behaviour is influenced by many factors, the main ones being the following:

- Biological factors
- Environmental stimuli
- Interpersonal situations
- Cultural and social factors
- Psychological and spiritual factors

All these factors, independently and in interaction, influence our behaviour. Each personality theory highlights one or more of these factors. Each one offers a possible explanation of behaviour from the perspective of the particular theorist. Each theory can contribute towards a better understanding of people's behaviour. It is not possible to know everything there is to know about human functioning or to predict behaviour totally.

2 Concepts

Although most of the basic concepts in personality theories, such as 'personality', 'character' or 'temperament', form part of our everyday language, personality theorists have specific meanings for these concepts (Coon, 2004; Weiten, 2001; Morris and Maisto, 2003).

2.1 Personality

When we use the word 'personality', we usually refer to whatever it is that makes people who they are. In this sense, personality is the sum of all the physical, psychological and spiritual characteristics that influence the behaviour of an individual. Theorists have different views about exactly what kind of characteristics determine people's behaviour and this is why there are various theories of personality. It is important to note that, although people change with time, personality characteristics remain relatively unchanged. Another important point is that a person's personality does not exist in isolation; personality is integrated with other attributes to influence behaviour. For example, two people may have the same intellectual ability but they may attain different levels of achievement depending on factors such as their levels of motivation, perseverance, interest and involvement (aspects of personality). Context, such as social and cultural factors, also influences behaviour.

2.2 Character

The word 'character' has a narrower meaning than personality and refers to those aspects of the personality involving the person's values and his or her ability to behave according to those values. It implies that the person has been evaluated, whereas personality is merely a description. Character refers to a person's moral attributes and values that are largely influenced by education and experience in the social environment.

2.3 Temperament

Temperament refers more specifically to people's emotions and the way in which they express them and deal with them. It can be defined as a person's 'relatively consistent and distinctive emotional character, moods and reaction style' (Jordaan and Jordaan, 1998). Temperament focuses on the emotional aspects of a person's biological and psychological self and may be referred to as the 'raw material' from which personality is formed. It refers to the inherited, biological aspects of the person. However, the way temperament is manifested in behaviour can be changed through learning and socialisation. For example, people who are very shy can be helped to overcome this to some extent. However, they will always tend to be shy and are not likely to become very outgoing, because shyness is their basic disposition. People are born with the potential for a certain temperament. The way that temperament is expressed in behaviour depends on the kind of interaction they have with the environment.

Temperament is regarded as having four main dimensions or characteristics:

- *General activity level* – ranging from very high activity to extreme passivity
- *Emotionality* – ranging from being easily upset or agitated to being very calm
- *Sociability* – ranging from being very outgoing or gregarious to being very shy and aloof
- *Impulsivity* – ranging from having a great deal of self-control to lacking self-control

Most people have a moderate level of these four dimensions of temperament. Relatively few people show extreme levels.

2.4 Traits

Traits are stable qualities that mostly remain consistent in various and changing situations. For example, words like 'friendly' or 'aggressive' refer to traits. When we say that someone is friendly (has the trait of friendliness), we mean that person is friendly to most people and that the person's friendliness does not change much over time. Traits are generally inferred from behaviour. For example, if you see someone at a party talking to strangers, you might infer that person is 'sociable'. Traits can also predict behaviour. For example, students who are agreeable, outgoing and hardworking tend to make more friends and have less conflict with other students.

2.5 Type

A personality type refers to people who have several traits in common. It is a way of labelling a person who supposedly has several key traits in common with others. For example, if you say someone is the motherly type, you probably mean that person has traits such as being warm, caring, nurturing, protective and so on. Several psychologists have proposed ways to categorise personality into types. Carl Jung proposed the theory that a person is either an introvert (a shy person whose attention is focused inwards) or an extrovert (a bold, outgoing person whose attention is directed outwards). Although you may think of people as being one type or the other, we also know that there are times and situations when you are extroverted (for example at a party) and times when you are introverted. For this reason, type does not offer a full explanation of personality.

2.6 Self-concept

Your self-concept consists of all your ideas, perceptions and feelings about who you are. We build our self-concepts from our daily experiences and revise them in the light of new experiences. Once a self-concept is established, it tends to shape the way we see things and can affect our adjustment to life. This is particularly true when the self-concept is inaccurate or inadequate. For example, if a young boy has a negative self-concept (that is, he views himself as worthless and a failure) even though he gets good marks in class, it is likely that he will remain anxious or depressed, no matter what he does.

2.7 Self-esteem

Self-esteem refers to the way we evaluate ourselves. A person with high self-esteem is usually confident, proud and self-respecting. A person with low self-esteem is very critical of the self, insecure and lacks confidence. Self-esteem rises when we experience success and are praised by others. Can self-esteem be too high? Yes. Some people may overestimate their own abilities and think highly of themselves without any real reason. Such people appear arrogant and put other people off. People who function well are realistic about their own abilities and have accurate self-knowledge.

Bibliography

Coon, D. 2004. *Introduction to psychology.* 10th edition. California: Wadsworth.

Jordaan, W. and Jordaan, J. 1998. *People in context.* 3rd edition. Johannesburg: Heinemann.

Meyer, W., Moore, C. and Viljoen, H. 2002. *Personology: From individual to ecosystem.* 3rd edition. Johannesburg: Heinemann.

Morris, C.G. and Maisto, A.A. 2003. *Understanding psychology.* New Jersey: Prentice Hall.

Weiten, W. 2001. *Psychology: Themes and variations.* 5th edition. California: Wadsworth.

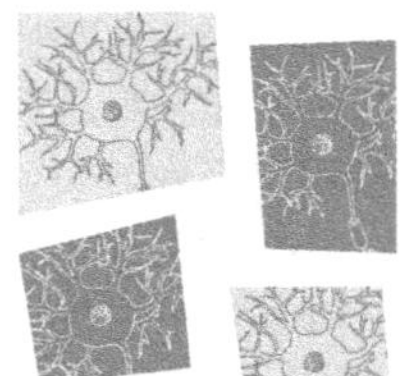

Personality theories

A personality theory is 'a system of concepts, assumptions, ideas and principles proposed to explain personality' (Coon, 2001:483). There are many theories of personality and a brief overview of five different theoretical approaches will be presented here.

1 Trait theories

Trait theories of personality are more concerned with describing people in terms of traits than explaining the origins of traits (Weiten, 2001). There are many important trait theories of personality and two of the main ones are included here.

1.1 Allport's trait theory

Gordon Allport (1937) believed that the best way to understand and predict people's behaviour was to find out what they value – that is, the things they will strive to attain. His view was that the most important traits are motivational traits related to values. For example, a man who values money more than family life would be expected to accept a promotion at work that would mean getting more money, but would require spending more time away from home.

For all trait theories, one of the important aspects is the way traits are organised or related to each other. Allport believed that there are cardinal, central and secondary traits, ranked in order of importance. Cardinal traits are those that are so important to an individual that they dominate that individual's life. For example, the desire for social justice is the trait that dominated Mahatma Gandhi's behaviour. Allport believed that very few people have cardinal traits. Central traits are more common – these are important traits that influence and organise most of our behaviour. The desire for power is an example of a central trait. Secondary traits are much more specific and are less important as a description of a person's behaviour. For example, a specific food preference is regarded as a secondary trait. In Allport's terms, a personality description may look like this:

- Name – S.A. Citizen
- Age – 22
- Cardinal traits – none
- Central traits – possessive, artistic, trusting
- Secondary traits – prefers colourful clothes, likes to work alone, always late

Try doing this exercise for yourself!

1.2. Cattell's source traits

Another major approach to traits is found in the work of Raymond B. Cattell (1950). He wanted to learn how traits were linked and began by studying visible aspects of personality or surface traits. He obtained data on the surface traits of a large number of people, analysed the data and observed that surface traits often appear in clusters or groups. Some traits appeared together so often that they seemed to represent a more basic trait or underlying personality characteristic, called a source trait. Cattell developed a list of 16 source traits that provide a description of a person's personality.

1.3 The five-factor model of personality

Many trait models of personality have been proposed. None of them was widely accepted until recent years, when advances in statistical methods and experimental strategies were used to study personality traits. There is now a fair amount of consensus among trait theorists that five basic traits provide a description of our personalities.

According to the five-factor model of personality (Weiten, 2001), personality can be understood in terms of five innate, universal dimensions, which are stable over time and have important consequences across the lifespan. These five traits are a reduction of Cattell's 16 source traits or personality factors. The so-called 'big five' personality traits are neuroticism, extroversion, openness, agreeableness and conscientiousness. It is believed that we all possess these traits, each one to a different degree and that the combination of the traits describes our personalities. For example, people who score high on conscientiousness tend to be safe drivers and are unlikely to have car accidents.

The five traits are described as follows:

- Factor 1: *Extroversion* – how introverted or extroverted a person is
- Factor 2: *Agreeableness* – how friendly, nurturing and caring compared to being cold, indifferent, spiteful or self-centred
- Factor 3: *Conscientiousness* – how self-disciplined, responsible and achieving as opposed to irresponsible, careless and undependable
- Factor 4: *Neuroticism* – how negative or having upsetting emotions (people

who are anxious or unhappy) as opposed to being calm, even-tempered and comfortable
- Factor 5: *Openness to experience* – how intelligent, imaginative and open to new ideas as opposed to being conventional and lacking in curiosity and creativity

The five-Factor model of personality does not address the issue of human nature directly, but the model seems to indicate that the core of human nature is represented by the five factors described here. These basic dimensions underlie all human behaviour, across cultures and different age groups. The way people vary on these dimensions accounts for individual differences.

2 The psychoanalytic approach

Psychodynamic theories arose from discontent with just examining personality traits as a way of understanding behaviour. Psychodynamic theories try to probe under the surface of personality to examine what makes us behave the way we do. Psychoanalytic theory, the best-known psychodynamic approach, emerged from the work of Sigmund Freud (Meyer, Moor and Viljoen, 2003).

Freud was a medical doctor. On the basis of talking to his patients about their thoughts and feelings, he concluded that ill health resulted from conflict about sexuality and aggression. The central theme of Freud's theory is that behaviour is the outcome of the wishes, desires and feelings that people are unaware of; in other words, their so-called unconscious thoughts. According to Freud's theory, people have three types of primitive unconscious instincts:

- *Sexual instincts.* These influence the experiences and behaviour that generate pleasure.
- *Ego instincts.* These influence experience and behaviour associated with preservation of the self.
- *Hostility instincts.* These influence aggressive experience and behaviour.

In Freud's view, these instincts are innate. They generate tension and energy that cause the person to behave in a way that releases the tension. There are two principles that regulate this instinctual energy:

- *The pleasure principle* directs energy in the direction of immediate gratification of needs, wishes and desires.
- *The reality principle* enables the person to delay the immediate gratification of needs so that greater pleasure may be experienced later on.

The psychoanalytic approach sees personality as a dynamic system directed by three mental structures – the id, the ego and the superego:

- The *id* refers to innate biological impulses and urges. These impulses are unconscious, irrational and self-serving. They demand immediate gratification. Examples of id impulses are the uncontrollable desires for food or sex, or to hurt someone.
- The *ego* refers to the executive part of the self that regulates the expression of the id's instinctual energy. The ego is in touch with reality and can foresee the consequences of behaviour. The ego is part of the system of thinking, planning and problem solving. It has conscious control of the self.
- The *superego* refers to the conscience. The superego is like a judge or censor. If someone does not adhere to society's standards for acceptable behaviour, the superego allows the person to experience guilt feelings and anxiety.

These are psychic systems that regulate the way instinctual energy is expressed. According to Freud, most behaviour involves the activity of all three systems. He theorised that there is a dynamic balance of power among the three. The ego acts as a mediator between the id and the superego. The ego has to make compromises to find a way to satisfy unconscious id impulses in an appropriate way that satisfies the superego. For example, you may see a very expensive pair of shoes that you really want to buy. The id says: 'Go for it!' but the superego says: 'Do not even think about it' and the ego says: 'Maybe there is a plan'.

2.1 Personality structure

The id is made up of innate biological instincts and works on the basis of the pleasure principle – that is, it looks for expression of pleasure-seeking urges. If we were solely under the control of the id, the world would be totally chaotic. The id provides energy for the psyche or personality. This energy is called *libido,* which underlies efforts to survive, as well as our sexual desires and pleasure seeking. Freud also described a death instinct, called *thanatos*, that produces aggressive and destructive urges. According to Freud, our long history of wars and violence is evidence of such urges. In terms of the psychoanalytic view, most id energies are aimed at discharging tensions related to sex and aggression.

The ego is often described as the 'executive' because it directs the energies supplied by the id. The id can be described as a blind king or queen who has considerable power but who must rely on others to carry out orders. The ego directs power by linking the desires of the id to external reality. We say that the ego is guided by the reality principle – that is, it delays action until the activity is practical or appropriate. The ego is the conscious control of the personality and can prevent the world from being chaotic!

The superego is the judge or censor for the thoughts and actions of the ego. Part of the superego is regarded as the conscience. When you do not keep to the standards of your conscience, you are punished with guilt feelings. The other part of the superego is the ego ideal, which is a reflection of behaviour that has been approved of or rewarded. This is the source of your goals and aspirations. When we attain these goals and aspirations, we feel pride. The superego acts as a kind of parent to bring behaviour under control. In Freudian terms, people with weak superegos may be delinquent, criminal or antisocial. On the other hand, a very strict superego may result in too much control and may lead to inhibition, rigidity or excessive guilt.

2.2 Development of personality

According to Freud's theory, the core of an individual's personality is formed before the age of six years, in a series of psychosexual stages. At each stage, a different part of the body becomes the primary area capable of producing pleasure. For example, the oral stage occurs during the first year of life. During this stage most of the child's pleasure comes from stimulation of the mouth (for example during breast or bottle feeding). Freud believed that many personality traits can be traced to unresolved conflicts or emotional issues related to a particular stage. For example, in terms of this theory, adult expressions of unresolved oral needs include nail biting, smoking, overeating and alcoholism.

Freud's theory was influential because of his idea that the first years of life help shape the adult personality. There are still psychologists who embrace his theory today despite evidence that, in some instances, he was not correct. Although psychoanalytic theory may have some clinical value, it is almost impossible to verify scientifically.

3 The behaviourist approach

The behaviourist approach to personality emphasises that personality is no more or no less than a collection of learned behaviours (Weiten, 2001).

According to this approach, personality, like other learned behaviour, is acquired through classical and operant conditioning, learning through observation, reinforcement, extinction, generalisation and stimulus discrimination.

Because they believe that personality is acquired through learning, the behaviourists reject the idea of personality traits. They are more interested in the situational determinants (or external causes) of behaviour. They may agree, for example, that a person is honest (which is a trait) but they would not agree that you can predict the person's honesty in any situation. In other words, they believe that being honest is related to a particular situation and is not an inherent or stable aspect of the personality. The behaviourists prefer replacing 'traits' with 'prior learning' to explain behaviour. Behaviourists are not interested in a person's experience of a situation and how the experience may influence behaviour.

Social learning theory explains behaviour in terms of concepts such as psychological situation, expectancy and reinforcement value. The *psychological situation* refers to a person's particular interpretation or understanding of a situation. For example, if you get a low mark in an exam, do you see it as a challenge to work harder or a sign that you should drop the course? These are different interpretations of the situation. An *expectancy* refers to your anticipation that whatever you do will lead to reinforcement. For example, if you have found in the past that working harder leads to getting good marks, then this is likely to be your reaction to getting a low mark, because you expect to get a better mark if you work harder. That would be the expected reinforcement. The notion of *reinforcement values* means that people attach different values to various activities or rewards. For some people, getting a better mark is a reward; for others, getting praise and respect may be the reward they want. There is another factor and that is *self-reinforcement.* Self-reinforcement refers to praising or rewarding yourself for having made a particular response. For example, the pride you feel in getting a better mark may be the only reward you need. Self-reinforcement can be viewed as the behaviourist's equivalent to the superego. The concepts discussed here are regarded by behaviourists as the factors that shape personality.

3.1 Behaviouristic view of development

Behaviourists agree with Freud that the first six years of life are crucial for personality development, but for different reasons. Instead of looking for psychosexual urges and fixations, they see childhood as a time of active drives, powerful rewards and punishments, as well as frustrations. Social reinforcement, based on praise, attention and approval, is also important. These forces are believed to shape the core of personality through learning.

According to social learning theory, the processes of identification and imitation contribute greatly to personality development. *Identification* refers to a person's emotional attachment to someone they admire. Children, for example, identify with a parent or someone who provides love and care. When a mother says: 'Nice girls do not climb trees', she serves as a model and in this way shapes her daughter's personality. Identification encourages *imitation* or a desire to act like the admired person. According to behaviourists, many male or female traits are the result of children's attempts to imitate the same-sex parent with whom they identify.

3.2 Rate yourself

Indicate whether you agree or disagree with the following statements (adapted from Coon, 2001):

- I often think positive thoughts about myself.
- I frequently meet standards that I set for myself.
- I try not to blame myself when things go wrong.

- I usually do not get upset when I make mistakes because I learn from them.
- I can get satisfaction out of what I do even if it is not perfect.
- When I make mistakes, I take time to reassure myself.
- I do not think talking about what I have done right is too boastful.
- I do not think I have to be upset every time I make a mistake.
- My feelings of self-confidence and self-esteem stay quite steady.

If you agree with most of these statements, you probably have a high rate of self-reinforcement. Self-reinforcement is related to self-esteem and is associated with less depression and greater life satisfaction. From the behaviourist viewpoint, there is therefore value in learning to be good to yourself!

4 The humanist approach

Human nature consists of the traits, qualities, potential and behaviour patterns considered most characteristic of the human species. Humanism, therefore, focuses on human experience, problems, potential and ideals (Coon, 2001). The theoretical orientation of humanists focuses on the unique qualities of humans, in particular their freedom and potential for growth. They look for answers to the question: 'What does it mean to be a person?'. The humanists rejected trait theory as being too rigid, psychoanalytic theory as being too pessimistic and learning theory as being too mechanical. The core of humanism is the positive image of what it means to be human. Humanists see people as creative beings, capable of free choice. They see people as conscious and rational beings who can control their innate impulses. According to the humanist approach, people should be understood and studied as holistic beings. To do this, attempts should be made to describe people in their worlds as they see them. This means that the subjective experience of the individual and his or her world is more important than so-called objective reality. This is an example of the phenomenological approach, based on the idea that behaviour can only be understood by appreciating a person's personal, subjective experiences.

Humanists look for ways to encourage us to develop our potential. To humanists, a person is the product of all the choices he or she has made.

4.1 Carl Rogers's person-centred theory

One of the best-known humanists is Carl Rogers, who based his theory on clinical experience. Rogers' view was that '[t]he best vantage point for understanding behaviour is from the internal frame of reference of the individual himself' (Rogers, 1951:494). Because of the emphasis on a person's subjective point of view, his approach was called person-centred theory. Rogers developed the term 'the fully functioning person' to describe someone who lives in harmony with his or her deepest feelings and impulses. Fully functioning people are open to experiences and they trust their own inner feelings and intuition. Rogers believed that becoming fully functioning is most likely to occur when a person receives a great deal of love and acceptance from others.

The main aspect of Rogers' theory is the concept of the *self,* a flexible and changing perception of personal identity. The self is made up of experiences that fit our own perceptions of ourselves and excludes experiences that are labelled 'not me' and do not fit our perceptions of ourselves. Today, this idea of the self is generally known as the *self-concept* and refers to the total subjective perception of beliefs about one's own nature, unique qualities and typical behaviour. Much of our behaviour is the result of attempts to keep a balance between our self-concept and our actions. For example, if you think of yourself as kind, you are likely to act in a kind and considerate way most of the time.

According to Rogers, when we have experiences that match our self-concept (in other words, they are *congruent),* they are admitted to awareness and contribute to gradual changes in the self. Because of the subjective nature of the self-concept, it may not be entirely consistent with experience. Most people tend to distort their experiences to suit a positive self-concept, but sometimes there is a gap between the self-concept and reality. Information or experiences that do not match the self-concept are said to be *incongruent.* Incongruence arises, for example, when you say you are not angry but all the time you are feeling very angry inside. The person who is incongruent (in other words, there is a big gap between the self-concept and reality) can become confused or dissatisfied, or have adjustment difficulties.

Rogers also considered it essential to have an ideal self. The ideal self is the image of the person you would like to be (similar to Freud's ego ideal). Although we never fully attain all our ideals, the greater the gap between the way we see ourselves and the way we would like to be, the more tension and anxiety we are likely to experience. In order to develop our potential, we have to accept information about ourselves as honestly as possible and be realistic about what we can become. Research has shown that people with a close match between their self-concept and ideal self tend to be socially confident and resourceful, while those with a poor match tend to be depressed, anxious and insecure.

4.2 Maslow and self-actualisation

Another humanist theorist, Abraham Maslow (1968), referred to the process of fully developing personal potential as self-actualisation. A self-actualiser is someone who is living creatively and fully using his or her potential. Self-actualisation is a process that requires hard work and patience.

According to Maslow, human behaviour is motivated by needs, arranged systematically in a motivational hierarchy. According to this hierarchy, basic needs must be met before the person can progress to meeting less-basic needs. The most basic needs are physiological, like hunger and thirst, or the need for security.

Once the basic needs are met, the person becomes aware of the need for belonging, or for self-esteem. When needs on one level are satisfied reasonably well, this activates needs at the next level. If needs are not satisfied, the person may regress to a lower level. At the top of the hierarchy is the need for self-actualisation, which refers to the need to fulfil one's potential.

In terms of Maslow's theory, self-actualising persons have a healthy personality. Self-actualising people are characteristically open and spontaneous, have a clear perception of reality, appreciate the world around them, are independent, are sensitive to the needs of others and have good interpersonal relationships (Weiten, 2001).

4.3 Developing potential

If you want to develop your potential and live a more creative life, you might consider the following as a beginning (adapted from Coon, 2001):

1. Be willing to change. Ask yourself: 'Am I living in a way that is satisfying to me?' If not, be prepared to make changes. This does not necessarily refer to physical aspects of your life, but rather to the way you see things.
2. Take responsibility. Do not blame others for your shortcomings.
3. Examine your motives. Try to make each life decision for growth, not to escape fear or anxiety.
4. Experience honestly and directly. Do not distort information to fit your way of seeing things. Try to see yourself as others do and do not rely on wishful thinking.
5. Make use of positive experiences. Repeat experiences that have given you feelings of amazement, renewal, humility or joy.
6. Be prepared to be different. Accept your uniqueness. Think about the standards you use to judge yourself.
7. Get involved. Give some attention to problems outside yourself.
8. Assess your progress. Look at yourself and, if necessary, renew your efforts. If you are bored with something, see it as a challenge and do something about it. You have opportunities for self-enhancement.

5 The biological approach

Up to the early 20th century, it was believed that particular regions of the brain controlled specific psychological functions and it was assumed that the shape of sites on the skull (like bumps, for example) indicated the size of those brain areas. Intellectual and personality functions were assessed by studying the size and shape of the skull. For example, if you had a big bump on your skull in the region thought to be related to kindness, then you would be a kind person. This theory did not stand up to scientific examination. Although we no longer believe that specific areas of the brain control specific personality characteristics, we cannot ignore the evidence for the biological underpinnings of human behaviour. This is why many people have adopted a biological approach to understanding personality.

There are many theorists who believe that heredity shapes personality. (Heredity refers to inherited biological characteristics.) This view is based on the idea that we have inborn behavioural tendencies that differ from one person to another. Support for this view comes from studies of newborn babies who clearly show differences in temperament. Some are emotionally placid (for example, they are peaceful and calm and adjust easily to changes in routine) while others are emotionally reactive (for example, they cry a lot, fuss and become distressed by changes in routine). You may wonder how these early differences in temperament contribute to the development of differences in personality. Temperament can influence how the infant responds to other people and in the same way how others respond to it. For example, an infant who cries a lot may demand attention from others.

Whether the caregiver can cope with a demanding infant or not influences the kind of care the infant will receive. Inherited differences in temperament also contribute to the development of differences in specific personality traits (such as introversion or extroversion).

A British psychologist, Hans Eysenck (1967), is a proponent of the biological approach to personality. He believed that personality was determined largely by a person's genes. Eysenck's theory is based on the idea that individual differences in physiological functioning result in some people being more easily conditioned than others. This influences the personality traits that people acquire through the conditioning process. For example, he suggested that introverts have higher levels of physiological arousal and are more easily conditioned than extroverts. Some research has shown differences in the electrical activity of the brain in introverts and extroverts, but the physiological basis for introversion/extroversion has not been confirmed.

Considerable attention has been paid to the assessment of genetic aspects of personality. In general, the closer the genetic relationship between two people, the more they will be alike in terms of personality characteristics (Weiten, 2001). You may think that this similarity may be the result of the fact that the people share the same environment or have common life experiences. To investigate this, studies have been undertaken with children who were adopted early in life. With regard to personality, it was found that adopted children are more like their biological parents than like their adopted parents. Another way of investigating the role of heredity in personality is to examine twins who are separated early in life and grow up in different environments. Thomas Bouchard (Bouchard and Segal, 1985) of the University of Minnesota has conducted studies of identical twins (that is, twins who share the same genetic material) reared apart and then reunited later in life. Amazing similarities between identical twins were found in these studies. Identical twins were also more similar than non-identical twins (whose genetic material is not exactly the same). The conclusion was reached that personalities were strongly, although not entirely, influenced by heredity.

6 African perspective

The theoretical approaches to understanding personality described here were developed in Europe and America and at present there is no specific theory of personality developed from an African perspective. In the past, psychological knowledge of the self has been based on the Western view of the individual as an independent, autonomous entity. More recent cross-cultural approaches have focused on the way in which people define themselves in terms of their relationships to others and groups. This implies fundamental differences in the way people view themselves.

The Western view of the self is regarded as individualistic. This means that emphasis is placed on the individual. In contrast to the Western approach of describing a person in terms of individual self-concept or self-esteem, in traditional cultures such as those of Africa and Asia, the self is seen as an integral part of a social group. This is called the collectivist view, which regards people as interdependent. Interdependence means that people's behaviour is guided by consideration for the well-being of others and the community. According to this view of the self, people take care of the needs of others and, in doing so, their own needs are also taken care of because they are part of others. The African worldview implies that people are not separate from the cosmos, which includes the spiritual world, nature and living things and the communities in which they live. The identity of the traditional African is part of collective life. The person exists only because he or she is part of a community: 'I am, because we are; and since we are, therefore I am' (Mbiti, 1990).

Whereas most Western approaches to personality emphasise the individual as the basis for understanding and explaining behaviour, the African perspective is based on the importance of the community and collective forces that shape it. Western-oriented theorists, such as Freud, explain behaviour as the result of internal factors (such as individual needs or wishes). The African perspective attributes behaviour to external agents. According to this view, people cannot hold themselves responsible or accountable for their behaviour. The causes of behaviour are attributed to external, supernatural powers. For example, according to the traditional African view, an illness or disability may be regarded as the result of witchcraft or as caused by enemies rather than being caused by the individual's own actions. In terms of the African worldview, this is why factors such as the wishes of ancestors or beliefs in spiritual forces have an important role to play in influencing the way people behave.

Table 1 The specific characteristics of the individual according to the individualist and collectivist viewpoints (Van der Walt, 1997:31):

Collectivism	Individualism
(First the community, then the individual – I am because we are)	(First the individual, then the community – we are because I am)
1. A high regard for the group elevates the importance of the group above the individual	1. A high regard for the individual elevates the importance of the individual above the group
2. Dependence on people	2. Individual independence
3. Strong group pressure	3. The opinion of the group is not as important
4. Individual initiative is not appreciated – good human relations are a priority	4. Individual initiative is highly regarded – personal achievement is more important than attention to the community
5. Co-operation	5. Competition
6. Duties towards the community are emphasised	6. The rights of the individual are emphasised
7. Values such as friendliness, helpfulness, hospitality, patience and brotherhood are highly regarded	7. Values such as formality, independence and self-sufficiency are highly regarded

When considering an African perspective of the self, one has to be careful not to generalise. The traditional African view should not be regarded as applying to all people of African origin. Many African people are in a state of transition from a traditional to a more modern and/or Westernised way of life and ways of thinking. There are different views within the African perspective, in the same way that there are differences between individuals (Meyer, Moore and Viljoen, 2003). It is important to remember that there is no theory or perspective that is more accurate or better than another – each has relevance in certain situations and for certain people.

Bibliography

Allport, G.W. 1937. *Personality: A psychological interpretation.* New York: Holt.

Bouchard, I. and Segal, N. 1985. Environment and IQ. In B. Wolman (Ed), *Handbook of intelligence: Theories, measurements and applications.* New York: Wiley.

Cattell, R.B. 1950. *Personality: A systematic, theoretical and factual study.* New York: McGraw-Hill.

Coon, D. 2001. *Introduction to psychology.* 9th edition. Belmont, CA: Wadsworth/Thomson Learning.

Eysenck, H. 1967. *The biological basis of personality.* Springfield, IL: Charles C. Thomas.

Kagan, J. 1998. Biology and the child. In W. Damon (Ed), *Handbook of child psychology, volume 3: Social, emotional and personality development.* New York: Wiley.

Maslow, A.H. 1968. *Toward a psychology of being.* New York: Van Nostrand.

Mbiti, J. 1989. *African religions and philosophy.* London: Heinemann.

Meyer, W., Moore, C. and Viljoen, H. 2003. *Personology: From individual to ecosystem.* 3rd edition. Johannesburg: Heinemann.

Rogers, C.R. 1951. *Client-centered therapy: Its current practice, implications and theory.* Boston: Houghton-Mifflin.

Van der Walt, B.J. 1997. *Afrocentric or Eurocentric? Our task in a multicultural South Africa.* Potchefstroom: PU for CHE.

Weiten, W. 2001. *Psychology themes and variations.* 5th edition. Belmont, CA: Wadsworth.

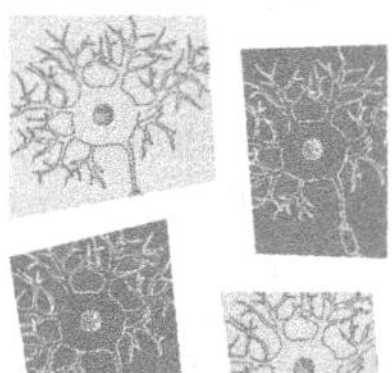

Presentations

1 What is a presentation?

A presentation is a live display in which one or more individuals presents information to an audience. Presentations can take a number of different forms and the delivery of presentations can involve a variety of different technologies. In this case, we will concentrate on the basic scenario of an individual having to provide a verbal presentation to a live audience. This scenario is common to most forms of presentation.

2 Why do people present?

Presentations occur for a variety of reasons:

- To inform
- To report
- To request

The aim of an informative presentation is to inform the target audience about a particular topic. This is a very common form of presentation. Informally, it happens so frequently that we hardly notice it. It happens every time somebody tells somebody else something. In its formal form, we often see informative presentations in the work environment and at conferences, when people are informed about new developments in their fields of interest. In the socio-political context, we see informative presentations on a daily basis, when politicians and economists are informing us about life circumstances.

Report-back presentations are informative, but are more restricted than purely informative presentations. They tend to be structured according to particular rules. The audience is normally aware of the circumstances of and the reasons for the presentation. The audience has usually been a partner to the history behind the report-back.

Request presentations are informative, but also harbour a request. This kind of presentation usually provides information (it informs) about the background or context of the request, as well as information that legitimises and justifies it. The request may be openly presented towards the end of the presentation, or it may be implicitly embedded in the entire presentation. For example, if the presentation is aimed at requesting financial help for a particular project, the presentation may explain the need for and the usefulness of the project and may then explicitly state the request for financial help. A presentation aimed at convincing people to make use of services offered by the presenter may provide a lot of information about the quality and timeliness of the offered services, but may refrain from explicitly making the request for people to use the offered services because everybody present understands the purpose of the presentation anyway.

3 The recipe for a good presentation

1. Find out what is expected of you.
2. Make sure that you know your subject matter.
3. Prepare the presentation thoroughly.
4. Deliver the presentation as well as you can.

Remember, a presentation is not a platform for realising your secret desire to win the Oscar for best actor. The needs of the audience are paramount. From the audience's point of view, the presenter is merely the vehicle for satisfying their needs. Before agreeing to present, make sure that you know exactly what the reasons are for the presentation and what expectations the audience has. Also make sure that you know who the audience will be, because one has to adapt one's presentation to suit the nature of the audience. Many excellently prepared and delivered presentations have failed because they missed the audience.

Do not agree to do a presentation if you do not know what to say. One has to know one's subject matter, or at least have the opportunity to research the topic. You have to know the topic well, to the extent that you really feel yourself in control of it. As long as you have the feeling that it is a struggle to put together the information for the presentation, you are not in control of the topic – the topic is controlling you! A singer once said that you cannot interpret a song if you have to concentrate on remembering the words. Likewise, one cannot interpret the information for a presentation if one is concentrating on getting to know the topic.

Never deliver a presentation that has not been thoroughly prepared. You are likely either to ramble on and on, or to stumble your way through vaguely defined and loosely tied notions and ideas. Either way, you are guaranteed to lose the audience as well as your chance ever to present again.

One does not have absolute control over the delivery of a presentation. There are always circumstances beyond one's control. One cannot control the audience and one may have to rely on technology that suddenly decides not to co-operate. Your venue may be changed at the last moment and people take their time to move to the new venue. As it is, you have too little time to do your presentation. Do not get flustered. Think on your feet. Try to see the situation from the audience's point of view. What do they need most? Do not get bogged down by points that you find interesting. Talk with the audience, not to it.

4 How to prepare material for a presentation

1. Formulate the aim of the presentation.
2. Research the topic.
3. Structure the information.
4. Prepare the information for presentation.

Make sure that you understand exactly what is required. Formulate a clear and precise aim for the presentation. For example, suppose the aim is to provide information to line managers about the topic of creative thinking. Note the structure of the formulation. It says: The aim of the presentation is to do something to somebody. In other words, the key aspects of the purpose of a presentation are the nature of the assignment (what needs to be done) and the nature of the target audience. It is crucial that one knows what needs to be done, but it is equally crucial that one should understand precisely who the target audience is. A presentation on creative thinking for line managers may differ extensively from a one on creative thinking for top management.

If you want to talk about something, make sure that you really know what you want to say. One always has to read and explore much more widely than the immediate limits suggested by the talk. For example, if you want to present on the topic of creative thinking, it is a good idea to read widely about thinking processes in general and to explore the notion of creativity in contexts other than that of cognition.

Once you have finished your research, you can start outlining the topic for presentation. First decide on the main ideas. Ask yourself what the main points are that need to be conveyed. Formulate each point as a single statement. Do not clutter your formulation with unnecessary detail. Keep the detail on separate speaker notes. Remember the famous Five plus/minus Two rule. People can fairly easily entertain five points at a time, but find it difficult to entertain more than seven points simultaneously. However, one should not go with too few points. If a presentation makes one or two points only, people feel that it was not worthwhile attending, so try to formulate between three and seven main points and structure your presentation around them. Then repeat the process for each main point. Take a main point and try to formulate between three to seven supporting or secondary points. Repeat this for each of the main points. Keep detailed information that you would like to mention when you deliver your presentation as separate speaker notes. Of course, this suggestion is for an ideal structure. Things do not always work out in practice as theory suggests. It is more important to let the nature of your subject material guide the presentation than it is to stick to a rigid theoretical schema. However, the Five plus/minus Two rule is a handy structure to keep in mind.

Information can be presented in various ways. It can be presented verbally without using any supporting visual material. Nowadays, most people will refrain from just standing in front of the audience without using slides to summarise the talk. People get bored easily. Keep in mind that few people can sit still and listen to a talking figure for longer than 20 minutes. Here are some hints for visually supporting a verbal presentation:

1. Prepare summary notes as handouts.
2. Summarise the main points on one or more overheads.
3. Consider using electronic slides to animate information.
4. Use film slides or short video clips to illustrate your talk with images of real-life events.

If you use overheads and electronic slides, try not to put too much information on a single slide. Remember the Five plus/minus Two rule. You may want to structure your slides as follows:

- Slide 01: Show the main points of your talk (highlight the first main point).
- Slide 02: Show the secondary points of the first main point.
- Slide 03: Show the main points of your talk (highlight the second main point).
- Slide 04: Show the secondary points of the second main point.
- Slide 05: Show the main points of your talk (highlight the third main point).

A final note: This way of structuring information works very well for verbal presentations, because it structures and condenses information to main points, but the method is not restricted to verbal presentations. One can use this approach effectively when structuring information for written presentations such as essays and written reports. In these, the main points would constitute the main headings of the text and the secondary points would constitute the subheadings. The speaker notes for the various points would constitute the paragraphs that fit under these headings.

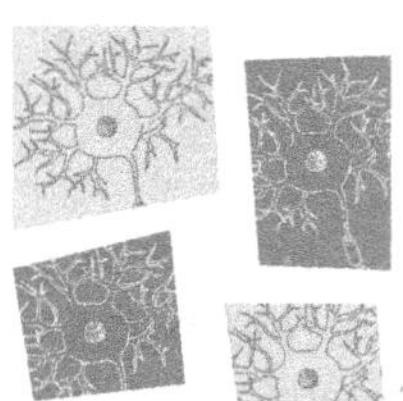

Psychological disorders

1 Criteria for psychological disorders

How do psychologists and other professionals determine whether a person has a psychological disorder? Although psychological disorders vary a great deal in terms of presentation and degree of severity, there are certain generally accepted criteria for determining the presence of a psychological disorder. The criteria are abnormality, maladaptiveness and personal distress (Lahey, 2002).

1.1 The criterion of abnormality

Behaviour is defined as abnormal when it is different from what we consider to be the behaviour of the typical person. This is called the norm. If we look at the Latin derivation of the word 'abnormal', *ab* means 'away' and therefore 'abnormal' means 'away' from 'normal'. We all know what is generally considered to be normal behaviour in our society, but it is sometimes difficult to decide what is abnormal. Abnormal behaviour may be expressed in inaccurate ways of thinking (for example ways of seeing the world and interpreting events in it), emotional instability, difficulties in interpersonal behaviour and poor impulse control.

Behaviour is generally regarded as abnormal when it deviates from culturally accepted standards. For example, it is normal to wash one's hands about three times a day, but if someone washes his or her hands 30 times a day, this would probably be regarded as abnormal. However, if the person who washes his or her hands 30 times a day is a doctor who works with patients all day, the behaviour no longer seems abnormal. We have to look at the context in which the behaviour occurs before we can decide whether it is abnormal and symptomatic of a psychological disorder. For example, wild shrieking would not be appropriate behaviour in a university library, but it may be appropriate at a rugby match. This is why abnormality is not the only criterion we use to decide on the presence of a psychological disorder.

1.2 The criterion of maladaptiveness

Let's look at the origin of the word. In Latin, the prefix *mal* means 'bad' or 'wrong', therefore maladaptive refers to bad or wrong adapting. If you do not adapt well, your life becomes distressing and you do not function properly. The criterion of maladaptiveness implies that you would have a psychological disorder if your behaviour seriously disrupted your life. For example, if a person used alcohol excessively, that person would be considered psychologically disordered because the behaviour (alcohol abuse) would interfere with everyday functioning. However, again we have to look at the behaviour in context. Driving at 220 km per hour is a maladaptive behaviour, but it is not necessarily symptomatic of a psychological disorder. One of the features of abnormal behaviour is that the person's behaviour is generally inflexible, irrespective of the situation. If behaviour is inflexible, this would interfere with the person's ability to adjust successfully to changing demands and situations.

1.3 The criterion of personal distress

Personal distress refers to the subjective feelings of anxiety, depression or other unpleasant emotions. However, personal distress is not a sufficient criterion for determining the presence of a psychological disorder. For example, a serial killer who murders six women but expresses no guilt may have a psychological disorder, but not feel any personal distress.

Remember that behaviour that is abnormal, maladaptive and personally distressing may indicate that a person has a psychological disorder but it does not necessarily mean that the person is insane (or mad, a term that is commonly but incorrectly used).

2 Theoretical viewpoints on psychological disorders

2.1 The biological viewpoint

The biological viewpoint favours the study of the biological causes of psychological disorders. Interest in the biological causes of psychological disorders was stimulated in the late 19th century when researchers discovered that a condition marked by severe mental deterioration was caused by syphilis. Researchers are now interested in the role of heredity, brain structures, brain activity and brain chemistry in the development of psychological disorders. Support for biological theories of abnormal behaviour has come from the successful treatment of psychological disorders with psychotropic drugs.

2.2 The psychoanalytic viewpoint

The psychoanalytic viewpoint grew out of the bio-psychological viewpoint. Instead of looking for underlying biological causes of psychological disorders, the psychoanalysts looked for unconscious causes. Freud's theory emphasised the continual conflict between the demand to express innate biological drives (such as sex and aggression) and the norms of society that inhibit the expression of those demands. Psychoanalytic theorists believe that, if the drives are not expressed, conflicts may be pushed out of awareness into the unconscious mind. This can lead to feelings of anxiety caused by stored up sexual or aggressive energy. Freud also emphasised the important contribution of anxiety-provoking childhood experiences in the development of psychological disorders. Psychoanalytically oriented therapy is based on identifying unconscious thoughts and emotions and bringing them to consciousness in order to help people understand their thoughts and actions.

2.3 The behaviourist viewpoint

The behaviourist viewpoint rose in opposition to viewpoints that looked for mental or biological causes of behaviour. Behaviourists look to the environment and the learning of maladaptive behaviours as the causes of psychological disorders. Social behaviourists like Albert Bandura suggest that a psychological disorder may be developed by observing other people's behaviour. For example, a person may develop an unrealistic fear of all dogs after being bitten or seeing someone else bitten by a dog. In behaviour therapy, behavioural goals are set (such as breaking a bad habit) and then attempts are made to achieve those goals through learning.

2.4 The cognitive viewpoint

The cognitive viewpoint is that psychological disorders arise from maladaptive ways of thinking about oneself and the world. It focuses on the thoughts and beliefs that underlie emotional reactions. Cognitive theorists are more concerned about what people are thinking in the present moment than about the early experiences that led to those thoughts. Depressed people, for example, have distorted negative thoughts about themselves, the world and the future and often look for ways to confirm these thoughts by adopting negative behaviours. Cognitive therapy is aimed at improving people's psychological well-being by changing their thoughts and beliefs (in other words, their cognitions).

2.5 The humanistic viewpoint

Psychologists who support the humanist viewpoint emphasise the importance of self-actualisation, which is the fulfilment of one's potential. According to this view, psychological disorders occur when people fail to reach their potential because others discourage them from expressing their true desires, thoughts and interests.

The distress caused by their failure to act according to their own desires, thoughts and interests can then lead to the development of a psychological disorder. The distress is caused by the mismatch between their self-concept and their ideal self. Humanist theorists believe that people can solve their own problems once they are freed from the inhibiting influence of other people who reject them.

2.6 The community psychology perspective

The community psychology perspective emphasises the importance of social, political and cultural contexts in understanding, identifying and treating psychological problems (Swartz, De la Rey and Duncan, 2004). In order to fully understand people's behaviour, we need to consider social factors, like socio-economic environment, availability of resources and social interaction in the community, that impact on mental health. The way people experience distress or psychological problems also depends on cultural beliefs and practices. In some cultures, it is believed that abnormal behaviour is the result of religious or ancestral forces and witchcraft. While there is no proof of this (as with the other theories), different cultural viewpoints should be taken into consideration in order to understand people's behaviour.

2.7 The African perspective

The traditional African worldview is one of holism, in which wholeness and integrated experiences play a fundamental role. In this world, the body and mind form a unit. Psychological experiences (for example negative emotions such as stress or depression) are not differentiated from bodily experiences. Physiological symptoms are equated to the corresponding psychological feelings. The mind is never experienced as separate from the body (Maiello, 1999). Healthy people experience harmony within themselves and in relation to their world. However, the experienced harmony may be disrupted by ancestors, sorcerers and malignant spirits and when this happens the whole body and not only part of it is affected by pathology. Pathological behaviour is seen as the result of disharmony between a person and his or her ancestors, or the evil spells of malignant spirits of sorcerers.

3 Conclusion

Today, it is generally believed that abnormal behaviour is a natural phenomenon with natural causes (Lahey, 2002). There is an increasing amount of research evidence that both biological and psychological factors play a role in the origin of psychological disorders. Sometimes the main reason for disordered behaviour may be biological (like a brain injury) and sometimes it may be psychological (for example chronic grief resulting from the traumatic deaths of loved ones). The psychological factors that play a role include stress, abnormal social learning, ineffective coping strategies, insufficient resources and a lack of social support. Often, both biological and psychological factors influence psychological disorders. For example, people with an autonomic system that reacts excessively to stress will have problems if they live in a stressful environment, but if they manage to avoid major stressors, they may be able to lead normal lives.

Bibliography

Lahey, B. 2002. *Essentials of psychology.* Boston, MA: McGraw-Hill.

Maiello, S. 1999. Encounter with an African healer. Thinking about the possibilities and limits of cross cultural psychotherapy. *Journal of Child Psychotherapy*, 25(2), 214, 217–238.

Swartz, L., De la Rey, C. and Duncan, N. 2004. *Psychology: An introduction.* Cape Town: Oxford University Press.

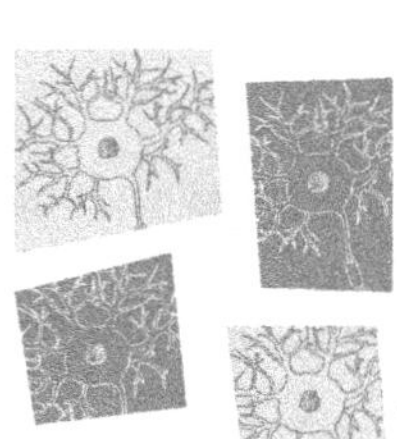

Psychological programme: Content for stress management

1 The relevance of the concept of stress

Two aspects of stress are vitally important for a programme on stress management:

- Information about the concept of stress
- Guidelines to manage stress

1.1 Relevant information about the concept of stress

1. Provide a definition of the concept of stress.
2. Provide information about the basic concepts that are important for understanding the process of stress (for example the concepts of tension, emotional ability and temperament).
3. Explain how basic processes in the body contribute to stress (for example the regulation of basic tension and the general adaptation syndrome).
4. Provide a stress model to explain how particular stress values are attributed to external environmental events and how people cope with stress. Provide information about the principles of the model as well as the processes described by the model (for example phases of a stress process).
5. Explain the relationship between stress and performance.
6. Provide information about the term 'effects of prolonged stress exposure' (for example the relationship between stress and disease).

1.2 Guidelines to manage stress

- Provide guidelines to cope with everyday stress.
- Provide guidelines to prevent the long-term effects of stress (for example burnout).

2 The relevance of the meaning of work

The concept of work and the meaning that work has for people are relevant for a stress management programme for two reasons: (1) work plays such a major role in the lives of most people that it is highly likely that work-related events and situations contribute to their everyday stress experiences; and (2) if the programme is developed for use in a work environment, the work situation constitutes the context in which stress occurs. In both cases, the stress management programme should provide an overview of the concept and meaning of work and also indicate the factors that make the current work situation more stressful than it was in the past.

2.1 Relevant information about the concept and meaning of work

- Information about the concept of work
- Information about the psychosocial meaning of work
- Information about important factors in the current work situation

2.2 Stress-bearing factors in the current work situation

2.2.1 Diminished security

In ancient times, work was directly linked to survival. There were no jobs to be gained or lost. Everybody had to work together to feed themselves and to defend their habitats. Later on, jobs became professionalised, but the socio-political structures within which these workers operated were such that one could be in trouble for not doing things right, but one could hardly lose one's job. The hierarchical structures within which workers performed their jobs were harsh but provided security.

The market ethic, the ethic of freedom and the protestant ethic led to the accumulation of capital (surplus money) that could be reinvested to create more wealth. The Industrial Revolution brought accelerated economic growth and increased numbers of jobs. Throughout these developments, the idea of the personal career developed and established itself. People trained for their jobs and then spent an entire lifetime doing them. The mechanistic worldview perpetuated the idea of predictability. Then came the post-industrial era with its emphasis on quick change. A number of developments during the 20th century undermined the predictability promoted by the mechanistic worldview. The world became seen as less predictable – as a complex chaotic system in which organismic systems represent small islands of order. In this world, people cannot expect to remain in the same job for life. In the fast-changing world, there is a constant process of jobs becoming obsolete and new ones being created. The idea of a single career for life is disappearing. Companies cannot guarantee the security they used to offer in the past. Employees have to look after themselves and become self-reliant to a much greater extent than before. This kind of work environment is much less secure and much more stressful than the work environment of the past.

2.2.2 Individualisation

The postmodern era brought the flattening of hierarchical structures and a much greater focus on the individual. In hierarchical structures, people have to take less personal responsibility because the final responsibility for decision taking always lies higher up in the structure. In flat structures, responsibilities are spiralled down to lower levels. Although this approach offers greater opportunities for self-actualisation in the workplace, it also means people have to take on new responsibilities and they constantly have to expand the range of responsibilities they are willing to handle. In a fast-changing world where knowledge grows exponentially, qualifications become obsolete within a couple of years of obtaining them. People have to keep on learning to stay abreast of new developments and to qualify themselves for new job opportunities. The emphasis on individualisation necessitates continuous self-development and emphasises an acute awareness of personal responsibility. This kind of environment is much more stressful to handle than one in which one can prepare oneself to face a predictable future.

2.2.3 Increased competition

The globalisation of markets, the fast-changing environment and the efficiency of modern communication systems mean that companies have to operate in a much more competitive world than before. Companies have to be effective and efficient to succeed in this kind of environment. The technologies of the post-industrial era are used to increase the effectiveness and efficiency of production and this often means the automation of jobs that were previously done by humans. Nowadays, companies look for highly qualified and multi-skilled people to run their automated production processes. This means fewer jobs and a constant pressure on the individual for qualification and re-qualification. The fact that more people compete for fewer jobs also has to do with the fact that companies operate on a multinational level. Apart from being a highly competitive world, the work environment of multinational companies is multicultural and diverse. Working in this kind of environment and managing processes at multinational levels requires multicultural and diversity-management skills over and above the qualifications required to do the job itself. This kind of environment is much more stressful than that of the slow-moving local companies of the past.

3 The relevance of motivation

The experience of stress influences motivation. Stress can have a positive influence on motivation, but it can also influence motivation negatively. For example, the phenomenon of burnout clearly illustrates the motivational incapacity of people who experience prolonged stress. People who are highly motivated are much better prepared to handle stressful situations than those who are not, therefore it is important to consider the following in a stress-management programme:

- Information to help programme participants understand what motivated behaviour is about
- Information to help programme participants understand how theoretical ideas on motivated behaviour describe and explain their personal behaviour

4 The relevance of emotions

Two aspects of emotions are important for a stress management programme, namely the various types of feelings and the expression and recognition of emotions.

4.1 The various types of feeling

Emotions are intimately involved in the experience of stress. It is important to differentiate between various kinds of emotions. People who work in high-pressure environments are likely to experience a range of different emotions and are likely to have more intense experiences of these emotions. Participants in a stress management programme need to learn to identify and name their emotions and moods. The cognitive-appraisal theory may be useful to help people cope emotionally with stressful situations by applying effective secondary appraisal and coping strategies and by learning how to take direct action in particular situations. They may benefit from debriefing sessions based on benign reappraisal of stress-proving situations.

4.2 The expression and recognition of emotions

Learning to recognise emotive signs provided by others helps people to understand one another better. If we are sensitive to other people's body language, the context in which emotions are expressed and the cultural background of the person displaying emotive behaviour, we are much more able to initiate and maintain appropriate communication with the person in question.

5 The relevance of interpersonal relationships

Interpersonal relationships are vital in a work situation and they play an important role in stress. Work will not happen if employees do not interact. Poor interpersonal relationships can contribute significantly to the experience of stress. Socio-affective needs cannot be satisfied in an environment where people have poor-quality interpersonal relationships. If socio-affective needs are not sufficiently satisfied, it is unlikely that people will be able to satisfy their needs for self-esteem and self-actualisation. Good interpersonal relationships are required for proper communication. Concepts that are particularly relevant in the field of interpersonal relationships are the following:

- The process and determinants of interpersonal attraction
- The nature of close relationships, especially the nature of friendships
- The nature of interpersonal communication, especially an understanding of the elements of interpersonal communication
- The dynamics of communication

Employees working in a high-pressure environment could benefit from exploring their interpersonal communication skills and from practising how to communicate effectively. It is important to communicate clearly and effectively in an environment where things happen quickly and situations change constantly. Communications have to be clear, precise and congruent and show mutual understanding. Workers have to learn that their interpersonal communications form processes and patterns that persist beyond immediate exchanges.

6 The relevance of group functioning

Poor intergroup relationships and functioning can be major sources of stress. The notion of a group is widely relevant. Groups exist at many different levels in our world. Most people are aware of groups in the context of society (society consisting of different groupings of people), but groups appear in many other contexts, such as the work context. The work environment is an important context for groups, which are often called work teams. The concepts that apply to groups in the context of the broader society are also true for groups in any other context. Good co-operation between groups is necessary for effective and efficient functioning. The absence of good co-operation could be a major source of stress in a high-pressure environment. Good intergroup co-operation presupposes properly constituted groups. We can expect intergroup conflict if group purposes are not clearly defined and if groups are not properly constituted to enable them to achieve those goals.

The following information is relevant for a stress-management programme:

1. People who select and manage groups should know the attributes of groups when they select and maintain them. It is impossible to work with groups if one is not aware of these attributes.
2. People who select and manage groups should understand how groups differentiate.
3. People who select and manage groups should know how to manage groups so as to allow them to co-operate effectively and efficiently.

If groups are selected and managed taking their structures, characteristics and dynamics of groups into account, one could claim that the groups are properly structured and one could then expect these groups to co-operate effectively and efficiently.

7 The relevance of self

The notion of the personal self appears in basic human needs, such as the need for self-esteem and the need for self-actualisation. In high-pressure environments, it is vitally important that individuals have knowledge about their selves and the way in which they participate in the constructions of their selves. The stronger an individual's self, the better that individual's ability to handle stressful situations. From a stress management programme point of view, one should include information about the dynamics of self-construction.

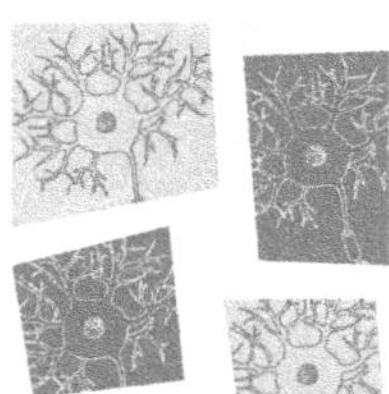

Psychological programme for stress

Programme title	**Psychological stress management programme**
Programme type	Psychological advisement programme
Version	Version 01
Programme developed for	InfoTech SA
Programme developed by	SocSci Information Services
Date of initial development	2012-04-10
Date of last revision	Not applicable
Revision notes	Not applicable

1 Aim

Employees at InfoTech SA work long hours under high pressure in a very competitive environment. The aim of introducing some form of intervention is to help them maintain high performance levels in stressful situations. A careful analysis of the work environment at InfoTech SA has shown that the best form of intervention would be a psychological advisement programme. The reasons for such a programme are as follows: The company has excellent work procedures in place and would not benefit from a programme aimed at improving work and management procedures. Also, it has become clear that employees show signs of stress and that some form of psychological intervention may be useful.

2 Target population

It was decided that all employees at the company could benefit from a psychological advisement programme. Initially, participation will be voluntary, but eventually all employees will have to sign up for the programme.

3 Programme objectives

3.1 Needs analysis

Employees were selected randomly from each sector in the company. In this way, a representative sample of employees was obtained. The selected employees completed various questionnaires and were interviewed individually. The aim of the questionnaires and the interview was to get an idea of the kinds of difficulties employees experience at work and how they react to them. Virtually all employees agree about the pressure factors in their various work environments. They do not mind working under pressure. What bothers them is that they often feel overwhelmed by the pressure. Most of the employees do not recognise the feelings they experience as feelings of stress. They are unable to describe how they feel. They think of themselves as individuals with particular knowledge and skills and the work environment is merely an environment in which they use them. They have no understanding of the work environment as one of interpersonal relationships that are formed and governed by the deeper meaning that work has for each of them. They do not consider themselves as individuals who have personal experiences and who react to these experiences in terms of their personal motivations and in terms of individual cognitive and emotional styles. It is clear that most of these employees do not have a psychological vocabulary that they could use to describe themselves. This makes it impossible for these employees to understand themselves psychologically and to think about their psychological well-being. They become physically sick because they do not recognise the emotional discomfort they experience. There is a tremendous need among these employees for a psychological vocabulary that could help them describe their behaviour in the work situation.

3.2 Objectives

Based on the needs analysis conducted at InfoTech SA, it was decided to design a psychological advisement programme that would aim at increasing the psychological vocabulary and self-awareness of people working at the company. In addition to this objective, the advisement programme would help them to recognise signs of stress and would provide them with strategies to cope with pressure in a way that would lead to lower personal stress levels. It was decided to call the advisement programme the Psychological Stress Management Programme, or PSMP for short.

4 Programme content

The needs analysis conducted at InfoTech SA showed that employees lack a psychological vocabulary to describe their personal experiences. A more detailed analysis of information obtained from these employees provided important indicators of the specific terms and concepts they require to increase their psychological awareness and self-understanding:

1. *The concept of stress.* Although most employees used the word 'stress', they were unable to explain what it meant, where it came from and how to deal with it.
2. *The meaning of work.* All the employees used the word 'work'. However, when asked to elaborate on the meaning of work, most of these employees could not explain what it means for them. The best they could come up with was the idea that work means earning money and that money means that one can buy the things one needs. There was no concept of the fact that work takes place within a work environment in which interpersonal interaction plays an important role.
3. *The concept and meaning of motivation.* Owing to employees' impoverished descriptions of the meaning work has for them (in other words, they found it difficult to motivate why they work), they were asked about their general motivations in life. Although most of them had a fairly good idea of their personal motivational factors, their explanations were limited to things that make them happy and things they do not like. They concentrated on external factors. Few individuals were able to describe the inner reasons behind their likes and dislikes.
4. *The nature of feelings.* The scarcity of descriptions of inner feelings and motivations seems to be linked to a lack of proper vocabulary. These employees do not mention their inner feelings and states of mind because they do not have the words for labelling and describing them.
5. *The nature of interpersonal relationships.* None of the employees seem to be aware of the fact that the place in which they work, together with their manner of work and their behaviour there, constitutes a work environment. This lack of awareness prompted questions about interpersonal relationships at work. Although most employees could indicate whom they liked and disliked, they were unable to describe their likes and dislikes in terms of interpersonal relationships. Their descriptions focused on the actions performed by the individuals in question. They did not seem to be aware that actions constitute interactions – that people become related via their actions and that these are governed by their relationships. There does not seem to be an awareness of the possibility of mutual interpersonal support on an emotional level. Interpersonal support seems to be limited to helping each other out with work tasks.

6. *Group functioning.* Despite the fact that most of the employees work in teams, they demonstrated little awareness of group functioning. In the individual interviews, they would often refer to 'us' and 'them' when distinguishing between their own team and another, but when pressed to explain how their own team differed from another, they could explain the differences only in terms of tasks and not group dynamics.
7. *Self-concept.* Many of the employees were at a total loss for words when asked to describe themselves. The questionnaire on self-awareness, as well as the information gleaned from the personal interviews, shows a limited ability to describe the self. Most of the employees used general statements to describe themselves. For example: I am good; I am friendly; I like people; I do my work well; I get angry quickly; My wife thinks I am great; I think most people like me; I like to laugh; I can be quite emotional, etc. When asked to elaborate on this kind of general statement, most of the employees reacted by providing further general statements. They were not able to provide descriptions of themselves in terms of personal understandings of their selves and the dynamics of these selves.

Based on this information, it is clear that the PSMP has to provide basic psychological vocabulary about stress, work, motivation, feelings, interpersonal relationships, group functioning and the self to enable employees to express their feelings and to describe their behaviour. In addition, the programme has to provide skills training in stress management.

5 Programme method

The PSMP is designed to be offered as a stand-alone self-study package, or as a self-study package complemented by a series of three workshops. The programme components are available in printed as well as electronic formats. The printed and electronic components can be combined in various ways to suit the needs of the user. Table 1 lists the programme components and their descriptions.

Table 1 Components of the Psychological Stress Management Programme

Quantity	Component	Description
1	Manual	The manual explains the objectives of the programme and also provides a programme outline, as well as a list of resources. It contains eight study units, one for each of seven fundamental psychological concepts and an eighth on stress management. The manual is available in printed as well as electronic format.
1	Reader	The reader contains the basic knowledge required for the programme. Concepts like stress, emotion, motivation, self, etc, are explained in the reader. The reader is available in printed as well as electronic format.

1	Workbook	The workbook contains exercises based on the information provided in the reader. It also has progress and score charts. The progress chart tracks the participant's progress through the course and the score chart shows the participant's performance on assessment exercises. The workbook is available in printed as well as electronic format.
3	Workshops	The first workshop explores the participants' experiences in the work environment. The second workshop introduces participants to the relevant psychological concepts and builds participants' psychological vocabulary. The third workshop explores methods of stress management and helps participants develop skills in personal stress management. Each workshop requires two days.
5	CD-ROM disks	The CD-ROM package consists of five disks. The first contains the electronic versions of the manual, reader and workbook. The electronic versions are fully interactive and contain additional video clips that are not available in the printed versions. The second, third and fourth disks contain material and exercises that can be used for the workshops. The fifth contains the software required to run the electronic version of the PSMP.
1	DVD	The DVD contains three study units, each divided into three parts. Each unit contains workshop video examples and exercises. The DVD material can be used to replace the workshops in a self-study package.
1	Assessment and certification package	The assessment and certification package contains an assessment test, a memorandum and scoring instructions for the certification of participants. The package includes four parallel forms (i.e. four different versions) of the assessment test. The assessment package is available in printed and electronic format. The electronic version uses an online automated assessment procedure.

Table 2 shows how the programme components can be combined to form four different versions of the programme:

1. A print-based version with live workshops
2. A print-based version with workshop examples and exercises on DVD
3. An electronic version with live workshops
4. An electronic version with workshop examples and exercises on DVD

The components marked with X are included in the particular version of the programme.

Table 2 The configurations of the Psychological Stress Management Programme

Component	Programme type			
	Print-based with workshops	Print-based self-study	E-format with workshops	E-format self-study
Printed manual	X	X		
Electronic manual			X	X
Printed reader	X	X		
Electronic reader			X	X
Printed workbook	X	X		
Electronic workbook			X	X
Live workshops	X		X	
DVD workshops		X		X
PSMP software			X	X
Printed assessment test	X	X		
Electronic assessment test			X	X

6 Programme resource requirements

The programme requires the following resources:

1. Development funding (the development costs are listed in Table 3)
2. Programme material (printed material; CD-ROM-based material; DVD-based material)
3. Custom-written software (for the electronic version of the programme and assessment package)
4. Programme presenters (workshop presenters)
5. Workshop venues
6. Programme administrators (people who handle programme administration)
7. Computers with multimedia capability (to run the electronic versions of the programme)
8. Assessors (to assess and certify programme participants)

Table 3 Programme development costs

Component	Description	Cost in ZAR
Printed material	Research of content (topics) to be included	10 000.00
	Instructional design (teaching method and exercises)	8 000.00
	Authoring of primary text	30 000.00
	Layout and graphics design	8 500.00
	Editing	5 000.00
	Production	35 000.00
Electronic material	Instructional design (interactivity of material)	9 500.00
	Preparation of electronic text (interactive)	22 000.00
	Preparation of audiovisual material	55 000.00
	Production	15 000.00
Live workshops	Research of content	8 000.00
	Instructional design	5 500.00
	Presenter training	18 300.00
DVD workshops	Instructional design (interactivity of material)	7 500.00
	Preparation of electronic text	15 000.00
	Preparation of audiovisual material	37 000.00
	Production	24 800.00
PSMP software	Software design	15 500.00
	Programming	18 000.00
	Production	4500.00
Assessment package	Design of assessment test	3000.00
	Development of assessment test	12 500.00
	Total production costs	364 600.00

7 Programme implementation plan

The programme is developed and implemented in five phases. Six months are allowed for programme development (phase 1) and a further three months for production (phase 2). The first two presentation cycles and revision of the programme are viewed as a test phase (phase 3). During these cycles, employee participation is voluntary.

The programme becomes provisionally operational during the next phase (phase 4). A revision period of three months is included at the end of this phase. The programme becomes fully operational in phase 5. It is expected that a fully operational programme will have a five-year lifespan at minimum. Table 4 lists the programme implementation phases and cycles.

Table 4 Programme development and implementation plan

Phase	Cycle	Duration	Description	Employee participation
1	0	6 months	Develop programme components	Not applicable
2	0	3 months	Produce programme components	Not applicable
3	1	3 months	First test cycle	Voluntary
	2	3 months	Second test cycle	Voluntary
	0	3 months	Programme revision	Not applicable
4	3	3 months	First provisional operational cycle	Compulsory
	4	3 months	Second provisional operational cycle	Compulsory
	5	3 months	Third provisional operational cycle	Compulsory
	6	3 months	Fourth provisional operational cycle	Compulsory
	0	3 months	Revision	Not applicable
5	7–27	5 years	Fully operational cycles 1 to 20	Compulsory

The material covered in the manual and reader requires 32 notional hours of study. One notional study hour means that a programme participant of average ability would require one hour to complete the work intended for one notional hour of study. The DVD-based workshops require an additional 18 notional study hours. Participants who do the 'Print-based with workshops' or the 'Electronic format with workshops' versions of the PSMP are required to register for the programme at least three weeks before the presentation of the workshops. It has been estimated that people who do self-study average about two hours of study per day during the week and four hours per day on weekends. The three-week period is required for self-study before the workshops begin. The workshops are presented one per week over a three-week period. Each workshop requires two full days. The workshop series are presented at three month intervals. Participants who register for the 'Print-based self-study' or 'Electronic format self-study' versions of the programme do not attend live workshops and are therefore not bound by registration deadlines. However, these individuals are expected to complete the PSMP within a timespan of two months. The programme concludes with a three-hour assessment session, which is scheduled once per three months. However, participants who register for the 'Electronic format self-study' version of the PSMP are allowed to complete their assessment online. The continuous availability of the electronic online version of the assessment package means that these participants can undergo their assessment at any date and time of their choice. All participants have to achieve the required standards to qualify for certification. Table 5 lists the comparative implementation schedules for the various configurations of the PSMP and Table 6 indicates the costs associated with the implementation, running and revision of the programme.

Table 5 Comparative implementation schedules for the configurations of the Psychological Stress Management Programme

Week	Day	Activity	Programme types			
			Print-based with workshops	Print-based self-study	E-format with workshops	E-format self-study
1	1	Register for course	X	X	X	X
		Receive course material				
	2–3	Complete Unit 1	X	X	X	X
	4–5	Complete Unit 2	X	X	X	X
2	1–2	Complete Unit 3	X	X	X	X
	3–4	Complete Unit 4	X	X	X	X
	5–6	Complete Unit 5	X	X	X	X
3	1–2	Complete Unit 6	X	X	X	X
	3–4	Complete Unit 7	X	X	X	X
	5–6	Complete Unit 8	X	X	X	X
4	1–2	Attend Workshop 1	X		X	
	Any	Complete DVD		X		X
		Workshop 1 Part 1				
	Any	Complete DVD		X		X
		Workshop 1 Part 2				
	Any	Complete DVD		X		X
		Workshop 1 Part 3				
5	1–2	Attend Workshop 2	X		X	
	Any	Complete DVD		X		X
		Workshop 2 Part 1				
	Any	Complete DVD		X		X
		Workshop 2 Part 2				
	Any	Complete DVD		X		X
		Workshop 2 Part 3				

6	1–2	Attend Workshop 3	X		X	
	Any	Complete DVD		X		X
		Workshop 3 Part 1				
	Any	Complete DVD		X		X
		Workshop 3 Part 2				
	Any	Complete DVD				
		Workshop 3 Part 3		X		X
7	1	Undergo assessment	X	X	X	
	Any	Undergo online assessment				X

Table 6 Programme implementation and revision costs for phases 3 and 4

Component	Description	Cost in ZAR
Printed material	Additional reprint of existing materials	10 000.00
	Revision of text	9 500.00
	Revision of graphics design	3 000.00
	Additional editing	2 000.00
	Reproduction costs	20 000.00
Electronic material	Revision of instructional design	3 000.00
	Revision of electronic text	4 000.00
	Additional audiovisual material	15 000.00
	Reproduction	6 000.00
Live workshops	Training of additional presenters	5 000.00
	Running costs	5 000.00
DVD workshops	Additional material	15 000.00
	Running costs	500.00
	Reproduction	5 800.00
Software	Additional programming	5 000.00
Assessment package	Revision of assessment technique	2 000.00
	Editing of assessment test	6 500.00
	Total implementation and revision costs for phases 3 and 4	117 300.00

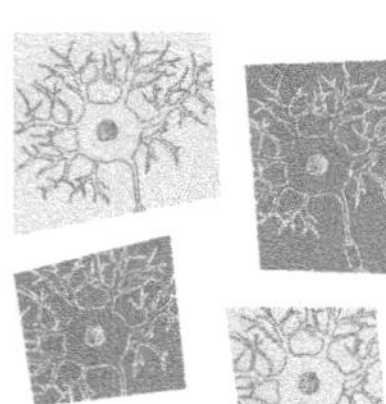

Psychological programme for study management

1 Aim

The student studies part time while working full time and pursuing social interests. The aim of introducing some form of intervention is to help him study effectively and manage his available time better. A careful analysis of his situation has shown that the best form of intervention would be a psychological advisement programme. The reasons for this are as follows: The student would like to study further so that he can obtain promotion to another section in the company. The company supports his efforts. The student has failed his exams and it is clear that he is having difficulty identifying his problem and taking appropriate action. In this situation, some form of psychological intervention may be useful.

2 Target population

In this situation, the programme will be designed for an individual student, therefore that student is the target population. His participation is voluntary because the programme was initiated at his request.

3 Programme objectives

1. *Needs analysis.* The student's needs were established in an interview. A thorough investigation was made of his perceptions of his difficulties and his needs. The student thinks his problem is that he did not pass his exams and this is what stands in the way of the progress he would like to make. It is clear that he has not really identified or recognised his problem. He has ideas about reasons for his lack of progress, but these are fallacies. The student does not understand the impact on his situation of his ways of thinking, reasoning and

problem solving. He also does not know how to study effectively in terms of time management and by using techniques to enhance learning and memory. The student does not have a psychological vocabulary that he could use to describe and understand himself and his situation in order to do something about it. There is therefore a need for a psychological vocabulary that could help him describe his behaviour and his study problem.

2. *Objectives.* Based on the needs analysis, it was decided to design a psychological advisement programme that would aim at increasing the psychological vocabulary and self-awareness of the student. In addition to this objective, the programme would help the student to identify and understand his problem and provide him with strategies to manage his studies effectively in a way that would help him attain success in his studies. It was decided to call the advisement programme the Psychological Study Management Programme, or PSMP for short.

4 Programme content

The needs analysis conducted with the student showed that he lacks a psychological vocabulary to describe his personal experiences. A more detailed analysis of information obtained from him provided important indicators of the specific terms and concepts he requires to increase his psychological awareness and self-understanding:

1. *The concept of thinking.* Although the student knew that he had been thinking about his situation, he was unable to explain the relation between thought and language and the important role that inner speech plays in successful problem solving.
2. *The concept of reasoning.* The student stated his reasons for failing his exams, but he was not aware that he was using fallacies as a basis of his reasoning. He did not have knowledge of critical reasoning processes or an understanding of the importance of critical reasoning. Because of this he was unable to identify his problem properly and work out reasons for the problem.
3. *The concept and meaning of problem-solving strategies.* The student was aware that he needed to do something about his situation, but he had no knowledge of problem-solving strategies. Owing to the student's inaccurate description of the nature of his problem, he was unable to identify and work out problem-solving strategies to deal with his situation.
4. *The nature of learning.* The student has already passed some of his exams, so he is familiar with the concept of learning; however, he was unable to explain how he learns. He was also unable to describe the conditions for effective learning, such as the importance of association and reinforcement in the learning process. He seemed unaware of possibilities of steps that could be taken to manage his studies better.

5. *The nature of memory processes.* The student recognised that memory processes play a role in studying but could not indicate how they could be made more effective. He was not aware of the nature of forgetting and the factors that influence it. Because of this, he did not realise the implications for his studies.

Based on this information, it is clear that the PSMP has to provide a basic psychological vocabulary about thinking, reasoning and problem solving, as well as learning and memory, to enable the student to describe his behaviour. In addition, the programme has to provide skills training in problem-solving strategies and study management, including behaviour modification to reinforce the study programme.

5 Programme method

The PSMP is designed to be offered in the form of 10 individual consultations, together with printed material. The programme components and their descriptions are listed below.

1. *Ten individual consultations.* The consultations cover different topics. The first one will introduce the student to the relevant psychological concepts. Thereafter, problem-solving strategies will be implemented through understanding the problem, considering alternative solutions, choosing an appropriate solution and applying and evaluating the solution. Once the appropriate solution has been decided on (together with the student), the solution will be applied by means of a behaviour-modification programme to reinforce the study programme. This programme comprises specifying target behaviours, developing a baseline (database) for measuring progress, selecting a suitable strategy for behavioural modification, ensuring adherence to the programme, carefully recording progress and evaluating and amending the programme where necessary. Each consultation requires one hour.
2. *A reader.* The reader contains the basic knowledge for the programme. Concepts such as critical reasoning, problem solving, learning and memory are explained in the reader. The reader is available in printed and electronic format.
3. *A workbook.* The workbook contains exercises based on the information provided in the reader. It also has progress and score charts. The progress chart tracks the student's progress and provides a database that records his progress toward the target behaviour. The score chart shows the student's performance on assessment exercises. The workbook is available in printed as well as electronic format.
4. A programme usually contains an *assessment and certification* package. In this instance, there is no formal assessment because the student's success is measured in terms of being able to achieve his goal (target behaviours).

6 Programme resource requirements

The programme requires the following resources:

1. Development funding (the programme development costs are listed in Table 1)
2. Programme material (printed material)
3. Custom-written software (for the electronic version of the reader and workbook)
4. Programme presenter and assessor (counsellor)
5. Consultation venue

Table 1 Programme development costs

Component	Description	Cost in ZAR
Printed material	Research of content (topics) to be included	2 000.00
	Instructional design (teaching method and exercises)	1 000.00
	Authoring of primary text	3 000.00
	Layout and graphics design	1 500.00
	Editing	1 000.00
	Production	5 000.00
Electronic material	Instructional design (interactivity of material)	3 500.00
	Preparation of electronic text (interactive)	1 500.00
Consultations	Research of content	3 000.00
	Instructional design	1 500.00
Total production		23 000.00

In this table, you will notice that no provision has been made for training a presenter. The counsellor's professional training would have included programme presentation and therefore no additional costs are required. Because the student is registered with the university, the student does not have to pay the counsellor for assistance with study management. However, it is important to remember that, even though the student does not have to pay for the programme, it still costs money to produce it (as shown in Table 1). In this case, the costs would be carried by the university.

7 Programme implementation plan

No initial time is required for programme development because the counsellor is already trained and the materials are already available. To implement the programme, provision must be made for 10 individual consultation sessions. The counsellor knows that the consultation sessions cannot be too far apart, otherwise the necessary progress will not be made. The recommended implementation time is two consultation sessions per week.

After the initial consultation session, the student has to do self-study before the next session. There should be a self-study session before each subsequent consultation. The self-study involves reading (the reader), completing exercises in the workbook and recording activities in order to assess progress. The material covered in the self-study package requires 10 notional hours of study. One notional study hour means that a student of average ability would require one hour to complete the work required. The student will therefore have to do two self-study sessions a week (one before each consultation). The programme should be completed within a timespan of six weeks. This depends on the progress made by the student and may need to be adapted with each evaluation.

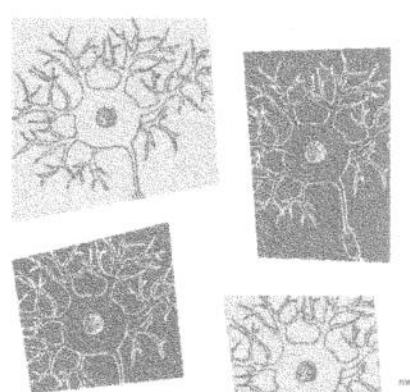

Psychological programmes

1 The new world and training programmes

People attend school to study and write examinations to get certificates. There was a time when these certificates equipped one for a broad range of jobs. Those who were fortunate attended universities, because university degrees equipped people for the really good jobs, but the world has changed significantly since that time. Nowadays, people are not assured of a job simply because they have the required diplomas, certificates and degrees. Furthermore, these qualifications do not carry lifetime guarantees. The knowledge one gathers when studying for a particular qualification becomes obsolete within a couple of years after completing one's studies. This is because the world changes at a tremendous rate. Nowadays, people have to keep on learning throughout their entire lives. Large numbers of people enter training programmes each year to update their knowledge in a particular area or to equip themselves with the knowledge and skills of a new field. Because training costs money and because people have little time to spend on it, these training programmes have to be efficient and effective. Therefore they are carefully designed and tailored towards the needs of those who enter such programmes.

2 Psychological training programmes

One kind of training programme that has become very popular in recent times is the psychological training programme, which focuses on the psychological well-being of people. Such programmes are popular because they provide underlying knowledge and skills. In other words, they provide knowledge and skills that help people to improve their general abilities. For example, a training programme that aims to improve memory can help people to do better in other training programmes where they have to memorise information. Psychological training programmes provide psychological information and skills that help people function better as human beings.

3 Programme differences and similarities: About elements, attributes and attribute values

There are many kinds of training programmes, and they come in a variety of sorts and sizes. For example, programmes may differ with regard to objectives and content. The objectives and content of a training programme for security guards would differ widely from those of a programme aimed at training aircraft pilots. Programmes also vary with regard to length and complexity. For example, it takes much less time to train a supermarket cashier to use a till than it takes to train a radiologist to use a scanner to X-ray the human brain. Some training programmes may be completed in a matter of hours or days, while others may take three to four years because the complexity of the required knowledge and skills differs widely. For example, it is much easier to use a till and to interpret till slips than it is to use an X-ray scanner and to interpret X-ray plates.

Despite the differences between programmes, they are called training programmes. In other words, they have certain things in common – things that identify them as training programmes. For example, cars may differ widely in model and in size, but they all have an engine, a body and four wheels, which are, among others, the elements of cars. Likewise, the elements of a training programme are the bits and pieces that a training programme is made of. For example, all training programmes are developed for an individual or a group of individuals. The person or persons that the programme is developed for is called the programme's target population. A programme must contain a description of its target population. Such a description is an element of a training programme.

Programmes also have attributes, which are not things. They form part of the description of things. For example, cars are painted in different colours, but a car does not have a thing called colour. The car has a body, which differs from the bodies of other cars in terms of colour, shape and size, which are attributes of cars. Therefore, unlike elements, the attributes of a programme are not something contained within the programme. They are aspects that characterise a programme. For example, some programmes can be completed within a day whereas others take weeks or years, thus they differ with regard to the attribute of length. Likewise, some programmes may cost more than others, thus they differ with regard to the attribute of cost. Attributes provide information about programmes and elements are the things that programmes are made of. One should note that elements can have their own attributes, which provide information about them.

Attributes have values. For example, if a car is blue, the car's colour attribute has the value 'blue'. The values of programme attributes describe how programmes differ from each other. For example, length is a programme attribute. All programmes have a programme-length attribute, because all programmes take a particular amount of time to complete. The amount of time that it takes to complete a programme is the value of the programme's length attribute. If a training programme for supermarket cashiers takes five days to complete, the value of the length attribute is five days. In the case of a radiologist training programme, the value of the length attribute may be four years. In other words, programmes differ from one another not in terms of their attributes, but in terms of the values of these attributes.

4 The basic elements of training programmes

There are basic elements that any training programmes must have in order to be called a training programme. These are the primary constituents of any training programme and the following table lists six basic elements.

Table 1 Six basic elements of training programmes

Target population	An indication of the person or persons who stand to benefit from taking part in the programme
Objective	An indication of what the programme aims to achieve
Content	The knowledge and skills that the programme offers to programme participants
Method	The way in which the programme conveys its content
Resources	The things required to run the programme
Implementation	The processes of running the programme

The following sections provide more detail about the basic programme elements.

4.1 Target population

A programme should contain a description of its target population. The target population consists of everybody who can benefit from participating in the particular programme. These individuals are identified and described in terms of their characteristics and their needs.

4.1.1 Characteristics

A characteristic is anything that may be relevant to identify an individual as a member of the target population. For example, geographical location and level of income are relevant characteristics if the training programme in question targets citizens in a particular suburb. Being a woman is a relevant characteristic if one wants to enrol for a training programme called 'Corporate world etiquette for women'. In other words, the programme targets women. Note, however, that the emphasis is on the relevance of a characteristic. Characteristics are not necessarily relevant under all circumstances. For example, marital status is an individual characteristic as some individuals are married and others are not. Although marital status may be a relevant characteristic for a programme concerning legal matters for married couples, this characteristic is not relevant for a training programme in postgraduate psychology, as marital status does not affect one's participation in a training programme in postgraduate psychology. In this case, one's graduate status is a relevant characteristic. One has to have a degree in psychology before one can enter into a postgraduate psychology training programme.

4.1.2 Needs

The needs of a target population are not always easy to obtain. It may be difficult to define particular needs. The members of a target population may not be aware of their needs, or they may have only a very vague idea. For example, a group of employees may register for a team-building training programme because the manager has decided that they do not perform well as a team, but this does not mean that the individual members of the group know what they lack in good team membership. People may also be unrealistic about their needs. For example, a self-help programme may target a poor community to help them increase their level of income. The members of the community may think they need capital to improve their situation, but the programme developers may think that the community needs entrepreneurial skills. If the needs of a target population are not clearly defined, a thorough analysis may be required to clarify them.

4.1.3 Needs analysis

Needs analysis requires one to (1) identify the relevant stakeholders; and (2) define the different stakeholders' needs. A stakeholder is anyone who is involved in the situation – that is, anyone who has a stake in the situation.

The needs of the different stakeholders have to be compared in order to get a clear idea of the needs of the target population. For example, a training programme to increase the effectiveness of security personnel may target the security personnel of big office buildings. In this case, the stakeholders are the security personnel, the tenants of the office space, clients, visitors to the building and maintenance and cleaning staff. The different stakeholders may have different security needs and these have to be taken into consideration when a training programme for security personnel is compiled. The tenants of office space may have security needs that the security personnel (that is, the target population) are not aware of. All stakeholders have to contribute when the needs of the security personnel (target population) are defined.

4.2 Programme objectives

The objectives of a programme indicate what it wants to achieve. Programme objectives are designed to address the needs of a target population, therefore they are closely linked to the target population needs. For example, consider a training programme for HIV/AIDS counsellors. The target population (the counsellors) clearly needs factual information about HIV/AIDS as a medical condition, as well as basic counselling skills, therefore imparting these would be the primary objectives of the programme.

Because programme objectives are closely linked to the needs of the target population, the descriptions of these objectives contain justifications. In other words, the description of an objective explains how the objective is linked to a need of the target population and how it satisfies this need. For example, consider a programme aimed at reducing aggressive behaviour. One of the needs of the target population could be the need to reduce aggressive acts in interpersonal behaviour. One of the objectives of the training programme could be to provide information about aggressive behaviour – that is, to explain what kind of behaviour is seen as aggressive and why. The link between this objective and the target population need is fairly straightforward and clear, but another objective of the training programme could be to increase self-knowledge. It is not obvious how this objective relates to the reduction of aggressive behaviour, therefore the programme objective needs to be justified by indicating its link to the target population's need. In this case, the objective justification would read as follows: 'Self-knowledge helps people to understand why they display aggressive behaviour. Awareness of the nature of their behaviour enables individuals to alter their behaviour patterns.'

4.3 Programme content

The content of a programme refers to the knowledge and skills that participants should gain through it, which should be in line with the programme objectives. In other words, participants should be able to realise the programme objectives through the knowledge and skills provided in the programme.

Training programmes can err in various ways. They can provide too little or too much content. If there is too little content, participants cannot achieve the set objectives. If there is too much, the superfluous information is a waste of time. Programme content can also be irrelevant. Content is irrelevant if it does not contribute to the achievement of programme objectives. Another way in which programmes err is by including content that is not at an appropriate level of complexity – that is, either too simple or too complex. This does not mean that content can never be simple or complex. Some objectives may require very simple content, whereas for others this may need to be highly abstract and difficult. The point is that the level of complexity of content should match the requirements of the corresponding programme objective.

To summarise: Programme content should be sufficient to allow participants to realise the objectives. Programme content is sufficient if the necessary knowledge and skills are provided at the appropriate level of complexity.

4.4 Programme method

The method of a programme refers to the manner in which the programme content is conveyed. It refers to how the programme manifests itself in reality, for example the format of presentation. The programme can be a self-study unit, printed on paper, a multimedia study unit presented on computer, a series of lectures presented by a tutor, or a workshop. Another attribute of programme method is the sequencing of programme activities. A programme requires both participant and presenter actions (that is, activities performed by participants and by presenters), which can be put together in a variety of ways. The particular sequence in which activities appear in the programme defines the process of the programme. Different sequences of activities define different processes and processes take time, as does running through the sequence of events that constitute the programme. The amount of time it takes to complete the programme is a function of the method used to convey the programme's content.

Programme methods should be appropriate and should fit the circumstances in which the programme is presented. In other words, the format of presentation should fit the needs and means of the target population. It is useless to have a multimedia, computer-driven programme if the target population does not have access to multimedia computer technology. In addition, the process of the programme should be logical and realistic. In other words, the sequence of participant and presenter actions should form a logical process. A participant should be able to work through the programme from beginning to end in a progressive manner and sufficient time should be allowed to complete the required activities. In other words, the programme length (the amount of time allowed to complete the programme) should be realistic.

4.5 Programme resources

Programme resources refer to anything (for example material, machines, people, apparatus, funds, venues) required to run the programme. For example, if a programme contains printed material, this constitutes a programme resource. One would not be able to present the programme if the printed material were not available. Likewise, one would not be able to present it without presenters and participants. Another significant resource is the funding required to cover development and running costs. One has to budget for these costs and indicate how programme funds are to be spent.

The various resources required by a programme have to be listed. To compile a full list, one has to consider each of the various activities that constitute the programme method. In other words, one has to consider in detail the way in which the programme conveys its content. The resources required by the different activities of the programme method make up the list of resources required by the programme as a whole.

4.6 Programme implementation

Programme implementation refers to processes involved in running it, one of the most important of which is time management. The programme needs to be executed within particular time constraints. In other words, it requires a time schedule, which links the sequence of events and actions to particular hours or dates. It indicates the time required to complete the various actions and events that constitute the programme and it lists deadlines and beginning and finishing dates. Other implementation processes that play a major role in most programmes are processes concerning the budget, the presenters and the participants. One has to manage the programme budget – that is, one has to indicate how, when and where money is spent and how spending is being monitored and controlled. As for presenters, one cannot implement a programme without a sufficient number of properly trained presenters, so the recruiting and training of presenters is an important part of the implementation process. As for participants, one cannot run a programme without them. One has to recruit and enrol participants for the programme in question and consider the logistics of programme participation. In other words, one has to indicate how the programme and its participants are brought together. For example, is the programme to be offered as a distance-learning self-study package or in a face-to-face, contact-learning context?

Note that the difference between programme resources and programme implementation is sometimes subtle and not always obvious. For example, the money required for a programme (that is, the programme funds) is a programme resource, but the way in which the funds are spent is a matter of implementation. In general, anything required for the implementation of the programme is a resource, but when the focus shifts from the resource (that is, the thing itself) to the process of handling the resource, it becomes a matter of implementation. For example, a resource is always listed as a resource, but its availability at a particular time is a matter of implementation. A study guide could be listed as a resource for a particular programme, but the date on and the way in which it is to be delivered to participants are matters of implementation. A programme cannot be implemented successfully if the necessary resources are not available.

5 Summary

The psychological programme must be comprehensive and must be implementable.

A psychological programme is comprehensive if

- the target population is indicated.
- the needs of the target population are described.
- the programme objectives are indicated.
- the programme method is indicated.
- the required programme resources are listed.
- an implementation plan is provided.

A psychological programme is implementable if

- the set of target population needs are comprehensive and relevant.
- the set of programme objectives meets the needs of the target population.
- it has sufficient content to realise the set of programme objectives.
- the list of required resources are comprehensive and relevant, the programme structure is appropriate and the implementation plan is executable – that is, the programme is accessible to the target population, the plan can be executed practically and the required resources are available.

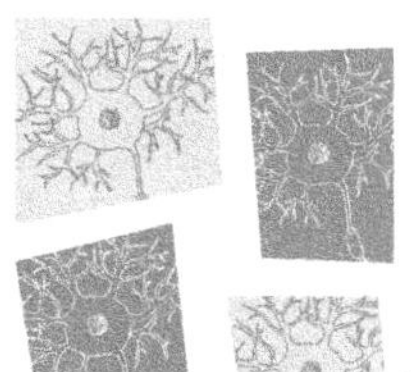

Psychological science

Psychology is a discipline, which means it consists of a body of scientific knowledge, which is made up of factual statements and theories. Factual statements are information that has been collected and analysed in a systematic and controlled manner. Theories are logical arguments that aim to explain phenomena on the basis of scientific facts.

The point is, psychology is not a haphazard collection of popular beliefs. Psychological statements are based on knowledge that has been carefully researched. This knowledge is used by people who have been trained in psychology and provide psychological information and services to their clients. Not only do they know and understand psychological information, but they have also been trained to think psychologically. In other words, their thinking has been disciplined. They have been taught how to think in terms of psychological concepts and this requires a scientific approach. To think like a psychologist means one has to think scientifically.

This section introduces four components of scientific thinking – the ontological component, the epistemological component, the methodological component and the ideological component (Mouton and Marais, 1991; Jordaan, 1998).

1 The ontological component of scientific thinking

The *ontological component* of scientific thinking refers to the basic nature of the object of research. In psychology, the object of research is the behaviour and experience of human beings. We often ignore the basic nature of the object of interest because we concentrate on certain aspects of the object. For example, when we concentrate on the behaviour and experience of humans, we ignore the fact that the human being is the basic reality of these behaviours and experiences. Behaviour and experience are characteristics of a more fundamental object of interest, namely the human being.

The mainstream view of the human being is in terms of a physical body and a mind.

The problem is the relationship between the body and the mind. Is the mind an epiphenomenon of the body, or is it something separate and apart from the body? These questions imply different ontologies. If the mind is merely an epiphenomenon of the body, the human person is fundamentally a physical being. On the other hand, if the mind has a separate existence from that of the body, the human being is made of both physical and mind stuff. This difference in ontology influences psychology. Broadly speaking, *behavioural psychologists* accept the physical body as the ontological reality of their object of study. They study the way in which the physical body behaves, biologically as well as psychologically. Emotional and cognitive activities are seen as behaviours and experiences of the human body. *Psychoanalytic and cognitive psychologists,* on the other hand, are interested in the psyche of the person and study the structure and processes of the human mind. The human mind is the ontological reality of these objects of study. *Social constructionists* have a very different ontology. They are interested in the way in which things like the body and the mind are constructed in our social and interpersonal interactions. The ontological reality of their object of study is language (that is, the process of signification).

The ontological component of a psychological object of study is not always clear, because psychologists do not necessarily stick with a specific school of psychological thinking. Nowadays, psychological science is more eclectic. For example, a psychologist who is interested in a particular kind of emotion may consider the psycho-physiological aspects of emotions, explore unconscious factors involved in emotional reactions and examine the social expression of emotions in an attempt to understand what role the particular kind of emotion plays in our lives, thus presupposing all three of the ontologies referred to above.

2 The epistemological component of scientific thinking

The *epistemological component* of scientific thinking refers to the knowledge we have about the object of research. Scientific knowledge differs from popular beliefs in being based on facts. A scientific fact is a statement that all researchers agree about. The problem is to know whether these facts are really true. Some researchers believe that, if one follows a proper scientific method, one will be able to distinguish between statements that are true and those that are false, but this only shifts the burden of truth from the outcome of the method (the scientific fact) to the method itself. The assumption is that if the method is true, the facts produced by it will be accurate. So the problem then becomes: How does one find the true or proper scientific method?

The core of the problem is the *concept of truth*. What does it mean to say that a statement is true? The traditional scientific approach is to define truth in terms of correspondence with reality. A factual statement is true if it corresponds to the real situation, but this raises a new problem, namely that we do not know reality. In fact, the point of science is to uncover reality. If we think carefully about this, we quickly come to the conclusion that the notion that there is a reality is a presupposition.

The researcher assumes that there is a reality and that this reality can be uncovered by conducting a scientific study. The way in which scientists work around this problem is to view reality as *objective reality*. In other words, they shift the idea of reality from something that lies beyond our perceptions to something that we can be objective about. An objective reality is something that is not tainted by personal interpretations. It appears the same to everybody regardless of what they think, or how they feel about it. This changes the criterion used to judge the truth of a statement. Now a factual statement is true if it is an objective one. The challenge for scientists is to arrive at objective statements, therefore scientific studies have to be designed to limit the researcher's interpretations in order to let the facts speak for themselves. Research studies are designed to minimise subjectivity in order to maximise objectivity. The ideal of science is to eliminate subjectivity.

However, the ideal to eliminate subjectivity is just that – an ideal. Philosophers of science, such as Karl Popper (1963; 1980), have argued convincingly that a scientific fact can never be an entirely objective fact. Scientific facts are always already embedded in one or another theoretical frame of reference. In other words, the theories that researchers use always play a role in their interpretations of research findings. This led Popper to the conclusion that a scientific statement can never be confirmed as true, only as false. A scientific statement becomes true only if we fail to show that it is false, thus we can never show that something is absolutely true. We can only say that it seems to be true because we failed in our attempts to show that it is false. Technically, we would say the truth of a statement is corroborated with each failure to prove it false. This is an *epistemology of falsification*.

When it comes to the ideal of objectivity, there is another kind of epistemology, namely the constructivist epistemology, that is even more radical than Popper's epistemology of falsification. According to constructivists, factual statements are not statements about a presupposed or an objective reality. They are statements that reflect shared meanings. The kind of reality that is constituted by statements of shared meanings is a reality of consensus. A statement is true if everybody agrees that it is true. This reality is similar to a text. Like an ordinary text, the content of a consensual reality can be interpreted, or it can be analysed for hidden discourses, or it can be deconstructed to explore the nature of its structure.

The epistemological component of scientific thinking is not independent of the ontological component. Our understanding of truth (epistemology) is intertwined with our understanding of reality (ontology).

3 The methodological component of scientific thinking

The methodological component of scientific thinking follows from the ontological and epistemological components. The ontological component concerns the reality that constitutes the psychologist's field of study. The epistemological component involves the criteria according to which scientific knowledge is considered true knowledge.

The *methodological component* of scientific thinking concerns our understanding of the methods that we should use to get proper scientific knowledge when we explore a given domain of reality (Jordaan, 1998).

All research studies go through definite phases, regardless of the particular methods used in them. There are certain activities that are essential in every study. All researchers have to identify the research topic, formulate a research problem, conceptualise and operationalise the key concepts of the problem, plan and design the study, collect the relevant information, analyse the information, interpret the findings and report the outcomes of the study. We look at these phases or steps below.

3.1 Identifying the research topic

The first step in a research project is to identify the research topic. Humans have inquiring minds. We are curious and we like to investigate new things simply because we like to explore. For example, we spend huge amounts of money to explore the planet Mars to satisfy our curiosity. However, there are sometimes pressing needs that we have to pay attention to, not for the sake of satisfying our curiosity but for the sake of survival. For example, global warming may have disastrous consequences and therefore we are forced to research its possible causes. The need is not always about a particular issue, though. We may have to do research for the sake of it, as when a research project is required to obtain a particular degree. Regardless of our reason for embarking on a research study, we have to *identify* the research topic and we have to make sure that it falls within our field of expertise. For example, if a psychologist is interested in factors that enable people to be successful in their work, his or her interest has to be limited to psychological factors that influence work success. We would not expect a psychologist to explore the economics of work success or the technical engineering of the work environment.

3.2 Formulating the research problem

The second step is to formulate the research problem clearly and unambiguously. It is not possible to conduct a research project if it is not clear what the problem is. To suggest that we are interested in psychological factors that influence work success does not indicate a problem. We have to read about the topic to find out as much as we can. In other words, we have to consider the knowledge that already exists about the role of psychological factors in work success. We may, for instance, learn from these explorations that work success may be influenced by the ability to learn quickly. Based on this information, we could ask whether there is a relationship between learning potential and work success. This question would then constitute a *research problem.*

3.3 Conceptualising and operationalising key concepts

The third step is to conceptualise and operationalise the key concepts of the problem.

The key concepts play a major role in the research study. They determine what information has to be collected to enable us to answer the research question. If the concepts are not clearly defined and if they have not been operationalised, we would not know what information to collect. *Conceptualisation* involves defining and clarifying these concepts until it is clear what they mean. The *operationalisation* of a concept refers to specifying the kind of information that is required to describe it. For example, the key concepts in a study about the relationship between learning potential and work success are the concept of learning potential and the concept of work success. Learning potential may be conceptualised as the ability to learn new information and work success may be defined as the ability to perform adequately in the workplace. However, these concepts have to be operationalised to enable a researcher to collect the correct information. The ability to learn new information may be operationalised in terms of the number of new things learned in a particular time period (for example 10 things learned in five minutes). To get a measure of learning potential, the researcher has to count how many new things a research participant learns in five minutes. Work success may be operationalised in terms of the speed (the number of minutes required to produce a certain number of responses) and the accuracy (the number of correct responses versus the number of wrong ones) with which a work task is completed.

3.4 Planning and designing the study

The next step is to plan and design the study. A research *plan* indicates when and where the study is to be conducted, who the research participants will be, how much the study will cost and where the money for the study will come from. The *design* of the study describes how the study is executed. For example, a study about the relationship between learning potential and work success may be designed as follows: 30 research participants will each be asked to complete a learning task and a work task.

3.5 Collecting the information

The fifth step in a research project is to collect the *correct information.* In the example indicated above, learning potential has been operationalised as the number of new things learned in a certain time, therefore the number of things learned in a particular time (say five minutes) is the information that the researcher has to collect for each participant. Work success has been operationalised as speed and accuracy. For each participant, the researcher has to record the number of minutes the participant takes to complete the work task, as well as the number of mistakes he or she makes during its completion.

3.6 Analysing and interpreting the information

After this, the sixth step for the researcher is to prepare the information for analysis and interpret the findings. The measure of learning potential is a single score (the number of things learned) that does not need further preparation. However, work success is indicated by two scores, namely the number of minutes it takes to complete a work task and the number of mistakes made during its execution. Work success can be indicated by the sum of these two measures. In other words, success is the total number of minutes plus the total number of mistakes. The smaller this number (fewer minutes and fewer mistakes), the higher the degree of work success. To *analyse* the data, the researcher calculates the relationship between the learning potential score and the work success score. The calculation yields a correlation coefficient of –0.67. The researcher now has to *interpret* this finding. Based on his or her knowledge of statistical measures, the researcher knows that a correlation of this magnitude is statistically significant. The researcher also knows that the negative sign in front of the correlation coefficient indicates an inverse relationship. An inverse relationship means that the two concepts are related in an opposite manner. As the learning potential score increases (a higher number of new items learned), the work success score decreases (fewer minutes required to complete a work activity and fewer mistakes made), therefore the researcher concludes that there is a relationship between learning potential and work success.

3.7 Reporting the research outcomes

The last step is to report the outcomes of the research. A research report is structured around the various phases of the research process. It describes the research topic, indicates the research problem and explains how the key concepts were operationalised, what information was collected, how it was analysed and what the findings were. A research report is written in scientific style, thus the writing style is formal and serious. A research report does not look like a letter written to a friend. Also, when we write a research report, we invariably rely on former work done by other researchers. We have to indicate where we found the information. In other words, we have to reference the sources and provide a list of references at the end of the report. It is also a good idea to provide a very short summary of the study (called an abstract) at the beginning of the report. The report should also have a title that clearly indicates what the study has been about.

4 The ideological component of scientific thinking

We have seen above that the ideal of science is to minimise subjectivity and to maximise objectivity. The aim of this ideal is to produce factual statements that are true and free of subjective interpretation. However, 20th century philosophers of science have shown that this ideal is not attainable. In the 1960s, a physicist interested in the history of science published a book that became most influential in demolishing the idea that science is an objective and neutral activity. The scientist was Thomas Kuhn and the book was called *The structure of scientific revolutions*

(Kuhn, 1970). Kuhn's historical analysis revealed science as a psychosocial project. Science has never been a neutral activity. It is the activity of humans who find themselves in particular social contexts. Researchers' subjective frames of reference and the social contexts in which researchers find themselves play a major role in the way in which these individuals conduct their studies. Nowadays, Kuhn's arguments are echoed by researchers who support a constructivist epistemology. They argue that it is not only the content of science (that is, the knowledge produced by scientific studies), but also our understanding of what science is (that is, science itself) that is embedded in the shared meanings that constitute our reality.

There are many psychosocial factors that play a role in our production of scientific knowledge, but they can be divided into two main categories, namely the *domain of science* on the one hand and the *socio-economic and socio-political environments* on the other hand.

Socio-economic and socio-political factors play a major role in the formulation and execution of research agendas. Most research-funding organisations identify and prioritise research fields. Areas of study are prioritised based on the needs of organisations and communities. Researchers are more likely to get research funding for studies about prioritised topics, but sometimes it is not a matter of need, but rather of politics. Some topics may be politically unpopular, as, for example, when a study is critical of the management of an organisation or the government of a country.

Factors that play a role in the domain of science itself are the popularity of theories and the perceived importance of experts. Researchers are more inclined to explore a topic that involves a popular theory than one that is based on old or obscure ideas. This is not only because they want to jump on the bandwagon but also because research based on contemporary theory is considered a more valuable contribution to the discipline than studies that involve dated theory. Research agendas are also swayed by the opinions of experts, who are supposed to be objective due to their in-depth knowledge. This is not the case, because experts are humans with personal agendas, living in particular socio-economic and socio-political contexts.

Bibliography

Jordaan, W.J. 1998. The science of psychology. In W. Jordaan and J. Jordaan, *People in context.* 3rd edition. Johannesburg: Heinemann.

Kuhn, T.S. 1970. *The structure of scientific revolutions.* 2nd (enlarged) edition. Chicago: University of Chicago Press.

Mouton, I. and Marais, H.C. 1991. *Basic concepts in the methodology of the social sciences.* Pretoria: Human Sciences Research Council.

Popper, K.R. 1963. *Conjectures and refutation.* London: Basic Books.

Popper, K.R. 1980. *The logic of scientific discovery.* London: Hutchinson.

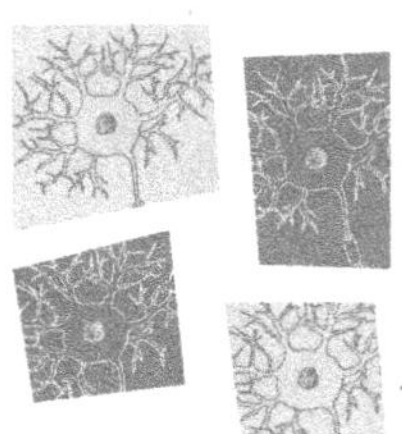

Psychology: What is it all about?

This section indicates how psychology fits into the three worlds framework. It gives a broad outline of the field of psychology and describes how the study of psychology should be approached.

1 The three worlds framework and psychology

The three worlds framework suggested by Mouton (2001:137–142) is a useful way to understand how psychology fits into the world we live in. The three worlds framework divides the world into three worlds, namely the world of everyday life and lay knowledge (World 1), the world of science and scientific research (World 2) and the world of meta-science (World 3). Figure 1 illustrates these three worlds graphically.

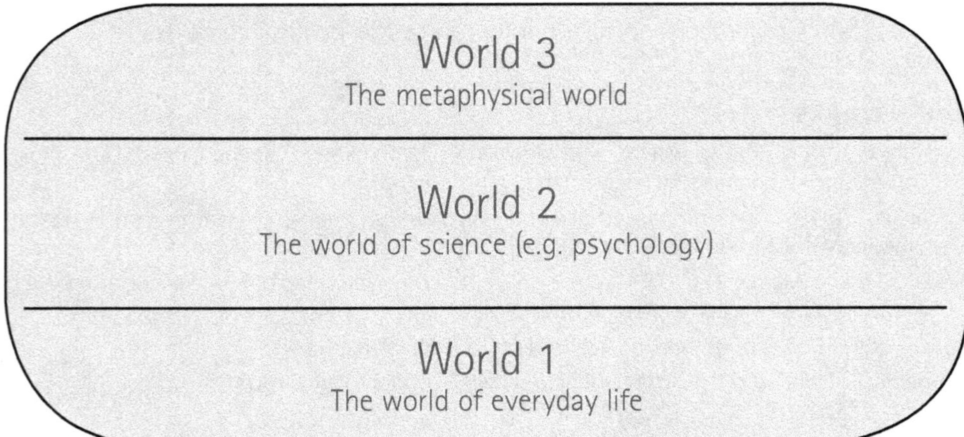

Figure 1 The three worlds framework

The table below describes the characteristics of each of the three worlds, the type of knowledge that is found in each of them, how that knowledge is achieved and what it is used for.

Table 1 The characteristics of each of the three worlds

World 1	Characteristics of World 1	World 1 is the world of everyday life. It is the ordinary social and physical reality that we find ourselves in. There are various living domains in this world, for example the family domain, the work domain and the recreation domain.
	Type of knowledge found in World 1	The type of knowledge found in World 1 is lay knowledge. It is also called common sense, insight and know-how. It is the kind of knowledge one needs in order to cope effectively with one's daily tasks, for example the knowledge required to drive a car, to buy goods in a supermarket or to milk a cow.
	Methods of achieving World 1 knowledge	We achieve lay knowledge through learning, experience and self-reflection – in other words, through normal interaction with people, events and phenomena in our everyday-life world.
	Use of World 1 knowledge	We need lay knowledge to solve problems and to gain insight into everyday tasks.
World 2	Characteristics of World 2	World 2 is the world of science. In this world, one finds scientific disciplines such as physics, psychology and archaeology. One also finds scientific theories and methods because these are part of scientific disciplines.
	Type of knowledge found in World 2	The kind of knowledge found in World 2 is called scientific knowledge. Scientific knowledge differs from lay knowledge because it is the product of systematic and rigorous inquiry. Whereas lay knowledge is embedded in subjective beliefs and best practices, scientific knowledge is objective (facts agreed upon by everybody) and truthful (aiming to uncover facts that are universally valid and reliable).
	Methods of achieving World 2 knowledge	World 2 knowledge is obtained through systematic and rigorous inquiry. The objects of World 1 (for example people, interpersonal relationships, rocks, chemical reactions and so forth) are made into objects of inquiry. Scientific methods are employed to make valid and reliable observations and to analyse and interpret the gathered information.
	Use of World 2 knowledge	World 2 knowledge is used to accurately describe objects in World 1 and to make reliable and valid predictions about the behaviour of these objects. For example, the theories and observations of psychology are used to describe the nature of human beings and to predict how groups of people may behave under particular circumstances.

World 3	Characteristics of World 3	World 3 is the world in which one reflects about one's scientific practice. In this world, one finds philosophies of science, research methodology, research ethics and deliberations about the histories of scientific disciplines.
	Type of knowledge found in World 3	World 3 contains knowledge about the ways in which we do science. In other words, it contains knowledge about scientific practice.
	Methods of achieving World 3 knowledge	World 3 knowledge is obtained through rigorous philosophical and conceptual analysis of the objects in World 2. The objects in World 2 are the theories and methods of scientific disciplines. In other words, knowledge in World 3 is achieved through constantly questioning the ways in which we do science.
	Use of World 3 knowledge	World 3 knowledge is used to identify the mistakes we make in science and to improve the quality of scientific inquiry.

Considering the three worlds framework, it is not difficult to see that psychology fits into World 2. Psychology is a science about human beings and the ways in which humans interact with one another and with their environments. As such, psychology is a discipline of theories and methods – psychological theories about humans and scientific methods to inquire about humans. Psychological knowledge is World 2 knowledge – knowledge that aims to offer accurate descriptions about humans and to make reliable and valid predictions about their behaviour. The next section gives a broad overview of the field of psychology.

2 The field of psychology

The field of psychology is very large. Literally thousands of scientific articles are published each year about a huge variety of topics in psychology. People often think of psychology in terms of its professional application in the fields of clinical and counselling psychology, industrial psychology and educational psychology. These fields are the professional domains of psychology; however, the professional application of psychology forms only a small part of the world of psychology. Psychological knowledge is used in virtually every aspect of people's daily lives. The field of psychology is much broader than what is normally perceived to be the professional domain of psychology.

Because the field of psychology is so large, it is useful to divide it into different contexts, for example the biological context, the intrapsychic context, the social context and the metaphysical context (Jordaan, 1998). The biological context focuses on the psychophysical aspects of the human body. The intrapsychic context considers the various psychological aspects of an individual and the social context looks at the social behaviour of humans in interaction with one another and with their environments. The metaphysical context considers the unique ability of humans to reflect on the origin and meaning of life. Each of these contexts delimits a broad domain of study in psychology and within each of these broad domains of study one finds a number of subfields that are disciplines in their own right. The following paragraphs provide a very general description of the various contexts of psychological studies.

The *psychobiological* context of psychology typically covers topics like the body cell, the neuron, the nervous system and the roles of genes and environmental factors in the constitution of a person. In these fields of study, one would be interested in the relationships between neurological functions and psychological experiences. One would investigate the links between the nervous system and consciousness. One would like to know how neurological activity relates to sleep and wakefulness, goal-directed behaviour, experience of stress and optimal functioning. One would like to know how the body receives and analyses stimuli to enable one to see, hear, feel, smell and taste objects in the environment and one would like to know how the various structures in the brain relate to different psychological experiences.

One may decide to explore the psychological aspects of an individual without direct reference to his or her biological body. This would mean that one chooses to focus on the *intrapsychic* aspects of an individual. In this regard, one's main areas of interest would be the processes of perception, thinking, emotional experience, learning and memory and self-reflection (thinking about who, what and how we are). Each of these domains is a vast area in the field of psychology. For example, the field of thinking covers such topics as the nature of thought, reasoning, problem solving, intelligence and creative thinking. Emotional experience involves deliberations about the nature of feelings, stress processes and motivation. The field of learning concerns classical and operant conditioning, cognitive learning and social and moral learning. In addition, the ability of human beings to think about themselves requires considerations of the nature of consciousness, self-consciousness and personology (the study of personality).

When one's inquiry into the nature of people shifts from a focus on the individual to the interaction between individuals and between people and their environments, one's attention turns from intrapsychic considerations to the social aspects of human functioning. The *social* context includes broad fields of study such as environmental psychology, interpersonal psychology, the psychology of work, the psychology of groups and group functioning and community psychology.

A further context of consideration in the study of human nature is the *metaphysical* context. In this domain, one studies how and why people grapple with and try to understand phenomena that lie beyond the physical world. People's constructions of ultimate reality and their understandings of the philosophical, aesthetic and religious characteristics of the world are the kind of topic that one explores in this domain.

The various contexts within which one can view and explore human nature do not exhaust the field of psychology. These contexts are like snapshots. Like still pictures, they freeze aspects of human life within particular frames of reference. Sometimes one wants to study processes that extend across one or more of these contexts. For example, in the field of developmental psychology, one explores how people develop during their lives, from birth to death. The fields of psychological well-being and psychopathology deal with processes that lead to healthy or psychologically sick people. When exploring these kinds of phenomena, one has to consider various aspects of human nature from the perspective of more than one context.

From this very brief summary of the field of psychology, it should be clear that psychology is a vast discipline, touching all aspects of human life. Although this discipline is less than 130 years old, it has accumulated a vast body of knowledge and impacted significantly on the ways in which we live our daily lives.

3 How to study psychology

It is easy to learn about psychology, but it is not easy to learn psychology. Learning about psychology is getting to know psychology. It is to read about the terminology and the theories of psychology, but having done so is no guarantee that you have been learning psychology. To learn psychology is different from learning about psychology. To learn psychology is to learn to see and understand the world through psychology. Psychology is a discipline. This means that, embedded in the terminology, facts and theories of psychology, there are ways of thinking and doing that are particular to psychology. To learn psychology is to discipline your mind to think and to act according to the discipline of psychology.

The three worlds framework is useful to demonstrate the difference between what it means to learn about psychology and what it means to learn psychology. According to the three worlds framework, psychology lives in World 2. Learning about psychology is to explore psychology as a discipline in World 2. People who have learned about psychology can tell other people one or two things about it; however, to learn psychology means something very different. To learn psychology is to learn to view the events and phenomena of World 1 from the perspective of World 2 (psychology). It is to understand the events and phenomena of World 1 in terms of psychology – to gain a psychological understanding of World 1. People who have learned about psychology can talk about it, but people who have learned psychology have a psychological understanding of everyday life events.

The traditional approach to studying psychology is first to learn about psychology and then to learn how to apply your psychological (World 2) knowledge to everyday (World 1) events and phenomena. It is, however, much more effective to begin with World 1 events and phenomena and then to explore how psychological (World 2) knowledge helps one to understand the World 1 events and phenomena in question. In other words, it is much more effective to learn psychology in the context of everyday-life events and phenomena.

Bibliography

Jordaan, W. 1998. Contextualization in psychology. In W. Jordaan and J. Jordaan, *People in context.* 3rd edition. Johannesburg: Heinemann.

Mouton, J. 2001. *How to succeed in your Master's and Doctoral studies: A South African guide and resource book.* Pretoria: Van Schaik.

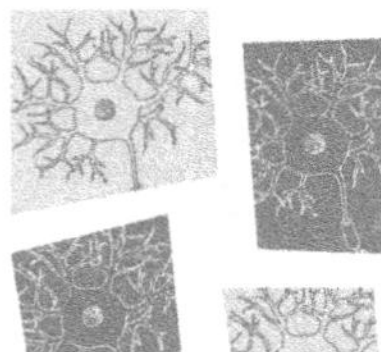

Research essays

1 What is a research essay?

A research essay is a text about a scientific topic. The essay describes the topic and argues particular points about the topic. A research essay has a definite structure.

It has:

- a title
- an abstract
- an introduction
- a body
- a conclusion
- a reference list

1.1 Title

The title of a research essay is a short, concise, yet meaningful, statement containing key words from the topic. The reader should be able to discern what the essay is about from the title.

1.2 Abstract

A research essay has an abstract, which provides a summary of the essay. The abstract briefly refers to three aspects of the essay:

- The problem (a brief outline of the issues at hand, the point(s) to be discussed)
- The argument (a very brief indication of how the discussion is conducted – not the discussion itself)
- The conclusion (a brief indication of the outcome(s) of the discussion)

Research articles are often papers reporting on research findings. If the research article reports on a research project, the abstract covers the following:

- The problem part of the abstract states the problem that was researched.
- The argument part of the abstract indicates how the research was done.
- The conclusion part of the abstract gives the research findings.

1.3 Introduction

The introduction of the essay consists of one or more introductory paragraphs. The introduction introduces the topic by

- contextualising the topic (that is, providing background information about the topic and putting it in perspective)
- stating the argument (that is, indicating the issues under discussion, the research issues and the author's standpoint about them)
- previewing the presentation (that is, outlining how the topic is dealt with in the essay)

1.4 Body

The body of the essay contains the main description or argument. It consists of information that supports the writer's argument and standpoint. In a good essay, the body continues from the introduction (which states the argument), gives the details of the argument in a systematic and logical way and leads to the conclusion. The issues under discussion have to be argued as objectively as possible. An argument that does not take counter arguments into account or that is based on the author's emotional feelings about a situation is not a good argument. The argument has to be conducted by means of logical and rational reasoning. Factual statements have to be justified. If the article is a research report, the factual information comes from the research project itself. If the facts come from somewhere else, the author has to indicate where they come from so that the reader can check them if he or she wishes to do so. This is the reason why an author may refer to other documents in the text and provide a reference list indicating the sources of the documents he or she referred to. If the source of the factual statements is a research project (in other words, if the research essay is a research report) the nature of the project has to be indicated. The reader has to understand how the information was gathered and analysed, so that he or she could replicate the research project to verify the results.

1.5 Conclusion

The essay's concluding paragraphs always follow logically from the argument that forms the body of the essay. The conclusion involves a brief summary of the main points of the argument(s) and a careful reformulation of the standpoint that formed the point of departure in the introduction. No new information (that is, information that was not included in the introduction or the body of the essay) should be introduced in the concluding paragraphs.

1.6 List of references

The reference list provides the references to the source documents of the factual information that the author referred to in the text. There are standard systems of referencing. The one developed by the American Psychological Association (APA) is widely used in psychology.

2 How to write an essay

2.1 Explore the topic

Never write an essay on a topic that you do not know much about. Always *research* the topic before you start writing. Make sure that you identify the main issues and that you understand the arguments behind them. Remember, one always has to read much more than what seems to be required. One has to gain a wide perspective on the topic to be able to write about it. It is easy to identify the lazy authors who do not read widely before writing. They tend to get caught up in the details of the topic without being able to provide a proper perspective on it. If one considers a topic to be like a river, the lazy author who does not read widely about the topic is like a swimmer in the middle of the river, unable to identify the currents or to fathom the depth and breadth of the river. One has to view the river from the outside to perceive its currents and to appreciate its depth and breadth.

2.2 Observe, describe, define and refine

Exploring a topic requires observation of facts, ideas and arguments; descriptions of these observations; and clear definitions of one's understanding of one's observations. A *description* is a statement about what is observed. The statement can be proved, qualified or disproved through *observation*. If I come home and tell my family that it is raining, I am telling them something on the basis of what I have observed. Any of my family can go outside and use personal observation to find out whether my description of the weather conditions is correct. They can *verify* my description of what I have observed. Likewise, a researcher reports on (provides a description of) what he or she has observed under controlled conditions. The fact that the conditions were controlled in a particular way enables other researchers to repeat the observations to verify the description. However, one has to distinguish between the observation of something and the description of it. Because we see in terms of what we know and understand, the description of what we have seen may not be an exact or complete record of reality.

We use basic concepts, related concepts and terms indicating the relationship between concepts to describe observations. Examples of basic concepts are 'rain', 'yellow' and 'people'. Examples of related concepts are 'rain and hail', 'yellow flower' and 'friendly people'. The terms indicating relationships between concepts may indicate physical relationships such as distance or direction, or relationships of time, or complex combinations of these.

Something to watch out for in descriptions is vagueness and ambiguity in the use of concepts. A concept is vague if its meaning cannot be accurately determined. A concept is ambiguous if it could have more than one possible meaning. In scientific discourse, one tries to prevent vagueness and ambiguity by creating subject terminology and by defining terms very carefully. A *definition* is an exact and accurate description of a phenomenon and it is exact and accurate if it applies to all possible examples of the phenomenon. In addition, it must not apply to anything that is not an example of the phenomenon. It is a great advantage to have clear definitions of terms and concepts because these definitions prevent misunderstandings in communication.

Observation, description and definition can lead to a lot of information. One cannot entertain loads of information simultaneously. One has to *refine* the information in terms of main and secondary points. A main point is a main idea or major theme in a text. To identify a main point in a description, one has to ask: 'What is the point of the description?'. In other words, what is the core idea that the description tries to bring across? Once the core idea has been identified, it is easy to see how the rest of the description supports or extends the main point.

2.3 Construct proper paragraphs

There is no simple definition of a paragraph. A paragraph can consist of a single sentence, or even a single word, but this is very rare. A paragraph usually consists of a collection of sentences organised around two or more ideas related to a single main idea. The main idea is expressed in the *theme sentence* and the ideas are related to the main idea are expressed in supporting sentences. The theme sentence often appears at the beginning or at the end of the paragraph. Only experienced authors can construct paragraphs that do not begin with theme sentences. If one is still learning how to construct good paragraphs, it is a good idea to start one's paragraphs with the theme sentence. Supporting sentences support the theme sentence in a variety of different ways.

A paragraph forms a tightly bound unit. There has to be a strong bond between the main idea and the supporting ones. In addition, the supporting ideas have to follow each other in a fluent manner. One should also take care to construct the last sentence of a paragraph in such a way that it links with the first sentence of the next paragraph.

2.4 Get the essay structure right

The information in the research article should be presented in a logical and fluent structure. In other words, the reader should never have to go back or search forward to try to understand what he or she is reading. At any point in the text, one should be able to understand what is being said if one has read the foregoing text. The broad structure described here (introduction, body and conclusion) should go a long way towards helping you structure the essay in a logical way. Here are some tips to keep in mind if the essay you write is a research report:

- Remember the research report has the same form as a research article, namely a problem, a critical analysis and discussion of (that is, an argument about) the problem and the conclusion reached by means of the discussion.
- In the case of the research report, the argument in the body of the essay requires a description of the research project. This description should provide:
  - a brief outline of the design of the research project
  - an indication of who the research subjects were
  - an explanation of how the research information was obtained from these subjects
  - an indication of how the research information was analysed
  - the results of the analysis
  - a critical discussion of the meaning of the results in terms of the problem stated in the introduction.

2.5 Pay attention to your style and tone of writing

One can complete the first draft of an essay without paying too much attention to language, but language begins to play a major role from the second draft onwards. One has to make certain that all spelling mistakes have been corrected and that proper grammar has been used. It is a good idea to edit long sentences and to try to make the text more readable.

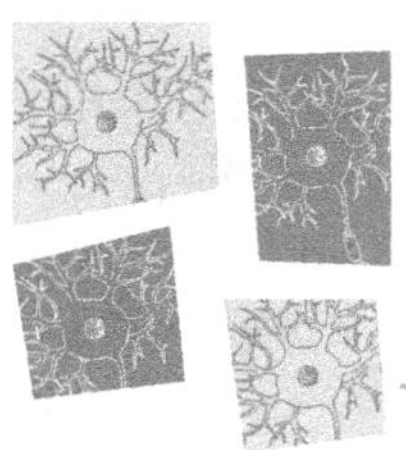

Self: The concept of self

In everyday language, we do not have a problem with the meaning of the word *self.* The word refers to ourselves in an obvious way. It is implicitly there when we use the words 'I' and 'me'. It is not something that we get confused about. However, the term *self* also appears in psychology and when a term like 'self' appears in a scientific discipline, it has to be defined accurately and unambiguously. It is not an easy task to define the notion of self. In everyday language, we skip seamlessly between two very different meanings of this term. We sometimes refer to the self as an object. For example, we say: 'I will do this myself'. What we actually say is: 'I am the person who will do this'. In other words, we refer to the self as an object called 'the person', but on other occasions we use the word 'self' to indicate the perception we have of ourselves, such as when we say: 'I am not good at telling jokes'.

In psychology, we have to distinguish between the *nature of self* and the *content of self.* The nature of self has to do with the concept of self. The question to ask is: What is the nature of the thing that we refer to as a self? In other words: What is the concept of self in psychology? The content of self, on the other hand, refers to the self-concept. Here the question is: How do people perceive themselves? In other words: What do they think of themselves and how do these self-perceptions come about? It is important to keep the difference between the concept of self and self-concept in mind when we talk about the self in psychology. In this section we will consider the concept of self.

1 The concept of self

We all have a sense of self. We think of the self as the core of our being and as something that is continuous over time, but it is also the totality of our personal experience. It includes our thought processes, our physical body and the experience that we are separate and unique from others (Gazzaniga and Heatherton, 2003:418).

However, if we look closely at this description of the concept of self, we can identify two issues that really complicate matters. The first is the difference between the self as (1) the core *of our being;* and (2) the *totality of our experience.* The second issue concerns the fact that we are selves *thinking of our selves.*

1.1 The stable self versus the changing self

When somebody refers to a past situation and remarks that she was a different person, we understand that she does not mean this literally. In some sense, the person is still the same person, yet she is also different in the sense that she would experience things differently given the same situation now. She has changed as a result of new experiences and new knowledge, yet deep down underlying the various ways in which she has changed, she knows that she is still the same person. The concept of self embodies both these ideas simultaneously, but in doing so it covers up a certain mystery. The problem is that we do not know which comes first – the stable core or the totality of experience. Is there first of all a stable core that has a totality of experience, or is there first a totality of experience out of which a stable core develops and differentiates itself? We cannot answer this question and in the next section we shall see why. What we do learn from this, though, is that the self is understood as identity in the midst of constant change.

One of the most influential theories of *identity formation* comes from the work of Erik Erikson (1968). One's identity becomes fixed during the developmental stage of adolescence when one experiences the pressures of one's transition from being a dependent child to becoming an autonomous adult. During this stage, one's body changes physically and one's cognitive capacities become fully developed. According to Erikson, identity is a solid sense of one's ideologies, philosophies, values and beliefs. This notion of identity describes the self as the stable core that differentiates itself through one's having to resolve conflicting situations by committing oneself to particular beliefs and values, thus it looks as though we are delivered to our *circumstances.* Our selves develop as we try to make the best of the situations in which we find ourselves.

However, humanist psychologists such Carl Rogers (1971) and Abraham Maslow (1970) have different ideas about this. According to these thinkers, the ultimate goal of personal development is *self-actualisation.* This is the process through which people realise their potential, thus one is not delivered to one's circumstances. The conflicting situations one has to deal with are not seen as crises, but rather as challenges that one seeks out in one's attempts at actualising one's self. People with high levels of self-actualisation are open to new experiences and can function independently. For Erikson, experience comes before the self and change develops into a stable core. For the humanists, the self comes before experience and a stable core changes. We need both of these perspectives for a comprehensive picture of the self.

1.2 The double self

When I talk about myself, I am a self talking about itself. The way in which we intuitively understand this is that I am a person who is aware of myself. In other words, I am a self that has a mental picture of itself. I am real and the thoughts I have about myself make a mental picture. The problem is that this description (the description of a real self maintaining a mental picture of itself) is also already a picture. This is a philosophical problem of *ontology* and *epistemology.* Ontology refers to the essence of things, the way things really are. Epistemology refers to how we understand things. Our problem is that we can only get to the ontology through the epistemology. When I try to get to my own essence and see myself for what I really am, I have to go through thought. I have to make a picture of what I am through thinking about myself. Obviously, the picture that I get in the end depends on how I make the picture. In other words, what I see of myself is *a function of the way in which I think.* There is no way out of this problem. We are stuck with a double self, namely the subject who thinks and the self who appears as the object of thought. The self is both the subject and the object of thought, and, although I think of myself as subject (the one who is thinking) and myself as object (the one who is thought about), as the same self they are logically not one and the same thing. I experience myself as a single self, but when I really think about it, I am a split self. According to the psychoanalyst Jacques Lacan (1977), we need the interplay between the subjective self and the objective self to form an understanding of ourselves.

In our everyday lives, we are very good at being ourselves and handling the interplay of the subjective and the objective selves. Normally, we do not even think about ourselves. In these instances, we simply take the role of the self who is the subject of our thoughts and our actions. In other words, we think and act without thinking about ourselves as thinkers and actors. However, sometimes we become very much aware of ourselves. In these moments of self-awareness, we become the object of our thoughts and we think things like: 'I am happy' or 'I am not a good person'.

Although we do not experience any problems in maintaining a sense of self, the concept of self is not as simple as it may appear at first. The self is simultaneously constant and changing and it is both the subject and the object of our thoughts and actions.

Bibliography

Erikson, E.H. 1968. *Identity: Youth and crisis.* New York: Norton.

Gazzaniga, M.S. and Heatherton, I.E. 2003. *Psychological science: Mind, brain and behaviour.* New York: Norton.

Lacan, J. 1977. *Ecrits: A selection.* (Translated by A. Sheridan.) London: Tavistock.

Maslow, A.H. 1970. *Motivation and personality.* 2nd edition. New York: Harper & Row.

Rogers, C.R. 1971. A theory of personality. In S. Maddi (Ed), *Perspectives on personality.* Boston: Little Brown.

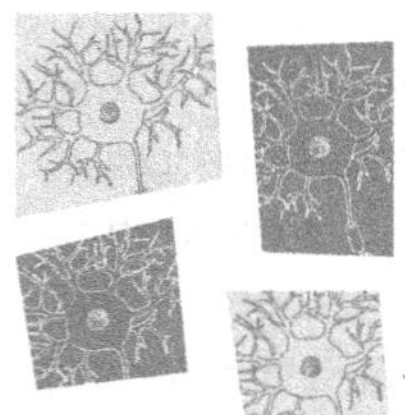

Self: The dynamics of self

It is not easy to understand the concept of the self. We can consider the self as the core that underlies all our experiences. From this perspective, the self is fundamental to our experiences, but we can also look at the self as something that condenses from our experiences. In this case, we view the self as that which is consistent within our experiences. These are conflicting views of the self, which make it difficult to form a concept. We need to consider both views because the notion of the self is too complex to be considered from a single perspective.

However, it is the complexity of the self that makes it so dynamic. The self is not rigid and unchangeable. Human beings are flexible and able to adapt to a variety of circumstances in their daily lives. If the self were nothing but a stable core at the basis of our existence, we would be stagnant beings, unable to change in ourselves. On the other hand, if the self were merely the common denominator in a stream of constantly changing experiences, we would be too fluid. Having a self that is both a core at the basis of experience as well as a common denominator of experience allows us to accommodate new experiences within ourselves and to develop in a consistent manner, avoiding uncontrolled, erratic changes in ourselves. However, this does not mean that the development in ourselves is without tension. In fact, we change and develop through the tensions between consistency and change.

There are no absolute certainties in the self. The process of self-construction is characterised by moments of ambivalence and the dynamic way in which we construct ourselves is due to these moments. Four such instances of ambivalence are identified by Jordaan (1998). These can be pictured as dimensions of self-construction. Each dimension has two opposing poles (that is, the dimension is bipolar), and ambivalence occurs on each one of these dimensions because the person is pulled in opposite directions on the continuum of the dimension. The dimensions that Jordaan identifies are the following:

- Self-insight versus self-deception
- Self-regard versus self-disregard
- Self-identity versus self-alienation
- The autonomous self versus the collective self

In the following sections we shall consider each of these dimensions separately.

1 Self-insight versus self-deception

We have all been in a situation where we did not act properly and then convinced ourselves that it did not mean that we were really bad. However, at the back of our minds we knew that we were trying to deceive ourselves. This demonstrates the tension between what we should have done (what we should be) and what we actually did (what we turned out to be). The self forms and knowledge of the self grows, as one incorporates more and more experiences of this kind into one's self.

Self-insight and *self-deception* are everyday terms that we are familiar with and that we understand intuitively, but when we try to define these terms more accurately (as we have to do in psychology), certain difficulties crop up. Self-insight refers to how much insight one has about oneself. It begs the question of whether one really knows who one is. If the answer to this question is yes, one has self-insight. If the answer is no, one is not in touch with oneself and one may tend to be self-deceptive. Although this sounds quite logical, there is a difficult problem here, namely that there is no way to fully know who we really are. We do not know ourselves in full, as we do not fully know one another. If we do not fully know who we are, we cannot determine self-insight in terms of who we are. All we can do is to consider self-insight in relation to self-deception. We have self-insight if we display more self-insight than self-deception and we lack self-insight if our self-deception is greater than our self-insight.

However, this does not solve the problem. Comparing self-insight to self-deception indicates the degree of self-insight (that is, how much self-insight there is), but it does not explain what we mean by self-insight. The obvious definition of self-insight is insight into the self, but then we have to ask: Whose insight? We have already indicated that neither we ourselves, nor others, have full insight into ourselves. There is no absolute insight and thus we have to accept a position of relativity. We have to consider self-insight (insight provided by one's self) in relation to insight provided by others. This means we can only know ourselves in relation to the way in which others know us. This should not surprise us, because we saw at the beginning of this discussion that the self is too complex to be defined from a single perspective. What we see here is that we ourselves are too complex to be known from a single perspective. The self forms and grows from the tension between what we know about ourselves and what others know about us. We have a high degree of self-insight if what we know about ourselves corresponds to what others know about us and we lack self-insight if there are large discrepancies between our self-knowledge and the knowledge others have of us.

The relationship between the knowledge I have about myself and the knowledge others have about me can be summarised in a table that is often called the Johari window (Luft, 1970). Jordaan (1998) uses the Johari window to explain the dynamics of self-insight and self-deception as a function of one's interpersonal relationships. Table 1 illustrates the Johari window.

Table 1 The Johari window

	What I know about myself	**What I do not know about myself**
What others know about me	Open knowledge	Blinded knowledge
What others do not know about me	Hidden knowledge	Unavailable knowledge

There is a tight connection between insight and knowledge and between deception and knowledge. More knowledge means more insight, but less knowledge means a higher possibility of deception, because it is easier to deceive in the absence of knowledge. Therefore, to increase insight, knowledge has to increase. The more I know about myself and the more others know about me, the higher the level of insight. The common denominator between what I know about myself and what others know about me is called *knowledge*. Open knowledge reflects the degree of correspondence between self-knowledge and the knowledge others have of me. In other words, it shows the degree of self-insight. To increase self-insight (open knowledge), I have to work on decreasing *blinded knowledge* as well as *hidden knowledge*. To decrease blinded knowledge, I have to listen to what others tell me about myself and to decrease hidden knowledge, I have to provide others with knowledge about myself. Jordaan (1998) indicates two processes that play a significant role in this regard. Firstly, if I am serious about changing my blinded knowledge into open knowledge, I have to listen carefully to and think seriously about what others have to say about me. This requires a process of critical self-reflection. The second process that plays an important role in increasing self-insight is clear and honest interpersonal communication. I have to communicate my personal feelings and ideas to others so as to reveal hidden knowledge (what others do not know about me) and increase open knowledge.

There is a third process that is important for self-insight and that is to expose oneself to novel circumstances. This is the only way to explore what one does not know about oneself (*unavailable knowledge*). One has to be prepared to experience new and unexpected events in order to allow oneself and others to discover formerly unknown aspects of oneself and to be surprised by oneself.

2 Self-regard versus self-disregard

One of the basic substantive needs that humans have is the need to feel worthy in the eyes of others (Davies, 1991). We want others to treat us with respect, because it reflects on the way in which we experience ourselves. If we are constantly ignored or treated with contempt, it is difficult to experience self-worth. We need the acceptance of others. We need to feel appreciated and we need to feel that others like us, not for what we have or what we can do for them, but simply for who we are.

Self-regard is the general feeling we have about our self-worth. This does not mean that an individual feels equally good or equally bad about all aspects of his or her life. Somebody may feel very good (that is, have a high level of self-regard) about his or her ability to play music, but a very poor opinion about his or her ability at sport. However, we all have a certain general level of self-regard versus self-disregard. Some people generally feel much more positive about themselves than others do. They are more positive about their abilities and they seem to have an implicit trust of other people. It is possible that people with lower levels of self-regard have experienced rejection more than those with higher levels of self-regard. People with lower levels of self-regard find it difficult to distinguish between failure in a particular task and failure as a person. They tend to equate failure in a task with low levels of self-worth. This may cause a vicious circle in which somebody with low self-regard expects negative outcomes and therefore puts little effort into the exercise. This leads to high levels of anxiety, which cause the person to perform poorly and this increases the chance of failure. When the person fails, it confirms his or her feelings of low self-regard (Jordaan, 1998). The same process of confirmation helps people with high levels of self-regard to become successful. Expectations of success lead to higher levels of effort, lowered feelings of anxiety, a higher probability of success and finally confirmation of self-worth. The self forms and develops through this kind of circular process that confirms and disconfirms our feelings of self-regard. We all experience failure at one stage or another, but when we do we have to distinguish between failing in a task and failing as a person.

3 Self-identity versus self-alienation

Self-identity refers to the identification of and with the self. Strong self-identification means knowing who one is (identification *of* the self) and also being satisfied with this (identification *with* the self), thus one's self-identity has a cognitive component (knowledge about oneself), as well as an emotional component (being content with oneself).

Self-alienation occurs when you feel that you do not really know who you are. This does not mean that you experience memory loss – it simply means that you have a feeling of estrangement. You feel like a stranger to yourself. Self-alienation may be accompanied by feelings of anxiety. In some cases of self-alienation, a person may become estranged from his or her body, indicating a serious psychopathological condition. However, most of us experience mild forms of self-alienation only. We all go through stages in our lives when we feel that we do not really know ourselves, but we normally grow out of these stages and emerge as stronger and more experienced people. Going through stages of self-alienation is part of normal human development.

The self-identify versus self-alienation dimension is fundamental in the construction of the self. Inherently, self-identification is a process of reflection. The self is reflected to itself. Any process of reflection contains a moment of alienation. When the self is reflected to itself, it is also already alienated from itself. This kind of logic is difficult to grasp, but is demonstrated in Lacan's (1977) mirror stage theory. Lacan explains the development of identity in terms of the reflection of one's image in a mirror. When the child recognises itself in the mirror, it looks from inside itself and sees its exterior form in the mirror. The child identifies itself, but it is not the interior form that appears in front of it. In the very moment in which the child identifies with itself, it is already alienated from itself in the sense that it sees the outside of itself. The point is that our self-identification always contains a measure of self-alienation. This means there is no absolute self-identification, as there is no absolute self-alienation. We cannot construct ourselves in total isolation within ourselves. In constructing ourselves, we have to be open to what is outside ourselves, but the converse is also true. We cannot construct ourselves if we are totally alienated from ourselves – that is, if we are totally open to what is outside ourselves. Self-construction takes place somewhere between the two extremes of being totally closed off within ourselves and being totally open to what is outside ourselves. People who construct themselves at the extremes show signs of psychopathology. One is likely to show narcissistic tendencies if one focuses on oneself too much and constructs oneself in isolation from others. On the other hand, if one is too open to what is outside oneself, one is likely to be over-dependent on others and over-anxious and in danger of losing perspective of reality.

Lacan's mirror stage theory focuses on the actual situation of a child recognising itself in the mirror, but this event of self-recognition is an example of the process that happens throughout our lives. We recognise ourselves in the image of ourselves that is reflected back to us in our social milieu. We see ourselves in the remarks that others make about us and through the effects and consequences of our behaviour. The process is similar to the event described by the mirror stage theory. We look from inside ourselves, but the image that is reflected is an indication of what we look like from the outside. The inside image is our personal identity and the outside image is our social identity. In constructing ourselves, we have to balance and align our personal identity with our social one. Our social identity is determined by the position we occupy in the community and by the various social roles we fulfil (Jordaan, 1998).

We all have a social identity, but the more visible we become in our community the stronger it becomes. Think, for example, of the priest of a local church, or the actress who plays a leading character in a television series. People expect their priest to behave in a manner that suits their image of what a priest is like and celebrities often complain that in real life people confuse them with the characters they portray.

In our daily lives, the social roles we play are not as visible as those of the priest or the television celebrity. The roles we play are, for example, those of being a parent, an employee or a friend. These roles are the ways in which we act out our various social identities, namely the way in which we see ourselves as parent, employee or friend.

Our social identity influences our personal identity. To a certain extent, we become who we are in the community, but the converse is also true. The social roles we play are determined by our personal identity. The way in which we act as a parent, for example, is determined by our personal values and ideas, so our self-identity is formed through the circular processes of reflection between our personal identity and our social identity. Unless our personal identity is balanced and aligned with our social identity, we are unable to construct a proper self-identity.

4 Self-autonomy versus self-collectivity

Self-identity concerns the question: Who am I? There are two very different kinds of answer to this question. The first focuses on the self as an individual entity, whereas the second considers the self in relation to others. In the first perspective, a healthy self means somebody who is autonomous and independent from others. However, according to the second point of view, the self should be inclusive of others and find its worth in relation to others. The first is an autonomous self and the second is a collective self.

Some theorists – for example Markus and Kitayama (1991) and Triandis (1989) – ascribe the divergent notions of the self to cultural differences. However, many of these studies implicitly accept stereotypical ideas regarding the cultural aspects of groups in the research. These studies tend to gloss over the differences among the group members and the specific contexts in which the groups exist (Jordaan, 1998). For example, the socio-economic context of a group plays a significant role in its culture. If the socio-economic environment provides easy access to basic resources, individuals do not need to rely on others for their survival. In socio-economic environments where basic resources are not within easy reach of the individual, people have to work together and support one another to ensure their survival.

The history of humankind shows how we became increasingly individualised as we developed from hunting groups into societies based on agriculture and industry. The growth of capital and the development of socio-economic structures empowered individuals and replaced autocratic leadership with democratic dispensations. In modern states, citizens are governed by constitutional law instead of being subjected to decrees issued by autocratic leaders. Constitutional law regulates the relationships among individuals, as well as the relationship between individuals and society as a whole. In societies based on constitutional law, the freedom of the individual is a major benchmark to test the justification of laws and regulations.

The individualisation of society plays a fundamental role in its development. As group support diminishes, individuals becomes increasingly responsible for their own well-being. Individuals are more productive when they work on their own than when they have to combine their efforts to complete a task (Williams and Karau, 1991). However, individuals can never become totally autonomous and absolutely independent of others, because they have to share their living and working environments with them. One is always a member of society, regardless of one's level of individualisation. Over-individualisation leads to a mechanistic and inhuman society in which people lose respect for one another. In this kind of society, the right of the individual is over-emphasised and people fight one another in courts of law instead of establishing mutual understandings of each other's needs. Over-individualised societies emphasise the differences between individuals rather than the similarities of our commonly shared humanity. People have to respect one another and tolerate differences if they want to live together as a society. In other words, a society can only exist if the freedom of its citizens is accompanied by equal measures of *interpersonal responsibility.* As our freedom as a citizen increases, so does our responsibility towards our fellow citizens.

South African society has strong roots in both individualism and collectivism. Jordaan (1998) summarises the difference between the individualised and the collectivist paradigms in South African society in terms of three dimensions, namely psycho-behavioural modalities, values and customs and ethos. This summary is shown in Table 2.

Table 2 Comparison of individualism and collectivism

	Individualism	**Collectivism**
Psycho-behavioural modality	Individuality, uniqueness, differences, individual rights	Groupness, sameness, communality
Values and customs	Competition, individual rights, separateness, independence	Solidarity, dependence, collective responsibility, co-operation
Ethos	Survival of the fittest, control over nature	Survival of the group, at one with nature

The healthy self is neither an entirely autonomous self, nor an entirely collective self. The healthy self is a self that can function autonomously while acknowledging its dependency on and its responsibility for, its fellow human beings.

5 A picture of the self

Each of the four dimensions indicated above plays a role in the construction of the self. We find ourselves at particular points on these dimensions, therefore we can plot the points and draw a diagram to show a picture of our self. In situation A (Figure 1), I may have high self-regard and a fair level of self-autonomy, but I may be prone to self-deception and feelings of self-alienation.

In situation B (Figure 2); however, I may be self-autonomous, have high self-regard, experience a strong sense of self-identity and have good self-insight.

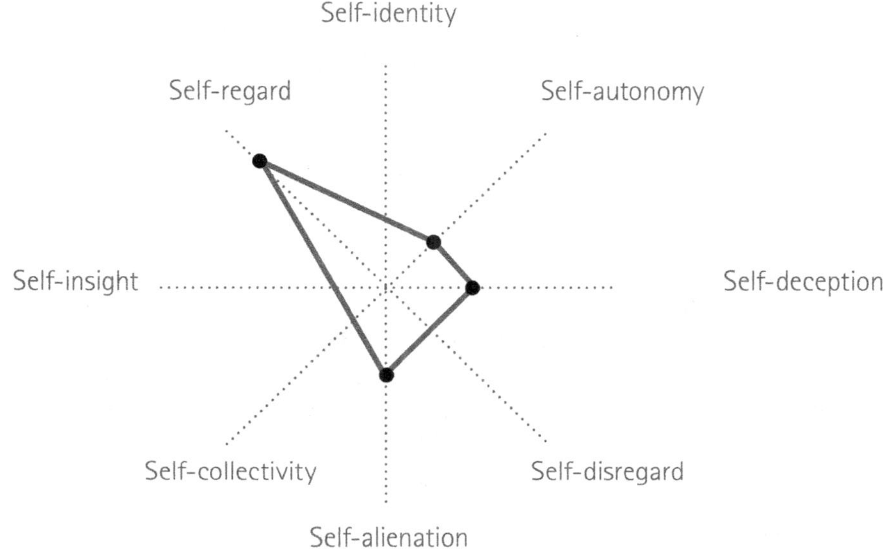

Figure 1 Situation A

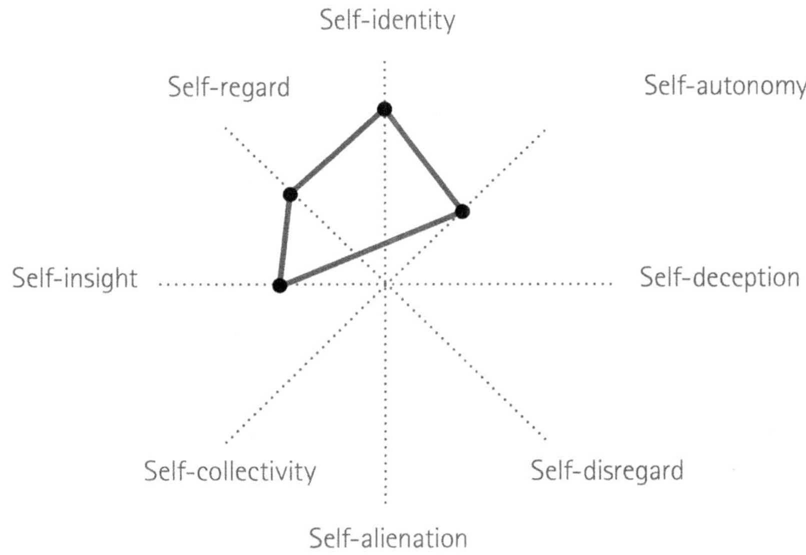

Figure 2 Situation B

Thus we construct ourselves in dynamic ways. We are not stuck at particular points on the dimensions of self-construction, but we do display characteristic dynamics in particular situations and thus we tend to hover close to particular points on the dimensions of self-construction. These points are the points where we feel comfortable with ourselves, given the situation in question. If we connect up the points as in figures 1 and 2, we see a picture of our self in the given situation.

Bibliography

Davies, I.C. 1991. Maslow and theory of political development: Getting to fundamentals. *Political Psychology,* 12(3), 289–420.

Jordaan, W. 1998. The self. In W. Jordaan and J. Jordaan, *People in context.* 3rd edition. Johannesburg: Heinemann.

Lacan, J. 1977. *Ecrits: A selection.* (Translated by A. Sheridan.) London: Tavistock.

Luft, I. 1970. *Group processes: An introduction to group dynamics.* New York: Mayfield.

Markus, H.R. and Kitayama, S. 1991. Culture and the self: Implications for cognition, emotion and motivation. *Psychological Review,* 98, 224–253.

Triandis, H.C. 1989. Self and social behaviour in differing cultural contexts. *Psychological Review,* 96, 269–289.

Williams K.D. and Karau, S.I. 1991. Social loafing and social compensation: The effects of expectation of co-worker performance. *Journal of Personality and Social Psychology,* 61, 570–581.

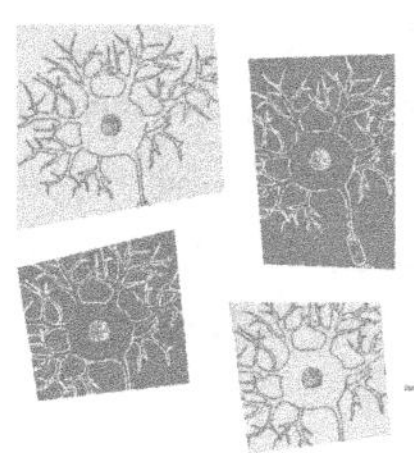

Self: The foundations of self

Broadly speaking, the aim of psychology is to find out who we are and therefore many of the questions in psychology boil down to a question about ourselves. Unfortunately, most of the questions we ask about ourselves are not easy to answer. It is perhaps not so difficult to explore the ways in which we describe our selves, because these descriptions are about what we think of ourselves. In fact, they are actually about how we exist as our selves. They are questions about *ourselves* (spelt as one word), not about *our selves* (spelt as two words). For example, I may describe myself as a caring, friendly and an intelligent person. In other words, I exist as a caring, friendly and intelligent person, but this is not really a description of myself, of the thing I call a self. Things get really difficult when we start to ask about ourselves because the question goes to the heart of the mystery that psychology is supposed to solve, namely to find out who we are.

Any question that deals with foundations in psychology is difficult because it immediately raises questions about the foundations of psychology itself. One has to ask: What kind of psychology is relevant here? What are the foundational terms and concepts of this psychology? Is it a psychology rooted in the biology of the body, or in the structure of the psyche, or perhaps anchored in interactions between individuals? There is no overarching psychology in which these different foundations come together in a unified description. When we ask about the foundations of the self, we have to explore different domains for answers and we cannot expect to combine these into a single answer.

In this section, we consider three foundations of the self. The first of these is the *physical domain.* It describes the self as the product of a biological process. The second foundation is the *intrapersonal domain.* It describes the self as the product of a process of consciousness. The third foundation is the *interpersonal domain.* It describes the self as the product of a process of symbolic interaction. Each of the processes through which the self comes into being is a process of reflection, thus in the following sections we consider the process of reflection within each of the foundational domains.

1 The process of reflection

The self is a process of reflection. Technically speaking, the concept of reflection is quite complex, but we have an intuitive understanding of what it means. In our personal experience, self-reflection is the process that occurs when we think about ourselves. We do not find the concept difficult to understand. If pressed to think about it, most of us would liken it to looking in a mirror. We reflect our emotions, ideas and behaviour in our minds much as we see our physical bodies reflected in a real mirror.

However, when one inspects reflection in more detail, there are two components to the process. Looking in a mirror, I see myself *deferred* from myself and I also see myself *differed* from myself. I see myself deferred from myself in the sense that there is some sort of distance between me and my image and I am differed from myself in the sense that my image is not really me. It is an image. The French psychoanalyst Jacques Lacan described this process in his famous mirror stage theory of self-development (Lacan, 1977). The mirror stage theory is based on the observation that children between six and 18 months of age are still fairly helpless. They are unable to speak properly and they do not have full control over their motor activities, but they do recognise themselves in a mirror. However, the image that the child sees in the mirror differs from its inner experience of itself. In the mirror, it sees a complete child. It sees itself as a functional unit, but, in reality (that is, inside itself), its real experiences are fragments of images and uncoordinated motor activities. The image the child sees is not only different from itself, it is also itself deferred from itself. It is a projection into the future. The image the child sees of itself is not what it is at the moment of looking. The image is what it will become in future. At the moment of looking, the child is a body in bits and pieces (fragmented experiences), but in future it will be a functional unit, thus the child recognises itself in something that is different from itself and that is also deferred from itself. According to Lacan, the mirror stage describes the basic process of self-production. Whenever I reflect about myself, I identify with a mental image that is differed and deferred from myself. I pitch my current self against my potential self.

Now we get to the real crux of the matter. The self is not the source of the process of self-reflection – it is the product of this process, thus one cannot say that a self exists before the process of reflection. One should not think in terms of a self that reflects upon itself. The process of reflection comes first. The self grows out of this process. In other words, my understanding of who or what I am (myself) comes from a process of reflection and this process is one of difference and deference. The self thus comes into being through a process of difference and deference.

What we see as the foundation of the self and the way in which we describe the construction of the self, therefore depends on the kind of reflection we consider. In the following sections we consider three kinds of reflection, namely *biological, intrapersonal* and *interpersonal* reflections.

2 The biological foundation of self

Biological systems live in an action-reaction relationship with their environments. This means they act upon their environments and react to stimuli they receive from their environments. According to the biologist Humberto Maturana (Maturana and Varela, 1980), the way biological systems interact with their environment is determined by their biological structures. The biological structure determines how environmental changes impact on the biological system and it also determines what kind of actions the biological system is capable of. The biological system undergoes structural changes in its interaction with the environment.

One of the most important structures of a biological system is its neural system because this system integrates sensations and actions. The neural system develops and becomes more complex as the biological system matures and as it gains experience through interacting with its environment. The neurons form networks (called neural networks) that establish relationships between sensations and actions. These relationships establish patterns in the organism's behaviour which are characteristic of the organism. They develop through the reflections between actions and sensations. The reflections between actions and sensations can be understood as follows: An action has an impact on the environment. It changes something in the environment and this change is reflected in a sensation. We can compare this to a mirror reflection and view the sensation as the 'image' of the action. The neural system is the 'mirror' that reflects the 'image'. In other words, actions are reflected as sensations in the neural system. The patterns of behaviour are a primitive self that develops from the reflections between actions and sensations.

Schwalbe (1991) describes how the self emerges through a process of self-organisation in the neural system. He refers to this as the *auto-genesis* of the self. According to Schwalbe, the formation of neural networks is the first step in the process of self-organisation. Neurons become connected and form neural networks as they differentiate actions from sensations (a process of difference) and relate actions to sensations (a process of deferring actions as sensations). These processes of differing and deferring (that is, the process of reflection) are captured in the neural system as neural networks.

The second step involves the unique way in which neural impulses flow in an individual's neural networks. How individuals act and what they sense of their environment, depends on their neural impulse patterns. Actions and sensations are characteristic to individuals due to the unique ways in which impulses flow in their neural networks.

The third step in self-organisation involves higher-order organisation in the neural networks. The patterns of neural impulses are organised as images, one of which is the image that the system has of itself.

The fourth stage requires an even higher order of organisation in the neural system. At this level of organisation, images are replaced by symbols and names are given to the images. In other words, the fourth stage of self-organisation involves the use of language. At this stage, the system is able to name the image it has of itself as its self.

3 The foundation of self in consciousness

Consciousness is possibly the most challenging and pervasive source of problems in the whole of philosophy (Blackburn, 1996:76). Consciousness is an abstract concept. It is not a substance that one can isolate and look at. For each of us, our consciousness is what underlies every thought we can think, but it is impossible to say what consciousness is. Yet we know that our consciousness is the theatre in which our experiences and thoughts exist, where our desires are felt and where our intentions are formed. We see consciousness in the behaviour of the body. If somebody is in a coma, we say the person has lost consciousness and when he or she comes round again, we say the person has regained consciousness. Thus we associate consciousness with an individual and we often think of consciousness as something that the person possesses. Strictly speaking, however, consciousness is merely an indication of the condition or state of a person, namely that the person is conscious or unconscious.

When we look at consciousness as a state of being (in the sense of being conscious versus unconscious) it is not difficult to see consciousness as a state of awareness, thus the basic nature of consciousness is to be conscious of something. We have seen above that the most basic thing that we are conscious of is our consciousness, therefore, in its most basic form, consciousness is consciousness being aware of itself as consciousness; in other words, it is a process of reflection.

Consciousness is like a mirror. The mirror is something that enables the process of reflection, but one never really sees the mirror. All one sees is the object in front of and the image in the mirror. The mirror itself disappears between the object and the image. The mirror is the invisible glass surface that separates the object from its image. Like the mirror, consciousness reflects the I who is conscious (the object in front of the mirror) as a me in consciousness (the image in the mirror).

In psychology, this kind of self-reflection is called *introspection.* The self is formed and shaped through a process of introspection in which I pitch my current state against my potential state. Myself is formed and shaped when I consider who I am or what I have done in the light of who I should be or what I should have done.

4 The linguistic foundation of self

In 1966, Peter Berger and Thomas Luckmann published a book called *The social construction of reality.* Since then, social constructionism has become a major influence in psychology. It maintains that we understand the world in terms of social constructions. Social constructionists are interested in the way in which we describe things around us, including our behaviour. They maintain that our discourses (the ways in which we talk about things) create the things we talk about, including ourselves. There are two ideas that are fundamental to a constructionist approach, namely *power* and *meaning*. These notions are philosophically complex, but we can greatly oversimplify the matter and say that meaning is created within a network of relationships, where this network is in fact one of power differentials (Foucault, 1969). The difference in power is alleviated and balanced out around a shared meaning.

To understand how this works, we have to consider an aspect of Lacan's mirror stage theory that we have not yet paid attention to. When the child looks in the mirror, it does not only recognise itself, it also identifies itself with the image in the mirror. So strong is this self-identification that the child considers the image to be as real as it is itself. This implies a *symmetrical relationship* between the child in front of the mirror and the child reflected in it. The one becomes the image of the other. Neither of the two can be considered more real than the other. This may sound foolish when we think in terms of a real child in front of a mirror, but it is not at all foolish when one uses the mirror stage as a model for understanding interpersonal interactions. In the interpersonal domain, I am as real as you are and you are as much an image to me as I am an image to you. In this sense, we maintain a symmetrical relationship with regard to each other.

The next question is how a symmetrical relationship comes about. This is another one of those tough philosophical questions that we cannot argue here and for which we simply accept the answer at face value: A symmetrical relationship is a relationship in which the power difference has been alleviated by balancing the power around a shared meaning. When you and I agree about something (when we share the meaning of something) we maintain a symmetrical relationship with each other. In other words, we construct meaning by negotiating symmetrical relationships with each other and we negotiate symmetrical relationships with each other through our discourses. However, our discourses also position us as subjects of the discourse, thus everything happens in language and you and I are reflected in language. Even when I think about myself, I am busy with inner-speak and 'I' and 'me' are positions in language. However, I am not only reflected in an inner (or intrapersonal) discourse with myself, but also in the interpersonal discourse with you, my community and the society in which I live. For example, Michel Foucault (whose ideas are fundamental to this discussion) is often described as a philosopher and historian (society's construction of his self), but he described himself as a specialist in the history of systems of thought (his personal construction of himself) (Macey, 2000:133, 135). Foucault has also been described as a 'gay philosopher', but has seen himself as 'a philosopher who is gay'. This example shows the subtle way in which language constructs very different identities. A 'gay philosopher' is somebody who philosophises about gay issues. A philosopher who is gay is a philosopher who happens to be homosexual.

Bibliography

Blackburn, S. 1996. *Oxford dictionary of philosophy.* Oxford: Oxford University Press.

Foucault, M. 1969. *The archaeology of knowledge.* (Translated by A.M. Sheridan Smith, 1972.) London: Tavistock.

Lacan, J. 1977. *Ecrits: A selection.* (Translated by A. Sheridan). London: Tavistock.

Macey, D. 2000. *The Penguin dictionary of critical theory.* Harmondsworth: Penguin.

Maturana, H.R. and Varela, F.J. 1980. Autopoiesis: The organisation of the living. In H.R. Maturana and F.J. Varela (Eds), *Autopoiesis and cognition: The realization of the living.* Dordrecht, Holland: Reidel.

Schwalbe, M.L. 1991. The autogenesis of the self. *Journal for the Theory of Social Behaviour,* 21, 269–295.

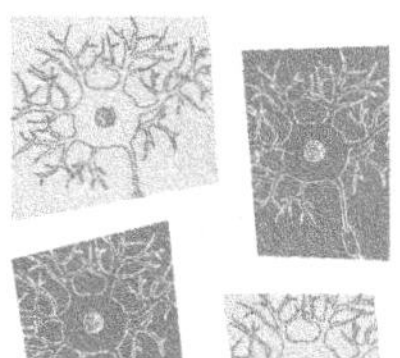

Sensation and perception

People are in continual interaction with the environment, influencing and being influenced by it. This implies that there is constant change, both in terms of what we do and what we are. In order to adapt to an ever-changing environment, we need to process information effectively. This means that we have to be able to receive and select information from the environment, determine differences between bits of information, integrate them to make meaning, get new ideas and understanding from the information we have integrated, store the information for later use and respond appropriately to the information we have processed.

This section deals with the way we receive information and make it meaningful. It covers the processes of sensation (sensory reception), orienting to and monitoring incoming information, forming perceptions (interpreting the meaning of information), organising information and paying attention.

1 Sensory systems

There are five sensory systems that provide us with information necessary for survival and adaptation:

- The *visual system* allows us to see. Light activates the visual receptors in the eye where it is converted into nerve impulses that send information to the brain for interpretation in the occipital cortex.
- The *auditory system* allows us to hear. Sound waves are received by the auditory receptors in the ear and are encoded before being sent along the auditory pathway to the brain. The messages are interpreted in the temporal lobe.
- The *proprioceptive systems* provide people with information about their movements and orientation in space. Kinaesthetic information comes from

the muscles, tendons and joints. Vestibular information comes from the ear and provides information about head movements.

- The *somaesthetic system* provides information about the environment immediately outside the skin, relating to touch, pressure, heat, cold and pain.
- The *chemical systems* allow us to experience taste and smell. The receptors for taste are the taste buds on the tongue that determine tastes such as sweet, sour, salty and bitter. The sense of smell (also called the olfactory sense) depends on the activation of receptors in the nose by chemicals in the air. The olfactory nerve sends information directly to the olfactory bulb at the base of the brain.

The process of receiving sensory information is called *sensation*. It is a general term that refers to a sensory experience that occurs after a sensory stimulus is detected. Sensations are not specific and can be associated with any sensory modality. Once the sensory information is received in the brain, it is interpreted and given meaning. The process of interpreting and making meaning from sensory information is called *perception*. Perception therefore refers to a higher level of information processing.

1.1 Receptors

Certain cells that are specially adapted to receive information from the environment are called receptors. For example, taste buds on the tongue are receptors and so are hair cells in the nose. Receptors differ in their sensitivity. A stimulus needs to have a certain amount of intensity if it is going to lead to a sensory experience. There is a critical point, called the *absolute threshold,* which determines whether the stimulus is intense enough. If the stimulus is below the threshold, it will not generate a response. In addition to a certain level of intensity, a stimulus has to act on a receptor for a certain length of time in order to activate it.

The intensity of a stimulus can easily be measured, but it is much more difficult to determine the intensity of the person's subjective sensory experience, which is referred to as the psychological intensity of the stimulus. Research has shown that people can compare two sensory experiences and determine the difference in intensity between them. However, there has to be a certain amount of difference between two stimuli in order for the difference to be detectible or noticeable. For example, in a dark room it is fairly easy to detect the difference between the amount of light given by one candle in comparison with two candles. If there were 10 candles and one candle was added, it would be difficult to see the difference between the amount of light provided by 10 or 11 candles. The size of the increase in intensity that results in a noticeable difference (also referred to a 'just-noticeable difference') is called the *differential threshold.* This threshold is different for the various sensory modalities.

1.2 Transduction and generator potentials

Environmental stimulation comes in various forms of stimulus energy (such as light or sound energy). In order to be processed by the nervous system, stimulus energy has to be transformed to electrical energy, because that is what the firing of impulses in the nervous system is based on. The function of the receptors is the transformation of one form of energy to another and this is called *transduction* or *conversion*.

Receptor cells are like all nerve cells in that they have a cell nucleus and a membrane surrounded by ions. The resting potential in receptor cells is called the *receptor potential.* Whereas other neurons convert a resting potential into action potential when they are stimulated, receptor cells convert receptor potential into a *generator potential* when they receive the kind of stimulus that they are most sensitive to. An action potential is an all-or-nothing event, but a generator potential is a graded potential (like a postsynaptic excitatory potential) because the energy comes from the stimulus. The receptor cell transmits the generator potential across the synaptic cleft to a sensory neuron, which can then send the information to the brain if sufficient stimulation is received. If a receptor cell keeps on receiving stimulation, the generator potential decreases to prevent overstimulation. This decrease is called *adaptation.* Adaptation occurs in receptor cells and is different from habituation, which is a decrease in the frequency of firing in neurons.

2 Monitoring – the orienting reaction (OR)

The next step in the process of perception is monitoring the available information. Monitoring refers to the brain's ability to process incoming information very rapidly and below the level of awareness, so that the person can respond quickly to potentially important events. Monitoring starts when the receptors receive stimulus energy. The energy is changed into electrochemical impulses and the brain responds by comparing the incoming information with information stored in memory. Monitoring ensures that changes in the internal and external environment are brought to the person's attention. In this way, the person organises and selects information and this influences any conscious experience, action or response that follows. One of the effects of monitoring is the orienting reaction (OR).

The OR is a state of arousal that follows any sudden change in environmental stimulation. There are several indicators that the OR is taking place:

- *Bodily signs* are increased muscle tone and movement of the eyes, head and body toward the stimulus.
- *Vegetative signs* are a brief decrease in heart rate, held breath, contraction of blood vessels in the limbs, decreased salivation and enlarged pupils.
- *Sensory signs* are provided by increased sensory sensitivity.

The purpose of these changes is to allow the person to obtain as much information as possible about the environment in a short space of time. Once the information is obtained, the responses become directed to the specific stimulus modality and other responses are subdued. If the person's responses to a stimulus increase, sensitisation has occurred. However, if the person realises that the stimulus is not important, all responses will decrease. If the stimulus then keeps on occurring, the person does not stay in a heightened state of responding, but becomes habituated to the response. Habituation is a basic form of learning and tells the person that the stimulus can be ignored or that certain responses can be stopped. For example, a sudden loud sound may startle you and cause you to stop working for a moment, but if the noise continues you ignore it and carry on working because it is not important. In other words, you have become habituated to the noise. Habituation therefore refers to the disappearance of ORs after repeated stimulation by the event that initially triggered them. However, if the stimulus that initiated the OR then re-appears in a slightly different form or in a different situation, the OR is triggered again and this is called dishabituation. Using the previous example, if the noise you became used to suddenly changes to a higher pitch, you will again become aware of it (become dishabituated). Dishabituation is a form of OR that allows us to become aware of potentially important changes in an environment that we have become used to or familiar with. All these responses occur before the stimulus has been recognised or given meaning – that is, the response is below the level of awareness.

3 Perceptual organisation

Once sensory information has been received, it is processed further so that attention is given to relevant or important information rather than irrelevant or less important information. This process is called *perceptual organisation.*

3.1 Laws of perceptual organisation

The process of perceptual organisation is regulated by certain laws that determine what aspect of incoming information is relevant and what is not. This kind of organisation is spontaneous and takes place on a low level of awareness. That means that we are not fully aware or conscious of organising the information. The factors that influence perceptual organisation are as follows:

- *The characteristics of the stimulus.* According to the nature of the stimuli, some are regarded as more important than others and this influences the way we perceive them (this is discussed in the following section).
- *The state of the nervous system.* The nervous system has to be in a state of readiness to perceive information.
- *The individual person's characteristics and past experience.* We interpret the information we receive in terms of our own experience. For example, a

woman who is always nervous and who has had bad experiences in the past may get a fright when she hears a sudden shout because it may mean danger, but a woman who is very sociable and happy-go-lucky may feel happy when she hears a sudden shout because she thinks it is someone greeting her.

3.1.1 Figure and ground

When we perceive visual information, we often organise it into a meaningful *figure* (relevant information) against a less meaningful *ground* (irrelevant or less relevant information) without being aware of doing so. In Figure 1a, you see the map of Robben Island as a meaningful figure in a relatively meaningless background (the sea). This is a basic law of perceptual organisation. The relevant information is at a higher level of awareness than the less important information and therefore the relevant information is the first to be processed further. Figure and ground are not necessarily fixed. They can be reversed (see Figure 1b), but this requires more conscious effort. Figure–ground perception does not only apply to the visual system, but also to other kinds of sensory information. For example, when you are at a social gathering, the voice of the person you are talking to is the figure against the general background noise. This is an example of auditory perception. An example of olfactory perception is the smell of meat cooking (figure) against the smell of smoke from the fire (ground) at a braai.

In Figure 1b, you may see a white goblet or vase (figure) against a black background (ground). However, if you change your perspective, you can see two profiles in black (figure) with a white background in between them (ground).

Figure 1a Map of Robben Island, showing the island as the figure and the sea as the (back)ground

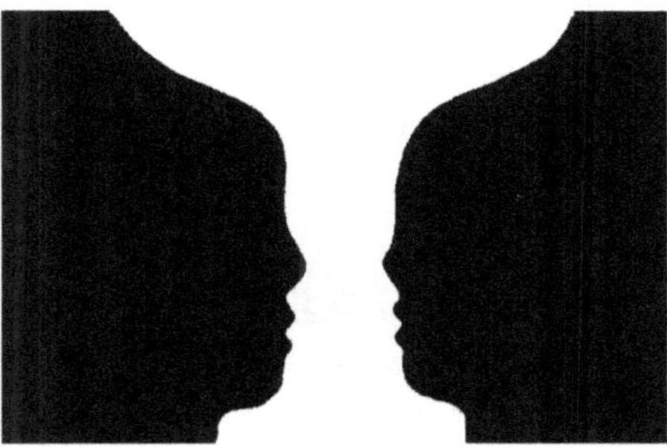

Figure 1b Reversible figure and ground

3.1.2 Contour, closure and grouping

There are other laws that influence perceptual organisation, namely the laws of contour, closure and grouping. *Contour* refers to the boundary or other feature that separates figure from ground. The perception of contour often depends on abrupt changes in brightness and colour, which provide contrast. Figure 2a provides an example of this phenomenon. When there is a gradual change in the stimulus (see Figure 2b), there is no definite contour and therefore no figure.

Figure 2a Sharp contrast between black and white provides the contour or outline of the star

Figure 2b The effect of gradually changing brightness is that there is no contour

Closure refers to our tendency to complete something spontaneously so that it has meaning. Closure depends a great deal on our experience in the world. For example, if you see someone talking while holding an object next to his or her ear, you perceive this as someone talking on a cellphone. However, if you did not know what a cellphone was, you would not know what the object was. Another example of closure is the tendency to read a familiar word correctly even if there is a letter left out of it (proofreading error). An example of visual closure is provided in Figure 3.

Figure 3 Visual closure – you see a cup even though the lines are sketchy and broken

People tend to perceive stimuli spontaneously in a way that makes sense to them. *Perceptual grouping* refers to the tendency to group stimuli in a pattern or shape in a way that is most likely to help you interpret them. There are four types of perceptual grouping, according to the following principles:

- The *principle of proximity* is the tendency to group elements that are close together as though they represent a figure (see Figure 4a).
- The *principle of similarity* is the tendency to group elements that are similar in colour, shape or texture as though they represent a figure (see Figure 4b).

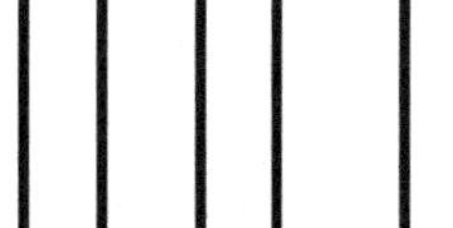

Figure 4a
Principle of proximity – you tend to see two sets of two lines and one of one line, rather than a random arrangement of lines

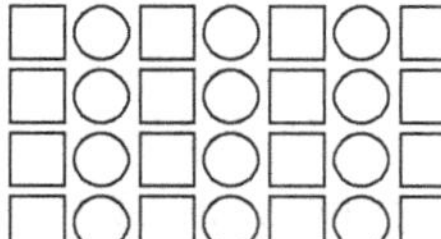

Figure 4b
Principle of similarity – you tend to see vertical columns of circles and squares, rather than rows of alternating circles and squares

Figure 4c
Principle of symmetry – you see a straight line crossing a wavy line rather than one shape with odd angles

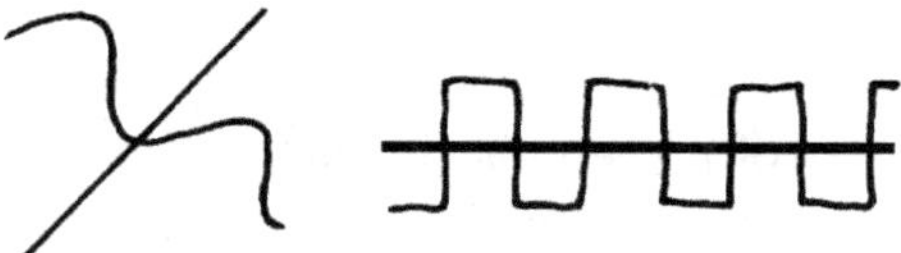

Figure 4d
Principle of continuity – you see the continuation of a pattern rather than two separate lines

- The *principle of symmetry* is the tendency to group elements in a way that creates a symmetrical or balanced figure (see Figure 4c).
- The *principle of continuity* is the tendency to perceive stimuli in such a way that elements that are continuous form a figure (see Figure 4d). These principles do not only apply to grouping in visual perception (visual grouping). For example, when listening to a choir, you can often hear the separate harmonies and rhythms coming from different groups in the choir (auditory grouping).

3.2 Spatial organisation

The spatial organisation of visual information also helps us to make sense of what we see. Spatial organisation explains why we see the world in three dimensions (height, width and depth) although the actual image on the retina is flat (two dimensional, in terms of width and height). Depth cues are detected automatically through the process of accommodation (changes in the shape of the lens that allow you to focus on objects at varying distances) and according to head movements. Although the size of the image on the retina gives a fairly good indication of the size of the object (the retinal image is large for close objects and gets smaller as the object moves further away), we can judge the relative size of objects by comparing them with other information in the environment. For example, an object that is behind another one is seen as being further away than the one in front. In addition, the further away you are from something, the smoother the texture appears to be. For example, when you look out of the window of an aircraft, the fields below look smooth and even, but when you are up close to them, you can see that the ground is rough and uneven. Shadows also provide depth cues.

3.3 Perceptual constancy

The world is viewed as a fairly constant and unchanging place and this is a function of perceptual constancy. Perceptual constancy means that we see things as having a particular size, shape, colour and brightness, irrespective of changing conditions. Perceptual constancy is spontaneous and we are seldom aware of it.

There are four attributes of perceptual constancy:

- *Constant size.* This refers to the fact that familiar objects are perceived as having a constant size as long as there are enough cues in the environment to provide information about distance and depth. We need these cues to judge the size of the object relative to that of other objects in the environment, therefore the image on the retina is only one cue for judging size. You make a judgement based on information in the environment and your own knowledge of the size of objects (familiarity) and then you make adjustments to the size of the retinal images. For example, when you are watching a soccer game, you see the ball as being a particular size, no matter whether it is close to you or far away. This is an illustration of constant size.
- *Constant shape.* When you stand in front of a closed door, you see it as a rectangle. When the door is open, the shape you see is trapezoid, although you still perceive it as a rectangle because you know from past experience that it is a rectangle. This is an example of constant shape. Shape constancy depends on making a compromise between the retinal image, the angle of the object you see and your past experience.
- *Constant brightness.* A white shirt may look slightly grey when you are standing in the shade but you still perceive it as white, even though it reflects less light than it would if you were standing in the sun. This is an example of constant brightness. That means our perception of brightness does not change when conditions change.
- *Constant colour.* Similarly, our perceptions of colour are constant despite changing conditions. Coloured lighting at a club may make your blue T-shirt look brown but it still looks blue to you. Familiarity with objects plays an important role in colour constancy.

Perceptual constancy is actually a perceptual error, in that the perceptions are not the same as retinal information, but they are necessary for effective functioning because they provide our worlds with some stability. Imagine, for example, how you would struggle to put together the bits of a computer if they looked too big or small depending on the angle or distance from which you were looking.

3.4 Illusions

Illusions are a form of mistake in perception. An illusion is not a vision of something that does not exist. The object or stimulus does exist, but we perceive an illusion because the object's attributes are combined and perceived incorrectly. One of the best-known illusions is illustrated in Figure 5a. The line on the right appears to be longer, even though the two lines are exactly the same length. The explanation for this illusion may be that the inward and outward flowing lines suggest three-dimensional objects and, on the basis of our experience, (see Figure 5b) we interpret the line on the right as being longer. Films provide another example of an illusion – a film is a rapid sequence of still pictures that we perceive as movement. Illusions are perceived spontaneously and even though there is objective evidence that the perception is incorrect, the illusion is still there.

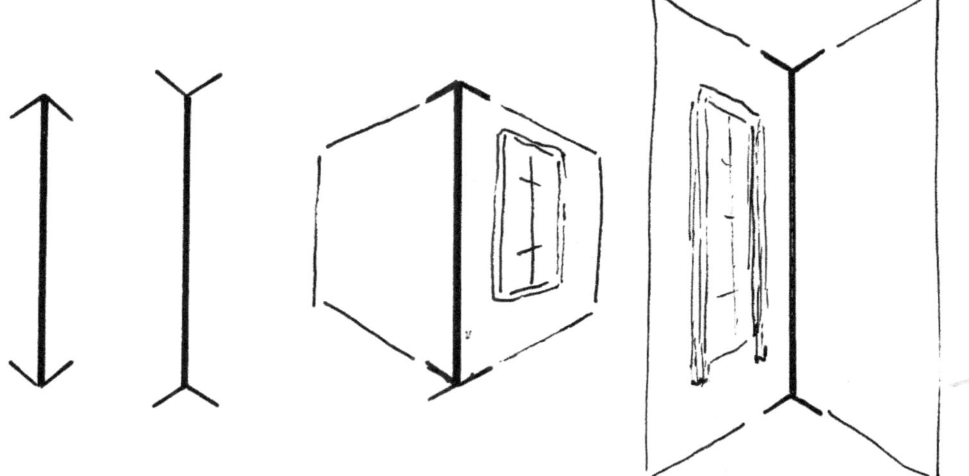

Figure 5a Although the lines are the same length, the one on the left appears shorter

Figure 5b We use depth cues (based on our experience of the everyday world) to interpret the length of the lines

4 Recognition

After the perceptual organisation of information into figure and ground, the relevant information is given a meaningful name or description based on the individual's own knowledge and experience. Whereas perceptual organisation occurs on a low level of awareness, attributing meaning to something requires a higher level of awareness. The process of recognition is an example of attributing meaning to something. Recognition occurs because we have built up a store of concepts and groups, which we use to classify information that is perceived. In this way, a person knows 'what' has been seen or heard by comparing new information with information obtained from past experience. For example, you are able to recognise a small rectangular object as a cellphone because you know what they look like, but a person who has been in solitary confinement in prison for the past 15 years may not be able to recognise one.

Once meaning is established, the person then has to decide whether it is necessary to pay attention to that information or not.

5 Attention

Paying attention occurs at a high level of awareness. Until this point, the selection and organisation of information take place at a lower level, either below or on the threshold of awareness. When you pay attention, you consciously decide on what should be dealt with. Paying attention is a form of conscious control over what is being perceived. For example, if you are paying close attention to reading this section of this book, you are probably not aware of noises in the street or elsewhere in the building. The material you are reading is the relevant information and the noises outside are irrelevant to what you are doing. However, if there was a sudden and loud shout for help from outside, you would probably be alert to the noises outside because they have become more relevant. Relevant and irrelevant information can switch places spontaneously, because the brain is constantly monitoring the environment for potentially important changes. Monitoring is an automatic process. You are not aware of it and it does not prevent you from attending to a particular task at the same time as you are monitoring the environment.

Most of the time, we are exposed to a great deal of information that competes for our attention. Competition between two different messages leads to divided attention. People have a limited capacity for attending to more than one thing at a time. When you concentrate on only one thing, you are able to deal with it efficiently. It becomes very difficult when you have to give attention (at a high level of awareness) to more than one thing at a time, although it is possible to do so. The process of simultaneous perception of different sets of information is called parallel processing. There are situations in which parallel processing is possible. Parallel processing is easier when the tasks to be dealt with are similar, when you have had considerable practise or training for them and when both tasks do not require much attention. If information is presented slowly, you can alternate your attention between the two sets of information and attend to both quite efficiently. If the information is presented too fast, you are unable to switch between them fast enough to allow for efficient processing. In addition, when one task is so familiar that it becomes automatic, you are better able to attend to another task simultaneously.

5.1 Determinants of attention

Certain situations, events or stimuli are more likely to demand your attention than others. There are internal (factors within yourself) and external (outside) determinants of attention.

5.1.1 External determinants

The following are external determinants that catch our attention:

- *More intense stimuli.* These are strong stimuli (like loud noises or bright lights) rather than weak ones.
- *Size.* This refers to large stimuli (like advertisement boards) rather than small stimuli.
- *Distance.* Things that are close up are more likely to catch our attention than those at a distance.
- *Change, movement and contrast.* We are very sensitive to movement in the perceptual field and respond well to novel, unexpected and unusual stimuli.
- *Repetition.* This may lead to habituation, but repetition can be used to establish an idea, followed by something different to hold attention.
- *Complex stimuli.* These are generally more interesting than simple ones, but the amount of interest differs from one individual and situation to another.

5.1.2 Internal determinants

Your attention will be attracted by something that is important or inherently interesting to you personally, therefore internal determinants of attention relate to aspects such as individual disposition, personality, needs and interests. If you have a particular field of interest, you may develop a *perceptual set* that allows an involuntary focus on only those things that are of interest. A perceptual set is defined as a state of perceptual readiness that makes the formation of certain perceptions and actions more likely than others. For example, if you have a particular interest in psychology, you are able to skim through a magazine and notice only the sections that deal with topics related to psychology, not paying much attention to other sections. A perceptual set provides a kind of framework for seeing things and therefore influences the way we perceive situations and events.

6 Intersubjectivity of perception

From this section, you can see that perception is a process of creating meaning. However, the meaning we give situations is not necessarily a reflection of reality, but is rather our own interpretation of it. Perception is a very subjective process because the meanings we give to situations depend on our individual dispositions and our experiences. Our perceptions are private, but through the use of language we can share them and develop shared meanings. We can describe our perceptions and communicate experiences through language and behaviour, therefore language allows us to make sense of the world and in ways that makes sense to others. For example, you know what a bicycle is because you have learnt through interaction with others what the characteristics of a bicycle are, so various people can talk about a bicycle and know that everyone understands what they mean.

We use the term *intersubjectivity* to describe the shared or agreed meanings of the way events in the world are interpreted. In South Africa, for example, many people use the word 'robot' when referring to traffic lights. To people in other countries, a 'robot' means something different. For South Africans, there is an intersubjectively shared meaning for the word. Intersubjectively shared meanings are very important in everyday life. For example, the fact that drivers know that a red traffic light signals that they should stop (on the basis of intersubjectively shared meaning) helps to bring some order to the flow of traffic and regulate it in busy streets.

Bibliography

Coon, D. 2004. *Introduction to psychology.* 10th edition. Belmont, CA: Wadsworth.

Davey, G. (Ed). 2004. *Complete psychology.* London: Hodder & Stoughton.

Jordaan, W. and Jordaan, J. 1998. *People in context.* 3rd edition. Johannesburg: Heinemann.

Morris, C.G. and Maisto, A.A. 2003. *Understanding psychology.* Englewood Cliffs, NJ: Prentice Hall.

Weiten, W. 2001. *Psychology: Themes and variations.* 5th edition. Belmont, CA: Wadsworth.

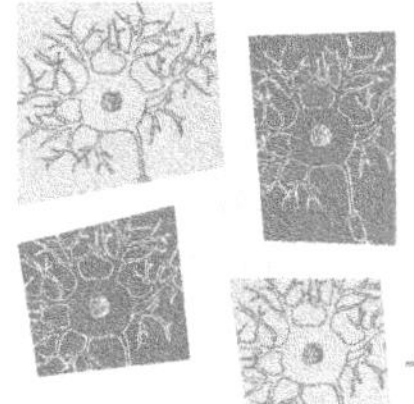

Sensation: The visual system

There are several sensory systems but only one will be discussed in detail here and that is the visual system. Light is the stimulus for the visual system. However, the human nervous system can only detect a very small segment of the electromagnetic spectrum, between the ultraviolet and infrared rays.

1 Visual information

Light waves have certain physical characteristics (Jordaan and Jordaan, 1998):

- Wavelength (the distance between the peaks of waves)
- Amplitude (the height of the waves)
- Purity (the mixture of light waves that reaches the eye)

These characteristics of light waves are associated with the observer's psychological experiences. Wavelength (a physical property of light waves) determines the colour (psychological experience) that people see. Amplitude determines brightness – the greater the amplitude, the brighter the light experienced. Purity is associated with saturation or clarity of colour. Pure wavelengths (that is, only one kind of wavelength) are experienced as pure or clear colour, while mixed wavelengths are experienced as less clear or less pure (saturated) colour.

2 Parts of the eye

Visual receptors are found in the eye (see Figure 1). Light enters the eye through the outer layer or cornea, which is transparent and passes through a fluid into the front part (called the anterior chamber) of the eye. This front part is divided from the rest of the eye by the iris, with its small opening called the pupil. The iris produces the colour of the eye. The white area around the iris is called the sclera, the part that helps to maintain the shape of the eye. There are six ocular muscles attached to the sclera and their function is to move the eye. The muscles of the iris can change the size of the pupil, making it smaller in bright light to limit the amount of light that is allowed in and larger in poor light so that more light can be admitted. The muscles of the iris respond reflexively to the amount of light. The light that is admitted through the iris is then projected by the lens onto the retina, the inside surface of the eyeball. The lens bends the rays of light so that they fall on the retina. The actual visual receptor cells are found in the retina. The ciliary muscles can change the shape of the lens to keep the object that is being looked at in focus. The adjustment of the lens is called accommodation. Although we are not aware of it, we have a blind spot in each eye. This is found in the optic disc, which is the place on the retina where axons are grouped together to form the optic nerve. The optic disc has no receptors and is therefore a blind spot. Each eye compensates for the blind spot in the other eye and this is why we are not aware of having them.

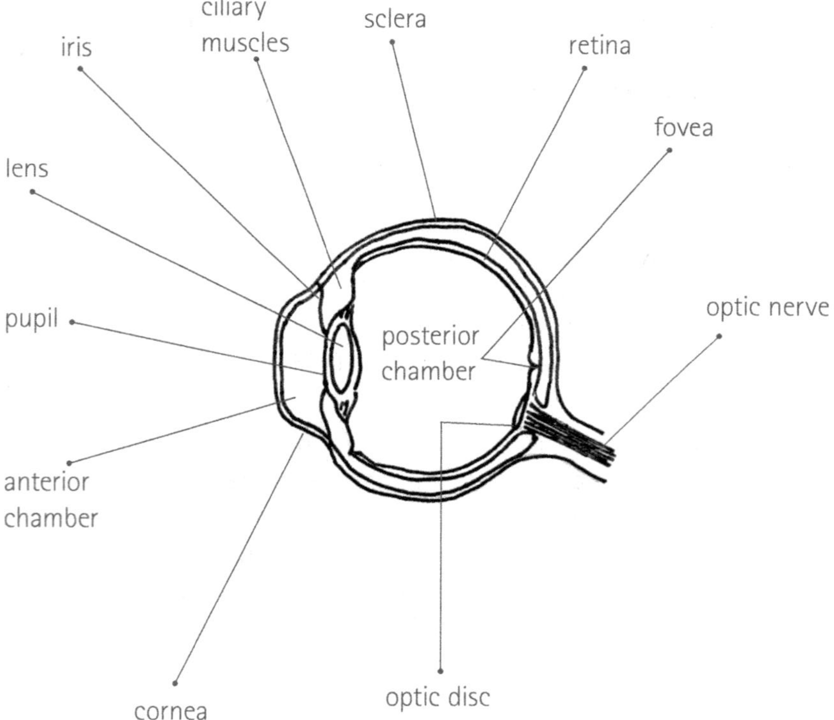

Figure 1 Diagram of a cross-section of the eye

2.1 Visual receptors

There are two kinds of visual receptor: the *cones* are responsible for vision in daylight as well as colour vision and the *rods* are important for vision at night and when the light is poor. Most of the cones are found in the fovea, which is a small dent in the retina. The cones allow us to obtain a sharp image of what we see (called visual acuity). This is why we turn our heads to look closely at something so that the light falls on the fovea. The rods, on the other hand, are distributed more on the periphery (the outside or areas further away from the fovea). The rods are more sensitive to light and can function when the level of light is poor. Because the cones are used for bright light, they have a higher sensitivity threshold than rods. This means that cones are less sensitive to light than rods and require more intense light stimulation to be activated.

The rods contain a chemical called rhodopsin. When the rods receive light, it is absorbed by the rhodopsin, which is broken down into two parts: retinene and rod opsin. This chemical process is called bleaching. When light stimulation stops, the rhodopsin is resynthesised (or made up again). The cones also contain a chemical called iodopsin. When light falls on the cones, iodopsin is broken down into retinene and cone opsin. When it is darker again, the iodopsin is resynthesised. Rods contain only one kind of opsin but there are three kinds of cone opsin, which absorb either red, blue or green wavelengths.

Bleaching is the process that allows us to adapt to abrupt changes from light to dark situations. In bright light, the rhodopsin in the rods remains in a bleached state. It is resynthesised only in darkness. When you go from bright sunlight into a dark room, at first you cannot see anything but soon you are able to make out things around you. This happens because in darkness, the rhodopsin is quickly resynthesised and the receptors are more sensitive so that you can see, even in poor light. This process is called *dark adaptation.*

3 Colour vision and colour blindness

There are several theories of colour vision (Morris and Maisto, 2003). Centuries ago, the *trichromatic theory* was developed by Thomas Young and Herman von Helmholtz (also named the Young-Helmholtz theory). According to the trichromatic theory, colour vision is the result of three retinal systems – one each for red, green and blue. When all three systems are stimulated at the same time and intensity, we see white. Different combinations of red, green and blue are seen according to the system that is stimulated the most. More recent research has confirmed that there are three kinds of cones in the retina and that each is most sensitive to either the red, blue and green wavelengths.

In contrast to the Youn-Helmholtz theory, Ewald Hering proposed the *opponent process theory* (also called the Hering theory). According to Hering's theory, colour vision is the result of three opposing processes: a green–red process, a yellow–blue process and a white–black process. The particular colour is experienced according to the wavelength of the light that stimulates it. Black or white depend on the brightness of light. Subsequent research has confirmed this theory. It is important to note that the opponent process theory does not apply to the photoreceptors but rather to the cells in the optic nerve and thalamus.

There is one phenomenon that these two theories do not explain and that is the fact that we usually do not perceive colour in isolation. We compare the colour of something in relation to other objects around it. For example, imagine that you are looking at a large white screen that is illuminated by green light in a darkened room. Is the screen white or green, or any other colour? As soon as someone wearing a red shirt and blue jeans stands in front of the screen, you can see that the shirt is red, the jeans are blue and the screen is white, even though green light is falling on all of them. This tendency of an object to appear nearly the same colour under a variety of lighting conditions is called colour constancy. This phenomenon led Edwin Land to propose the *retinex theory* of colour vision. Retinex is a combination of the words 'retina' and 'cortex'. In terms of the retinex theory, we perceive colour through the cerebral cortex's comparison of various retinal patterns. In other words, the visual cortex compares the pattern of light coming from different areas of the retina and forms a colour perception for each one. Support for this theory has been obtained from people with certain types of brain damage – the damage to one region of the cortex destroys colour constancy.

Each theory describes a different aspect of colour vision. The trichromatic theory accurately describes events at the level of the retina (three types of cones). The opponent-process theory best describes how the activities of neurons in the rest of the visual system organise colour information. The retinex theory shows how the cortex compares colour information from different parts of the visual field. If you put these theories together, they all provide information about the processes involved in colour vision.

There is one more aspect of colour vision that is of interest and that is colour blindness. The opponent-process theory explains colour blindness, a phenomenon that the trichromatic theory or the retinex theory alone cannot explain. People with normal colour vision have three kinds of iodopsin (red, blue and green) but most colour-blind people have two kinds of iodopsin. The most common form of colour blindness is the inability to distinguish between red and green. People with red–green colour blindness have cones with blue iodopsin but their red and green cones have the same iodopsin so that they see red and green as the same. Colour blindness is quite common and this is why traffic lights always have the red light on top, so that colour-blind people will know when to stop or go, even if they cannot see the colour.

4 The visual pathway

The area that the eye can see is called the visual field. Light stimuli coming from the visual field are projected onto the retina. The area of the retina that receives the light rays is called the retinal field. The axons of neurons that link the receptors to the brain are grouped together in a bundle called the optic nerve. The optic nerve and optic tract carry information from the visual receptors to the visual areas of the brain in the occipital lobes. There are two optic nerves (one from each eye) that come together at the base of the midbrain where some of the axons cross over at the optic chiasm. Some of the axons end in the midbrain (where they provide input for the size of the pupils) and some end in the superior colliculus for the control of head and eye movements, but most end in the thalamus, where visual information is relayed to the occipital cortex. Because of the crossing over of some axons at the optic chiasm, the thalamus projects information from the right side of the retinal fields of both eyes to the right visual cortex and from the left retinal fields to the left visual cortex (see Figure 2). This explains why a person can have poor sight or blindness in certain parts of the visual field, according to the part of the optic nerve that has been injured.

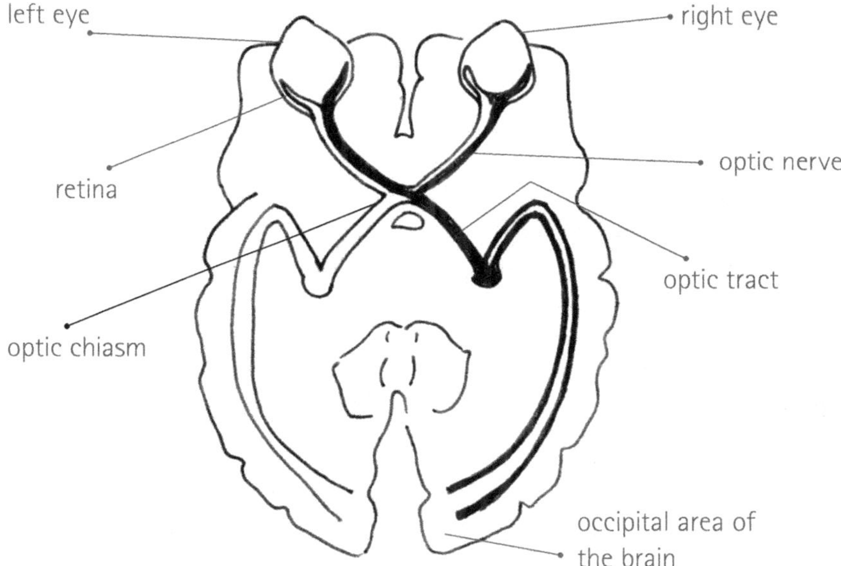

Figure 2 The visual pathways from the retina to the visual cortex in the brain (horizontal cross-section of the brain)

The visual tracts that are marked in black lead to the right hemisphere and the white tracts lead to the left hemisphere.

Bibliography

Coon, D. 2004. *Introduction to psychology.* 10th edition. California: Wadsworth.

Jordaan, W. and Jordaan, J. 1998. *People in context.* 3rd edition. Johannesburg: Heinemann.

Morris, C.G. and Maisto, A.A. 2003. *Understanding psychology.* New Jersey: Prentice Hall.

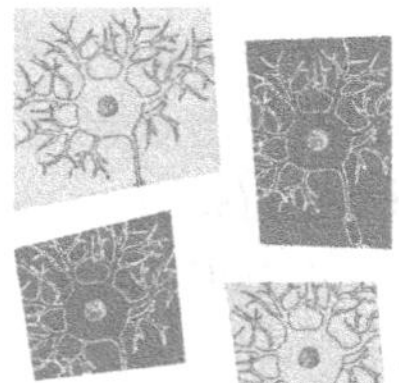

Social issues

The psychologist Kurt Lewin (1890–1947) was one of the pioneers of social psychology. He developed a theory, called field theory, which emphasised the interplay between personal characteristics (such as habits and beliefs) and environmental elements (such as the physical environment, social situations and group dynamics). This approach focused psychologists' attention on the societal aspects of human behaviour (Gazzaniga and Heatherton, 2003:24–25). In this section, we shall look at four issues that are pertinent to contemporary society. These are violence, discrimination, poverty and land ownership.

1 Violence

Violence begins when one person fails to esteem the other person, stops respecting the other person's dignity and starts to abuse him or her (Freire, in Jordaan and Jordaan, 1998). Violence becomes part of daily life in subtle metaphoric forms. These include psychological violence (showing itself in violent talk and intolerance of others), structural violence (showing itself in the unfair distribution of commodities as a result of class- or race-based stratification in society) and violence of poverty (showing itself in the indignity of subhuman living standards). These metaphorical forms of violence are often the source of physical violence. In this way, violence creeps into the very fabric of society (Degenaar, in Jordaan and Jordaan, 1998). Today, violence is the leading cause of death in the 15 to 44 age group worldwide (Naidoo, Van Wyk and Carolissen, 2004). In South Africa, at least 3.5 million people per annum require health care as a result of trauma (Higson-Smith, 2004).

There are many kinds of violence, but the following broad types are perhaps most evident in contemporary society:

- Violence for material gain (for example muggings and armed robberies)

- Domestic violence (for example neglect of children, battery of spouses and abuse of the elderly)
- Sexual violence (for example rape and sexual harassment)
- State and collective violence (for example colonialism and apartheid)
- Self-directed violence (for example suicide and self-mutilation)

These acts of violence do not occur in isolation. They affect one another on an individual, group, community and society level and so we need an ecological model to describe a phenomenon as complex as violence (Higson-Smith, 2004).

There are three main theoretical approaches to understanding violence. These are the following:

1. Instinct or socio-biological approaches
2. Frustration–aggression approaches
3. Observational learning approaches (Feldman, 2003:462–463)

The *instinct* or *socio-biological approaches* see violence as an inborn survival strategy. In the past, instinct enabled humans to hunt for food and to react to a threat. *Frustration–aggression approaches* explain violence as the outcome of frustration. When people are frustrated they become angry and anger leads to violent acts, especially if the frustration occurs in contexts that have previously been associated with violence. According to the *observational learning approaches,* we learn to be violent through direct reinforcement and through modelling our behaviour on that of others. When I see somebody getting his way through acting violently, I am likely to imitate his behaviour when I find myself in a similar situation. However, when I see the opposite happening, namely that somebody is punished for displaying violent behaviour, I am unlikely to imitate his behaviour (Feldman, 2003:463).

Violence has severe repercussions on all levels, ranging from the individual level to society as a whole. It is both fragmenting and disempowering. Violence causes fragmentation in the sense that it breaks up and destroys important linkages and relationships in communities and it is disempowering in the sense that it undermines people's ability to fulfil their appropriate functions in their groups and communities (Higson-Smith, 2004). Violence also has alienating effects in society and it impacts significantly on children (Jordaan, 1998).

Alienation is a consequence of societal violence. Societies are normally organised around rules in terms of which people accept personal responsibility for their conduct and expect others to do the same. Violence goes against this orderly, rule-bound existence and, in the long run, creates a state of lawlessness that threatens people's psychological well-being. One of the effects of such a state is alienation. There are three interrelated aspects to alienation:

- The fear that you yourself, or your family or friends, will fall victim to violence.

- The avoidance of all kinds of behaviour that used to be spontaneous (for example not travelling on certain roads, or not travelling at all at night).
- The experience of being at the mercy of forces beyond your control, which gives rise to feelings of helplessness, isolation, lack of commitment to society and mistrust of people (Jordaan, 1998).

Violence has a negative impact on children. The effect of violence depends on how children experience it and on what coping mechanisms they apply. Children need a supportive home life with firm norms for behaviour (Ramphele, in Jordaan and Jordaan, 1998). A culture of violence, intimidation and terrorism is damaging to the psychological well-being of children and can result in various forms of maladjustment. *Maladjusted behaviour* refers to a behaviour pattern that is displayed in response to a certain situation (adjustment) but that fails to serve the purpose (maladjustment).

The first form of maladjustment as a result of violence is when the behaviour becomes a permanent pattern, which is continued long after the violence has already disappeared. For example, a child may leave his parents' house and roam the streets over weekends to escape his drunken father's violent behaviour, but then continue to stay away over weekends after the father has left the family. A second form of maladjustment in reaction to violence is identification with the instigators and perpetrators of violence. The imitation of violent behaviour lies at the root of youth gangs who engage in unlawful behaviour. Children may also become mentally lethargic in the presence of recurrent violence. This third form of maladjustment is characterised by an uncritical acceptance of reasons why an individual or a group is branded as the enemy. There is also an uncritical acceptance of the situation of violence as a way of life and an inability to see the necessity of education. The fourth form of maladjustment is the development of a skewed morality that comes from fanatical adherence to a particular ideology. Children do not have the opportunity for a balanced, critical and objective approach to life if they grow up in an environment where they are not allowed to hear anything that does not square up with the dominant ideology.

2 Discrimination

Discrimination is negative behaviour towards members of a particular group. It is usually based on stereotypical ideas about the group, which lead to prejudice against its members. Prejudice is a specific form of attitude. It is negative and is characterised by hatefulness and irrational beliefs. Stereotypical ideas about a group are based on ignorance and faulty or incomplete knowledge about it. Stereotypes and prejudice are belief systems. Discrimination happens when these beliefs are translated into practices that result in privilege, status and power for one group at the expense of another (Stevens, 2004). For example, a manager may believe that women do not have good business sense (stereotypical idea about women) and therefore decides to appoint a man instead of a woman (discrimination based on prejudice against women).

Discrimination based on the gender of a person is called sexism or gender bias. Discrimination usually occurs against women rather than men because of the ideology of patriarchy. In a patriarchal system, manhood is seen as the basic standard of being a person (that is, of personhood), thus personhood is equated with manhood. It is not considered a combination of manhood and womanhood. Womanhood is viewed in relation to the basic standard of manhood and not in relation to a neutral and overarching concept of personhood. These views of manhood and womanhood are entrenched in society and are perpetuated by discursive practices in society. (A discursive practice is a way of talk that constructs the thing that is being talked about in a particular way). Discursive practices that perpetuate patriarchal stereotypes (that is, talk that constructs men as superior and women as submissive) unwittingly legitimise discriminatory practices against women (Jordaan, 1998).

The notion that discursive practices play a cardinal role in discrimination has shifted the focus from ideology to ideological practice. Following this trend, contemporary studies about racism emphasise the role of racist discourse in the way that we understand race. For example, in liberal newspaper articles about violence, black people have been depicted as innately violent and untrustworthy sub-humans that should be tamed; racially biased against whites; child-like in the sense of not acting responsibly; and unreasonable (Duncan, in Foster, 2003).

The former is an example of overt (traditional) racism, in which the black person is seen as primarily bad and inferior to the white person. However, racism is not always so explicit. Modern (also called symbolic) racism is more subtle. When, in 1991, a group of black people formed a new township in a former white area of Hout Bay, Cape Town, an analysis of the discourses of the time shows little use of the labels 'black' or 'white'. A more neutral and impersonal language was used to depict the township as 'out of place' and its inhabitants as 'foreign' and 'alien'. The town of Hout Bay was classified as 'beautiful', 'picturesque' and 'unspoiled' and the township was described as a 'scar', an 'eyesore', a 'festering sore' and a 'sprawl' (Foster, 2003).

In *modern racism,* there is no direct denigration of black people. Modern racism occurs in racist remarks and jokes that groups of all colour make among themselves about other groups. It manifests itself in the following ways (Jordaan, 1998):

- Unwittingly perpetuating negative stereotypes through highly selective perceptions of situations (such as thinking that black people are bad drivers because the driver who skipped the stop street was a black person)
- Apparently supporting the principle of equality, while resisting its implementation through some kind of rationalisation (such as suggesting that a black colleague does not as yet have sufficient experience to be appointed as a manager)

- Implementing non-racial policies, yet withholding vital enablers of performance (such as creating opportunities for promotion but withholding training opportunities)
- Maintaining distance in interpersonal situations (such as being friendly but not being interested in getting to know the person better)
- Passively resisting support for another person by withholding normal supportive actions (such as not forwarding an important policy document to the person)

The difference between traditional and modern racism is a symptomatic change (that is, a change in the way in which racism is expressed), but not a real change in attitude (that is, a change in racist feelings) (Jordaan, 1998).

3 The development of poor communities

Poverty is a worldwide phenomenon. Globally, as many as one in five people is poor and, in some regions, this figure is as high as one in two. Although South Africa is classified as a middle-income country, most South Africans are poor. In 2004, of the 44 million South Africans, eight million live below the internationally recognised poverty line (Terre Blanche, 2004).

Poor countries have a high infant mortality rate and low life expectancies. They also have higher than normal incidences of physical and mental illnesses. Most of these problems are caused by undernourishment, high levels of environmental pollution and poor sanitary conditions (Terre Blanche, 2004). However, the most devastating effect of poverty is its cyclic dynamic. This means that people get caught up in a cycle of poverty. It becomes a way of life, carried over from parents to children, increasing the poverty level of each generation (Jordaan, 1998). The victims of cyclic poverty tend to become desperately passive. Their passivity is characterised by a learnt helplessness, in the sense that they feel that nothing can be done about their situation. They uncritically accept advice from outside experts. They do what is dictated to them, because they believe that they do not have choices and bargaining power. However, there is also a passive resistance, demonstrated in the resistance against taking responsibility. Because development projects often focus on the acceptance of self-responsibility, there is a reluctance to take part in development projects. Passivity does not mean that people do not experience anger and frustration. Deprivation and hardship may be loaded with aggression and hostility. Individuals in such circumstances can be provoked easily and encouraged to act violently (Jordaan, 1998).

Poverty is not simply about being deprived of necessities such as food, medicine and clothing, but also about living a situation of hopelessness, uncertainty about the future and alienation from 'mainstream' society (Terre Blanche, 2004). People feel hopeless because they cannot see a way out of their circumstances. They live with uncertainty on a day-to-day basis because they have no means to buffer themselves against unexpected events threatening their existence. They feel alienated from mainstream society because their experience is that the institutional structures of society do not serve them. Societal institutions like banks and courts serve the middle and upper classes, but are neither accessible to nor affordable by the poor (Terre Blanche, 2004). Liberating people politically and freeing them from social oppression do not automatically free them from a spirit of dependence (Seedat, in Jordaan and Jordaan, 1998). The development of a community requires careful collaboration with community members and the tapping of local knowledge. In other words, what is required is a process of participatory appraisal. Knowledge and experience should be gained through co-operation with the community.

A community is more than a physical or geographical entity. It consists of people who experience a sense of belonging to the physical place as well as to one another. There is a transactional relationship between a community and its members. This means that the community and the members of the community play in on each other. The identity of the community members is determined by the community, but at the same time the community gets its identity from the individuals who belong to it. Community members are not only co-creators of the community in which they live, they are also responsible for the community that they create (Jordaan, 1998). The development of a sense of community involves four characteristics, namely membership, influence, need fulfilment and shared emotional connectedness (McMillan and Chavis, in Jordaan, 1998).

There are three aspects to community membership. The first is that people feel they have contributed to the community and *invested* in it. The second aspect involves *boundaries.* Boundaries may be physical or psychological, but they create a distinction between us (the members of the community) and them (those who are not part of the community). The third aspect refers to the *advantages of membership.* Being a member of a community offers emotional security, as well as a sense of belonging to it and fulfilling a certain position in it. Influence involves the influence that members have over community matters, as well as the influence of the community over its members (for example to live by the community's regulations and norms). Need fulfilment refers to the community's ability to fulfil its members' current and future needs. To the extent that the community can fulfil the needs of its members, the community becomes more cohesive and better integrated. The last aspect of community membership is the degree to which individuals share a common history, experiences of places and future prospects. The greater the degree of sharing in these aspects, the deeper the experience of community membership.

4 A place to stay

Colonialism did not only mean the political subjugation and economic exploitation of people. It also caused tremendous psychological harm by alienating people from their land. Today we understand the strong feelings that fuelled the anti-colonialist movements and people's need to return to the land of their forefathers. The environment has significant psychological value in terms of its physical, personal and social features (Grieve and Jordaan, 1998). To take people's land away from them is not simply to rob them of a physical location, but also to take away a piece of their personhood and a chunk of their social belonging. People's environments are extensions of themselves. They are the physical locations in which their entire social networks are anchored.

4.1 The environment as a physical place

When people move into a new environment for the first time, they are acutely aware of its characteristics, such as its shapes, noises and colours. As they settle into the environment, the physical features become less obtrusive, but the environment continues to influence them. Its physical characteristics determine how people move and interact in the environment. Some influences are more subtle. Colours, textures and smells create atmospheres that influence people's moods. Environmental influences can be so strong that they cause identification with and attachment to the environment. People are drawn to particular places because they find a place aesthetically beautiful, or because they experience an inner sense of satisfaction when they are there, or because of a combination of these two reasons (Grieve and Jordaan, 1998).

4.2 The environment as an extension of the self

An environment may cause us to experience strong emotions attached to all aspects of that environment, to the extent that we feel as though our inner being is expressed in and through it. The environment feels like part of our being. It becomes something through which we can express ourselves; in a sense, it is an extension of our self-identity. Who or what we are is expressed in terms of the qualities of the environment. When we are so closely tied to a particular place, it is very hard to let go of it, therefore people find it difficult to move from a place to which they have become strongly attached (Grieve and Jordaan, 1998).

4.3 The environment as a social system

There are four elements that characterise the social aspects of an environment. These are privacy, personal space, territoriality and crowding.

The desire for *privacy* is not a need to be alone, but rather a need to control how much interaction we have with others. Privacy has three functions:

- It establishes boundaries between us and others, creating personal space. These boundaries can be physical (for example a closed door) or psychological (for example refraining from answering a question that we find intrusive).

- It enables us to control how much others know about us. The control can be formal or informal. Informal control is how much you tell others about yourself. Formal control refers to the official agreements you sign with organisations to keep your information private.
- Privacy also allows us the opportunity for self-reflection. We need time on our own to regain our sense of self.

Personal space refers to the amount of space we need between ourselves and other people. We all keep people at a certain physical distance from us. If they come too close, we begin to feel uncomfortable and we may turn or move away. The minimum distance that we allow between ourselves and somebody else is called our personal space. Different individuals have different personal spaces. Some people are more comfortable than others in allowing people close to them, but we also have different personal spaces for the different people we interact with. For example, you will allow a friend to come much closer to you than you would a stranger. Personal space has two functions. First, there is practical value in keeping people at a distance. For example, it is not easy to communicate with somebody if they stand too close to you. Second, personal space is one of the non-verbal ways in which we communicate intimacy. If you allow somebody into your personal space, you indicate that you find intimate social interaction with them acceptable (Grieve and Jordaan, 1998).

Territoriality refers to a place we select and that we demarcate as our own. When others get into this space, they have to adhere to our rules. Our living spaces are places that we are normally territorial about, but we also display territorial behaviour in more subtle ways. We often have a favourite chair in a friend's house, where we prefer to sit every time we visit. Territoriality is sometimes used to maintain social order and also to establish relative status in groups. For example, the head of the household often has his or her place at the head of the table (Grieve and Jordaan, 1998).

Crowding is our subjective experience of the number of people around us. It is important to note that crowding is a psychological experience of a physical situation. In other words, it is not just the number of people in a particular area, but our experience of the number of people that is important. For example, you and I may be in a room with 20 people and I may experience the situation as crowded, whereas you may not. Experience of crowding also depends on the circumstances. I may feel crowded in a room with 20 people if we are all waiting to be interviewed for the same position, but may not find the room crowded when we are all watching a sports game on television. However, although crowding is a subjective experience, the number of people in a given area does have certain consequences. People show an increased tendency to withdraw and reduce interaction with others as the number of people increases. There is also the tendency of reduced personal responsibility when there are others around. In other words, people are less inclined to personally take responsibility (for example to help somebody in need) in the presence of other people (Grieve and Jordaan, 1998).

Our environments are deeply important to us. Individuals attach physical, personal and social significance to their environments. It is therefore not surprising that people will sometimes negate economic realities to get a place that they can call their own, or to regain possession of and return to land that belonged to their forefathers.

5 Preventive interventions

Research indicates that most emotional or behavioural problems have their origins in environments characterised by poverty and violence. Early exposure to negative social contexts may limit optimal social development and could result in later adult pathology.

Preventive measures are necessary to counter these effects. However, despite the fact that numerous studies have pointed to the positive benefits of preventive interventions, this area has been neglected. Psychology as a profession has continued to apply its energies to the treatment rather than the prevention of illness. For example, services are aimed at victims of violence, which is a curative approach. This kind of treatment focuses on the symptoms of problems and does not address the root causes. Strategies of prevention, apart from delivering services, also aim to combat the development of psychosocial issues They focus on entrenched cultural forces that perpetuate gender and racial inequalities. In addition to delivering services to victims, they seek to offer rehabilitation programmes for perpetrators. Prevention interventions should be multilevel and multidisciplinary, involving the family, school, church, traditional healers, clinics, hospitals, government departments, the public media and the workplace. Prevention does not merely address the symptoms; it also confronts the deep-seated structural inequalities that lead to mental health problems in society (Naidoo, Van Wyk and Carolissen, 2004).

Bibliography

Feldman, R.S. 2003. *Essentials of understanding psychology.* 5th edition. New York: McGraw Hill.

Foster, D. 2003. Social psychology. In L. Nicholas (Ed), *Introduction to psychology.* Cape Town: UCT Press.

Gazzaniga, M.S. and Heatherton, T.F. 2003. *Psychological science: Mind, brain and behaviour.* New York: Norton.

Grieve, K. and Jordaan, W. 1998. The living environment. In W. Jordaan and J. Jordaan, *People in context.* 3rd edition. Johannesburg: Heinemann.

Higson-Smith, C. 2004. Violence and traumatic stress. In L. Swartz, C. de la Rey and N. Duncan (Eds), *Psychology: An introduction.* Cape Town: Oxford University Press.

Jordaan, W. 1998. Societal patterns. In W. Jordaan and J. Jordaan, *People in context.* 3rd edition. Johannesburg: Heinemann.

Jordaan, W. and Jordaan, J. 1998. *People in context.* 3rd edition. Johannesburg: Heinemann.

Naidoo, T., Van Wyk, S. and Carolissen, R. 2004. Community mental health. In L. Swartz, C. de la Rey and N. Duncan (Eds), *Psychology: An introduction.* Cape Town: Oxford University Press.

Stevens, G. 2004. Ethnicity. In L. Swartz, C. de la Rey and N. Duncan (Eds), *Psychology: An introduction.* Cape Town: Oxford University Press.

Terre Blanche, M. 2004. Poverty. In L. Swartz, C. de la Rey and N. Duncan (Eds), *Psychology: An introduction.* Cape Town: Oxford University Press.

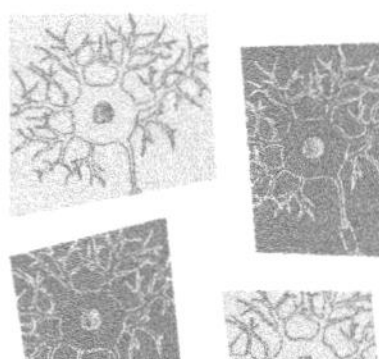

States of consciousness

1 The nature of consciousness

Many people have different definitions of consciousness, but the generally accepted one is the awareness of all sensations, thoughts and feelings at a particular time. To be conscious therefore means to be aware (Coon, 2004). We spend most of our time in waking consciousness, which is a state of clear, organised alertness. However, states of consciousness can change when, for example, we are tired, under hypnosis or experiencing the effects of drugs. These states can be very different from what we consider normal awareness.

Consciousness can be examined in terms of levels of arousal. States of consciousness vary from very little to high levels of arousal (Jordaan and Jordaan, 1998). Immediately after a brain injury, a person may have a very low level of arousal or awareness of what is happening. On the other hand, a state of intense emotional excitement represents a high level of arousal. These states are not entirely separate from one another and that is why we refer to a continuum of arousal (that is, its structure is continuous or ongoing) from low to high. At the lowest level of arousal, a person would be in a coma or unconscious. As we move up the continuum, the person would be in a state of very deep sleep, moving from deep sleep to light sleep, drowsiness and then wakefulness. Moving further up the continuum, arousal increases and the person is highly alert. Intense emotional excitement characterises the highest state of arousal.

1.1 The nature of sleep

Sleep is not a lack of consciousness. The brain actively maintains sleep and this is indicated by the physiological measurement of brain activity. A recording of brain activity (brainwaves) is called an electroencephalogram (EEG). There are different types of brain waves (see Figure 1), classified according to amplitude (or size) and frequency (the timing or how often they occur). The categories are the following:

- Delta waves, which have a high amplitude and a frequency of 0.5 to 3 Hertz (Hz)
- Theta waves, which have a slightly lower and irregular amplitude and a frequency of 4 to 8 Hz
- Alpha waves, which have a medium amplitude and a frequency of 8 to 12 Hz
- Beta waves, which have a low amplitude and a frequency of 13 to 30 Hz

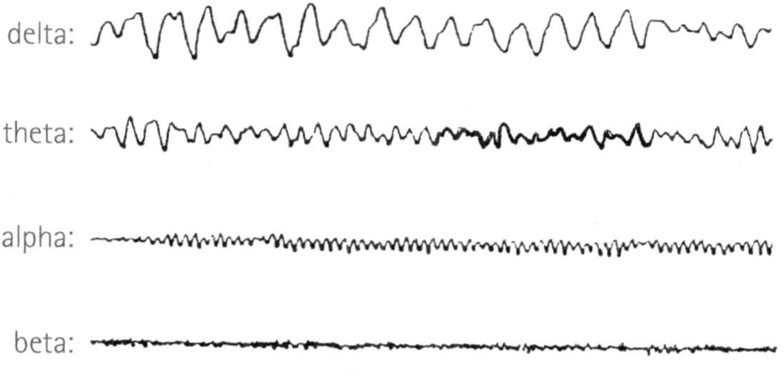

Figure 1 Illustration of delta, theta, alpha and beta EEG activity

The EEG provides some indication of arousal levels during wakefulness and sleep. There are mostly alpha waves when people are awake and relaxed (particularly if they have their eyes closed) but as soon as people pay attention to things happening around them, beta waves replace the alpha waves. As people become drowsy and fall asleep, there are more delta waves. Different types of sleep are characterised by different brain waves.

1.1.1 S-sleep

During S-sleep, the wave patterns are synchronised (high amplitude and low frequency) and this is called restful sleep, which occurs in four phases (Coon, 2004):

- *Phase one* sleep is a state of drowsiness or light sleep. The EEG indicates alpha and delta waves with a little theta activity (3.5 to 7.5 Hz). The person can still be easily aroused but the body is relaxed, the heart rate slows and breathing is deep and regular.
- *Phase two* sleep follows approximately 10 minutes later. This is deeper sleep and the wave frequencies are mixed, as indicated by the presence of sleep spindles, which are sporadic increases in frequency. There may also be K-complexes, which are occasional waves with sharp peaks. It is believed that these are mechanisms that prevent the person from waking by reducing sensitivity to sensory input.

- *Phase three* sleep is deep sleep. Almost half of the EEG recording consists of delta activity. The person is very relaxed and autonomic activity slows down.
- *Phase four* sleep is very deep sleep. More than half of the EEG consists of delta activity and it is very difficult to rouse the person out of sleep. If people are woken up during this stage, they are confused, their speech is slurred and their motor co-ordination is poor.

1.1.2 D-sleep

There is another type of sleep called D-sleep because the wave pattern is desynchronised (low amplitude and high frequency). This is actually the same pattern that characterises wakefulness, although the person is asleep and this is the type of sleep when dreaming most often takes place. During D-sleep there are rapid eye movements, even though the eyes are closed and it is sometimes called REM (rapid eye movement) sleep. Muscle tone is very low during D-sleep and the sleeper is unable to move. However, when people are woken from D-sleep, they are instantly awake and know what is happening around them.

1.1.3 Functions of sleep

No one is really sure what the functions of sleep are. Various theories have been suggested, for example, that regard sleep as a period of restoration and as having a survival function. It is generally believed that sleep is essential for normal functioning. Sleep deprivation is a form of stress and can have negative effects on concentration and coping ability. The effects of sleep deprivation also vary according to the person's physical and mental health. Two theories on the functions of sleep are discussed here:

- According to the *cognitive theory* (Jordaan and Jordaan, 1998), REM sleep allows the brain to withdraw from the outside world and reorganise the millions of bits of information collected during the day. The information is not lost, merely reorganised in a more meaningful way.
- The *neurobiological perspective* (Crick and Mitchison, 1983) is based on neuronal networks that support memory. The cortex has an enormous number of interconnections and the theory holds that memory information is encoded in these networks. When an aspect of the networks is triggered by a stimulus, related information is remembered. When there is an overload of information, the networks do not function well. REM sleep is suggested as the mechanism for cleaning up the networks by deleting unnecessary information. For this reason it is thought that people should not be encouraged to remember dreams because they actually contain information that the brain wants to get rid of.

1.1.4 Sleep disorders

- *Insomnia* is the term given to the inability to sleep. This may refer to difficulties falling asleep at night, or waking in the middle of the night and being unable to get back to sleep, or waking very early in the morning without having slept enough.
- *Narcolepsy* is the term used for symptoms of sleep that occur during wakefulness. A narcoleptic sleep attack is an overwhelming need to sleep. It can happen at any time and usually lasts for a few minutes.
- *Catalepsy* is a sudden collapse, when the person is awake but unable to move. It is usually triggered by an intense emotional experience or sudden movement. Another symptom of catalepsy is sleep paralysis that occurs just before falling asleep or waking in the morning. The person is awake but unable to move, but the paralysis ends when they are touched or called. During the paralysis they may have a sort of dream, called hypnogogic hallucinations.
- *Sleep apnoea* refers to a condition of breathing difficulties during sleep. People with this condition wake up gasping for breath and then go back to sleep. The problem is that sleep is frequently disrupted and the person experiences a form of sleep deprivation.

1.2 Hypnosis

Hypnosis is a definition given to a situation in which people's behaviours are involuntary or hypnotic. It occurs because of increased suggestibility in the context of a special relationship between a person and the hypnotist. The term *hypnosis* comes from Hypnos, the Greek god of sleep, although hypnosis and sleep are very different conditions. Hypnotised people can walk around and respond to things in the real world. In addition, their EEG is like that of waking people, not those who are sleeping.

A person has to be willing to be hypnotised in order for it to succeed. Hypnosis is based on increased suggestibility of the person or patient and therefore they have to be willing participants.

1.2.1 What hypnosis can do

Hypnosis generally produces relaxation, concentration and temporary changes in behaviour (Coon, 2004).

One of the established effects of hypnosis is to decrease *pain*. For example, some people can have dental surgery under hypnosis and feel no pain. Pain has both sensory and emotional components. Hypnosis does not prevent the body from experiencing pain (the sensory component) but alters the emotional components so that the person does not feel it. A hypnotised person may say that he or she feels no pain, but in fact there are bodily symptoms of pain. For example, heart rate and blood pressure increase in response to pain in the same way as they do in non-hypnotised people.

Another use of hypnosis is *posthypnotic suggestion*. This refers to the suggestion to do or experience something in particular after coming out of the hypnotised state. Sometimes behaviour changes persist after the end of the hypnotic state and a person may follow many of the hypnotist's suggestions long after being hypnotised. Posthypnotic suggestion can help people change bad habits but only if they have already indicated that they wish to do so. For example, posthypnotic suggestion is used to help people stop smoking or nail biting. The effects of a single hypnotic suggestion decrease with time but can be reinforced with repeated suggestion. Note that the effect is produced because the person wants to stop smoking (indicating a willingness) and the hypnosis builds on that to produce the desired effect. Hypnosis works on the basis of using or strengthening abilities that the person already has. There is no evidence that hypnosis can give people new physical or mental abilities.

Sometimes people under hypnosis experience sensory experiences that do not correspond to reality. For example, when told 'your left hand feels numb', the person actually experiences a numbness, although the hand is in actual fact quite normal. The feeling of numbness is the result of suggestion.

1.2.2 What hypnosis cannot do

You may have read about spectacular claims of the powers of hypnotic suggestion. If you look at these carefully, they often turn out to be less dramatic than they are claimed to be. For example, people under hypnosis claim to become so strong that they can be suspended between two chairs with their head on one and their feet on another and keep their body so stiff that someone can stand on it. In actual fact, many people can do this without hypnosis. There is no evidence that hypnosis empowers people to do anything they could not do otherwise if they were sufficiently motivated.

The claim is often made that hypnosis can improve memory, but this is not the case. Hypnotised persons are highly suggestible and, when told that they will remember more than before, they generally respond with new information but information that is not correct. In other words, the information is not remembered as such. Instead, other information is produced. Research studies indicate that most of the new 'memories' produced under hypnosis are false (Weiten, 2001).

1.2.3 Is hypnosis an altered state of consciousness?

Some psychologists regard hypnosis as a special state of consciousness characterised by greatly increased suggestibility. Other psychologists point out the similarities between hypnosis and waking and conclude that hypnosis is therefore not an altered state of consciousness. One way to determine whether or not hypnosis is an altered state of consciousness is to find out whether non-hypnotised people can do everything that hypnotised people can do. Studies have found that people can pretend to be hypnotised and mimic the effects of hypnosis (Weiten, 2001), but this does not mean that hypnosis is nothing but imitation. The idea of hypnosis as an altered state of consciousness has been promoted by Hilgard (1992) who views it as a dissociation in consciousness. Dissociation means that hypnosis splits consciousness into two separate streams of awareness. One stream communicates with the hypnotist and the external world and the other with the person's inner thoughts. At present, there is no conclusive proof that this is so.

1.3 Effects of psychoactive drugs

Psychoactive drugs are chemicals that bring about changes in mood, thinking, perception and behaviour by affecting the activity of neurons in the brain.

1.3.1 Stimulants

Stimulants are drugs that increase alertness, boost energy and activity and produce a pleasant feeling. They activate motivational centres and reduce activity in inhibitory centres of the brain. *Amphetamines* are powerful stimulants that increase the release of dopamine in the brain. They work by preventing neurons from reabsorbing the dopamine they have released and in this way the effects of dopamine are prolonged. Because they increase activity at norepinephrine and serotonin synapses, amphetamines also increase heart rate, blood pressure and body temperature.

Cocaine is also a stimulant because it increases heart rate, makes people excited and interferes with their sleep. However, cocaine works by decreasing the activity of neurons that inhibit other neurons, so by slowing the neurons that are supposed to be inhibiting others, the cocaine actually results in stimulated behaviour.

A very common stimulant is *caffeine*, although it is less powerful and dangerous than amphetamine or cocaine. Caffeine blocks a chemical that inhibits glutamate synapses. In other words, it increases the activity of glutamate, which is an excitatory transmitter. Tobacco and cigarettes contain *nicotine*, which increases wakefulness and arousal (by stimulating acetylcholine receptors). When people smoke often, their stress and tension levels actually increase and they experience withdrawal symptoms after a relatively short period. When they have another cigarette, it reduces the withdrawal symptoms and this is why they think that smoking relaxes them.

There is no evidence that these drugs improve mental or physical performance. In fact, there can be a negative effect on performance because people become over-aroused, even to the point of exhaustion.

1.3.2 Depressants

The main effect of depressants is to decrease arousal levels. The two most common types of depressants are alcohol and tranquillisers. Many people think that *alcohol* is a stimulant because people who drink it often talk loudly and act in a more extroverted way. However, alcohol works by depressing the activity of the nervous system. It facilitates the effects of GABA, which is an inhibitory neurotransmitter. It is primarily a relaxant and, in moderate doses, can reduce tension, but it can also impair memory and judgement. In larger amounts, it can increase aggression and risk-taking behaviours, mainly by decreasing the fears and anxieties that would normally inhibit people from behaving in this way. *Sedatives* and *tranquillisers* are used to help people relax. They are prescribed to aid sleep and sometimes to overcome anxiety. They also decrease muscle tension. Tranquillisers such as benzodiazepine work by increasing the activity at synapses that use the neurotransmitter GABA. If alcohol and tranquillisers are taken together, they increase GABA so much that they can affect the areas of the brain that control breathing and heartbeat.

Narcotics are powerful depressants that produce drowsiness, insensitivity to pain and decreased responsiveness to events. A well-known example of narcotics is the group of opiate drugs. They generally make people feel happy and content and free of pain, but the person can also experience nausea and tends to ignore the real world, which can become very dangerous. Examples of opiate drugs are morphine, heroin and codeine. They work by binding to a specific set of neurotransmitter receptors (opiate receptors) in the brain and increasing the release of dopamine.

Depressants can have the effect of impairing cognitive ability and slowing performance because of lowered levels of arousal.

1.3.3 Hallucinogens

Hallucinogens are drugs that bring about distorted sensory experiences. People who take them have intense sensory experiences and can enter a dreamlike state. They generally alter perceptual experiences, but only cause vivid hallucinations in large doses. In these altered states of consciousness, people experience imaginary visions and realities. *LSD* is a hallucinogenic drug that works by attaching to brain receptors that are sensitive to serotonin. Unfortunately, LSD can result in a 'bad trip' in which the alteration of consciousness is so disturbing that it results in feelings of panic.

Marijuana (dagga) also falls into the group of hallucinogens. Its psychological effects include a sense of well-being and relaxation, as well as an altered sense of time and perceptual distortions. It is not as powerful as the other hallucinogens, but can have dangerous effects.

Ecstasy or MDMA produces stimulant effects like amphetamines at low doses and hallucinogenic effects like LSD at higher doses. In the process of stimulating dopamine and serotonin axons, ecstasy damages or destroys these axons, which results in brain damage. More recently (Coon, 2004), ecstasy was placed in a new category of psychoactive drugs called entactogens because of their unique effects that lie between those associated with hallucinogens and stimulants.

Because these drugs bring about altered states of awareness, their effects are likely to have a negative effect on attention, concentration and performance.

1.3.4 Inhalants

Inhalants are substances that produce a sense of intoxication when they are inhaled (sniffed through the nose). Examples of inhalants are substances like glue, cleaning fluid and paint. They are typically placed in paper bags and inhaled or sniffed. In South Africa, it has been found that street children resort to sniffing glue to escape the harsh realities of their lives (Swart-Kruger and Donald, 1994). Inhalants are highly addictive and extremely dangerous and can cause permanent brain damage and other serious complications. The use of inhalants can also lead to cognitive impairments.

1.3.5 Chronic drug effects

Most of these drugs appear to have an initial desirable effect, such as excitement or relaxation. However, the effect of the drug wears off as it leaves the brain. Some drugs may cause brain damage. When the drug leaves the brain, the person experiences withdrawal effects, which are usually the opposite of the initial drug effect. For example, some hours after taking the stimulant cocaine, the user becomes inactive and depressed. After the drug has been taken repeatedly, the effects of that drug get weaker and the person has to increase the dose to get the same effect. This is called drug tolerance. Withdrawal effects are usually very unpleasant and often the person feels compelled to use the drug again in order to reduce them. When this happens, the person develops a physical dependence on the drug. Psychological dependence refers to the strong desire to take a drug without the accompanying symptoms of withdrawal. When people are psychologically dependent on a drug, they feel that it is necessary to maintain their emotional or psychological well-being because of the drug's rewarding qualities. Any person who has lost control over his or her drug use, for whatever reason, has become addicted. People differ in their responses to drugs and the effects are usually the result of a combination of factors – biochemical, psychological and social.

Bibliography

Coon, D. 2004. *Introduction to psychology.* 10th edition. Belmont, CA: Wadsworth.

Crick, F. and Mitchison, G. 1983. The function of dream sleep. *Nature,* 304, 111–114.

Hilgard, E. 1992. Dissociation and theories of hypnosis. In E. Fromm and M. Nash (Eds), *Contemporary hypnosis research.* New York: Guilford.

Jordaan, W. and Jordaan, J. 1998. *People in context.* 3rd edition. Johannesburg: Heinemann.

Swart-Kruger, G. and Donald, D. 1994. Children of the South African streets. In A. Dawes and D. Donald (Eds), *Childhood and adversity.* Cape Town: David Philip:107–121.

Weiten, W. 2001. *Psychology: Themes and variations.* 5th edition. Belmont, CA: Wadsworth.

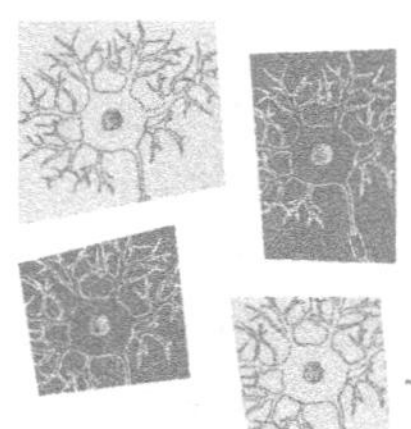

Stress: The effects of stress

Some degree of stress is normal, but too much stress can be detrimental to one's performance and prolonged stress has been indicated as a significant factor in illness.

1 The relationship between stress and performance

The basic relationship between psycho-physiological arousal and performance was established by two researchers, Yerkes and Dodson, in 1908 and the relationship became known as the Yerkes-Dodson law. This law states that performance increases as arousal increases, but this is only true when stress increases to a moderate level of arousal, where performance reaches an optimal level. When arousal is increased beyond this level, performance does not increase further – it starts to decrease. The meaning of this is quite clear. Performance is low when arousal levels are low. The person is under-stimulated and therefore finds it difficult to concentrate. As arousal levels increase, the person becomes more alert and reaction speed and concentration improve until performance reaches an optimal level of efficiency at moderate levels of arousal. If arousal levels are increased beyond this level, the person becomes over-stimulated, physically as well as psychologically. He or she becomes overly tense and loses concentration. At high levels of arousal, performance starts to drop to the same low levels associated with low levels of arousal.

Two other factors play a role in the relationship between arousal and performance, namely the complexity and the novelty of the performance tasks. As performance is optimal at moderate levels of arousal, we would expect that complex and novel tasks would still be performed most efficiently at more or less moderate levels of arousal and to a certain extent this is true. However, novel and complex tasks have a curiosity value that help people concentrate and focus despite lower levels of arousal. Complex and novel tasks, therefore, are most efficiently performed close to, but just below, moderate levels of arousal. Simple tasks, on the other hand, do not have a curiosity value. People get bored with simple tasks as well as with those that are well learnt, therefore, they require moderate to high levels of arousal. (Jordaan, 1998; Santrock, 2003a:426–427; Sdorow and Rickabaugh, 2002:343–344).

2 The relationship between stress and health

Numerous research studies have established a relationship between stress and illness. This does not mean that stress is the direct cause of disease, but it certainly acts as a catalyst for it. In other words, diseases start and develop in the presence of stress. The culprit seems to be prolonged periods of stress, or so-called chronic stress, rather than intense stress experienced over shorter periods of time. People who experienced stress over a two-year period before being exposed to a common cold virus were three times more likely to catch a cold than those who reported no stress (Cohen et al., 1998). The researchers attributed the greater vulnerability to disease to stress-triggered changes in the immune system. Stress can make one sick because the hormones and nerve pathways that are activated by stress change the way the immune system responds, making it less able to fight invaders (Sternberg, 2000:131). Stress has been linked to cardiovascular disease and to the development of cancer (Santrock, 2003b:480).

Chronic or repeated stress over a period of time can be harmful to physical health and may lead to the development of psychosomatic disease. A psychosomatic disease (*psyche* = mind and *soma* = body) is a condition where psychological factors contribute to physical damage in the body or to harmful changes in body functioning (Coon, 2001). Psychosomatic diseases are not imaginary – they are real conditions, but psychological factors, particularly the experience of stress, play a significant role in the cause of such conditions. Doctors in general practice estimate that almost half of the patients that consult them for physical problems have emotional problems that impact on their health (Jordaan, 1998). These may contribute directly to the development of health problems or may arise in reaction to a health problem (for example anxiety related to the impact of illness on work or family) and make the condition worse.

However, stress is not the only cause of psychosomatic diseases. The person who develops a psychosomatic condition often has a potential physical weakness in a particular organ of the body and then, in the presence of stress, that organ's functioning breaks down. For example, a man who has a hereditary heart condition is likely to develop a cardiovascular disease if he experiences chronic stress. People differ in the kinds of condition they develop. For example, some people may respond to stress with digestive difficulties and others with skin rashes. This is because people tend to respond to stressors in a certain way (with a certain physiological reaction pattern), which is called response specificity – that is, they tend to have a specific response pattern in reaction to stressors. Because certain people respond to stressors with a specific physiological reaction pattern, they develop specific weaknesses in these systems, thus specific bodily functions deteriorate in the presence of stressors and eventually physical symptoms appear that are related to particular systems such as the stomach or the heart (Jordaan, 1998). The link between stress and psychosomatic diseases such as high blood pressure, migraines, ulcers and asthma is well documented. Less severe complaints, such as backache and indigestion, may also be stress related. Psychosomatic diseases develop from experiencing cumulative emotional tension over a protracted period of time.

A more benign but equally serious problem that arises from prolonged experience to stress is burnout. The problem is serious because it affects economically active individuals. Burnout may develop unobtrusively over months or years. If the condition is allowed to continue without treatment, the individual can become seriously incapacitated. Burnout occurs when people are subjected to too much stress for too long a period of time. When this happens, people begin to complain that they feel emotionally drained, empty and alienated from the people around them. The feelings of alienation cause a sense of unreality, leaving people without hopes and aspirations in their work. They experience feelings of inadequacy because they feel that they have achieved nothing and that they are unable to do anything about it. Together, these feelings may lead to a decline in performance levels, which causes more stress and repeats a vicious circle.

One can reduce one's chances of burnout by trying to become more realistic in one's expectations regarding work and job satisfaction. Rely on colleagues, friends and family and share negative aspects of your work experiences with them. Evaluate the value of the work you do. Ask yourself whether the things you do now will be as important to you in a few years' time as they are now (the 'life-and-death' test). Make sure that you take time out. Restrict your exposure to work-related interactions and issues. This is known as the Restricted Environmental Stimulation Therapy (REST) programme (Jordaan, 1998).

Bibliography

Cohen, S., Frank, E., Doyle, W., Skoner, D.P., Rabin, B.S. and Gwaltney, J.M. 1998. Types of stressors that increase susceptibility to the common cold in healthy adults. *Health Psychology,* 17, 214–223.

Coon, D. 2001. *Introduction to psychology.* 9th edition. Belmont, CA: Wadsworth/Thomson Learning.

Jordaan, W. 1998. Stress processes. In W. Jordaan and J. Jordaan, *People in context.* 3rd edition. Johannesburg: Heinemann.

Lazarus, R.S. 1993. Coping theory and research: Past, present and future. *Psychosomatic Medicine,* 55, 234–247.

Santrock, J.W. 2003a. *Psychology.* 7th edition. New York: McGraw-Hill.

Santrock, J.W. 2003b. *Psychology: Essentials.* 2nd edition. New York: McGraw-Hill.

Sdorow, L.M. and Rickabaugh, C.A. 2002. *Psychology*. 5th edition. New York: McGraw-Hill.

Sternberg, E.M. 2000. *The balance within.* New York: Freeman.

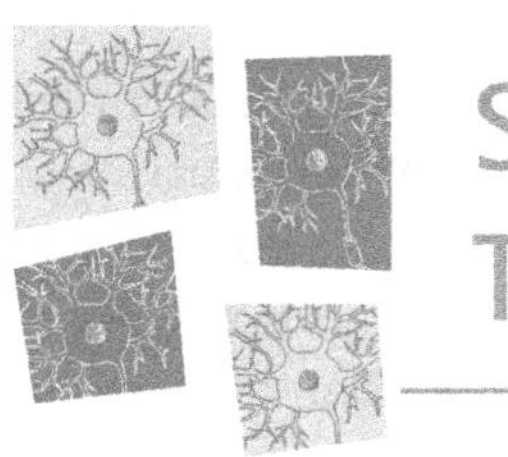

Stress: The process of stress

The feeling of stress does not appear overnight. It develops over time and follows a particular process.

1 The general adaptation syndrome

The stress process was first described by Hans Selye (1976; 1993), whose model of the stress process is known as the general adaptation syndrome – often abbreviated as GAS. The model is important because it suggests that there is a pattern in the way in which people react to stressors, regardless of the nature of the stressors. Therefore, although some stressors may cause more stress than others, the process of stress remains the same.

The GAS model considers stress as a three-phased process. These phases are (1) the alarm and mobilisation phase; (2) the resistance phase; and (3) the exhaustion phase. During the alarm and mobilisation phase, we become aware of the presence of a stressor. The first reaction is to be alarmed. We experience shock and our ability to cope with the stressor drops below our normal levels of coping. However, the body counters the effects of being alarmed by releasing hormones that help us mobilise against the stressor. As a result, our ability to cope increases to levels that exceed our normal level of coping. However, if the stressor persists, we move into the resistance phase. During this phase, we try to deal with the stressor and the coping level remains higher than normal. If the stressor is dealt with successfully, it disappears, but if we fail to cope, we ultimately reach the point of exhaustion. During this third stage in the stress process, our ability to cope declines sharply and quickly drops below our normal level of coping. If the situation continues, we finally reach the point where the negative consequences of stress begin to show. We may become physically ill, find it difficult to concentrate and suffer from a heightened degree of irritability (Feldman, 2003).

2 The contextual model of stress

The GAS model describes the process of stress in general terms only. It does not include finer details. For example, it does not take into account the fact that events and circumstances are not equally stressful to all people. Someone may find bungee jumping a pleasurable challenge, while others may be horrified at the idea of jumping off a high bridge attached to a rubber tether. It all depends on the context and our appraisal of the situation. Jordaan (1998) formulated a more comprehensive model that takes the context of stress into account. This model is called the contextual stress model. The main tenet of this model is that people perceive events in context and that their reactions to them occur in particular contexts, therefore an event needs to be contextualised before it can be seen as a stressor and the reaction to an event needs to be considered in the context in which it occurs. The GAS model does not explain how an event becomes a stressor and it does not consider the context of coping behaviour.

The contextualisation of the stress process is based on four assumptions (Jordaan, 1998):

1. An event does not have a universal meaning independent of the situation in which it occurs, or independent of the person who perceives the event. In other words, an event gains its meaning when it is perceived by somebody in a particular situation. This means that one person may perceive an event as a stressor, while another person may not. It also means that a person may experience an event as stressful on one occasion but may not see it as such in another situation.
2. Communities share beliefs and meanings. This means that communities may share interpretations of the stressfulness of certain events. The individual members of a community are likely to see an event as stressful if it is viewed as a stressor by the community as a whole.
3. When an event is perceived as a stressor, the person (or community) assigns a positive or a negative value to it, depending on the situation in which it occurs. Positive stress is associated with life-enriching events. The outcomes of these events are beneficial to the individual or the community, given the current circumstances. Negative stress is associated with life-threatening events. The outcomes of these events are harmful or detrimental in the situation in which the person or the community finds itself.
4. Events gain meaning through perception, therefore the process of perception is a key factor in the contextualisation of an event. We have to indicate how an event is perceived and appraised if we wish to describe the process of stress.

Jordaan (1998) describes the contextual stress model as a process consisting of five phases. However, these phases cannot be seen as independent steps that occur one after the other. The model is based on a theory of perception that describes the process whereby perceptual content changes into meaningful ideas in terms of information-processing loops. Forming an understanding of what we see requires information to be fed forward and backward in various loops in the neural circuits between the sense organs (for example the eye) and the cortex, therefore the phases of the contextual stress model are interdependent. They occur more or less simultaneously as we process the information coming from our senses.

Phase 1: Encountering potential stressors

The world we live in consists of various events, which are potential stressors when they are first encountered. They have the potential to be stressors, but they cannot be seen as stressors because they have not been interpreted as such. There are three categories of potential stressors (Jordaan, 1998; Feldman, 2003:362–332) These are: (1) *universal events* that affect the majority of people in society or in the world; (2) *personal events* that are specific to a community or an individual; and (3) *micro events* that affect the individual on an everyday basis. Examples of universal events are natural disasters, terrorist attacks like 9/11, the occurrence of epidemic diseases, a cure for a previously incurable disease, up-and-down swings in the world economy and new technological developments. Finding a job, getting married, being involved in a car accident and getting a new shopping mall in the neighbourhood are examples of personal events that affect the individual or a specific community. Examples of micro events are organising somebody to pick up the children from school, shopping for the right pair of shoes, negotiating an overdraft on a cheque account, repairing a leak in the roof and paying the electricity bill. In our daily lives, the events from these categories become connected. We may not feel directly involved in a natural disaster or an act of terrorism that happens on the other side of the world, but the effects of these events may change our mood and make us feel negative in general. As we form associations, the events become psychosocially connected. Owing to these connections between events, we may later experience a particular event as a stressor, not because the event is stressful in itself, but because we perceive it against the background of another stressful event. The psychosocial connections between events may thus contribute to the potential stress values of these events.

Phase 2: Performing a primary appraisal

When an event is encountered, we immediately experience it as positive, negative, neutral or ambiguous. This is the result of a primary appraisal of the event. The feeling we experience is the result of our psychobiology (for example whether we are feeling tense) and the psychosocial circumstances in which we find ourselves. For example, I may be praised for my courage to sit for a challenging examination. The way in which I perceive the praise depends on the psychosocial circumstances of the praise event. If the praise is offered by someone who I know really understands the challenge involved, I may perceive the praise in a positive light, but if it comes from someone who does not have the faintest idea of the complexity of the examination, I may simply dismiss the praise (feeling neutral), or I may feel angry at the person's audacity (feeling negative about the event of praise). Whether the feeling associated with an event differentiates as positive or negative also depends on whether the event is threatening or challenging (Lazarus, 1993). Threatening and harmful events evoke negative feelings, but an event that is challenging is more likely to evoke a positive feeling. However, whether or not we are likely to see an event as challenging depends on our personality. In the case of a community's reaction to an event, cultural rules and the prevailing emotive perceptions of the community play a significant role. An event that cannot be accommodated within the cultural ethos of a community is more likely to be experienced negatively than an event that fits the cultural rules and norms. Furthermore, if a general negative feeling exists in a community, the community is likely to experience demanding events as negative rather than to see them in a neutral or positive light.

Phase 3: Experiencing stress

The feeling of stress is associated with heightened psycho-physiological arousal. We feel physically and emotionally tense. There is a general feeling of pressure. If the event acquired a negative feeling in the primary appraisal phase, we associate the event with harm or threat. If the primary appraisal differentiated into a positive feeling, the event is likely to be associated with a challenge and opportunities that can be utilised to our advantage (Lazarus, 1993). A mixture of positive and negative feelings leads to events being experienced as both threatening and challenging.

Phase 4: Performing a secondary appraisal

In this phase, an event has been identified as a stressor and the individual (or the community as a whole) has to consider his or her ability to cope with the demands of the stressful situation. The outcome of the secondary appraisal depends on two factors, namely whether the event is experienced as threatening (negative) or challenging (positive) and whether the person feels that he or she will be able to cope. In the case of a threatening (negative) event, the stress will increase further and become even more negative if the person thinks that he or she will not be able to cope. However, if the person feels that he or she will be able to cope, the stress will diminish and become less negative. If the coping strategies promise to be successful, there may be a reversal from negative to positive stress. In the case of a challenging (positive) event, the stress will diminish and become more positive if the person feels that he or she will cope. However, the stress will increase and become less positive if the person is of the opinion that he or she will not be able to cope. When the coping strategies begin to fail, the positive stress may revert to negative stress.

The appraisal of our ability to cope is influenced by such factors as our explanatory style, our psychological hardiness, how resourceful we are, the type of conflict we are required to deal with, the relevance and reliability of the information we have about the situation and the degree of control we have over circumstances (Jordaan, 1998; Sdorow and Rickabaugh, 2002:466–468). Some people are inclined to explain events pessimistically rather than optimistically. It is possible that people with a pessimistic explanatory style are less likely to take action to counter the effects of stressful events, which may lead to more stress. Psychological hardiness refers to the tendency to commit ourselves, an aptitude for challenges and the ability to take control of a situation. People with high levels of psychological hardiness seem to be more resistant to stressors and are able to handle stress more effectively than those with lower levels of hardiness. People learn to be resourceful in the same manner that they can learn to be helpless. Learnt resourcefulness refers to the ability to try various approaches to find a way to work through a difficult situation. People learn to act in a helpless manner when they are constantly subjected to situations in which they feel they have no control. If this carries on for prolonged periods of time, they begin to feel apathetic and despondent.

We have to solve conflicts in our attempt to handle stressful situations and this means we have to choose between options. If two options are equally attractive, we are faced with an approach–approach type of conflict, which means we want to choose both options. This kind of conflict is the least stressful because either choice leads to a positive result. The type of conflict in which we are required to choose between two equally unattractive options is called an avoidance–avoidance conflict. This kind of conflict causes stress because we try to avoid making a decision, but postponing a decision does not solve the situation – it simply adds to our experience of stress. However, the type of conflict that is most difficult to solve and that causes the most stress is called an approach–avoidance conflict. This happens when we are faced with a single option that has both positive and negative consequences. We have to handle the situation in such a manner that the positive outcomes are maximised and the negative consequences minimised. This causes much stress because there are no guidelines to follow. We are solely responsible for the way that we choose to handle the situation. It is difficult to make decisions if we do not have relevant and reliable information at our disposal. Vague and unreliable information leads to doubt and doubt leads to lack of action and loss of control. The amount of control we think we have in a situation (perceived control) is an important factor in the way we handle stress. The more control we have, the less stress we experience, whereas loss of control leads to increased levels of stress.

Phase 5: Apply coping strategies

An extensive study (Amirkhan, in Jordaan, 1998) showed that people employ three kinds of strategies to cope with stress. These are problem-solving strategies, avoidance strategies and social support strategies. People who use problem-solving strategies accept responsibility and think things through. They deal with matters and adapt their behaviour in rational ways. This approach to coping with stress stands in stark contrast to people who handle stress by applying avoidance tactics. These individuals do not take personal responsibility, but try to find excuses for their lack of coping by blaming external factors. They do not react rationally, but prefer emotionally based arguments in attempts to lower their experiences of stress. The third approach to coping with stress is to muster social support, which can be tangible in the form of physical assistance. It can also be intangible in the form of advice (recommending actions and plans to help the person under stress cope more effectively) or encouragement (providing emotional support) (Taylor, 2003). People who have social support are better equipped to handle stressful situations.

Bibliography

Feldman, R.S. 2003. *Essentials of understanding psychology.* 5th edition. New York: McGraw-Hill.

Jordaan. W. 1998. Stress processes. In W. Jordaan and J. Jordaan, *People in context.* 3rd edition. Johannesburg: Heinemann.

Lazarus, R. 1993. Coping theory and research: Past, present and future. *Psychosomatic Medicine,* 55:234–247.

Sdorow, L.M. and Rickabaugh, C.A. 2002. *Psychology.* 5th edition. New York: McGraw-Hill.

Sellye, H. 1976. *The stress of life.* New York: McGraw-Hill.

Sellye, H. 1993. History of the stress concept. In L. Goldberger and S. Breznitz (Eds), *Handbook of stress: Theoretical and clinical aspects.* 2nd edition. New York: Free Press.

Taylor, S. 2003. *Health psychology.* 5th edition. New York: McGraw-Hill.

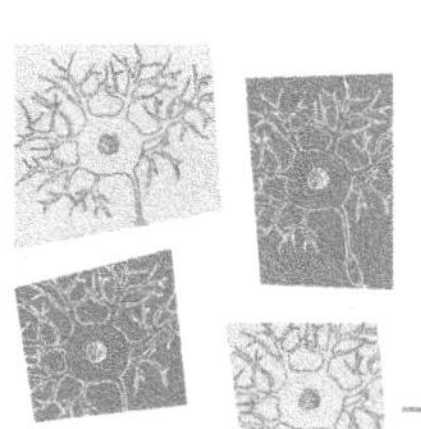

Stress: The psychophysiology of stress

Stress is the feeling we experience when things are getting too much. In other words, stress is an emotional response to circumstances and events that threaten us and challenge our coping abilities. It is a physiological response to physical and psychological demands (Sdorow and Rickabaugh, 2002:456). These demands are called *stressors.*

The experience of stress involves a combination of psychological and physiological factors. To understand the psycho-physiological processes involved, we have to consider both physical tension (the physiological part) and emotional tension (the psychological part).

1 Physical tension

All living bodies maintain some degree of physical tension. The sympathic and parasympathic divisions of the autonomic nervous system are responsible for physical tension in the body. Sympathic stimulation increases the body's degree of physical tension, whereas parasympathic stimulation decreases it. The relationship between sympathic and parasympathic stimulation determines the level of physical tension in the body.

In some individuals, the sympathic activity is generally more dominant than the parasympathic activity. In other words, their autonomic nervous systems are sympathically dominated. The higher the level of sympathic dominance, the higher the individual's basic tension level. There are also individuals whose nervous systems are parasympathically dominated and they have lower levels of basic tension, thus the higher the level of parasympathic dominance, the lower the basic tension level. One can express the sympathic versus parasympathic dominance in the autonomic nervous system as a ratio in which one pitches sympathic activity over parasympathic activity. The ratio has a numerical value of one (1) if the sympathic activity equals the parasympathic activity. It is higher than one (1) if the sympathic activity is more than the parasympathic activity and lower than one (1) if the sympathic activity is less than the parasympathic activity. It is important to note that the ratio does not tell us how much activity there is in total. It simply tells us how much sympathic activity there is in relation to the degree of parasympathic activity.

Everybody has a characteristic level of physical tension. My characteristic level of physical tension is expressed as the characteristic ratio of my sympathic activity to my parasympathic activity. My basic level of physical tension is higher than yours if the ratio of my sympathic activity to my parasympathic activity is higher than the ratio of your sympathic activity to your parasympathic activity. We can observe the difference in basic tension levels in people's behaviour. If my basic level of physical tension is higher than yours, I will display more restless behaviour than you do.

Although we have a natural basic level of physical tension, this does not mean that our degree of physical tension always stays at this level. When the senses are stimulated, the body's physical tension increases. Our level of physical tension is higher when we are active than it is when we are lying down and relaxing with our eyes closed. The physical tension of an alert body is higher than that of a relaxed body. This difference in physical tension is referred to as the body's level of physical arousal.

People differ in the way in which they react to incoming stimuli. High levels of basic tension may adversely affect our ability to react well to incoming stimuli. We may be too tense to react if we have a high level of basic tension. In other words, it is difficult to further arouse a tense body. People with low levels of basic tension tend to be more relaxed. They have more potential to react to incoming stimuli because they have more scope to be physically aroused.

A second way in which individuals differ in their reaction to incoming stimuli concerns the stability of their nervous systems. Some individuals have labile nervous systems, whereas others have nervous systems that are much more stable. If my nervous system is more labile than yours, my body is likely to react more quickly and more intensely to incoming stimuli because the balance between my sympathic and parasympathic systems is disturbed more easily. In technical terms, we would say that my nervous system has a lower degree of autonomic homeostasis and that my body is aroused more quickly and more intensely. If your nervous system is more stable, your basic physical tension level is less likely to be disturbed as severely as mine is, thus your nervous system has a higher degree of autonomic homeostasis and your body is not aroused as easily as mine is.

2 Emotional tension

The physical alertness level of the body is not the only factor that plays a role in physical tension. Physical tension also depends on the way in which we experience a situation, increasing when we experience a situation as threatening. Physical tension, together with the cognitive content of threat (the understanding that a particular situation is threatening), leads to the conscious experience of feeling tense. This feeling of tenseness about a situation is called *emotional tension* (Jordaan, 1998).

The degree of emotional tension that we experience is related to the autonomic homeostasis of our nervous system. If you have a high degree of autonomic homeostasis (a stable nervous system), your physical arousal is smooth and steady and therefore you are likely to experience less emotional tension than somebody with a low degree of autonomic homeostasis (labile nervous system) (Jordaan, 1998).

Our level of physical arousal, together with the amount of threat a situation holds for us, determines the degree of emotional tension we experience, therefore our emotional tension varies as our level of physical arousal and our perception of threat change. The difference between a feeling of no emotional tension and the level of emotional tension experienced in a particular situation is an indication of the level of psychological arousal in the situation.

3 Psycho-physiological arousal

We can now put physical and emotional tension together to form the concept of psycho-physiological arousal. Psycho-physiological arousal (usually just called arousal) consists of physical arousal (the difference between our basic and our actual tension level in a particular situation) and psychological arousal (the difference between our feeling of no emotional tension and the feeling of emotional tension that we experience in a particular situation).

Bibliography

Jordaan, W. 1998. Stress processes. In W. Jordaan and J. Jordaan, *People in context*. 3rd edition. Johannesburg: Heinemann.

Sdorow, L.M. and Rickabaugh, C.A. 2002. *Psychology*. 5th edition. New York: McGraw-Hill.

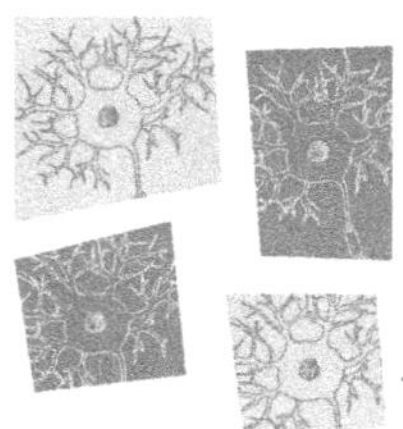

Work: Motivation in the workplace

The human workforce is part of the production capacity of an organisation The people employed by an organisation produce outcomes that make the organisation profitable, but they also cost money because they are paid salaries. The costs of an organisation's workforce therefore have to be balanced against their production outcomes. For an organisation to survive, its workforce has to produce more than what it is costing the organisation. The problem is that human beings are not machines. They cannot be mechanically tuned to produce outcomes in set and predetermined ways. Humans have personal reasons for the ways in which they behave. Individuals' levels of productivity depend on their motivation and therefore organisations have to keep their employees motivated. However, productivity is not the only reason for keeping individuals motivated. Motivation is also important for psychological reasons. Motivated workers have higher levels of self-esteem and they experience higher degrees of self-actualisation.

Any consideration of motivation in the workplace involves questions about what energises human behaviour, what directs it and how it is maintained and sustained (Steers and Porter, 1991). These factors depend on the personal meanings that people attach to work. Personal meaning of work can be understood in terms of three dimensions suggested by Lundberg and Peterson (1994). These are work centrality, social norms and valued work goals. Work *centrality* relates to how important a person's work is in his or her life. A high degree of job centrality implies that the person attaches a greater importance to his or her job than to one or more other factors in his or her life. Social *norms* relate to social rights and responsibilities in the context of one's work. For example, people may consider their work to be meaningful because they feel they contribute to society through it. *Valued work goals* relate to what one wishes to achieve through one's work. One person may want to become wealthy, whereas another may strive for fame. For these individuals, work is instrumental in becoming rich or famous.

So what motivates people? Kanfer (in Sdorow and Rickabaugh, 2002:526–527) identifies three categories of motivational theories. These are need-fulfilment theories, cognitive-choice theories and self-regulation theories, thus the causes, purposes and sustainability of behaviour in the workplace are explained in terms of the fulfilment of personal needs, people's intentions and choices and the way in which they regulate their own behaviour.

1 Need-fulfilment theories

Need-fulfilment theories argue that individuals are motivated as a result of their personality, disposition and values (Sdorow and Rickabaugh, 2002:326). People work to satisfy their own needs, but these are not fulfilled in a haphazard manner. According to Maslow (1970), there is a hierarchy of needs, which people fulfil as they work their way up. Physiological needs are the lowest layer in the hierarchy. These are primary drives, such as the need for water, food, sleep and sex. The next layer of needs comprises the need for a safe and secure environment (safety needs). Then comes the need for love and belongingness. This layer of needs concerns one's desire to obtain and give affection and to feel that one contributes to the groups and society that one belongs to. The fourth layer is the need for esteem – the desire to develop a sense of self-worth. And, finally, there is the need for self-actualisation.

All of these needs play a role in motivating people to work. However, according to Maslow's theory, people do not become aware of the next layer of needs before their current needs have been satisfied, either partially or completely, therefore we cannot expect somebody who works to fulfil needs at the lower end of the hierarchy to be aware of needs at the higher end. An individual who has to work just to satisfy his or her daily physical needs (for example to afford a meal) sees work as a means of survival. This individual is not able to experience it as a means of self-actualisation.

2 Cognitive-choice theories

Cognitive-choice theories focus on the idea that people make conscious choices, based on their appraisals and expectations of situations and thus are motivated to act if they see value in the outcomes of their actions.

Vroom (1964) distinguished three factors that play a role in the way that people choose to act, namely valence, instrumentality and expectancy. *Valence* is the value that people attach to an outcome, *instrumentality* is the potential that the valued outcome has to lead to more desired outcomes and *expectancy* is the attainability of the outcomes. Thus if you think that performing a certain task will lead to a valued outcome (the task has valence) and you believe that this outcome is likely to lead to other desired outcomes (the task is instrumental) and you believe that you can complete the task (expectancy of success), you will be motivated to perform it. However, if you expect that you cannot complete the task, you will not be motivated to execute it despite the fact that it may lead to valued and desired outcomes (Sdorow and Rickabaugh, 2002:326).

Motivation is also influenced by equity. Equity concerns people's perceptions of fairness (Van Deventer and Jordaan, 1998). Individuals compare what they put into a situation to what they get out of it. In the work environment, workers give knowledge, skills and experience and they receive salaries, fringe benefits and promotions. If the return provided by an activity (for example the salary) is too small in relation to the effort that goes into it (for example long working hours), people consider the situation to be unfair. They weigh the value of an outcome (for example the importance of a salary) against the cost of the input (the amount of work they have to do to earn the salary).

The situation is complicated further by the fact that equity is a matter of perspective. An individual's understanding of fairness is a personal perception. Such perceptions are not objective observations, but are based on social comparisons (Van Deventer and Jordaan, 1998). If I think I have to work harder than you do (that is, provide more input) to earn the same salary (similar return), I may consider the situation to be unfair. However, the salary I earn may seem fair to me if I know that the big salary you earn also requires you to work much harder than I do.

The problem with social comparison is that it requires one to be properly informed. If I do not really understand what your job entails, I may overlook important aspects of your work and think that you have to put in less than I to earn your salary. This kind of misunderstanding often occurs in companies where line workers are not informed about the responsibilities and pressures of a manager's job.

3 Self-regulation theories

Cognitive-choice theories focus on the way in which people choose to act in order to achieve the desired outcomes. Self-regulation theories describe the behaviours involved in attaining a goal. Cognitive-choice theories thus deal with the individual's intentions and choices and self-regulation theories concern the individual's agency and will (Sdorow and Rickabaugh, 2002:326).

Goal-setting theory is a well-researched example of self-regulation theory. The assumption of this theory is that people are motivated to work if they have goals to work towards. The goals have to be specific and clearly defined and should be challenging but attainable. To encourage co-ownership of their goals, employees should be involved in setting them. People should also be able to compare current levels of performance with those implied by the goals, therefore employees require regular feedback on performance and progress (Van Deventer and Jordaan, 1998). There is a vast body of research that suggests that individuals who are assigned difficult specific goals, who accept them and who receive feedback about their performance are more productive than those who are merely required to 'do their best' (Sdorow and Rickabaugh, 2002:326).

Attitude plays an important role in the self-regulation of behaviour. Our motivation to work is influenced by our attitude towards our job and our commitment towards the organisation as a whole. However, the relationship between attitude and behaviour is complex. There is no single attitude that is strongly related to a specific form of behaviour (Sdorow and Rickabaugh, 2002:327) and job satisfaction has been used as a general indicator of work attitude. One of the best-known of the theories that relate job satisfaction to work motivation is the motivational hygiene theory (Herzberg, Mausner and Snydermann, 1959; Herzberg, 1966).

Herzberg and his co-researchers identified two kinds of factors that influence individuals' experiences of job satisfaction and job dissatisfaction. These are motivating factors and hygiene factors. Generally speaking, *motivating factors* concern the content of the job itself, whereas *hygiene factors* refer to the context in which the job is executed. Motivating factors include such aspects as achievement in the job, recognition of one's performance and the nature of the job. Hygiene factors include things like company policy, supervision, working conditions and remuneration.

There is a complex relationship between the content and the context of the job and job satisfaction (see Table 1). Unfavourable hygiene factors (e.g. poor working conditions and low salaries) cause job dissatisfaction, but favourable hygiene factors do not necessarily lead to job satisfaction. Favourable working conditions and good salaries only keep people from being dissatisfied with their jobs. Motivating factors (for example opportunities to achieve and recognition of one's achievements) are required in addition to favourable hygiene factors for people to experience job satisfaction. However, the absence of motivating factors does not necessarily mean that people will become dissatisfied with their jobs. In other words, if your job does not provide opportunities to achieve, or if you do not receive recognition for your work, you are not likely to experience job satisfaction, but you will not necessarily become dissatisfied with your job.

Table 1 The relationship between job satisfaction and motivating and hygiene factors

Hygiene factors	**Motivating factors**	
	Present	*Absent*
Favourable	Satisfied	Not dissatisfied
Unfavourable	Not satisfied	Dissatisfied

Motivation is a complex topic, and to understand it in the context of the workplace, we have to broaden our considerations from a somewhat narrow focus on human needs to an emphasis on individual goals and self-regulation, viewed against the background of job satisfaction.

Bibliography

Herzberg, F. 1966. *Work and the nature of man.* Cleveland: World Publishing.

Herzberg, F., Mausner, B. and Snydermann, B.B. 1959. *The motivation to work.* 2nd edition. New York: Wiley.

Lundberg, C.D. and Peterson, M.E. 1994. The meaning of work in US and Japanese local governments at three hierarchical levels. *Human Relations,* 47(12), 1459–1487.

Maslow, A.H. 1970. *Motivation and personality*. New York: Harper and Row.

Sdorow, L.M. and Rickabaugh, C.A. 2002. *Psychology.* 5th edition. New York: McGraw-Hill.

Steers, R.M. and Porter, L.W. (Eds). 1991. *Motivation and work behaviour.* 5th edition. New York: McGraw-Hill.

Van Deventer, V. and Jordaan, W. 1998. The work situation. In W. Jordaan and J. Jordaan, *People in context.* 3rd edition. Johannesburg: Heinemann.

Vroom, V.H. 1964. *Work and motivation.* New York: Wiley.

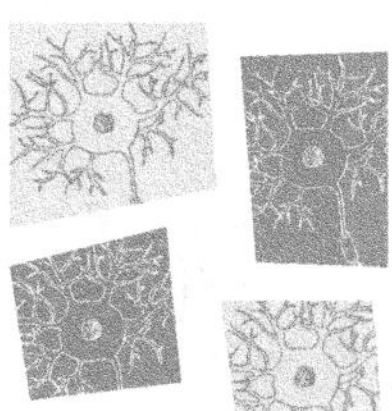

Work: The concept of work

Most of us have a traditional notion of work. We see it as a set of activities performed for our employer. We arrive in the morning and we leave in the afternoon and in between we perform the tasks required by our job descriptions. At the end of the month we receive a salary. However, not everyone thinks about work in this way. In underdeveloped rural areas where few people are formally employed, people find it difficult to distinguish between everyday activities and formal work (Sully, 1997). The socio-political circumstances under which people work also influence their perceptions of work. For some of the research participants in Sully's study, formal work was not only a means to earn a living but also a process of oppression and 'piece workers' who have to find jobs on a daily basis see job hunting as a form of work in itself (Gonzo, 2001).

Our contemporary notion of work has developed over thousands of years and cannot be divorced from the evolution of human intellect. The development of human intellect is characterised by the development of tools. What we see as work today has developed from the activities that people performed to meet their circumstances and to cope with the demands of their environment. These actions can be traced through four successive phases, namely the hunting and gathering phase, the agricultural phase, the industrial development phase and the information-processing phase (Retief and Cole, in Van Deventer and Jordaan, 1998). Each phase shows humans greater independence from and control over the environment. It was the tools humans developed that enabled them to gain the levels of independence and control we have today (Kinget, 1975).

The first tools were not really produced by humans, but were objects found in the environment. Hominoids (human-like beings) used objects like sticks and stone shards for hunting purposes and to dig for food and water. Although these objects were not manufactured, they were tools in the sense of being instrumental in the achievement of objectives. The fact that these early hominoids could recognise these objects as instruments shows that they were able to recognise an object as a thing in itself. The ability to recognise an object in this manner was a major step in the development of symbolic language (language in which the name of an object is used in the place of the object). The development of language enabled people to consider images of objects in their minds and to manipulate these images mentally. This ability allowed them to manufacture tools for specific purposes. The first purposely made tools were simple, such as a blade made from a sharpened piece of stone, but they encouraged the development of skills and of personal agency. In other words, as individuals mastered and developed the skills of using particular tools, they were recognised for this and were assigned roles associated with their mastery and skills. The differentiation of roles increased the social complexity of the groups and language developed further to support the social interactions within the group. Thus, even in these early groups, work was already characterised by skilful action, purpose and social role.

The agricultural phase began when hunting and gathering groups settled down and established communities around agricultural activities. This happened when people broadened their notion of tools from instruments of work to work mediators. Whereas hunting and gathering groups saw tools as extensions of the body, agricultural groups understood that tools could replace the body altogether by deferring the work to somebody else. In other words, they realised that they did not always have to execute a task themselves, but that something or somebody else could be used to do the work on their behalf. For example, animals were domesticated and used to accomplish work on behalf of humans, but humans, too, were used to work for other people.

Agricultural communities were larger than the former hunting and gathering groups and because their social structures were more complex, social layers and personal status developed in them. Social differentiation and greater specialisation of work roles resulted in people doing work for others. Settled communities also had vested interests in natural resources and often fought wars to defend or expand their territories. Those who lost the battles were used as slaves. However, in these communities, work differentiation was more complex than a division into masters and slaves. Unlike hunting and gathering groups who lived off the land, settled communities had to manage their resources – a process involving specialised tasks. Apart from the basic activities of planting and harvesting, produce had to be distributed and surpluses stored for future use. Accounts had to be opened and maintained to handle an economy of buying and selling. Thus, the agricultural phase introduced work as specialised jobs in a stratified socio-economic context.

Although the agriculturalists understood tools as work mediators, these mediatory tools were basically body-extension instruments put in the hands of other humans or attached to animals. For them, work mediation meant the application of biological power. Their ability to harness other forms of energy was limited to natural resources, such as a mill driven by water. It was the industrialists who developed work mediation tools that not only replaced humans and animals, but also outperformed them in the execution of a task. The development and rapid improvement of the steam engine was a major driving force in the advancement of industrial production. It powered both the production and the distribution of goods. Products were manufactured in huge factories and distributed widely by trains and ships driven by steam engines. The size of production facilities necessitated a hierarchy of jobs and required managers to oversee work performance. The constant emphasis on production efficiency required careful selection and training of workers to ensure a competent workforce. The industrial age brought the distinction between production and the management of production and it introduced such notions as qualifications, job description, selection, training and management into the workplace.

Although the socio-economic environment of work is infinitely more complicated today than it was ever before, work is still basically a purposeful activity executed in a socio-economic context and people still try to minimise their own involvement in work by devising tools that can work on their behalf. The information age is a further step in this direction. The industrial age was encouraged by our need for physical capacity, while the information age is fuelled by a need for intellectual power. The engine was the basic industrial tool, while the computer is the tool of the information age. The information society still maintains industrial activities, but it has begun to integrate the industrial capacities of the world's countries into a single global economy.

Major changes are sweeping through the world of work. The hierarchical structures that characterised the workplace of the past are flattening. Top-down communication structures are replaced by single-layer networks. Permanent jobs are taken over by temporary positions in project teams, requiring multi-skilled individuals instead of narrowly specialised workers. The notion that a career is a work-development path within an organisation is replaced by the idea that a career is the work-development plan of an individual, realised within various organisations through a variety of work opportunities. A job in the information age is one job in a series of jobs that constitute an individual's work history. The information society has introduced into the workplace such notions as the project team, the curriculum vitae, personal management, being multi-skilled and continuous training and development.

Bibliography

Gonzo, W. 2001. *The psychological repercussions of unemployment: A study of Windhoek's 'street unemployed'*. Unpublished Master's dissertation, University of Namibia.

Kinget, G.M. 1975. *On being human.* New York: Harcourt Brace.

Sully, M. 1997. The construct of work and non-work in rural South Africa. *South African Journal of Psychology,* 27(3), 127–133.

Van Deventer, V. and Jordaan, W. 1998. The work situation. In W. Jordaan and J. Jordaan, *People in context.* 3rd edition. Johannesburg: Heinemann.

Work: The dynamics of unemployment

Work plays a crucial role in the everyday lives of people. It provides a source of income and allows a measure of self-sufficiency. It is an outlet for creative accomplishment, it creates an environment of stimulating relationships with colleagues and it is a major source of self-esteem (Duncan and Van Niekerk, 2004). To lose one's job is devastating, not only financially, but also psychologically.

Although unemployment is a worldwide phenomenon, it takes on major proportions in developing countries. During the last decade of the 20th century, South Africa had an average unemployment rate of 30 per cent. The majority of the unemployed (55 per cent) came from the poorest sector of South African society and from rural communities (55 per cent) and 57 per cent were women (Duncan and Van Niekerk, 2004). When one considers these statistics in the context of the importance that work has for individuals, it is clear that unemployment is a phenomenon that impacts heavily on individuals as well as on society as a whole. It affects people economically, socially and psychologically. Excessive unemployment is a potentially explosive socio-political problem in any community (Van Deventer and Jordaan, 1998).

Research has shown that the loss of employment and income, or the inability to find work in the first instance, is extremely stressful and places individuals at risk of alcohol dependence, violence, suicide and psychological illness. Globalisation in the job market adds to the stress that workers and job seekers experience because it causes instability and fierce competition, exposing citizens of developing economies to exploitation (Duncan and Van Niekerk, 2004). Stress, together with poor socio-economic circumstances, often encourages socio-political unrest.

The adverse effects of unemployment on people's personal lives in terms of psychological and physical health are diverse and far-reaching. One's place, status and value as a person are often measured by one's job. Individuals who lose their job tend to question their personhood and their competence, even in circumstances where the job loss occurred for reasons outside the control of the individual. The greater the need for the job and the greater the person's commitment to it, the more adverse are the effects of the loss of employment. People experience symptoms akin to those associated with identity loss, namely feelings of inadequacy, self-mortification, social and emotional isolation and general existential anxiety and worry (Van Deventer and Jordaan, 1998).

However, the way in which individuals react to unemployment is related to their perceptions of work. Economic uncertainty, rapid social change and accelerated technological developments mean that fewer people can expect to have lifelong jobs and careers provided by the organisations they work for. Individuals have to build their careers out of a series of jobs (Davidson and Rees-Mogg, 1997). Job loss is not a lasting condition but a process of transition, marked by the re-evaluation of one's goals, retraining and up-skilling (Ezzy, 1993). However, it is not only for economic reasons that these transitional interludes are necessary. They also benefit the individual psychologically. The intense competition of the work environment and the fact that we base our self-worth on work success cause us to lose sight of the consequences of success and the adverse effects of achievement (Korman, in Landy, 1989:485). We believe that success gives us control over our lives, whereas in fact it leads to more responsibilities and increased involvement. We try to boost our experiences of self-worth and self-esteem through achievement, but forget the health risks associated with prolonged stress. When faced with an interlude between jobs, we have the opportunity to re-evaluate our values. In a study conducted by Moller (1993), those who experienced unemployment were able to report that, amidst the negative psychological impact, they also rediscovered their true selves, learned to be independent, discovered what skills they possessed and learned how to be useful to their community.

Bibliography

Davidson, D.J. and Rees-Mogg, W. 1997. *The sovereign individual.* London: Macmillan.

Duncan, N. and Van Niekerk, A. 2004. Adulthood and ageing. In L. Swartz, C. de la Rey and N. Duncan (Eds), *Psychology: An introduction.* Cape Town: Oxford University Press.

Ezzy, D. 1993. Unemployment and mental health: A critical review. *Social Science Medicine,* 37(1), 41–52.

Landy, F.I. 1989. *Psychology of work behaviour.* 4th edition. Pacific Grove, CA: Brooks/Cole.

Moller, V. 1993. Youth employment schemes urgently needed. *In Focus,* (HSRC), 2.8, 22–25.

Van Deventer, V. and Jordaan, W. 1998. The work situation. In W. Jordaan and J. Jordaan, *People in context.* 3rd edition. Johannesburg: Heinemann.

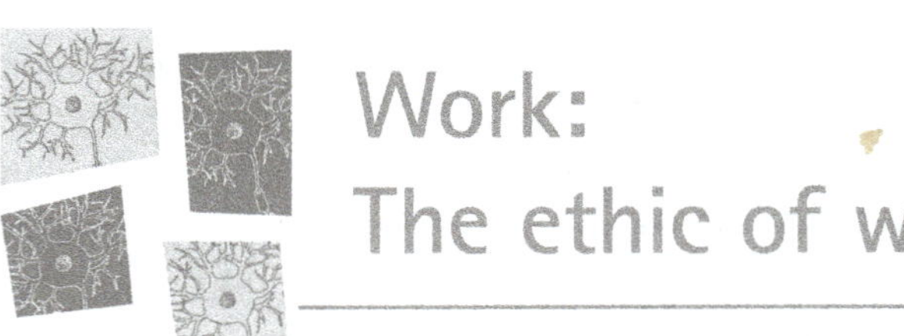

Work: The ethic of work

The work ethic refers to the principles of what is considered right and wrong in the work environment. These are principles that are widely accepted by individuals or groups of individuals. It includes what people regard as their duties and obligations, the nature of the relationship between employees and employers and the amount of freedom of choice they have. People's work ethic is a function of their socio-political circumstances as well as of their psychological makeup. Our work ethic has developed over thousands of years, from being forced to do a particular job to being largely free to choose the jobs we want to do.

In this section, we look at two aspects of the work ethic, namely the socio-politics of the work ethic and the psychology of the work ethic.

1 The socio-politics of the work ethic

Early tribes organised themselves into communal groups under the leadership of a single individual. The leader was usually a strong male who could physically fend off any challenges to his leadership. However, as the groups grew in numbers and as the complexity of their social structures increased, it was the social position of the individual rather than his physical strength that gave him his leadership. At first, the resources of the group belonged to the group as a whole, but later on everything became the property of the king, including the people he governed. The citizens of these kingdoms had no free choice and their lives were governed by royal decree. They had to do the work assigned to them or die. Most of them were soldiers, while others worked the fields in a feudal system.

The kingdoms, however, did not exist in isolation. Although there were many wars amongst them, they also traded with each other. Trading increased significantly in the 13th century when new trade routes opened between Europe and countries like India and China. The increased trade among kingdoms and city states created a *market ethic* (Wren, 1994:23–33). People learned to buy and sell and to make a profit in the process. The profits re-entered the economy as capital that got reinvested, expanding the economy and increasing production. This kind of economic cycle freed people from their agricultural existence, gradually eroding the rights of kings and the aristocratic stranglehold of landlords (Van Deventer and Jordaan, 1998). Increased economic freedom and greater levels of literacy coincided with the cultural and social revival that swept Europe at the time. This Renaissance of Europe brought an *ethic of freedom* (Wren, 1994) as people learned to take their own decisions and began to measure their worth in terms of personal achievement and wealth. However, these notions of freedom conflicted with the doctrines of the Roman Catholic Church, a major socio-political influence at the time (Van Deventer and Jordaan, 1998). The conflict came to a head with the Protestant Reformation, spearheaded by Martin Luther in 1530. The Protestants believed in the goodness of work and that one had to earn goodness through working for the glory of God. The Protestant worldview resulted in a *Protestant work ethic* (Wren, 1994).

The Protestant work ethic played an important role in the development of modern economic systems (Weber, 1958:157–173). It propagated the following ideas:

- People should not be idle. They should use their available time to work, because work is inherently good.
- One has to earn what one wants to use. One is not entitled to anything unless one has worked for it.
- Individuals should constantly improve their skills so as to work better.
- People should not waste and consume more than is needed to satisfy their basic needs. Surpluses should be saved or ploughed back to improve people's circumstances.

Protestants understood these ideas in a religious sense, that work was to be done for the glory of God, but we have come to see them as good economic principles.

The European Renaissance also cultivated a mechanistic worldview. The world was seen as a gigantic machine and everything, including people, fitted together into it like cogs. God was the one who had wound up the clockwork to let the machine tick away. This worldview was instrumental in the formidable advancements that followed in science. Scientific advances supported industrial development, but also led to a mechanistic view of people in the work environment. People came to be seen and treated as part of the production machinery. They were slotted into predefined jobs and their performance was monitored and managed in hierarchical control structures. Power and decision making were centralised in top management and were exercised and communicated from the top downwards. Planning was a mechanistic exercise in which management would set the goals and implement the processes through which employees lower down had to achieve them (Van Deventer and Jordaan, 1998).

Although this *mechanistic ethic* was successful from a production point of view, it negated the individualism and psychological needs of people.

It was not until the 20th century that the metaphor of the machine began to give way to the metaphor of the organism. An organismic worldview is based on the notion that the world is a system made up of other systems (subsystems), thus an organisation is a system within a larger system, which is the organisation's environment. By the same token, workers are systems within larger organisational systems that constitute their work environments. Human systems function like living organisms, which change dynamically and evolve in response to their environments. The organismic worldview encouraged freedom and led to a *post-industrial ethic*.

The machine metaphor and its mechanistic ethic was undermined when the workforce started to organise itself and gained a voice in organisational management through trade union representation. The atrocities of World War II and the emphasis on human rights that followed afterwards played a further role in changing organisational structures and the way people function within them. Today, organisations are changing from authoritarian environments into workplaces organised around participatory management, from hierarchically managed workers to self-determining work teams, from pre-described jobs to dynamic work roles and from the rigid implementation of predefined policies to flexible and adaptable procedures (Van Deventer and Jordaan, 1998). People reject organisations that seek to standardise their lives. They want activity and variety (Dumont, 1991).

The shift from people as machines to people as living, evolving systems is a shift from dependency to autonomy. It is a shift towards self-agency and greater self-reliance (Peavy, 1993), but this also means a change in work ethic. The work ethic is changing from the previously mechanistic ethic to an *ethic of self-development* (Savickas, 1993).

2 The psychology of the work ethic

Some people are enthusiastic about their jobs and identify with the missions and the visions of the organisations they work for. They are honest and reliable and often do more than is expected of them. These individuals have a good work ethic. However, there are also those whose aims are to do the minimum amount of work to get the maximum benefits, even if it requires dishonesty and theft. Their work ethic is poor. How should one understand this difference in the work ethic from a psychological point of view? Although cultural background influences people's work ethic, there are definite psychological factors that play a role. Locus of control, the need for achievement and self-actualisation and awareness of responsibility are prominent factors in work ethic.

An internal locus of control is associated with a strong Protestant work ethic (Furnham et al., 1993) and is backed by conservative attitudes and views, which in their turn make for commitment (Furnham, Kirkcaldy and Lynn, 1994). Individuals with an internal locus of control recognise and meet their obligations. They have a sense of duty and, when they enter into agreements and make commitments, they do their best to see these through. Individuals with an external locus of control feel their lives are dominated and controlled by circumstances over which they have no control. They do not like to commit themselves and they may fail to meet their obligations, blaming circumstantial issues for their actions.

The second psychological factor that plays a role in work ethic is the fulfilment of human needs. The needs for achievement and self-actualisation are important for an ethic of self-development. There is a close relationship between achievement and self-actualisation. In their need to achieve, people do not focus on external indicators like wealth, status and respect. The need to achieve relates to an internal locus of control. It is characterised by the desire to be successful, to overcome obstacles, to accomplish difficult tasks and to exercise power (Landy, 1989). The need for self-actualisation is marked by the desire to be free of both self-imposed and organisational constraints in order to develop and fulfil one's potential.

A third factor that plays a role in work ethic is the awareness of personal responsibility. Individual responsibility and being responsible for oneself are logical outcomes of people's desire to be free of enforced and standardised constraints in the workplace. Personal responsibility and rights are two sides of the same coin. Workers have been emancipated by a culture of human rights, determined by constitutional laws and work contracts, but the shift towards greater freedom and personal agency also means a shift to greater responsibility. The willingness to accept personal responsibility is closely related to an internal locus of control, the need to achieve and the desire to actualise one's self.

It is important to note that psychological factors should not be seen in isolation from the socio-political and cultural environments in which people find themselves. People are psychological beings within socio-political and cultural contexts. For example, Japanese culture and social traditions emphasise commitment, the ability to let the self take a backseat for the good of the whole, achievement through conscientious perseverance and attention to detail in order to do things properly. In Africa, there is the notion that 'I am because we are' (*ubuntu*). This approach values collective solidarity and interdependence through unconditional acceptance, respect, affirmation of human dignity, compassion, hospitality and stewardship (Van Deventer and Jordaan, 1998). Religious culture also plays a role. For example, there is a connection between Protestant religious views and work ethic (Giorgi and Marsh, 1990). Protestants have a good work ethic in the sense that they are dedicated and rigorous, consider leisure activities a waste of time, believe in hard work and strive for success (McHoskey, 1994), all of which relate strongly to the psychological needs for achievement and self-actualisation.

However, it is not always the context that influences the individual. It can also be the other way round. Psychological factors may significantly influence the socio-political and cultural contexts that people find themselves in. According to McClelland (1961), the need to achieve appears strongly in a society about 50 years before that society blossoms into rapid economic growth and prosperity. The golden age of ancient Greece, medieval Spain and the Industrial Revolution in England were all pre-empted by a strong need for achievement.

Bibliography

Dumont, F. 1991. Individual differences and institutional constraints. *International Journal for the Advancement of Counselling,* 14, 163–179.

Furnham, A., Bond, M., Heaven, P., Hilton, D., Lobel, I., Masters, J., Payne, M., Rajamanikam, R., Stacey, B. and Van Daalen, H. 1993. A comparison of Protestant work ethic beliefs in thirteen countries. *Journal of Social Psychology,* 133(2), 185–197.

Furnham, A., Kirkcaldy, B.D. and Lynn, R. 1994. National attitudes to competitiveness, money and work among young people: First, Second and Third World differences. *Human Relations,* 47(1), 119–132.

Giorgi, L. and Marsh, C. 1990. The Protestant work ethic as a cultural phenomenon. *European Journal of Social Psychology,* 20(6), 499–517.

Landy, F.I. 1989. *Psychology of work behaviour.* 4th edition. Pacific Grove, CA: Brooks Cole.

Peavy, R.V. 1993. Envisioning the future: Worklife and counselling. *Canadian Journal of Counselling,* 27(2), 123–139.

McClelland, D.C. 1961. *The achieving society.* Princeton: Van Nostrand.

McHoskey, J.W. 1994. Factor structure of the Protestant work ethic scale. *Personality and Individual Differences,* 17(1), 49–52.

Savickas, M.L. 1993. Career counselling in the postmodern era. *Journal of Cognitive Psychotherapy: An International Quarterly,* 7(3), 205–215.

Van Deventer, V. and Jordaan, W. 1998. The work situation. In W. Jordaan and J. Jordaan, *People in context.* 3rd edition. Johannesburg: Heinemann.

Weber, M. 1958. *The Protestant ethic and the spirit of capitalism.* New York: Charles Scribner.

Wren, D.H. 1994. *The evolution of management thought.* 4th edition. New York: Wiley.

www.ingramcontent.com/pod-product-compliance
Lightning Source LLC
Chambersburg PA
CBHW081356270326
41930CB00015B/3322

9780702189050